Liberating *the* GOSPEL

Also by Rev. Piazza

Liberating Word
Volume One: The Old Testament

Gay by God
How to be Lesbian or Gay and Christian

Prophetic Renewal
Hope for the Liberal Church

The Real antiChrist
How America Sold Its Soul

Queeries
Questions Lesbians and Gays Have for God

Liberating the GOSPEL

Matthew, Mark, Luke, John and Acts

a daily reflection for liberals

by Rev. Michael S. Piazza

SOURCES OF HOPE
PUBLISHING

Liberating the Gospel

Mathew, Mark, Luke, John and Acts: a daily reflection for Liberals

Published by Sources of Hope Publishing
5910 Cedar Springs Road
Dallas, TX 75235-6806
800 -501-HOPE (4673)

ISBN: 978-1-887129-15-2

Printed in the United States

Dedication

This book is dedicated to the Rev. Dr. G. Ross Freeman and Bess Freeman. Ross was my pastor as I finished high school and as I answered the call to ministry. He inspired me to answer that call. Bess gave me the courage to dare to believe I could. As this book goes to press, word came to me that Bess had died. What I know is that only her body has died. Who she was, and is, lives on in the hearts and souls of people like me, and now a bit of her will live in you, too.

Table of Contents

Acknowledgements

I'm not sure what ever possessed me to decide to write a daily anything. Life is so turbulent in the best of times, and my work with the Center for Progressive Renewal has kept me on the road more than ever in my life. The result is, while I have written these 350 or so reflections, that may have been the easier part of the task. My name appears on the cover, but this work is certainly not mine.

I am able to write this extensively only because of the faithful and diligent work of David Plunkett. Frankly, I research each passage and then dump my thoughts on a page. David makes it coherent and keeps me from sounding like the poor boy from South Georgia that I am. It isn't easy having someone "fix you" every day, so it is sometimes a thankless job. While it is not sufficient, it is important that I thank him here and place in the permanent record that this work is at least as much his as it is mine. I am deeply grateful he is my partner.

These thoughts have traveled around the world before they arrived in your hands in this form. Hope for Peace & Justice sends these Liberating Words to more than 10,000 people every day. They then are forwarded to others, often to those who do not agree with a liberated view of the Gospel. This task is managed daily by my longtime partner in ministry David McCollough and by one of my biggest sources of encouragement, Kevin DeCloux. I love working with them, and it is impossible to say how much it means to have people who believe in you and are willing to show it by their daily work. DeSorrow Golden is a member of the board of directors of Hope for Peace & Justice, and, for more than two years, he has worked as a volunteer in getting *Liberating Word* to almost one million email boxes.

Coy James also has been a partner with me in ministry for more than two decades. He is my publisher and friend. He is also someone who manages the business end of all of this, which is, indeed, a thankless task. Coy is the one person who won't let me quit. At least once a month during the past three years I have wanted to stop, but Coy wouldn't hear of it. He is the reason we have this in book form. He is a dear soul and a great friend.

You will find, right in the middle of John, the voice of someone I have known and loved for decades. Rev. Shelley Hamilton agreed to be my substitute while I was on vacation, and I am glad to have her voice heard here. I often have sought her wisdom and compassion, and it is only appropriate that I share a bit of her with you. We began our relationship when she took me for a walk on the beach after hearing a sermon that I preached to the denomination of which we were then a part. She had a critique of it and me, and we have been fast friends and colleagues ever since. We all need friends like Shelley in our lives, and I'm so glad she is in mine.

Finally, I must acknowledge Bill Eure. I have many partners in ministry and life, but the one who prays for me every day is the love of my life. I can't possibly thank him, but it would be impossibly arrogant of me not to acknowledge that any good that ever comes from me is rooted in the prayers of one whose love has sustained me for more than 30 years.

Introduction

I want to liberate Jesus. I want to liberate him from many of the things I was taught about him in Sunday School, and some of the things I was taught in seminary. For half-a-century now, I have lived with Jesus, and, as I am being liberated from my own prejudices, biases, presumptions and arrogance, it is amazing how much Jesus has changed.

While the following reflections contain some historic information and context, I trust that if that is what you seek you will buy a commentary by a better Biblical scholar than me. What I have tried to offer are daily thoughts designed to allow the stories and teachings in the Gospels and Acts to intersect with your own life.

It is my sincere hope that there will be times when you will say "Yes! That is what I always believed that meant." I also hope there will be many times when you will wonder if what you are reading might be a heresy. On other days, you may think I have gone too far, and if the writings don't make you angry or defensive a time or two then I have failed utterly. What should happen as you read these reflections is what happened to Jesus' original listeners. Sometimes they cried, and sometimes they laughed. They often went away reflected, and not infrequently mad. They didn't, however, hear Jesus and remain unchanged. The real power of this book lies in Jesus' words, not mine. My job is to get us to hear from Jesus in new, fresh and challenging ways.

At the start of a new year, we all have the best of intentions. This year we will be much better about our spiritual devotions. We will read the Bible (or, at least, *Liberating Word*) every day, and we will pray and be more generous and kind. We've all made these resolutions before, though. I'm always impressed by how crowded the gym is in January, but by February you have the place to yourself … or someone does. With this book in hand, you may have committed yourself to studying the New Testament this year.

Actually, "study" would be too strong a description for what we do. What I hope is that we will look at a verse or two in a new way and find some challenge or inspiration that will liberate us as progressive people of faith.

The first four books of the New Testament are called "The Gospels." The word "gospel," of course, means "good news." That is fairly common knowledge, but I'm not so sure the preachers I grew up listening to knew that the news was good.

After we finish with the four Gospels, we continue our study with the book of Acts. It is volume two of the Gospel of Luke. The Risen Christ makes a cameo appearance at the start but then "ascends into heaven" with a promise to return. Ten days later, he does. The second coming of Jesus happens on the day of Pentecost, which is described in the second chapter of Acts. The rest of the book is an account of the early Church, which is called the Body of Christ. In other words, Acts is a fifth Gospel that tells the story of the risen Body of Christ.

In the first meditation, we jump right in with the Gospel of Matthew, though it is my least favorite of the four Gospels. The first three—Matthew, Mark and Luke—are called the synoptic Gospels, which simply means that they can be looked at in parallel columns and that much of the material is shared. John is different in many ways.

Although the first three seem to repeat the same material, each has its own twist or spin. That is probably determined mostly by who the audience was. You know how you tell a story differently if you are telling it to your elderly mother as opposed to your most erudite friend. I think I'm going to pretend that this year I'm telling these stories to my sisters and brothers who, like me, are trying desperately to keep their New Year's resolutions.

Matthew

The first, and oldest, Gospel is believed to be Mark. It seems Matthew and Luke used Mark as a guide in writing their versions of the story of Jesus. However, it seems each of the three was written with a different audience in mind. Matthew's primary audience seems to be Jewish Christians.

It is tough to remember that Jesus was not a Christian. He was a Jew who sought to provide a liberating word to his people. Matthew's Jewish audience shaped his material in many ways. For example, he points back to the First Testament to illustrate how the life of Jesus was a fulfillment of prophesy. Like many preachers, Matthew really strains the scripture at times to make his point.

The Gospel of Matthew also begins with a genealogy, which would have been meaningful to Jewish readers who knew their history, but which makes keeping New Year's resolutions tough for the rest of us. I mean, how many of us have resolved to read the New Testament, only to run right into this long list of names right at the start? Luke has a slightly different genealogy and doesn't put it right up front.

Luke traces the lineage of Jesus back to Adam, but Matthew only needs to go back as far as Abraham. For the Jews, Abraham was their beginning as a people, and it was the covenant with Abraham that gave them their special identity. To Matthew, the fact that Jesus was descended from Abraham made him a Jew, and the fact that he was descended from David gave him a rightful claim to be the Messiah. That is how Matthew's Gospel begins.

He sets out to prove that Jesus is the Messiah expected by the prophets. Modern Christians buy that view entirely, though there is some evidence that Jesus didn't buy it. He was the son of God, but he thought we all are daughters and sons of God. Matthew is trying to sell you a certain historical view of Jesus. Your job over the next few weeks is to decide if you buy it, or to answer Jesus' primal question: apart from what these early witnesses say, "Who do you say I am?"

Matthew 1:1-17

A man was telling a friend about hiring someone to research his genealogy. When she asked how much it costs, he replied, "$12,000." Astonished, she said, "Wow, that is a lot." He then admitted that, "Well, it costs $2,000 to look it up, and then $10,000 to cover it up." Matthew's genealogy leaves us wondering, if his mission was to prove Jesus was the one sent from God, why he didn't cover up some of the characters in Jesus lineage.

In that day, lineages almost always were patriarchal since inheritance was exclusively through the father's line. Matthew traces Jesus' line through Joseph, even though, in a few pages, he'll acknowledge that Joseph had very little to do with the conception. And Jesus' genealogy in Matthew includes four women. One, Tamar, was the victim of rape; Rahab was identified as a harlot; Ruth, was a foreigner who made covenant with another woman; and the fourth, Bathsheba, was the wife of another man who became David's wife only after he committed adultery with her and arranged for her husband to be killed in battle. Not exactly a "who's who" list by the sexist standards of that day.

It is ironic that each of these women had their own sexual "scandal" that got them included in this list, yet the Gospels of Matthew and Luke both have been used by the Church to deprive Mary of her sexuality. It is nearly impossible to separate how much the authors are responsible for this and how much the idea of the "virgin birth" was a later interpretation of an anti-sex (especially for women) Church.

Since Christmas is behind us, perhaps I can dare to say that, given the genealogy of Matthew's Gospel, it might have been more consistent if we simply had been left to wonder just how Mary got pregnant. Yes, the messenger said to Joseph in a dream that the one conceived within Mary was "from the Holy Spirit," but that easily could be understood as a simple reassurance that, regardless of how Mary got pregnant, the child was from God. Without Luke's amplification, Matthew only tells us that Joseph wasn't the father. An out of wedlock pregnancy was the means of Jesus' birth, and that fits perfectly with the genealogy of Jesus. It is one more proof that God works in interesting ways. If you need another, take a careful look in the mirror.

Following the genealogy in the first chapter of Matthew is the very familiar story of how God talked Joseph down off a ledge. All of us probably have stories of unplanned or unexpected pregnancies. As the father of two teenage daughters, the story of Mary becoming pregnant by someone other than her fiancé makes me break out in a cold sweat. She might well have been younger than my 15- and 16-year olds.

Matthew tells us that a dream reassured Joseph, and he then follows by quoting a prophecy from Isaiah 7:14:

> *Behold, the virgin shall conceive and bear a son, and they shall name him Emmanuel, which means, "God is with us."*

Hebrew has a specific word, betulah, for a virgin, and a more general word, `almah, for a young woman. Since `almah is the word used in the Hebrew text of Isaiah, some scholars believe it is at least possible that Isaiah had in mind only a normal conception by a young mother and that Matthew simply applied this line of scripture to the birth of the one he believed to be the messiah. Matthew doesn't seem to argue, as Luke does, for a supernatural conception.

The important thing is not to debunk the doctrine of the Virgin Birth, but to ask why it is important. Some scholars, particularly Roman Catholics, argue that Jesus had to be born of a virgin in order to be free of the "infection of human sin." The doctrine of the Immaculate Conception was put forth in the Middle Ages as a way of explaining how Mary was conceived without sin. Though Protestants tend to confuse these two doctrines, what is clear is that both derive their importance from the Church being sex-negative.

Mary is held up as the perfect example of womanhood and virtue. Jesus' own sexuality has always been a taboo topic, but men never have been required to strive to be perpetual virgins. I wonder if that is because, for most of history, men have been the ones to make the rules and set the standards.

Matthew 2:1-12

January 6 is the Christian Feast of Epiphany. In many cultures it is a bigger holiday, or Holy Day, than Christmas. Epiphany celebrates the story we find in Matthew 2. Most of what we know about this story comes from the Christmas carol "We Three Kings," but much of what we know is simply wrong.

First, nowhere does it say they were kings. The magi, or "wise men," likely were astrologers from Persia (modern day Iran or Iraq). There is also no reason to believe there were three. Since the word used is plural, we know the author of the story indicated more than one. Traditions from the Middle Ages indicate that there were 12. Of course, thinking there were three comes from the three gifts the magi bring with them. In addition, we always place them around the manger at the inn with the shepherds. Matthew says they came to a house where the family was staying. He also indicates that the baby might have been up to two years old, since Herod had the male infants up to two killed.

This is a good, though relatively harmless, example of how much of what we believe is simply wrong. It becomes a part of our culture and takes on the value of "truth," but it isn't at all what the Bible said or meant. There are many examples of not-so-harmless, but equally mistaken, convictions that Christians hold.

This is a legend that was circulating by the time Matthew wrote his Gospel. Any possible eyewitnesses would have been long dead. However, the author of Matthew is writing to the Jews, and the important part of the story for him was that Herod had the male infants killed, in much the same way Pharaoh had done trying to eliminate Moses. He didn't succeed because Joseph had another dream, and, in Matthew 2:13, he takes the baby and his mother and flees to Egypt. After Herod died the family returned home to Nazareth.

Matthew cites this as fulfilling yet another prophecy—"Out of Egypt I have called my son." (Exodus 4:22)—and, in one fell swoop, he replaces God's covenant with Israel with Jesus. This is a perfect example of how Christians often refuse to allow history, facts or good theology to get in the way of a point we are trying to prove.

The Book of Matthew begins with the birth of Jesus and the flight into Egypt. After Herod dies, Joseph takes the baby and his mother home to Nazareth, and he is never heard from again. The next thing we know Jesus is a grown man being baptized by John in the Jordan. Chapter three begins with a couple of paragraphs about John. There is no story about him being a cousin of Jesus; that is found only in Luke. There is no account of John declaring Jesus to be "the Lamb of God who takes away the sins of the world;" that is found only in the Gospel of John.

In Matthew, John is described briefly as an ascetic prophet in the Hebrew style who was sent as a precursor to the Messiah. John is more than a warm-up act to the main event, but barely. His lines are limited to calling both the Sadducees and Pharisees a "brood of vipers." John's description of Jesus is equally severe. He said:

> *I baptize you with water for repentance, but one who is more power-ful than I is coming after me. ... His winnowing fork is in his hand, and he will clear his threshing floor and will gather his wheat into the granary; but the chaff he will burn with unquenchable fire.*
>
> Matthew 3:11-12

Much of fundamentalist Christianity has accepted this as a description of Jesus. They seem to delight in a messiah with a winnowing fork burning up the chaff. (Frankly, if you are reading this you probably qualify as chaff to most of them.) So, again, we are left to decide if we agree with this description of Jesus, or do we believe that the Bible is simply mistaken because this doesn't match the Jesus of our hearts? Well, I'd advocate for trusting the witness of the spirit in your heart over even Holy Scripture, but that may be an unnecessary choice.

What we have in John's sermonette to the Jewish spiritual leadership is a description of who John thought the messiah was going to be. His description is congruent with the expectations of his prophetic predecessors, but he may have been wrong. Actually, some months later, after he is arrested, John sends word to Jesus to ask if he really is the messiah, or if they should be looking for another. Apparently, John was just the first fundamentalist Jesus disappointed by not being venge-ful enough, but he won't be the last.

Matthew 3:13-17

The story of John baptizing Jesus in the Jordan is told in all four Gospels. This brief scripture historically has been the foundation of the inexplicable Christian doctrine of the Trinity. Here we have Jesus in the Jordan, the Spirit descending from the sky like a dove, and the voice of God from heaven saying, "This is my beloved with whom I am well pleased."

The doctrine of the Trinity teaches that God exists in three persons, but is one being. Now, if that sentence makes no sense to you then you are not alone. Only the ignorant claim to "understand" the Trinity. The word itself does not occur in the Bible, and the doctrine largely arose to explain how Jesus could be God incarnate, but also someone with whom God was pleased. It is an explanation of how we can believe that Jesus was divine but God was still in heaven. To most non-Christians, claiming Jesus to be divine makes us polytheistic. The doctrine of the Trinity is how Christianity holds both the divinity of Jesus/the incarnation and still believes in Judaism's radical monotheism.

Now, it is tempting to discard the whole thing as early church mumbo jumbo. Anything requiring that many big words and that much explanation is likely to be a cover up for a much simpler truth. However, before we leap to that conclusion, a little humility might do us well.

You see, despite all that the experts and theologians may claim, to say that God is simultaneously three and one is incomprehensible to the human mind. Still, that does not make it untrue; in fact, it may be evidence that it is true. Anything or anyone that we are capable of truly comprehending cannot be God. As smart as we like to think we are, claiming to understand and to be able to explain God is arrogance. It is this arrogance that has led to so much religious violence in the world. When we think we understand and possess all knowledge we are tempted to scorn or disregard anyone whose "knowing" doesn't match ours. Incredible freedom comes when we are secure enough to admit that we really don't know, and neither does anyone else. This journey for us all is a matter of faith, which seems to delight God's perverse sense of humor. Next time you are tempted to speak in absolute terms about God or matters of faith, pause and close your eyes and see if, in the darkness, you don't catch the hint of a smile on God's face ... or faces.

Matthew 4:1-11

In the three synoptic Gospels, the baptism of Jesus is followed immediately by the story of his being tempted or tested for 40 days and nights in the desert. The story is told in almost identical form in Matthew and Luke, but in Mark it only takes one verse.

The fact that this story exists at all is pretty remarkable. Since Jesus is alone during this time, if the story is historically factual, He had to have been the source. (Remember there is a great difference between a story being factual and it being true.) The fact that the story is true is not in dispute, because it has spoken powerfully to people for centuries. The idea of Jesus struggling greatly at the outset of his ministry is not so amazing, but for that struggle to be recorded and reported by authors whose purpose is to convince us to believe is impressive.

Jesus faces three basic "temptations":

- Turn stones to bread: use the power of your life to satisfy your own needs and greeds.
- Cast yourself down from the pinnacle of the temple: use sensationalism to convince people to believe in you.
- Fall down and worship evil: compromise for the greater good.

While few of us struggle with these specific temptations, we all struggle. The idea of Jesus being tested should be a source of encouragement when we are facing our own tests. When we are in the fires of life, it is challenging to remember that the word temptation shares its root with the word "temper." Steel that is tempered is stronger and sharper.

Does that mean there really is a devil that tests us so that we will be stronger? There is an old B-movie called "Voyage into Terror" in which one of the characters says something I've always remembered: "That there is a devil there is no doubt; the question is whether he is trying to get in or get out." Whether the testings are from within or without, remember that Jesus was tested, and, like him, the Spirit is with us, helping us to emerge stronger, if not because of the test then despite of it.

Matthew 4:12-17

Jesus emerges from the time of testing that followed his baptism with clarity and resolve. In this passage, Matthew provides a theological context for the ministry of Jesus and places it against a favorite prophecy from Isaiah: "The people who sat in darkness have seen a great light." Matthew also uses this transition passage to make some rather random historical notes. John has been arrested and Jesus moved from Nazareth to Capernaum. He then ends this passage with a sentence that describes what Matthew believed to be the theme of Jesus' ministry: "Repent, for the kingdom of heaven is at hand."

Repent was good news that has been turned into bad, having been screamed at us by preachers who want us to conform. The word simply means "turn around," and the good news in that is that Jesus believed in the human capacity to change, to grow, to become a person who lived under the reign of God.

That is essentially what "kingdom" means. Matthew uses "heaven" instead of "God" because he is writing to Jewish readers who, out of great respect, sought to avoid using the name of God. The term "kingdom" does not imply a place but the dominion or reign of God. Some modern scholars use the term "Empire of God," but that term has an uncomfortable meaning for many of us. Fr. Richard Chilson suggests the terms "Love's Domain," "Love's Dominion" or "Love's Rule" because the Kingdom of God is where the God who is Love rules. I like that.

So, if this is the theme of the life and ministry of Jesus, what does it mean for us to live under *Love's Rule* or in the *Domain of Love*? If we are honest, we must admit that, for this to be a reality in our lives, we must begin with the first step of Jesus' message. We must repent. We must be willing to admit that many of our attitudes, values and ways of living do not conform to love. We must admit that and change that. We must repent. Our job is not to call others to repent, but to so change our lives that the quality invites others to live with us in this Realm where God is love. So how have we been Christians so long without realizing this is what Jesus came to teach?

Earlier in this chapter, Matthew was careful to move Jesus from Nazareth to Capernaum in Galilee. Now he reports that the first disciples Jesus called were fishers on the Sea of Galilee. It will be a few chapters before Jesus calls a tax collector, who tradition identifies as the author Matthew, but Capernaum was where the region's tax office was located.

Today's passage is divided in two parts. The first part tells of the call of four disciples. The second part tells about how Jesus went all over Galilee proclaiming good news, healing people and generally gathering quite a crowd. The next several chapters, known as the Sermon on the Mount, summarize much of what Jesus is reported to have taught.

What seems odd to me about today's passage is the order of the two halves. I mean, it makes much more sense to me that Peter, Andrew, James and John left their nets and followed Jesus AFTER they heard Jesus' message and saw his healing power. The way the story is told Jesus saw the men (for the first time in his life) and simply said, "Follow me and I will make you fishers of souls." What made them go?

Maybe they were having a bad day on the lake and were ready for a change of careers. That is often how it happens. I'm never quite sure if God calls us only when we are miserable, or if we have to be miserable before we are sensitive to Life's calling us to make a change.

And what was Jesus thinking? Did he really think he could bring in the Reign of Love using people like fishers? They weren't scholars or leaders, and they weren't particularly spiritual. Was Jesus trying to prove that if he could use them he could use anyone to do the work of the Reign of Love? I've always believed that to be true in my life.

The truth is that the lifestyle Jesus came to teach wasn't just for the special … or maybe it was. Maybe Jesus came to teach us that we are all special and have something to do in building the Reign of Love. AMEN.

Matthew 5:1-12

Matthew 5, 6 and 7 are called "The Sermon on the Mount." Much of this material is shared with the other Gospels, but it is not arranged like it is here as a single set of teachings. Actually, it is a collection of teachings, and much of the material was not original with Jesus. That isn't to say he didn't believe it and teach it. We often find him taking an ancient teaching and twisting it slightly or expanding it greatly. The Sermon on the Mount begins with some of Jesus' most famous sayings, known as "The Beatitudes":

> *Blessed are the poor in spirit, for theirs is the Realm of Heaven; blessed are those who mourn ... the meek ... those who hunger and thirst for righteousness ... the merciful ... the pure in heart ... the peacemakers ... those who are persecuted ...*

Tom Long suggests that the Sermon on the Mount serves as the Constitution for the Realm of God, and that the beatitudes are the preamble that establishes the essence of the realm and the purposes of the principles that will follow.

We could, of course, spend many weeks unpacking each of the nine beatitudes, but that will need to wait for a more in-depth study. It might be most helpful today to think about the word with which each beatitude begins: "blessed." It is difficult to find an adequate English word for the Greek word *makarioi*. Some translations render it "happy are" or "how fortunate are." The tough thing with this translation is that it is difficult to see the persecuted as "happy" or "fortunate." In addition, Matthew's version of the beatitudes is substantially more spiritualized than those we find in Luke. Matthew says "Blessed are the poor in spirit." In Luke Jesus simply says "Blessed are the poor."

What is clear is that happiness and a blessed life are being redefined. Despite the popularity of this passage, it never has been taken seriously by Christians. Those of us who claim to be disciples of Jesus still pursue happiness in the same way as those who have no faith, and if we talk about our lives being blessed we generally mean the same thing any atheist would. Living in the Realm of God first requires a different set of core values, goals, hopes and dreams. That might be worth pondering at the outset of a new year. What SHOULD our goals be?

Matthew 5:13-16

The twin metaphors of salt and light have become a ubiquitous part of our common culture. That speaks to the power of these instructions to communicate, but the result is that they have become so common that they have lost their original power. Take salt for example. In Jesus' day salt was much less available and much more valuable. In a desert land without refrigeration or air conditioning, salt was not just a seasoning, it was vital for life. What salt brought to mind for the original listeners was using it to preserve fish and meat, more than as a mere seasoning.

I think one lesson from both salt and light is that a little makes a big difference. A little light dispels a lot of darkness, and a little salt can transform a whole meal. Perhaps what Jesus sought to do with these metaphors was not so much to define our roles in life as to disarm our excuses. In the face of enormous challenges like war, injustice, poverty, global warming, etc., we are tempted to believe our effort or contribution will make very little difference. That can help to soothe our conscience when we do nothing at all.

Jesus didn't call us to be the sun of the world, but a light in the world. The analogy of salt discourages the idea that we are called to do it all. A meal of salt is not appealing at all. This might be overstraining these two metaphors, but this is a rather common theme for Jesus. He also talked about the tiny mustard seed and about the pinch of leaven in the loaf. While we may have to struggle with grandiosity, Jesus is not expecting us to do any more than what we can.

In addition, a single grain of salt accomplishes little; a single light cannot brighten the whole world. Jesus was never deluded by the myth of individualism, but was clear that transforming the world was something we must do together. As I like to say, none of us can do everything, but all of us can do something. And what we can do we must do with all our strength. That seems to be Jesus' point in this very familiar saying from the Sermon on the Mount.

Matthew 5:17-20

No Christian keeps all the commandments of the Bible. None of us even try. There are many First Testament laws and regulations than most of us have never even heard of. There are things Jesus told us to do that the most rigorous fundamentalist doesn't do ... which raises some interesting questions given today's scripture:

> *Jesus said do not think that I have come to abolish the law or the prophets; I have come not to abolish but to fulfill. For truly I tell you, until heaven and earth pass away, not one letter, not one stroke of a letter, will pass from the law until all is accomplished. ... For I tell you, that unless your righteousness exceeds the scribes and Pharisees, you will never enter the Realm of Heaven.*

St. Paul and subsequent preachers have argued that Jesus replaced the law as the means by which we come to know the Realm of God. However, a frank reading of this text doesn't seem to indicate that this was what Jesus thought he came to do. So does that mean that Jesus expects us to give up shrimp and pork chops?

The truth is, if you only read this passage and fail to understand its content and what comes after it, you might well make the assumption that, as Christians, we are expected to keep the law and the prophets. That is an important thing to remember about scripture. Few verses actually stand alone without context, and almost any argument can be supported with a verse or two of scripture.

Remember, Matthew is writing to a Jewish audience. To win a hearing with them, Jesus must affirm the sacred value of the law and the prophets. Remember also that this verse occurs in the beginning of what is the Constitution of the Realm of God. New interpretations and understandings of the law are about to be offered, but first the old must be affirmed. Then Jesus challenges us to go beyond the law. While the average person couldn't keep the law, the scribes and Pharisees tried. Then Jesus told us that we had to do better than them. It is a clear indication of where Jesus is going. His teachings will not be about regulation and control, but about relationship and letting the presence of God burst forth as a Reign of Love in the world. That is what he means by exceeding the type of righteousness of fundamentalist rule keepers.

"Thou shalt not murder" is the sixth commandment. It is short and to the point, but Jesus can't leave well enough alone. This is one commandment that we all thought we could keep ... until Jesus got a hold of it. He says that our righteousness had to exceed that of the fundamentalist law keepers, and then he gives an example. For Jesus, not murdering someone didn't simply mean not killing someone; it means not taking life.

For Jesus, anger, hatred, division and strife all take life. Jesus expands the commandment to include our attitudes toward our sisters and brothers—the things we say to them, the way we treat them, and how we handle conflicts with them. Jesus takes a simple four-word commandment we could all keep and makes it into a lifestyle and value system that is a whole lot harder.

The formula he uses is, "You have heard it said ... but I say to you." He isn't discarding the law about murder, but he is trying to get at what lies beneath the ultimate act of violence. This is a pattern that will be repeated, though fundamentalists then and now seem to miss the point.

We are not murderers, but the rampant desire for revenge after the events of 9/11 ultimately led to the deaths of hundreds of thousands of people who had absolutely nothing to do with that event. According to Jesus, we, too, have broken the sixth commandment. And what about our over consumption? Tens of thousands of people starve every day in a world that produces enough food. In fact, our nation discards, wastes and turns enough food into fuel to feed them all. And what about the fumes from our convenient cars with their dirty fuel? Children in our cities are choking to death, and almost everyone is suffering the ravages of allergies, asthma and respiratory problems so we won't have to make sacrifices or hard choices.

Oh, the little bit we contribute to these issues doesn't matter. Have we so quickly forgotten the lesson of salt and light? If the good we do adds up to great good then the opposite is also true. Our anger takes life and adds up to great evil.

Matthew 5:27-32

First Jesus greatly expands the sixth commandment, and then he tackles the seventh. A strict interpretation of the Jewish law said that if a man had sex with another man's wife he was guilty of adultery. If a woman had sex with any man other than her husband then she was guilty of adultery. Jesus expands that definition to include lust. Well, technically he expands the definition to include heterosexual men who lust.

He then goes on to take a fairly firm stand against divorce. It appears to be an outright ban on divorce for any reason other than unchastity. I always have found it interesting that, while everyone agrees divorce is unfortunate and painful, even conservative Christians do not believe two bitterly unhappy people should not be allowed to get a divorce. Yet here it is in red letters. Jesus is very cut and dried about this, though he is silent about things like homosexuality, abortion and the ordination of women.

There was a day when the church legalistically opposed divorce for any reason. People who were divorced couldn't be ordained and, in some parts of the country, couldn't be elected to public office. Over the years, though, the church became more compassionate and tried to listen to the spirit of what Jesus was saying rather than twist his words into a new rule.

In Jesus' day if a man got tired of his wife or another woman caught his eye, he could simply, quickly and easily divorce her and move on. The divorced woman often ended up homeless and penniless, left to beg or become a prostitute. Jesus' words were spoken as a way of protecting women and calling men to greater accountability. His were principles of compassion and equity in a world where both those qualities were, and still are, too rare among people of faith. For a time, they were used as a weapon, but, eventually, the church moved toward a more compassionate interpretation of these words in red. One wonders when those values will find wider application by the Church.

Matthew 5:33-37

These verses deal with the laws about making an oath. This is the fourth expansion of righteousness by Jesus. Again he begins, "You have heard it said of old ... but I say unto you." Essentially Jesus is calling us to live with such integrity that we don't need to call heaven to bear witness to our promise.

Jesus goes beyond simply "You shall not lie." He calls his disciples to live with such a level of integrity that there would be no need to say "I swear." Certainly this speaks to us being consistently honest and truthful, but it goes beyond that. In verse 37, Jesus says, "Let your yes mean yes and your no mean no; anything more than this comes from the evil one."

What he is saying, of course, is that how we live should be so consistent with the values we claim that a simple yes or no is enough. It is true that life is complicated and nuanced, but, when we have fully and genuinely integrated what we believe into whom we are and how we live, navigating those complexities becomes simpler if not easier. It also becomes easier for others to know who we really are, and what our words truly mean.

We live in a politicized world where our leaders carefully parse every word, avoid direct answers, and are consistently deceptive and duplicitous. Long gone are plain spoken politicians who say what they mean and mean what they say. Their words are carefully chosen to avoid estranging voters by disclosing what the leader really believes or intends. The result is a complete loss of trust and confidence. While we might be able to dismiss this simply as politics, they have become the role model for modern communication.

A person who is plain spoken and direct is often dismissed as unsophisticated or even rude. Jesus is calling us to integrate our values so that our words can be simple, few, meaningful and true. While integrity is increasingly rare, I think the deeper problem is that few of us take the time to know what we believe and why, so we hedge our bets ... and who can depend on someone with those convictions?

Matthew 5:38-42

Here we have one of one of Jesus' most truly revolutionary teachings. If he never said anything else, but had been able to persuade the world to follow these precepts he still would have been the greatest teacher of humanity. The trouble is almost no disciple takes Jesus seriously, even those who claim to take him literally. Fundamentalist Christians are the leading supporters of capital punishment in America. Since study after study has proven it is not a deterrent to crime, the only rationale for it is revenge. That might be appropriate for those who don't believe in Jesus, but this is an absolute ban on retaliation.

And Jesus doesn't stop there. Not only should we not retaliate, but we should take affirmative steps toward those who would victimize us. On the surface, giving to someone who would take from you seems utterly irrational. What is Jesus thinking?

Well, clearly, he is not talking about people who are victims of abusive relationships. In fact, he is not encouraging us to be anyone's victim. He is giving guidelines for non-violent resistance to a people who are under the oppression of an occupying army. He is saying to them, "So you may not have the power to resist an armed Roman who would strike you or take your coat from you. You do still have the power to determine how you respond. When you decide who you are in every circumstance then you are never anyone's victim."

The whole of the Sermon on the Mount is a radical call to be a different type of person in the world. When we choose to be peaceful in the face of violence, or generous in the face of greed, we are living out of a place of true power. This might all be dismissed as Pollyanna thinking if Jesus hadn't proceeded to adhere strictly to his own teaching. Go back and read the verses again and think about how Jesus conducted himself when he was betrayed, arrested, abused and killed. Then remember whose power ultimately prevailed.

Matthew 5:43-48

Now here is a passage that needs no commentary at all. What it needs is application. People seem to be reacting to the age of globalization with increasing tribalization. Washington has become viciously partisan. Talking heads seek to utterly destroy those who hold different views. Activists seem utterly incapable of authentic dialogue with people who disagree. Far from learning to love our enemies and treat "the others" with the kindness instructed by Jesus, people of faith seem increasingly divided and divisive.

I recently wrote an editorial that was supportive of someone with whom I completely disagree. Scores of people reacted by attacking me as if I were the enemy because I didn't advocate for the utter exile of a person who holds different values and views. I wish I could say that I was simply obeying Jesus, but the truth is, as a person who has spent more than two decades being personally attacked by fundamentalists who disagreed with me, I simply didn't want to act like them.

This passage ends with Jesus' startling command for us to be perfect just as God is perfect. I will never forget my ordination in the Methodist church when the bishop looked me in the eye and asked, "Are you going on to perfection, **and** do you expect to be made perfect **in this life**?" I always wondered what would happen if a candidate honestly said, "Yeah right …" Fortunately, I had studied this passage, and I remembered the context for this command.

Jesus is telling us that, as we learn to love our enemies and treat those outside our family with compassion and kindness, we become perfectly the person God created us to be. We are not called to be perfectly God, but to be perfectly human and perfectly connected to the human family, not just our own tribe.

Matthew 6:1-4

Several years ago, I had a church member scold me because I didn't pray before eating at a public restaurant. They were never convinced that my thanking God did not have to be done so that everyone could see. Once, a member of the Board of Directors resigned because we "were not spiritual enough." As evidence, she cited the fact that we didn't always pray before we met. She was unconvinced by my explanation that, while we did begin most of our meetings with prayer, true prayer was best done before we arrived at the meeting.

Can I confess that this kind of piety makes me tired? It apparently made Jesus tired, too. In this passage, it is like he is saying, "I hope you practice your piety, but I don't want to see it!"

Actually, what Jesus is reflecting is that public piety is almost always done for reasons other than faith. When I was a kid prayer was outlawed in public school. (Okay, so I'm old.) Even back then I was amused by all the fuss because even a child knows that the Supreme Court can't stop kids from praying before they take a test. In addition, I never listened to the prayers the teachers read, so I figured God probably didn't either. Jesus knew this fight was never really about prayer.

In the midst of the controversy over who would pray at the presidential inauguration, I realized that I didn't think anybody should. This kind of public civil piety doesn't elevate our faith; it usurps it. It isn't like this or any administration is going to lead by the principles of Jesus, but by having a Christian minister pray at the beginning, our faith is hijacked for P.R. purposes and then can be safely ignored. Jesus knew that any real prayer that might transform our government and our world would need to take place in the hearts and minds of our leaders and our people. Public prayers for show might ease our conscience and satisfy a constituency, but then we have received our only reward.

Matthew 6:5-15

After instructing us to practice our piety, generosity and prayer "in secret," Jesus goes on to give us a pattern for praying. This pattern is commonly called "The Lord's Prayer." It has been prayed by individuals and congregations billions of times all over the world. My favorite version of this familiar prayer is found in *The New Zealand Book of Common Prayer:*

> *Eternal Spirit, Earth-Maker, Pain-bearer, Life-giver,*
> *source of all that is and that shall be, Father and Mother of us all.*
> *Loving God, in whom is heaven.*
> *The hallowing of your name echoes through the universe!*
> *The way of your justice be followed by the peoples of the earth!*
> *Your heavenly will be done by all created beings!*
> *Your commonwealth of peace and freedom sustain our hope and come on earth.*
> *With the bread we need for today, feed us.*
> *In the hurts we absorb from one another, forgive us.*
> *In times of temptation and test, spare us. From the grip of all that is evil, free us.*
> *For you reign in the glory of the power that is love, now and forever.*
> *Amen.*

After teaching us this pattern for prayer in which we are told to ask that we be forgiven in the same way we forgive, Jesus warns:

> *For if you forgive others their trespasses, your heavenly Parent*
> *will also forgive you; but if you do not forgive others, neither will*
> *your Parent forgive your trespasses.*

This message of forgiving seems to be an obsession of Jesus. He seems to know that the only way our souls ever will know freedom, release, restoration and healing is for us to learn to be forgiving and forgiven. I don't think that God won't forgive us, but that it doesn't do us any good if our souls remain clogged with resentment, bitterness and anger. Real prayer releases those things through forgiveness and releases us to be forgiven people. Now you see why Jesus wanted us to pray in private.

Matthew 6:16-18

The purpose of Jesus' lesson about fasting in this passage is again to repudiate the kind of public piety done to obtain admiration or praise for the one who is practicing it. Jesus again is clear that piety done for show is worse than worthless; it actually gives all people of faith a bad name.

Frankly, it would be easier to focus on the lesson than to acknowledge that Jesus said "WHEN you fast" not "IF you fast." While Jesus is not making fasting a law that must be followed, he is clear that it is a spiritual practice that should be a part of our lives in the same way that we should be generous and prayerful.

Few people who are serious about their spirituality would dispute that generosity and prayer are important components for a life of faith. However, fasting seems to be regarded as something only saints and professional Christians do. Jesus seemed to think that it was something all Christians should do. It is a discipline practice that is observed by devout Jews, Muslims and Hindus much more regularly than by western Christians.

One wonders if it is a coincidence that Western Christians are the most obese and materialistic people of faith. We live in abundance that is considered opulent by much of the world. Many days our greatest struggle is where to eat, or what to have for dinner. Dieting and exercise are inexplicable to a world where there is never an excess of food and where people must work from dawn to dusk to obtain what they do have. Jesus doesn't call us to practice fasting as a means of weight loss, but as a means of reflection on why we need to lose weight, our slavery to our physical life, our neglect of our spiritual life, our lack of appreciation for all we have, and, perhaps most importantly, our need to understand what it means to hunger. Hunger is vital if we are ever to find the motivation to become one of the spiritually serious.

This passage is meant to be heard against the teaching about fasting. Obviously, the point is to call us to refocus the hungers of our life. Ironically, all of Jesus' original audience probably would be considered poor by today's standards.

His statement "where your treasure is, there your heart will be also" is profound, but it has radically different meaning for those of us with equity, 401ks, checking accounts, stocks and investments. The majority of the people to whom he spoke carried their net worth in a purse at the waist, or maybe had buried or hidden what little extra they had scraped together through a lifetime of hard labor. Their wealth may have consisted of one set of fine clothes that moths might eat or a set of iron tools that rust could corrupt. The word "treasure" meant something very different.

But what does it mean to you? What is it in your life that you treasure? What are your valuables? What do you have in your life that you love? Are you clear that "what" is the wrong word for any of these questions? If we get Jesus' meaning' I probably should be asking "Who" is it you treasure. Who are your valuables? Who do you have in your life that you love?

Jesus is clear that we live in a world where money and possessions compete in our lives for the place that should be held by God. Both can't occupy the same place. The United States is sometimes erroneously called a "Christian nation." I say erroneous because of the arrogance and xenophobia implied, but there is another reason that statement is so wrong. The real religion of America is capitalism. We worship at temples of conspicuous consumption. I believe all the Christian religious-speak practiced in this country is an attempt to obscure this truth. Jesus calls us on this lie when he says, *"What you treasure owns your heart."*

Matthew 6:25-34

This is one of the tenderest and most pastoral passages in the whole Bible. Jesus uses a variety of illustrations to lure us from the trap of worry. It is no accident that this teaching about anxiety immediately follows Jesus' teaching about the impossibility of seeking to serve both God and money. Jesus knew that we could trust only one master or the other with our future.

That really is the key here: who/what do we trust? To whom/what do we entrust our lives? Where are our hearts or passions, our thoughts, our deepest desires? If the honest answer is money/wealth/savings/investments/income then there is little that can be done about the anxiety that wracks our thoughts and steals our sleep. That is why Jesus says, "Consider the lilies" and "consider the sparrows." He then very pointedly asks, if we can add a single moment to our life by our fretting. Jesus also asks how people of faith are any different from people with no faith if what we trust is money and wealth.

His prescription for anxiety is not medication but redirection. Matthew 6:33 is a cornerstone for anyone who wishes to live in the realm of God. "Seek first God's reign in your life and all the other things you need will come." How different that formula for success is from the one we pursue.

Most of the time we work hard, and *then* we ask God to bless what we are doing. What would it be like if we sought out what God is working on and sought to invest ourselves in those things? Maybe rather than trying to persuade God to care about the things that worry us, we ought to seek out the things God already cares about.

Someone recently asked me how she could discover God's will for her life. I'm not sure she appreciated my answer. I told her that the first step was to start doing those things that she already knows to be God's will. Otherwise it is like asking God for more light when we've refused to open our eyes and use the light we have.

The sixth chapter of Matthew is divided between how to practice our piety and how to handle our money. The seventh chapter is a bit less coherent and more of a collection of amplified aphorisms.

Jesus begins with a teaching about judging others, which has been one of the most widely neglected of the teachings of Christ. "Do not judge," Jesus says. Although we want to qualify that statement and justify our need to make moral evaluations, taken on face value, the verse is pretty black and white. Eventually, Jesus will offer some more nuanced teachings, like knowing people by the fruit of their lives and how to deal with a member of the community who has gone astray. Here, though, he seems to want to stop religious people in our tracks.

Having offered us an expanded understanding of traditional moral teachings, Jesus wants to make clear that evaluating how others live out those teachings isn't our assignment. After equating hate with murder and lust with adultery, Jesus then seeks to get us to use those standards to remove the planks from our own eyes before we start trying to get the speck out of our neighbor's eyes. (Mt. 7:3-5)

The principle here is based on the law of "sowing and reaping." Throughout scripture, that principle is as consistent and true an assumption as gravity. What you sow you also reap; what you give out in life comes back to you. Here Jesus is warning that living judgmentally comes back to us. I hate that.

Nothing makes you feel better than a little moral superiority. We liberals enjoy holding the moral high ground over those who don't care for the poor, or who support war, or who aren't concerned about the environment. We can be arrogant and condescending in our self-righteousness, discounting people who disagree with us as unsophisticated or unenlightened. Maybe Jesus is trying to warn us that fundamentalists are not the only ones who need to work on their own eyes/vision.

Matthew 7:7-29

The remaining teachings of the Sermon on the Mount are a rather random collection that includes what we know as the "Golden Rule." These teachings conclude with the commentary:

> *Now when Jesus had finished saying these things, the crowds were astounded at his teachings, for he taught them as one having authority and not as their scribes.*

Mt. 7:28-29

When I was in college, in ancient times, most of my professors required every assertion in a paper to be footnoted and substantiated by a scholar or authority. Then, in graduate school, I encountered a professor who would not accept any paper that did not have our own original perspective. He explained that, if we were earning a master's degree, we needed to demonstrate that we had mastered the material. He expected that we had integrated the ideas of others into our own thinking, and were now capable of expressing our unique view on the matter. It seems that Jesus was a graduate of that school.

The teaching tradition of his day was typical of the scribes who taught by quoting precedents and the teachings of other authorities. Jesus came into their midst "as one with authority." This closing assessment in the Sermon on the Mount reflects Jesus repeatedly saying, "You have heard it said of old, but I say to you ... ." He was someone who went beyond the rules and law to the spiritual principles beneath them and called us to integrate the principle, not just obey the law.

I believe that we who seek to be disciples of Jesus also ought to be people who speak with authority. Quoting scripture is worthless unless we have integrated into our lives the principles, values and ethics that are represented. Disciples of Jesus work to integrate into our lives who he was and how he lived. This goes beyond rule keeping. The identity of Jesus shines through us in unique ways.

Each of us is a unique piece of glass that has been colored/stained by our experiences. The light of Jesus shines through us, and, though it is the same light, its expression is as different as each of us is. We are not clones of Jesus, but people who live under the authority of Jesus.

This chapter begins Matthew's record of a series of miracles that Jesus performed. So, what is a miracle? Do we believe in them? How can we avoid the superstitions and magical thinking that were common in ancient times and still find meaning in these stories? How do we avoid the terrible theology that comes with believing that God randomly intervenes in human life? What does it mean that Jesus is credited with violating the laws of medicine and physics? If Jesus had special powers, was he really fully human? And, finally, what on earth makes you think I know the answers to these questions?

While people of faith traditionally draw comfort and hope from these miracle stories, a thoughtful consideration should leave us with more questions than answers. Ironically, as I write this, my iPod is playing Twila Paris singing "God is in Control." As I listen to that song, I realize that it conveys a message of conventional piety, but I wonder if those who sing it ever wonder why things are such a mess if God is in control. So, too, when something happens and we call it a miracle, do we pause to wonder at all about the people who did not get their miracle today?

It seems to me that the worst theology is that which has not fully considered the implications. Do we really believe that God is in control of a world where children are brutally raped? Can we honestly say that one person got a miracle while one person a second dies of starvation, 85 percent of them children? If we are not careful, our thoughtless piety makes a monster out of God. Does God play favorites?

On the other hand, to deny that there is such a thing as a miracle is arrogance. We dare not presume that we understand either God or the universe well enough to be able to explain all that happens. So, are we left with a choice between human hubris and Divine capriciousness? Do you honestly think I know? What I do know is that we dare not seek to study the miracles of Jesus without having thought about these implications.

Matthew 8:1-13

The first miracle Jesus performs in Matthew's account of his life is healing a leper. The word "leper" was applied to a variety of skin diseases, and, when diagnosed, the victim was considered spiritually unclean and then isolated from the community. This was a fate far worse than what that old commercial used to call "the heartbreak of psoriasis." The law was designed to limit contagion, but, since it was applied to almost anything other than a temporary rash, there were many victims. The leper said, "If you choose to you can make me clean." This, of course, reflected the belief that his skin disease had made him unclean, unfit for human community. Jesus' response was an unambiguous, "I do choose."

Throughout the Gospels, the witness of Jesus is consistently that God's will for all people is health and wholeness. In fact, nowhere in the Bible does it say that Jesus came to save souls. The witness of the miracle stories is that God is concerned about our physical wellness. Common sense tells us that, in our ideal state, we are created to be whole and healthy and that our bodies are wired to move us back to that state as efficiently as possible. There are times when we need help, but think of all the times you have cut yourself and your body has healed with little or no outside help. We are made to be healthy and whole. Every day we encounter billions of disease causing germs; however, our bodies defeat almost all of them with remarkable efficiency.

When it comes to our being healthy and whole, we can hear God say, "I do choose that for you." Yes, accidents happen; body parts wear out; germs come our way at a weakened time; we get sick; we all die. However, the witness of Jesus is that God's desire for us is health and wellness. You will never find Jesus saying that God made someone sick or punished someone with disease. You will never see anything in the actions or teachings of Jesus to indicate that anything other than wellness was God's will.

Of course, in teaching us to pray, Jesus taught us to pray that God's will would be done "on earth as it is in heaven," because Jesus knew that God's will is not always realized on earth. Like every mother, God wants her children to be healthy and strong and aches with love whenever we are sick, wanting to love us back to health. Although God's will isn't always done, Jesus' consistent witness is that wellness is God's choice for us all.

This passage describes how Jesus healed the servant of a Roman centurion. It is a scandalous miracle that speaks volumes about Jesus' compassion. First, it was outrageous that he responded to a request to help a commander of the enemy soldiers occupying and terrorizing his own country. Secondly, this request came from a gentile; that is a non-believer. Thirdly, and perhaps most interestingly, is the implied relationship between the Centurion and his "servant."

Episcopal Priest Tom Horner was one of the first scholars who dared to make the point that both Matthew and Luke use the Greek work *pais* to refer to the Centurion's servant rather than the word *doulos,* which both writers use in other places when referring to servants. The implication is that there is a different kind of relationship here. The word *pais* is used elsewhere in Greek literature to refer to a man's younger male lover. Many contemporary scholars, including Theodore Jennings at Chicago Theological Seminary, have concluded that this is exactly the meaning that Matthew and Luke are seeking to communicate.

Here, Jesus is asked by a military officer of an occupying army to heal his intimate servant who is paralyzed. The centurion tells Jesus that he doesn't need to come to his home to perform the miracle. As a person with authority himself, he recognized that Jesus was a person with spiritual authority who simply could give the command and it would be done. So, did this centurion not want Jesus to come to his home because it was messy? Or had he worked with the Jews long enough to know that entering a gentile's home would make him unclean? Or was it the relationship that he feared might be scorned by Jesus?

I do not think it was the latter because the centurion is the one who spills the beans. He tells Jesus matter-of-factly what kind of relationship this was. Without this note the readers of the story would have thought it very odd. No powerful military leader would ever have gone out of his way and humbled himself for a mere servant. The identifier is the only thing that makes sense. Note that far from rejecting this request because it came from a gentile or because of the relationship between the two men, Jesus commends the centurion's faith, saying, "In no one in Israel have I found such faith." (v. 10) People who have been marginalized and excluded have to exercise great faith to come to God when others say they can't. Here, early in Matthew, we find a stirring example of how that is done: with humility, courage and determination.

Matthew 8:14-17

Yesterday we examined the story of Jesus healing a centurion's male lover. Today's lesson, ironically, is the healing of Peter's mother-in-law. Without this story we would never know Peter was married. His wife is never mentioned, not even in this story, only his mother-in-law, by which we must assume a wife. The poor woman is sick with a fever.

It is probably important to remember the extreme sexism of the day in which Jesus lived. There are clues through out the Gospels of the women who were disciples and friends of Jesus, but very little is said directly of them. A careful reading reveals that Jesus resisted the kind of sexism of his day, which excluded women, treating them as property or worse. Those who recorded the stories of Jesus did not seem to get the message, or perhaps they assumed their readers would not understand.

This brief story is recorded in Matthew, Mark and Luke. In it, Jesus heals an older woman. As in the preceding story, this miracle is done for someone whom society did not highly regard. Like most of the women in the Bible, this woman is unnamed and is simply identified by her relationship with a man. All three versions of this story end by noting that, after Jesus healed this woman, she immediately got up and began to serve him. (v.15) It is as if they tried to explain why Jesus would "waste" this miracle by pointing out that she was still useful.

Throughout the Gospels, Jesus heals women and men without differentiation. Sexism is still very much a reality today, but it has lessened enough that we might miss that the way Jesus treated women was a revolutionary change. While the authors might have wanted to justify Jesus caring for one they regarded as insignificant, the total testament of the Gospels tells a different tale. Unfortunately, most of the scholars, theologians, preachers and priests of the past 2,000 years have been men who suffered similar sexism, so few of us have been invited to read the text with liberated eyes. Historically marginalized people like women have had to read between the lines to find themselves and to hear that Jesus regarded them fully as children of God. Like Jesus, we, who are people of faith, must seek to heal people of the wounds of exclusion. It is a fever for which there is a cure.

In the first three recorded miracles, Jesus heals people who were marginalized by his society: a leper, a gentile's servant/lover and a woman. The next set of miraculous signs includes stilling a storm, defeating demons, healing a paralyzed man, and healing a hemorrhaging woman. Before those stories are told, though, there is an encounter with possible disciples. Then, in the middle of the next set of miracles, is the story of Jesus calling Matthew. It is as if the power of Jesus is responsible for people believing and becoming disciples:

> *A scribe then approached and said, "Teacher, I will follow you wherever you go." And Jesus said to him, "Foxes have holes, and birds of the air have nests, but the Human One has nowhere to lay his head." Another of his disciples said to him, "Lord, first let me go and bury my father." But Jesus said to him, "Follow me, and let the dead bury their own dead."*

Jesus seems to discourage one follower who he seemed to think did not understand the cost. It is an interesting statement, given the popularity of the "Prosperity Gospel," which says that God wants us all to be successful and wealthy. Jesus is saying that, by that standard, his life was cursed because foxes and birds had more than he did.

While it is tempting to dismiss this as being only about Jesus, people like Francis of Assisi seemed to think that, since Jesus was making this statement to one who wanted to be his disciple, this was a more general expectation of Jesus. Today, we want to be disciples of Jesus, but we don't want to sacrifice or be inconvenienced. Be honest; would you be a Christian if Jesus said to you what he said to that scribe?

The second person asked for a deferment. To our modern ears, Jesus seems almost cruel in not wanting to let the man go bury his father. The truth is, though, the man was asking to delay his obligation to follow Jesus until his parents were dead and gone. That may have been many years, and Jesus knew that there was an urgency to the work he calls us to do. When we are comfortable, and have lost the sense of urgency and the challenge of sacrifice, we probably need to reflect on whether or not we are still answering the call of Jesus, or following another.

Matthew 9:2-7

Seven weeks into this study and we have made it through only nine chapters of Matthew. At this rate we certainly won't finish the New Testament. However, most of the material in Matthew is repeated in Luke, and almost all of it is in Mark. We will move quickly through those Gospels and then spend a long time with John before we move through the rest of the New Testament.

In the ninth chapter of Matthew we find several more miracles, beginning with Jesus healing a paralyzed man by forgiving his sins. The Jewish leaders consider this to be blasphemy since only God can forgive sins. It is easy to see their point, but it may be that, like the pious people of that day, we, too, miss Jesus' point.

The story is **not** a testimony to Jesus' power to forgive sins. While his opponents thought he presumed too much, today Jesus' fans make the opposite mistake. We put Jesus up on a pedestal, making him divine, therefore relieving ourselves of any obligation to emulate his example. Jesus doesn't make these claims for himself, and, when demons tried to testify about him, he silenced them. Perhaps he knew that more damage would be done by those who deny his humanity than by those who denied his divinity.

Jesus forgave this man and set him free. The Jewish leaders thought he was presuming to take the place of God. Actually, Jesus simply was acting out of the fullness of his humanity. His favorite title for himself was the "Human One" (Son of Man). We probably all have heard this story about healing the paralytic, but did you notice what the final verse says? It talks about how this miracle awed people, but notice what they were awed about: *When the crowds saw the man was healed, they were filled with awe and they glorified God,* ***who had given such authority to human beings.***

The main difference between Jesus and us is that he understood fully all that humans were created to be and accepted the authority that comes, not from being divine, but from being HUMAN. You have more power to set people free or paralyze them than you will ever know. Use it well today!

Matthew 9:9-13

This is a brief record of Jesus calling Matthew the tax collector to be a disciple. Today, people argue about whether or not lesbian or gay people can be disciples of Jesus, and only the United Church of Christ has consciously affirmed that gay people can be fully Christian and therefore eligible for ordained ministry. The irony is that, in Jesus' day, calling a tax collector was a much more radical act than calling a homosexual.

Tax collectors (IRS agents) are unpopular today, but in Jesus' day they were the most hated of people. The Roman oppressors were resented, but they were outsiders seeking power and control. Matthew was a Jew who betrayed his own people by collecting taxes for those oppressors. He had sold his very soul for a bit of gold. He would not be allowed in the temple and never invited to dinner by his family or any respectable people.

Matthew's call is described with the fewest words. Jesus said, "Follow me," and he did. What follows is a description of Jesus and his disciples eating with a whole bunch of tax collectors and "sinners." This apparently upset the Pharisees who criticized Jesus for the company he kept. Maybe they would not have been upset if Jesus had been "loving the sinner but hating the sin." He isn't lecturing or demanding anything. He is simply breaking bread. Notice that this isn't just Jesus eating with people of questionable standing, though; the disciples are all there, too. How has the church missed this point?

Jesus answered the criticism by saying, "I have not come to call the righteous but sinners." (Mt. 9:13) Do not miss what is missing here. Jesus does NOT add the words "to repent" to the end of that sentence. He simply came to call sinners. Given the context of Matthew's call to be a disciple of Jesus, we can presume that what is meant is that Jesus came to call sinners to be his disciples. Both from what he said and how he lived, it appeared that the righteous made him tired. Jesus enjoyed the company of sinners, and that is whom he called to come and follow him. In other words, Jesus didn't want to hang out with those who thought they had their act together and were insiders with God. Jesus came to be with those of us who know we need help and are willing to both ask for it AND offer it. Wanna go to dinner?

Matthew 9:18-26

The next story Matthew recounts actually is a miracle on the way to a miracle. A leader of the synagogue came to Jesus asking him to heal his daughter who had just died. He believed that if Jesus laid his hands on her she would return to life. This miracle story is similar to the story in the First Testament books of Kings in which Elijah and Elisha both raise children from the dead. What is different is that in those stories the kids were both boys. Here the child is a girl. Today we are not surprised by that, but it is obviously noteworthy to the author because he puts this story of Jesus raising up a girl with the story of Jesus healing a woman.

On his way to the leader's home, a woman whose menstrual flow had lasted 12 years decided that she would reach out and touch the hem of his garment. Luke fleshes this story out a bit, telling us that Jesus stopped and searched the crowd for the one who had touched him. Matthew simply says that Jesus turned and saw her.

That really is a point we've missed in our traditional readings of the Gospels. Jesus saw those people who are invisible in our society. When the Bible is interpreted only by representatives of the dominant culture—able bodied, white, middle class, heterosexual men—these truths are almost always missed.

This woman tried to obtain her healing surreptitiously. She no doubt knew that, according to the law, if she simply had walked up to Jesus and asked him to touch her, she would have made him unclean. Leviticus forbade a Jewish man to touch a woman when she was menstruating. This woman had no idea that compassion was Jesus' guiding value, and he would have done whatever he could to help her.

Jesus turns and sees her. He is probably the first man to do so in 12 years. Then he speaks to her and commends her faith: *Take heart daughter; your faith has made you whole.* Notice he doesn't claim responsibility for her healing. He affirms that her exercising her faith is what led to her wholeness. God may have been the one to heal her, but it was her courage to resist the oppression of society and seek out an answer to her problems that led her to wholeness. Jesus knew there was a difference between not being sick and being whole. Regardless of the role he played in healing her sickness it was her own faith that made her whole.

In this passage, the 12 male disciples of Jesus are named and sent out. This passage ends with one of my favorite verses in Matthew. Jesus tells his disciples to go out and do all the good they can, telling people the good news. He knew that not everyone would be receptive to good news since religion then and now had been so much about controlling behavior by threatening bad news. Perhaps he also knew that "no good deed goes unpunished." Human nature is a strange thing, and Jesus acknowledges that by telling them how to handle rejection.

What is probably important to see is that, while Jesus was a realist, he was not a cynic. He offers one of the best pieces of advice found anywhere: *Be as cunning as a serpent and as innocent as a dove.* (Mt. 10:16) Being cunning and wise without slipping into bitterness and cynicism is not a balance many people manage to achieve.

Religious people sometimes can be naïve and blame it on God. For example, caring for the poor doesn't mean unthinkingly creating dependency. Being compassionate with a homeless person doesn't mean that you let them use you, manipulate you, or steal from you. Rather it may mean investing your compassion, your time, and your resources into changing the systems that contribute to homelessness and poverty. It may mean confronting behaviors that are self-destructive and refusing to continue enabling that person's destruction.

I believe Jesus is saying that we must be wise, strategic and deliberate in how we live our lives. We must also be innocent or harmless. There is far too much truth in the little girl's question. Having witnessed an interchange in which one party was harsh and unkind she asked, "Are you mean because someone hurt you, or is it just because you go to church?"

I believe what Jesus is saying in this passage is that e*very day get up and go out into the world to do as much good as you can. Heal hurts and tell people good news. Not everyone will be entirely receptive so you are going to have to be strategically compassionate and kind, but never be anything less.*

Matthew 10:34-39

Yesterday we looked at one of my favorite passages in Matthew. Today we encounter one of my least favorites. I was tempted to skip it, ignore it or pretend it doesn't exist. This is what the passage says:

> *Do not think that I have come to bring peace to the earth; I have not come to bring peace, but a sword. For I have come to set a man against his father, and a daughter against her mother, and a daughter-in-law against her mother-in-law; and one's foes will be members of one's own household. Whoever loves father or mother more than me is not worthy of me; and whoever loves son or daughter more than me is not worthy of me; and whoever does not take up the cross and follow me is not worthy of me. Those who find their life will lose it, and those who lose their life for my sake will find it.*

As the president of a peace and justice organization, I particularly hate the first part of that verse. No wonder, in the next chapter, John the Baptist sends a messenger to ask, *"Are you the One or should we look for another?"* This seems to contradict the verse in Matthew 5:9 where Jesus said *"Blessed are the peacemakers,"* and Jesus himself refused every opportunity to take up the sword in his quest to establish his Kingdom. Even at the end, he rebukes Peter for trying to use his sword to defend him. Jesus is the one who said we must learn to love our enemies, so just why would we take up a sword against our sisters and brothers? Maybe Jesus was talking about how the Church he would establish would fight one another.

The truth is that Jesus isn't talking about what he intended, but acknowledging that his call for us to live life differently would create conflict and division even in families. Living by the guiding principles of Jesus—mercy, forgiveness, compassion, generosity and tolerance—puts us on an inevitable collision course with a culture whose guiding principles are acquisition, dominance, superiority by exclusion, and power. Jesus wasn't talking about peace as the absence of war, but he was clear that, for those who take their faith seriously, there will be conflicts. We must remember to be as cunning as a serpent in these conflicts, but we must also be as innocent as a dove … the symbol for peace.

In chapter 4, following the Baptism of Jesus, John the Baptist is arrested by Herod and thrown into prison. At his baptism, John declares Jesus to be the one sent from God with a "winnowing fork" in his hand. Apparently, he now is having second thoughts. John sends his disciples to ask, "Are you the One, or should we be looking for another?"

I know how John feels, don't you? I mean, I love Jesus, but when I'm in trouble or pain or distress he seems altogether too passive for me. John had read all the Hebrew prophets' predictions of the messiah, and he fully expected someone who would vigorously sort the wheat from the chaff. John came breathing fire and warning, "Just wait until the Messiah gets here … "

Then Jesus comes along suggesting that we needed to forgive our enemies, turn the other cheek, and go the extra mile. In answer to John's question, Jesus tells his disciples to go back and tell him what they have seen and heard:

> *Go and tell John what you hear and see: the blind receive their sight, the lame walk, the lepers are cleansed, the deaf hear, the dead are raised, and the poor have good news brought to them. And blessed is anyone who takes no offense at me.*

Jesus describes the work he is doing, and ends by saying "blessed are those who aren't offended" by this vision of the messiah. I don't think he meant John so much as all of those who are offended by a messiah who brings peace rather than a sword. The ancient Jews certainly were not the only religious people to believe that the "enemies" of God would be punished and the "friends" of God rewarded. They were not the last who thought that the good news was for the rich, powerful and successful, not the poor to whom Jesus came.

John isn't the last person who thought Jesus ought to be more judgmental, vengeful and just. Even now, Jesus is used to uphold our prejudices and to reinforce our righteous anger. Like John, few of us really want to be a disciple of a healing liberator who is on the side of the poor. We keep looking for another, or making Jesus into another type of messiah that better suits our needs.

Matthew 11:28-30

Chapter 11 ends with an invitation from the true Messiah:

> *Come to me, all you that are weary and are carrying heavy bur-*
> *dens, and I will give you rest. Take my yoke upon you, and learn*
> *from me; for I am gentle and humble in heart, and you will find*
> *rest for your souls. For my yoke is easy, and my burden is light.*

This is one of the most beautiful passages in scripture. It describes the mission and ministry of Jesus. Yet, I recently received an email from someone who was concerned that they might "go to hell" because they are gay. They had learned in church that Jesus said, "Come unto me some of you" or "Come unto me those of you who are heterosexual."

The witness of scripture is that Jesus came for the poor, the weary, the heavily laden, not for the rich, the powerful or the strong. The gentle, humble Jesus offering us rest seems quite foreign to the Christ many of us grew up learning about in church. Why is that? Is it possible that we would have met a different Jesus if the preacher or teacher was not one of the dominant members of society? Every mega-church in this country is lead by a man … most of them white men. They seem to have a different interpretation of who Jesus is than people who live at the margins of society.

If you hear Jesus' invitation as addressed to the over-worked members of society who are climbing the economic ladder, then we miss what Jesus meant by "weary." Oh, working hard for long hours can leave us all tired, but Jesus' invitation is to those whose very souls seem exhausted. It is an invitation to the oppressed who bear burdens that are beyond their control or choosing.

This is not "Come to me you over-worked, over-stressed, over obligated, over-extended." This is "Come unto me all those of you who bear the burden of oppression laboring long but not receiving the benefits. Come to me all of you who must bear burdens you did not choose." Jesus isn't offering a hammock, but a yoke, for he, too, was bearing the burden of others not of his own choosing.

Chapter 12 contains the first conflict between Jesus and the Pharisees over the observance of the Sabbath. These conflicts are difficult for modern readers to appreciate. Those of us that are a bit older remember the old "blue laws" that required stores to be closed on Sunday, or banned the sale of alcohol on Sunday. Household items could not be sold on Sunday in Texas until 1985.

For the Jews of Jesus' day, though, the observance of the Sabbath wasn't just an arbitrary rule based on one of the 10 commandments. For them, this rhythm of life was a corner stone of their identity. Surrounded by other religions and occupied by a Roman army, keeping the Sabbath was crucial to retaining their culture and their faith. When Jesus' disciples didn't strictly adhere to the law, or when Jesus healed the sick (practiced medicine), the Pharisees saw their core values being eroded.

There is a sense in which they were correct. While no one advocates returning to the days of blue laws, even a cursory consideration can see that our society has changed in ways that have not always been for the better. While Jesus did push back against the rigid legalism of the Sabbath observance, his own life modeled a rhythm of work and renewal. He tried to get his disciples to understand the principle behind the Sabbath without getting caught up in seeking to impose a legalism on others.

Jesus healed a man with a withered hand on the Sabbath, and the Pharisees were outraged. They thought he could have waited until the next day. Since the man was not suffering a life-threatening illness, they had a point. Obviously, Jesus is deliberately trying to challenge them to observe a higher law. For the second time he quotes the prophet Hosea through whom God said, "I desire mercy and not sacrifice."

In his conflicts around the Sabbath, Jesus isn't seeking to undermine the law, but to call us all to a higher law. The external piety of the old blue laws didn't satisfy the demands of higher demands of love. Jesus was trying to teach us that these God-given principles were given for our health and well-being, not our obedience.

Matthew 13:1-23

Matthew began with a long set of teachings attributed to Jesus that has been called the "Sermon on the Mount." Then there is a long series of miracles that are offered as signs of proof that Jesus was the Messiah. Now, in chapter 13, Matthew moves on to a collection of parables.

This section begins with one of my favorite parables. Jesus describes a farmer who is sowing seeds. In contrast to the careful, rigid and controlled religion of the fundamentalists of his day, this story is a depiction of a farmer on drugs. The farmer doesn't carefully plant the seeds in straight rows with stakes and identifying signs at each end. Instead, this extravagant, recklessly exuberant farmer flings seeds in every direction with scant regard for where they land. Some of the seeds land on the path, some in the bushes, some on the rocks, and some even land on good and fertile soil.

What kind of crazy farmer would work so inefficiently? Well, according to Jesus this crazy farmer is God. Is that your understanding of God?

How different this image of God is from the one with which so many of us grew up. The churches of our childhood left us with the impression that God only had enough love for those who believed and behaved the right way. Then Jesus comes along describing this eccentrically extravagant Sower of Life. Of course, this is shocking to our modern religious sensibilities, but it shouldn't be. After all, we have ample evidence that what Jesus says is true.

If you have ever looked through a microscope or a telescope, or if you re-member being a child with a magnifying glass, then you, too, have seen proof of the eccentric extravagance of this God of creation. So much variety, diversity, creativity … was it really necessary? Creation itself rises up to bear witness to this God who just doesn't know when to stop. For those of us who have spent a lot of our lives in the weeds and on rocky ground, that is good news. Our lives didn't take a straight path, but somehow this eccentrically extravagant God managed to fling a bit of grace into even our lives.

Following the extraordinary story of God as a reckless farmer, Matthew inserts a long explanation. It is almost as if he is trying to tame the story, even if he can't tame the God Jesus is revealing. Many scholars believe the explanation came from Matthew or some other teacher, not from Jesus.

Jesus next tells the parable of the wheat and tares (weeds). The parable sounds similar to the sower and seeds, because the farmer seems quite unconcerned about the weeds. He tells the servants to just let them all grow and sort it out later. However, when you read the explanation (Matthew 13:36-43) the tone is quite different, ending with the threat of weeping and gnashing of teeth.

The parables sound a lot like the Jesus I have come to know and love. The explanations sound much more like the followers of Jesus who find extravagant and uncontrolled grace too much to handle. I know because I have been one of those followers too often.

For much of my career I was more drawn to the explanation than to the parable. The explanation tames the parable, taking a spirituality of trust and turning it into a religion of control. Religious people like control. In fact, most people are religious because it gives them a feeling of control. If we think we understand, or can explain how life works and how God thinks, then we feel more in control of the chaos that is life.

The parables of Jesus don't depict a controlling God, so the later recorders of these stories added an explanation that made the stories less radical. Sadly, Christianity has worshipped a god of the explanation, not the God of the parable. Jesus kept trying, though. Next he says the Reign of God is like a treasure hidden in a field that is later found. The person who finds it sells everything **to buy the field.** Notice the treasure is just "found," and the finder doesn't buy the treasure but buys the field that contains the treasure. This religion of Jesus makes us uncomfortable because it isn't rigid, structured or controlled. It requires too much trust. I mean what if we don't find the treasure … or could it be that learning to truly trust the grace of God is the treasure?

Matthew 13:54-58

Matthew ends a chapter full of parables with a section in which the people in Jesus' hometown reject him. In Luke that is how Jesus starts his ministry. (Luke 4:16) What is interesting here is not so much that his hometown didn't embrace Jesus, but why they didn't. The rejection isn't based on miracles or other signs that Jesus performed, but on the teachings contained in the parables he told. They don't disagree with what he has to say, but wonder aloud where he got so smart:

> *Is this not the carpenter's son? Is not his mother called Mary?*
> *Are not his brothers James and Joseph and Simon and Judas?*
> *And are not all his sisters with us? Where did this man get all of*
> *this?*

What challenges them is not Jesus' divinity but his humanity. They know his family—father, mother, brothers and sisters. It seems that the people in the crowd in Nazareth are not the only ones bothered by Jesus' humanity. The early Church's teaching about the virgin birth was one of the earliest attempts to distance Jesus from his humanity. In this passage, it is clear that people thought of Joseph as his father.

In the 15th century, the pope declared as official doctrine the concept that Mary was herself immaculately conceived. The doctrine of Immaculate Conception is that Mary was conceived in her mother's womb without sex, which, according to the Church, would have made her sinful. The Church also taught that Mary was perpetually a virgin and that the relatives mentioned here are actually cousins or Joseph's children by another marriage.

The Protestant Church generally rejects this doctrine; however they do not reject the bad theology that it expresses. Unlike Jesus, the Church to which he gave birth has never embraced humanity as a good thing. In the King James Version of the Bible a favorite title for Jesus was "The Son of Man." A modern and more complete translation of that is "The Human One." Native American tradition understood that our choice was between being human and being savages. We need to insist on the full humanity of Jesus and to insist on the sacred value of our own humanity, regardless of what those in our hometowns may have thought of us.

Jesus' rejection by his hometown is followed by the story of the execution of Jesus' cousin John by Herod Antipas. The story of how John died and why Herod had him killed is told here, but John apparently had been dead for a while because Herod thinks that Jesus is actually the resurrected John come back to haunt him.

This story became a part of the common culture after Oscar Wilde wrote a play in French entitled "Salome." Richard Strauss turned it into a German opera in 1905, and, in 1923, it was made into a silent film. The film was considered the first "art film," and it became a cult classic.

Salome (not named in the Gospels) was the daughter of Herod and Herodias (Herod's brother's wife). Salome danced so seductively for Herod that he offered her anything she wanted. Prompted by her mother, she asked for the head of John the Baptist on a platter. Herod is said to regret having made the offer, but he was a man of his word. So, he had John beheaded.

No wonder Herod thought Jesus was John come back to haunt him. He was a man of integrity and wouldn't break his word to Salome, but this illustrates how often we have strict values that govern one part of our life, while still able to do great harm in another. Few people alive have ever considered themselves unethical or immoral. Hitler had great integrity in living out his warped value system. I'm sure you do, too, and so do I.

We wouldn't lie, but that doesn't seem to stop us from repeating rumors that we don't know are true. We wouldn't break a promise, but we have made so many to God that we can't even remember them. We wouldn't kill someone, but the rage we aim at them would if a weapon were behind it. We are legalists about certain values and generally expect other people to be as well. Yet, all of us have areas of our lives that are much less holy than we want to pretend. Maybe we all need for Jesus to come back and haunt us now and then.

Matthew 14:13-21

Here we have what must have been Matthew's favorite miracle story because he tells it twice. Here, Jesus feeds 5,000 men, plus women and children, (v. 21) with five loaves and two fish. In the very next chapter, Jesus feeds 4,000 men, plus women and children, with seven loaves and a few small fish. Mark also has two feeding accounts, and Matthew seems to follow Mark's pattern. It is possible that an editor had two versions of this story and included them here.

This story is told six times among the four Gospels, so perhaps there is something here that we should attend to.

One of the things we must note is that if we are looking for proof that the Bible is not inerrant/infallible we only have to read these verses where women and children are mentioned but don't really count. If the life and death of Jesus means anything at all to us, it has to be that everyone counts with God.

This story is told as a miracle, a sign that proved Jesus was the Christ. I've always thought that maybe what happened was that one person shared what they had brought. (Luke says it was a little boy, one of those who didn't count.) Jesus took it and gave thanks, despite how little it seemed in the midst of such great need. Maybe it was the faith that was great enough to give thanks for so little, or maybe it was the generosity of an uncounted one. Whatever it was suddenly people began to pull out the food they had kept hidden.

In a world that produces more than enough and yet millions starve, is it anything less than miraculous that Jesus could move people to generosity and sharing? When we make this into a story about magic it cannot speak to us because we can't do magic. However, we all have something to share.

In both stories, Matthew notes the abundance of "leftovers." Perhaps he knew that we would have a tendency to slip into a scarcity mindset and forget that there is more than enough to go around. The miracle of generosity and gratitude can feed us all as if everyone actually did count.

We next encounter the miracle of Jesus walking on the water. I'm never quite sure what to make of this story. How do we encounter this story without resorting to magical thinking? A careful reading of the text in the original language may be of some help. One perfectly reasonable translation of the story might say this:

> *And early in the morning he came walking towards them **toward** the lake. But when the disciples saw him walking **toward** the lake, they were terrified, saying, "It is a ghost!" And they cried out in fear. But immediately Jesus spoke to them and said, "Take heart, it is I; do not be afraid."*

> Mt. 14:25-27

This is a reasonable understanding of the Greek phrase used and makes the story less about a magical messiah and more a parable about how we often let our fears shape our perceptions. We very well may respond to help with fear rather than with faith. I can think of many times in my life when the circumstances became so tumultuous that support, care and compassion went unrecognized. However, I can't think of a single time when anyone ever walked on water to rescue me.

God has come to me many times via people willing to walk **through** storms to get to me. God has sent people into my life who shouted above the roar of the storm and challenged me to leave the security of my boat and to try doing something I'd never tried before.

There is much that rings true in this story, but the traditional magical interpretation leaves it as an ancient tale that was only about Jesus and not about us. While the ancients, and even Matthew, may have been telling the story in a way that would prove that Jesus was special, that isn't what is needed today. We all know Jesus was the son of God. What we seem unable to believe is that we are also sons and daughters of God. Jesus' ability to work magic only distances us from whom we are called to be. According to John, Jesus said we would do greater things than he did. That is hard to believe if we take stories like this literally, as they have been taught in the past. If we liberate them from magical thinking, we might hear them speak to us and about us ... which may be why we choose to think of Jesus as a worker of magic.

Matthew 15:21-28

Matthew 15 contains a story that I find to be the most difficult in the Gospels. I always try to avoid it when possible, but I know that isn't fair. This story makes me uncomfortable because, in my modern eyes, it seems to put Jesus in a bad light. A Canaanite woman came to Jesus seeking healing for her demon-tormented daughter. According to the story, Jesus ignored her until his disciples finally came and asked him to send her away because she kept shouting at them. Jesus said to them, "I was sent to the lost sheep of the house of Israel."

The woman would not be sent away, though, and she fell on her knees to plead her daughter's case. To her, Jesus says, "It is not fair to take the children's food and throw it to the dogs." And the woman rose up and slapped him silly … well, if I had been the woman pleading for my child that is what I would have done. She didn't do that, but she reminded him that "even dogs get to eat the crumbs that fall from their master's table." Jesus then commends her faith and heals her daughter.

Now you know why I avoid this story. We could talk about the historical context of this story—the conflict between Jews and Gentiles for whom "dogs" was the kindest of insults—or the sexism of the day where it was unacceptable for a woman to speak to a rabbi, or perhaps the messianic expectations of the One who was to come to rescue Israel, not to help their enemies. None of that makes me feel any better.

Is it possible that what we have here is a person at the very margins of life helping Jesus to recognize that he is not just the Jewish Messiah, but that he was anointed by God to help us all? Jesus initially responds to her as his role dictated, but, by her faith, her persistence and her relentless love for her child, this woman perhaps shifted Jesus' understanding of himself and his calling.

Does it make us think less of Jesus to imagine him learning and growing? Isn't that what healthy humans do? The Bible talks about him "growing in wisdom," and there is no indication that this growth ever stopped. It shouldn't for any of us. So, if today's meditation made you a bit uncomfortable, maybe you are closer to understanding what really happened in this story.

This passage marks a turning point in the Gospel of Matthew. The author begins this passage saying:

> *From this point on Jesus began to show his disciples that he must go to Jerusalem and undergo great suffering at the hands of the elders and chief priests and scribes, and be killed, and on the third day be raised.*

This passage was written, of course, long after the facts and hence with both the benefit and liability of hindsight. The benefits are obvious, but when we are reading the Bible we sometimes forget about the liabilities. What exactly Jesus said, and what it meant loses its original context. Matthew knew how it ultimately turned out, but, frankly, I am dubious about his claims that Jesus had complete foreknowledge of how things would unfold. If Jesus' humanity has any meaning, then, like the rest of us, he, too, had to make his way through life with limited knowledge about how this was all going to turn out.

Anticipating that there would be a price to pay for confronting the power structure and the status quo didn't require a divine revelation. Jesus was a most intelligent observer of human nature. He was aware of history and already had seen what happened to his cousin John the Baptist, so it makes sense that he would begin to prepare his disciples for the price that would be paid.

Peter responds to this new insight from Jesus by taking him aside and rebuking him. Jesus responds strongly, not to the rebuke but to the idea that paying a price was not in Peter's formula for being a disciple. By now, Jesus is probably growing frustrated that those closest to him are still expecting him to be the kind of Messiah who would overthrow their enemies and reward them. In contrast to those expectations, Jesus tells them that true discipleship involves self-denial and cross-bearing.

That was the last thing Peter wanted to hear, and it seems that it is a message that still hasn't penetrated Christianity. People are still more attracted by the prospect that those with whom they disagree will be punished (hell) while they will be rewarded (heaven). Would we follow Jesus without the bribery of resurrection?

Matthew 17:1-21

This chapter begins with an episode known as the "transfiguration." While this story is read in most churches every year on the Sunday before Lent begins, I'm still not sure anyone understands what happened or what it really means.

Jesus took Peter, James and John high up a mountain, presumably to pray together. While they were there, Jesus was "transfigured" before their eyes, and two strangers showed up who they identify as Moses and Elijah. If we were to take this story as literal history, we would be left to wonder just how they recognized these ancient figures. What is true is that this story is meant to relay to us that Jesus was the successor to both the great law-giver, Moses and the great prophet, Elijah.

Peter, ever the purveyor of bad applications of the faith, suggests to Jesus that they build three tabernacles, one each for Jesus, Elijah and Moses. That way they could just stay there and worship. Of course, Jesus would have none of that, so they return to the valley below. There, Jesus is promptly confronted by a man whose son seems to have the symptoms of epilepsy, but his disciples have been unable to heal him because of their lack of faith.

Matthew seems to offer this story as a reminder to the church that, as tempting as it is to get caught up in the ecstasy of prayer, study and worship, there are still hurting people who need our help. It is with those in need that we must exercise our faith if it is to grow.

Christians go to church their whole lives. Many attend Sunday School for decades without ever graduating. It is true that we will never fully master all there is to know about the things of God, but this story is a reminder that we cannot allow that fact to keep us from practicing what we do know. We don't need to worry so much about the things in the Bible that we don't understand (like the transfiguration), as we need to worry about not applying the things we do understand … like forgiving our enemies, serving others and helping the poor and the needy.

Jesus begins this chapter with a lesson on humility. Greatness for disciples is becoming childlike, Jesus says. He then talks about God's passion, which is not for the 99 safe sheep, but for the one who goes astray.

All of this precedes a long section in which Jesus teaches about how to treat "offenders," both in the church and outside. Again, this is a retrospective interpretation by Matthew since the Church as we understand it did not yet exist. Essentially, Jesus was talking about how to deal with conflicts with fellow disciples. He begins by saying, "If another member of the church sins against you … " Some manuscripts lack the phrase "against you," which makes this a teaching about how to deal with members of the community of faith who commit an offending sin.

First, Jesus says, meet with that person alone and tell them what you think is wrong with their behavior. His words are set against Peter having taken him aside to rebuke him. Peter was mistaken, but he did it correctly. Perhaps this is a model we need to remember. Often when we judge another person to be mistaken in their actions we are simply wrong, like Peter was. By doing it privately we do not damage their reputation or our relationship.

This seems to be one of those red-letter verses that almost all Christians have cut out of their Bibles. We are almost fanatically consistent about talking to others about what we perceive to be a sister's or brother's "sin" without EVER talking to the brother or sister directly. Direct dealing is a clear instruction by Jesus. It is advocated by every mental health profession. It is a cornerstone of healthy relationships and community building. NO ONE disagrees with this principle, and almost no one practices it, at least in the church.

We might find direct dealing at work or in our 12-step groups, but the behavior of Christians would make you think Jesus had commanded us to talk to everyone in the world before we talk to our sister/brother. It isn't that Christianity doesn't work, so much as it is that it is so rarely authentically practiced.

Matthew 18:15-20

Jesus teaches direct dealing when we have a conflict. It is the healthy thing to do, but even Jesus acknowledged that it wouldn't always work. For when that happens, he offered another frequently-ignored suggestion. Jesus says we should take one or two others along to talk to the person. If that doesn't work, then, and only then, do you get the community involved. Even then the purpose is not gossip, conflict or punishment, but reconciliation.

Finally, though, even that may not work. Then, Jesus says, we should treat the person like a tax collector or Gentile. Many traditions have interpreted this as the process for excommunication; however, I'm not so sure. Remember that this is the Gospel of Matthew, the tax collector.

It is true that there does come a time when it is unhealthy for both the person and the community to continue to seek to be in relationship. Like divorce, this separation is a most unfortunate outcome, and it is only appropriate after great effort is made. I think what Jesus is saying is that even if a divorce is the only way we must treat the person just as he treated Gentiles and tax collectors, with mercy and compassion.

I probably do need to add here that there are exceptions to this process. In cases of abusive relationships the first priority must be safety. In those cases separation must come first for the sake of the victim. However, even in those cases, the work of healing must bring even the victim to a place where they can wish the abuser healing too. We should not continue in an abusive relationship, which means we must work our way to emotional release as well as physical safety. It takes time, but, unless we can release our anger, hatred and bitterness, we allow the person to continue to abuse us.

Centuries before Freud, Jesus was trying to teach us how to deal with conflict in a way that brings healing, hopefully, to both parties. If the Church had ever taken these principles seriously the world might look to us to help them resolve conflicts and make peace. Maybe we could be a place where taking Jesus seriously could start.

Matthew 18:21-35

Speaking of not practicing the teachings of Jesus … just as dealing directly with our sisters and brothers seems impossible, this passage that compels us to forgive is equally neglected.

Peter asks what to do if reconciliation doesn't work. How often should we forgive? Seven times? No doubt Peter was learning, so what he was suggesting was incredibly generous. Imagine his shock when Jesus said, "Not seven times but 70 times seven."

Of course, Jesus isn't saying that we need to forgive 490 times, but that our forgiveness can't know limits. He goes on to tell a parable about a king who forgives his servant an inconceivably large debt of 10,000 talents. It would take the average laborer more than 15 years to earn a single talent. This servant owed a debt greater than the wealth of a king. However, he goes out and encounters a friend who owes him a sliver of the amount he has just been forgiven. Rather than forgive his friend's debt, though, he has him thrown into debtors' prison.

Jesus is trying to remind us that, when we are confronting sin, we need to remember that we are sinners; when we are forgiving debt, we cannot forget that we are very great debtors. We must offer unending mercy and grace to our sisters and brothers, because we need God's unending mercy and grace.

One core principle that disciples of Jesus MUST understand is that we can never be reservoirs or containers of God. We are either channels, or we are nothing at all. If God's blessings, mercy, forgiveness and grace don't flow THROUGH us, they cannot flow TO us.

There are many times when we do not feel forgiveness or mercy, especially after the sixth or seventh time it is needed. Then all we can do is "deny our self" and seek to be a channel of God's forgiveness. We may not be capable of forgiving, but God is. We can allow that relentless grace through us. The beautiful thing is you can't be a channel of living water without getting wet yourself.

Matthew 19:1-12

This chapter marks the beginning of the end. The opening verse describes Jesus leaving Galilee for Judea. This is more than a change of address; he is headed for Jerusalem and the closing chapter of his life. Some passages make it appear that Jesus had some kind of supernatural foreknowledge of how it all would end. In this case, though, it didn't take a psychic to know that the empire was about to strike back against one who was teaching large crowds to live free of religious controls.

In the next major teaching, we find Jesus speaking rather sternly against divorce. Far from setting up a new legalism, Jesus was trying to protect women who were completely vulnerable to the whims of their husbands. This passage also contains a unique teaching about eunuchs:

> *His disciples said to him, "If such is the case of a man with his wife, it is better not to marry." [11]But he said to them, "Not everyone can accept this teaching, but only those to whom it is given. [12]For there are eunuchs who have been so from birth, and there are eunuchs who have been made eunuchs by others, and there are eunuchs who have made themselves eunuchs for the sake of the realm of heaven. Let anyone accept this who can."*

Eunuchs are at the very least a close parallel in the Bible to gay and lesbian folk. Jesus begins this passage talking about a man leaving his mother and joining his wife. The teaching ends with an example of those who do not do this. Jesus talks about three types of eunuchs: those who were born eunuchs (homosexuals), those who were made eunuchs (castrated), and those who made themselves eunuchs for the sake of the realm of heaven (celibate).

It is fascinating that, for centuries, the Church used this passage to demand celibacy for priests and nuns, but never acknowledged that first category of "eunuchs." We all read scripture through our own biases and life experiences. The secret is knowing when you are doing that. I acknowledge that I am doing that now. How would you understand this passage in a homophobia-free world?

Matthew 19:16-30

This encounter with Jesus is known as the "Rich Young Ruler." It also is recounted by Mark and Luke, and these three descriptors are gained only by looking at the story in all three. Matthew only tells us that he was young and rich.

He comes to Jesus asking what good deed he needed to do to gain eternal life. Jesus responds by asking the young fellow why he called him good, when God is the only one who is good. (Mt. 19:17) This seems to call into question the proposition that Jesus understood himself to be uniquely divine. Jesus clearly thought of himself as a son of God, but also seemed to think that all of us are sons or daughters of God. I am not suggesting that Jesus isn't the incarnation of God, but just wondering aloud if that was Jesus' own self-understanding. You see, if Jesus knew he was divine in a unique way, then he is simply playing the role of a human. For Jesus' humanity to have true meaning to how we live our lives, Jesus must be human in the same way we are, and, in this life, we must be divine in the same way Jesus was. It seems to me that the unique characteristic of Jesus is that he knew he was a son of God and we all still secretly doubt it.

This young man came looking for something he could DO that would ensure his eternity. Jesus suggests that he keep the commandments, and the young man says that he has. Both the young man and Jesus seemed to know that something was still missing. The man was trying to be God's perfect son by keeping the rules, so Jesus said to him, "If you want to be perfect then go sell all you have and give the money to the poor. The young man went away sad because he had many possessions." (Mt. 19:21-22)

Jesus then talks about how wealth gets in the way of God's reign in human life. The disciples, like most people, are startled by the thought that what they have gets in their way of letting God rule their life. Jesus used their possessions to break through to them and to the young man. They ask, "Who then can be saved?" It is a silly question, because Jesus never was talking about salvation. He says, "With you it is impossible, but with God nothing is impossible." Jesus was trying to teach them/us how to live, yet they kept thinking he was talking about heaven and hell. I think Jesus was saying essentially: *If you can live in such a way that your wealth and possessions don't rule your life then you will be my disciple and you can leave eternity in God's very capable hands.*

Matthew 20:1-16

Keeping these meditations short is tough. There is so much more to say, and I'm not able even to begin to do the passages justice. My hope is that you will see something new in a scripture and be willing to engage it more on your own. It sometimes makes me anxious to raise complex issues and not get to develop them or look at both sides. Having said that: today's passage is remarkably clear and painfully radical in its implications. I can't decide if sports influence our culture or if they are simply an expression of our need to keep score. Either way, that orientation makes this parable startling, especially when you consider that money and possessions are one of the ways we like to keep score and that Jesus warned us about that in yesterday's lesson.

In today's passage, Jesus describes the reign of God as being like a landowner who hires workers throughout the day so they end up working varying lengths of time. The final ones only work one hour, yet all of the workers get paid exactly the same wage. Those who worked all day long felt cheated, but the landowner asks, "Am I not allowed to do what I want with what is mine? Or are you envious because I am generous?"

Philip Gulley, in his great book *If Grace is True,* suggests that this story is about how humans are invested in heaven and hell as the ultimate method of keeping score. We don't like the idea that God ultimately will treat us all the same regardless of what we "deserve." Yet that is what this parable means, **if grace is true.**

In the very next verses, Jesus predicts his crucifixion. I can't help but wonder if he understood how unpopular grace really is. Gulley, who is a Quaker pastor, talks about all the hateful responses he has gotten from Christians as a result of suggesting what life here and hereafter might be like if we really believed in grace. Just today, an agnostic friend of mine, reflecting on the church, said, "Someday you can explain to me how an organization built on Christian principles attracts so many without them." I guess Jesus knew that many would be envious if God were so generous, which is why he told his disciples this very parable.

Matthew 20:20-28

In this passage, Matthew tells us that the mother of James and John came to Jesus and asked if her boys could sit on Jesus' right and left hand. This story is taken from Mark, who recorded it first, but in Mark's earlier version James and John make the request for themselves. Here it seems Matthew wants to ease the embarrassment on James and John by blaming their mother for their ambition.

This is another of those contradictions in the Bible that infallibility claims deny. It also misses the point about how often women and people of color have been scapegoats of men. (The Bible is not immune from these cultural prejudices either.)

The point of the story, though, is that Jesus again reminds us that in the Reign of God the first are last and the servant is the great one. Time and again, Jesus turns the typical scheme of things on its head. This is the third time Jesus says this in the last 30 verses. He concludes by reminding them that he saw himself as a servant.

I sometimes wonder if Christians have exalted Jesus so highly as a defense against having to follow his example or take his teachings seriously. If Jesus is uniquely divine then we can't possibly live as he did. However, if we strip away the mythology and listen to what Jesus said about himself, we then have to decide if living as a servant is what we really are called to do.

James' and John's ambition was crass, but is it so different from those of us who see our faith as a means to gain heaven and avoid hell? They wanted some eternal reward from Jesus. What do we want? If what we want is guidance on how to live our lives, then what we are offered is a call to live as a servant.

It seems that much of Christianity is more concerned with eternal reward (and punishment for others) than with learning to live as a servant. We see ourselves as privileged guests in this world rather than as hosts who are servants of the Creator.

Matthew 20:29-34

This is the last miracle in Matthew's Gospel. The next chapter begins with Jesus' entry into Jerusalem, which we celebrate on Palm Sunday. There are still several more chapters containing parables, but no more miracles.

Jericho is the last major town Jesus will pass through before getting to Jerusalem. As he passes, two blind men begin to shout above the crowd trying to get Jesus' attention. In Luke's version of the story there is only one blind man (Lk. 18:35-43), and in Mark's older version there is one blind man who is clearly identified. His name is Bartimaeus, son to Timaeus. We are left to wonder why Matthew used a different version of this story.

The blind men raise such a ruckus that the crowd tries to silence them, but they would not be denied. Was it their need that was so great or their faith? Perhaps it was the junction of the two, but, either way, they were determined to seize the moment. It was a good thing, too, because, though no one knew it at the time, Jesus would never pass that way again. In Matthew's telling, this was Jesus' last miracle before he entered Jerusalem to die.

In the wake of 9/11, there were many stories about last words and missed opportunities. My own daughters started ending all their phone calls to me with the words "Love you." It isn't a bad thing to remember that each conversation may be our last or that opportunities often only come once.

These men decided that they didn't care what the crowds thought of them; they were going to do everything they could to get to Jesus. If only we made so much effort, we, too, might find new sight and insight. It seems that only anger motivates us that strongly, never healing. Jesus heard their cry and healed them, and they followed him. They had no idea they were following him to a cross … but we do.

Matthew 21:1-11

This passage describes what has traditionally been called Palm Sunday. The implication, of course, is that we have entered the last week of Jesus' life. Matthew places some significant teachings between this reading and the description of the crucifixion.

Jesus entered Jerusalem along with crowds of other pilgrims streaming into the city for the observance of Passover. Some estimate that the city's population swelled to more than two million, though that is a difficult number to comprehend given the size of the ancient city. Still, every Jewish man living within 20 miles of Jerusalem was supposed to come to the city for Passover, and pilgrims journeyed from much farther.

In their superb book *The Last Week*, Marcus Borg and John Dominic Crossan have a wonderful description of the two processions entering Jerusalem that day. The first, a peasant procession led by Jesus, the other an imperial procession led by the Roman Governor Pontius Pilate. It is a contrast in types of power.

Jesus came riding a donkey, and people threw their cloaks on the ground for him to walk over and waved branches torn from trees. It seems a conscious enactment of a prophecy right from the pages of Zechariah, which Matthew naturally quotes. Here was one whose power resided completely in the faith and devotion of the people.

Across town, Pilate's procession was just as deliberate. He rode on a charger with the imperial banners of the Roman Empire at the head of a column of cavalry and a sizable contingent of Roman soldiers. It was his deliberate intent to flaunt the military force that would ruthlessly keep the peace. It was also a reminder that they were under the power of the empire.

The week begins with a clear contrast of two types of power. They will clash before the week is out. One will win, and one will lose. But, just as Jesus tried to tell us, the loser is the one who ultimately prevails, as we can see 2,000 years later. What we can't seem to see is that we keep joining the wrong procession.

Matthew 21:1-11

Before we leave this passage behind, it is important that we understand the contrast that Jesus is trying to create between the power and empire that he came to establish and the power and empire embodied by Rome. His disciples participated in Palm Sunday, but they missed the point. That seems to be as true then and now.

Back then, they thought the triumphant entry into Jerusalem heralded Jesus overthrowing the Roman Empire and establishing Israel's independence. Even after his death and resurrection, the disciples ask Jesus, "Will you NOW restore the kingdom to Israel?" They were anxious that Jesus punish their enemies and give them what they deserve. They also were looking forward to their own coming to power and being rewarded.

That brand of religion swept like wild fire across America in the wake of the tragic events of 9/11. Even now one of the Christian radio stations in Dallas prays every day for "our troops," while never praying for peace, or for our enemies, or for the countless innocent victims of our war. Civic religion is regarded as orthodox Christianity by many, if not most, Americans.

If you are reading this, you have probably rejected that brand of Christianity, but I wonder how we will ever escape our expectation that if we are good God will reward us, and if we are bad we will be punished. How will we ever eradicate the secret wondering if somehow God is punishing us every time something bad happens?

The Reign of God that Jesus rode into town to bring is still far from what we pray will come on earth as it is in heaven. This Realm—where the rich are poor and the last are first—is not what our religion is all about. We may not ask God to annihilate our enemies, but our faith is still often about being rewarded and avoiding punishment. Jesus didn't come to give us power and reward, nor to put down and overthrow our enemies. Jesus came to create a reign where the lion lays down with the lamb in our hearts and peace comes to earth in our world. They didn't get that. Do we?

This passage is known as the "cleansing of the temple." Matthew offers it as one of the reasons the Jewish religious leaders decided Jesus had to go. It is not the kind of direct, causal explanation that John offers when he tells us that raising Lazarus was the final straw.

This story is an anomaly in the life of Jesus, but it is told in all four Gospels, though John places it at the beginning of Jesus' ministry rather than at the end. Our image of this event is rather violent, with Jesus overturning tables and tossing people out on their ears. What is interesting is that all the action is described in one long sentence. (v. 12)

Still, even with an economy of words, we are left struggling to reconcile our image of Jesus the peacemaker with this image of him using physical force to confront those in the temple who were exploiting the poor. My pacifist friends offer lots of explanations for this story, but the truth is I think this scene made Jesus mad enough to act in ways he never had before.

When I read this story, I recall that great scene in "The Color Purple" in which Shug, the blues singer says, "I think it pisses God off if you walk by the color purple in a field somewhere and don't notice it." Well, I think it pisses Jesus off when people walk by the poor being exploited and don't notice it.

It wasn't that money-changing and animal-selling in the temple was inappropriate; it was that the priests were profiting at the expense of the devotion of the poor. The peasants of Palestine sacrificed and saved to make their offerings at Passover, but when they had to exchange their Roman coins for temple currency, they often got cheated. Poor families raised animals to take for a sacrifice, and that animal represented at least one meal they would have to do without. The animal had to be without blemish to be offered to God. Priests often found faults and forced the family to buy another from the sellers in the temple, and, of course, the priests got their cut.

Dom Helder Camara said, "When I give food to the poor, they call me a saint. When I ask why the poor have no food, they call me a communist." Jesus might have added "And when you don't ask why the poor have no food in a word that has plenty, it really pisses me off."

Matthew 21:12-17

Jesus never condemned sinners, but he often rebuked the righteous and, particularly, the self-righteous. In the end, he reserved his greatest expression of anger for the righteous who made it difficult for the poor to worship God. Yesterday we talked about the expression of Jesus' anger about the neglect and abuse of the poor.

According to Matthew, Jesus explained his actions by quoting from Isaiah 56: "My house shall be called a house of prayer for all people." He then adds "But you have made it a den of robbers." That last part is not in Isaiah. What is in Isaiah, though, is a teaching of radical inclusion. The statement that God's house is to be "a house of prayer **for all people**" comes in the middle of an amazing statement of how the messiah will create a realm in which ALL are welcome.

Specifically, Isaiah singles out the foreigners; think immigrants and outsiders. Even more explicitly this passage promises to eunuchs—think those who are excluded because of their sexuality—a special place and "a name better than sons and daughters." The inclusion of daughters there makes it clear that Isaiah was not talking about males who had been castrated.

In quoting this radically inclusive passage from Isaiah, Jesus is defining again the kind of messiah he was, the work he had come to do, and the kind of reign he had come to establish. His disciples didn't get it, and I'm not sure we get it now. Even today the Church debates who can be allowed fully into the House of God. What part of "all people" don't we get?

Matthew then says, "The blind and the lame came to him, and he healed them." I can't help but wonder if the Church's lack of spiritual power is directly linked to the fact that we have spent so much time defining who is in and who is out. Or maybe we lack the power to heal because we aren't as passionate in our defense of the poor. Either way, what we have is a synopsis of what the Body of Christ ought to be about: fighting for the poor, including all people in the community, and healing the hurting. The one last image in this passage is how the chief priests and scribes got angry because the children were worshipping Jesus. That probably means it is something we should be doing, too.

Matthew 21:23-32

In this passage, Jesus is caught teaching in the temple, and the chief priest and elders demand to know by what authority he was doing that. It is unclear whether they are asking who let him do it there, or if they want to know where he got the authority with which he offered new understandings to old stories and scriptures.

Jesus turns it back on them and demands that they say where John the Baptist got his authority. This put them in a bind because, while they did not respect John, the people did, so they refused to answer.

Jesus then told a parable about two sons. Their father asked them to go work in the vineyard. One said he would but didn't, and the other said he wouldn't but did. Jesus then asked which one did the father's will. They said the latter, of course. Jesus then went on to say that tax collectors and prostitutes would get into the Realm of Heaven before them.

This outraged them, of course, because it was an insult. Notice, though, that Jesus didn't say they wouldn't get in. Maybe what he was saying was that those who know they need God's grace are more likely to experience it sooner than those who do not. What he is doing is rejecting external piety in favor of those who do the right thing.

Jesus is more likely to hang out with those who are doing good than with those who are saying good things. The external piety so highly valued then and now seemed to have little value to Jesus. From the Sermon on the Mount at the beginning of Matthew through this parable told at the end of his life, Jesus tried to make that point. He affirmed spiritual practices and disciplines and especially good works such as caring for the poor, but Jesus had great disdain for any religion that was purely external and public.

Jesus would say that the atheist who was kind and just and compassionate was closer to the realm of God than a deacon (or a preacher) who was judgmental and miserly with grace. Too often those of us who are people of faith are **religious in the worst way** … maybe that is why we have lost our spiritual authority.

Matthew 21:33-46

This parable is known as "The Wicked Tenants" and gets repeated pretty much verbatim in Mark 12 and Luke 20. The parable begins with a detailed word picture: vineyard, hedges, wine press, tower. It is tempting to try to determine what each of these represents, and preachers have been known to follow that path. Still, this is a parable not an allegory, and parables are told to make a single point.

While this might be interpreted as an apocalyptic parable that predicts the awful punishment to come when the Owner of the vineyard returns, it seems to me to be more of a parable of stewardship. Jesus is trying to remind his disciples that they have been given a great gift: to live in and from the vineyard that they did not design, build or plant. Like the Owner of the vineyard, God has done everything possible to remind us of our stewardship, even going so far as to send the Heir who was abused and rejected.

Unfortunately, the idea of "stewardship" has become inextricably linked to the Church's effort to raise money. Notice that in telling this parable, Jesus is not trying to encourage his disciples to tithe. Rather, he is telling a parable of life and living. He is trying to teach us of a pattern for going through our days that leads to life. Jesus is warning of the arrogance of presumption, of forgetting that we are all beneficiaries of gifts and graces that are not our own creation.

Someone once said that we have become a generation of self-made men and women who worship their own creator. Jesus is warning of the folly of such an ordering of life. In verse 43, he says, "Therefore I tell you, the Realm of God will be lost by such people and given to a people who produce fruit of God's reign. The one who falls on this stone will be broken to pieces, but the one on whom the stone falls will be utterly crushed."

Yes, recognizing that we are not the creators or sustainers of life is a humbling experience. It may require that our pride and arrogance be broken. On the other hand, our illusions that we are life's Atlas, holding up heaven and earth on our shoulders, is a crushing hubris. It isn't any wonder that this passage said that when the chief priests and Pharisees heard this they wanted to arrest Jesus. Stewardship is an attitude of servanthood and hospitality. Those of us who assume we know all about God and have all the religious answers sometimes think we are in control and slip into pretending we are owners not stewards. That attitude ultimately will crush you.

This parable of the wedding feast is found in a slightly different version in Luke, but not in Mark. The source seems to be a document that Matthew and Luke shared. Scholars call that document "Q," but, since we don't have it, we only can deduce what it was like from the material Matthew and Luke share that is not in Mark.

The inclusion of this parable is an interesting clue. The story is told in two parts. In the first we hear a description of a typical Jewish wedding banquet to which all the "right people" were invited. Everything has been prepared, but the invitation is insultingly rejected. They made light of it and sent word that they were all too busy to come. Others rejected or abused the messengers. As a result, the Host tells the servants to go into the street and invite everyone who wants to come to join the feast.

This story often has been interpreted as a parable of how the Jews rejected God's invitation to the feast and, therefore, God decided to invite everyone else, both good and bad. While that may have had meaning in the context in which it was originally told, I wonder if it isn't truer today that people generally miss the feast God has prepared for them because they are just too busy. The proper people may show up in church on Sunday mornings when it is expected, but their weeks are so full that there is no time to enjoy the festival of life they are offered.

The abused and rejected servants originally may have represented the prophets God sent, but I wonder today if they don't represent the rejection of the message of grace. Free, unconditional welcome to the table makes no sense to people whose true religion is Capitalism.

In the second part of the parable there is a harsh scene during which the host finds some in attendance who are not properly robed and throws them out. It seems especially harsh to us since the host was the one who invited everyone regardless of their financial means. It looks pretty graceless and is a stark contrast to the unconditional invitation to the feast. Jesus' original listeners would have understood, though, that the Host would have provided garments to all the guests, so the failure to be robed properly was an act of arrogance or ingratitude. Perhaps what Jesus is trying to communicate is that we are ALL welcome to come to the feast of life just as we are. We can come as we are, but we cannot stay as we were. An authentic acceptance of the invitation to new life is transformational. Rejecting that transformation has the same effect as rejecting the invitation to begin with.

Matthew 22:15-22

In this and the following sections we see the religious leaders trying to test, trick and trap Jesus. They come asking apparently sincere questions, but it is really an act of manipulation. The first question asks if it is lawful to pay taxes to Caesar.

We all have heard sermons on this text and know that if Jesus said yes he would be violating Jewish law, which prohibits paying tribute to anyone but God. If he said no then he would be violating Roman law and could be charged with treason and sedition. Of course, Jesus' answer is classic: "Show me your coin. Whose inscription is on it? Then render unto Caesar the things that are Caesar's and unto God the things that are God's." So brilliant is Jesus' response that it is reported almost verbatim by Mark and Luke, and the authenticity of this passage rarely has been questioned.

We like having a smart Messiah. We admire him greatly and obey him hardly. Oh, most of us render to Caesar the things that are Caesar's. That is we pay our taxes and even participate in the civic process that is our responsibility as citizens of our country. However, what about the other part? Do we give to God the things that are God's? What would that look like? What claims might God have on our lives?

In light of Jesus' recent teachings on stewardship, his followers ought to have known instantly what he meant. All that we have, all that we are, ultimately belongs to God. Even the breath we breathe came to us from God and returns to God. The question is, between that first breath and the last, how do we render the life we live to God?

Whenever preachers ask such questions, we immediately begin to think about volunteering in soup kitchens, or teaching Sunday school. To me that seems to be a pretty low and, frankly, boring opinion of God's expectations. I love the poster that says, "Until further notice celebrate everything!" In my weekly benediction at the end of services, I have tried to send people out to celebrate every moment of their lives "from now until the finale."

What a different approach that is than dutifully sacrificing and serving out of obligation. The exuberances, abundance, diversity and splendor of creation testify to the God to whom Jesus calls us to render our lives. Every moment we celebrate life we are rendering our very selves to the One who is Life! That is what made the faith of Jesus so different from the religious leaders of his day.

The second question by which Jesus was tested came from a religious group called the "Sadducees." They represented the upper-class in that day. They were wealthier and better educated, and the cultural leaders. The high priests were almost always Sadducees. They collaborated with the Romans in order to keep their positions of power, and Jesus made them very nervous.

It is ironic that in this country those who want political power now must make a public issue of their allegiance to Jesus. That Jesus named by the wealthy and powerful is almost totally unrelated to this Jesus who was, and is, a threat to those responsible for maintaining the status quo in which some have and others have not. It is blasphemy to name Jesus as a partner in a system that requires an underclass for profitability and that spends more resources on war than on the poor, the elderly, the sick and the children combined. I am convinced that only the grace of God keeps the tongues of politicians from falling out of their mouths every time they invoke the name of Jesus in their blasphemous value system. If they must rule in a callused, classist, racist, militaristic fashion so be it, but do not do so in the name of Jesus whose life was a repudiation of all those things.

That soapbox was to set the scene for this clash between Jesus and the power-brokers of his day. The Sadducees only held the Torah to be sacred and disregarded the Hebrew books of the poets and prophets as having any authority. In the end, that meant that they vigorously rejected the concept of resurrection. Hence, they were deeply invested in getting all the power and wealth they could in this life.

They come to Jesus with a story of a man who marries and dies without an heir. Subsequently, his seven brothers all marry his widow, one after another, and each dies without children. Then they ask, "In the resurrection, whose wife shall she be?"

This time, Jesus does not try a witty retort, but simply repudiates their entire belief system. Clearly, the Christian faith by the time the Gospels were written had rejected the Sadducee's faith system and embraced the resurrection as life that was wholly "other." Jesus quotes from the Torah God's claim to be the God of Abraham, Isaac and Jacob, and then reminds them that God is the God of the living not the dead. Using their own scripture, he challenges the kind of God they believed in.

I suspect Jesus would offer the same challenge to the defenders of the status quo in our day.

Matthew 22:34-46

So, the Pharisees tested Jesus by asking him a question about taxes, and the Sadducees asked him about the resurrection. Finally, a lawyer comes along to ask Jesus which law he thinks is most important. Perhaps they thought Jesus might toss out the law or offer a new teaching that they could use against him. They must have been very disappointed. Jesus' answer could not have been more orthodox: "Love God with all your heart, soul and mind, and love your neighbor as yourself. On these two hang all the law and the prophets."

In Matthew, this question is asked as a test, but in Mark the setting is very different. There is a collegial relationship between this lawyer and Jesus, and the question is asked almost as if to give Jesus an opportunity to prove that he was not such a radical as his enemies would make him out to be. (Mark 12:28-34) As someone who spent four years, and many thousands of dollars in graduate school, studying theology and religion, it seems more than a little ironic that, time and again, all religion is summed up so succinctly: Love God. Love your neighbor. I sometimes wonder if we preacher types don't make it more complicated as a means of justifying our student loans.

I say that only half-jokingly because I wonder if much of the problem isn't that religious leaders in our day, as in Jesus', have a vested interest in making faith more complicated than it has to be. What kind of world would we have if leaders of every faith saw their role as simply helping people experience and express their love for God and their love for their neighbors? Could any religious war be fought based on those two principles? Would any lesbian or gay teenager ever commit suicide because a preacher taught one of those lessons?

Could religion be just that simple? Love God. Love Neighbor. All else is commentary.

Oh, I know something that is "simple" isn't always easy. Love is complicated. If it were not there would be no marriage counselors and no divorce. However, I think religions of every brand have distracted us from working on the core things: How do I experience and express more fully my loving relationship with God? How do I experience and express more fully my loving relationship with my neighbor? All the rest is commentary.

Matthew 23:1-12

My face turns red every time I think about it. I was in an ecumenical meeting with a group of people I really liked. At some point, I called something "pharisaical." Later, a rabbi in the group, whom I regarded as a friend, explained that he found that term very offensive since he saw his vocation as descending from the Pharisees. All I could do was stammer an apology and resolve to increase my own sensitivity.

It is tough because Jesus was so often in conflict with the Pharisees. Part of this may be the authors' anti-Semitism, but the truth is that Christianity as it has evolved, and our understanding of the teachings of Jesus, conflicts with Judaism at certain points. Of course, Protestant Christianity conflicts with Roman Catholicism, too.

In this passage, Jesus warns his disciples against following the example of the scribes and Pharisees. Interestingly, he acknowledges that they "sit on the seat of Moses" and therefore deserve their respect, if not their emulation. Jesus goes on to cite how their teachings and their example "tie a heavy burden on the shoulders of others." His concern was that the practice of the Pharisees made religion a burden for those who already were terribly burdened by life. Jesus also warns about the external piety they show and the artificial respect and reverence they demand. Matthew then records Jesus as saying:

> But you are not to be called rabbi, for you have one teacher, and you are all students. And call no one your father on earth, for you have one Father—the one in heaven. Nor are you to be called instructors, for you have one instructor, the Messiah. The greatest among you will be your servant.

These verses are not found in Mark or Luke. One wonders how traditions in which pastors or priests are called "father" deal with this passage. Of more importance, though, may be the call to humility by any who would dare to teach or preach in Jesus' name. The call to servanthood is placed upon the whole Church, but it is a call we often forget. Nothing is more revolutionary to a congregation than to finally recognize that in everything they do they are to be the servants, not the served, the hosts not the guests. I keep asking out loud how life would change if we ever managed to get that all turned around right.

Matthew 23:13-39

This passage follows Jesus' warning that we are not to practice our religion for show and that we not allow our faith to make life more burdensome for others. According to Matthew, he cites the Pharisees as an example of what not to do. Then Matthew follows with six "woes" that Jesus pronounced against those who missed that lesson. He begins by saying, *"Woe to you, scribes and Pharisees, hypocrites! For you lock people out of the Realm of Heaven. For you yourself do not go in and when others are going in, you stop them."*

While Matthew directs this rebuke at the Pharisees of Jesus' day, he could well have directed it at religion in general. As children, we came from God, but our ability to live in that relationship has been more often inhibited than facilitated by religion in its various forms.

I love Phillip Gully and James Mulholland's books *If Grace is True* and *If God is Love*. While I do not always agree with them theologically, I relish the fact that they are calling Christians to take those two tenants literally AND seriously. What would the Christian faith be like if we all acted as though *grace is true*? How would Christians live if we actually did believe that *God is love?*

Jesus is warning against religion that gets in the way of others embracing the reality of God's grace and love. He seems to believe that we do it because we have not been able to fully know God's grace and love.

After these rather harsh repudiations of the religion practiced by the Pharisees in his day, and most Churches in ours, Jesus ends with a powerful and deeply moving lament. He looks out over the city of Jerusalem, the people he loves and longs to love back into relationship with God and says, *"Jerusalem, Jerusalem ... how often have I longed to gather your children together as a mother hen gathers her brood under her wing, but you were not willing."*

This is the heart cry of a man who is feeling his maternal instincts and longing simply to hold us so close to his heart, safe and warm and loved. Perhaps Jesus believes that if he could do that we might again hear the heartbeat of our Heavenly Mother, and, who knows, maybe our hearts would beat once more in time with hers.

Matthew 24

In this chapter, Matthew seems to throw together all the loose stories and teachings of Jesus that he had heard and read about how things would end. Taken together, it is a confusing and convoluted picture. It also challenges us to consider our own understanding of Christian apocalyptic literature.

This chapter is a collection of the things that Jesus was reported to have said about the end of time. Naturally, there always has been a great deal of interest in any insights that might be gained from how this will all turn out. The challenge is that the Jewish tradition of apocalyptic literature is that it is written is highly symbolic and contextual language.

After centuries of repression, there was an expectation that the only way things ever would be made right for the Jewish people was for God to come in person and reorder all things. David's throne thus would be re-established in fulfillment of the covenant that God had made with David.

The irony is that Christians understand Jesus to be God coming to earth to reorder life and believe that, as the descendent of David, Jesus fulfilled that great promise. All of that makes apocalyptic Christian literature even more complicated. The early Church believed that Jesus would return again, though there is some indication that Pentecost was understood to be the fulfillment of that promise.

Still, although life was forever changed by Jesus and the birth of the Resurrected Body of Christ—the Church—things were not magically and miraculously fixed. In fact, for centuries, Christians were as persecuted and oppressed as the Jews were. Therefore, this future hope for themselves and the world became a survival mechanism. This divine intervention was longed for and greatly anticipated.

We read this literature 2,000 years later and in a vastly different context. The great irony of the fundamentalist Christian's teachings about the second coming is that they now are a part of the status quo. They are the unofficial official religion of the state. Far from anticipation, a naive and brutally honest reading of this literature ought to make the modern Church quake because Jesus ends all this talk about the judgment at the end by saying, "What you did to the **least** you did to me."

Matthew 25

Matthew clusters many of Jesus' teachings into the last week of his life. Perhaps it was his way of telling us these were important. In this last chapter, before the telling of the end, Matthew includes three big stories.

The first is the parable of the bridesmaids. The groom was delayed. Five bridesmaids were prepared, having brought extra oil for their lamps, and five were caught unprepared. Written decades after Jesus was gone, stories like this were important to members of the early Church as they were suffering persecution while they waited for Jesus to return and rescue them. For us, these stories are a reminder that we always must live as one who is prepared to meet Jesus. How many times have we heard that??? Well, that is how many times we have ignored it. Matthew could have saved this space, I'm afraid. We all tend to live as if we are the one exception to the "Everyone Dies" rule.

The second parable is about the owner who gives three servants five, two and one talents respectively. It is also a parable about the coming of Jesus and how our lives ultimately will be evaluated. It is also told in Luke, and we will look at it in more detail there.

The last parable of Matthew is also one of Jesus' more famous. It appears only in this Gospel. Although it is a story about judgment, that isn't how it is known by most. It is of course the parable in which Jesus concludes, "What you did unto the least, you did unto me." It is a powerful teaching that, just as God is incarnate in Jesus, God is incarnate in the "least."

Just in case we might miss whom he is talking about, Jesus lists them: the hungry, the thirsty, the stranger, those without clothes, the sick and the prisoner. How we treat them, Jesus says, is how we treat him; not the pretty hymns and songs we sing, or the prayers we pray, or the statues we erect, or the buildings we build, or the pious reverence we give, but how we treat those in need. Having just read an article about the Texas prison system, I think those of us in the Lone Star State ought to be living in mortal fear if Jesus really meant the part about how we treat prisoners. By making it Jesus' last teaching, Matthew is trying to warn us that this really might be one teaching we should pay attention to.

So the curtain rises on the final act. This chapter begins with a description of how "the chief priests and elders gathered in the palace of Caiaphas the High Priest and conspired to arrest Jesus by stealth and kill him." In the next scene Jesus is eating in the house of Simon, and a woman named Mary anoints Jesus with costly, perfumed oil. In Matthew's version, the disciples got angry by the waste of such costly ointment. John says it was Judas who got angry, but Matthew acknowledges that the others were angry as well. They suggested that the oil could have been sold for a large sum of money and given to the poor. Jesus tells them to give her a break because there will always be poor, and she was doing a kindness for him preparing him for his death.

Although Matthew doesn't blame Judas for reacting negatively, he does follow this incident with a description of how Judas went to meet with the chief priests to strike a bargain. Judas is the consummate villain. Few of us can conceive the level of cynicism or narcissism, or greed, required to sell out a friend to his or her death. True friends are one of life's greatest treasures. We share our joys with them, and they are near in times of sorrow. Gay author E. M. Forster once wrote, "If I have to choose between betraying my country and betraying my friend, I hope I should have the courage to betray my country."

That may be a bit strong for some of us, but there is little in life that is more reprehensible than betraying a trusting friend. Friendship is such a sacred treasure that to desecrate it is evil, which is why history has been so unkind to Judas. Dante suggested the lowest level of hell was reserved for Judas. Contemporary Christian singer Michael Card wrote:

> *Why did it have to be a **friend** that chose to betray the Lord?*
> *And why did he have to use a kiss? That's not what a kiss is for.*
> *Only a friend can betray a friend; a stranger has nothing to gain.*
> *And only a friend comes close enough to ever cause so much pain.*

If you've ever been betrayed by someone you trusted and cared for, you know firsthand the searing pain that Judas caused Jesus when he betrayed him with a kiss. Why would Jesus kiss Judas knowing what he was about to do? Probably the same reason that if you will be still enough you can feel Jesus kissing you.

Matthew 26:17-35

The Thursday of Holy Week is known as Maundy Thursday. It is a commemoration of Jesus' last supper with his disciples and friends before he was arrested. Each Gospel tells this story slightly differently. They even conflict over whether or not this was the Passover meal.

In Matthew, Jesus talks about the fact that one of them will betray him, and, while we like to make Judas into evil incarnate, all of the disciples are deeply distressed, wondering aloud if they are the one. What amazing honesty, to acknowledge your own capacity for evil. The truth is there is a bit of Judas in us all.

At the end of the meal Jesus predicts that Peter—the star disciple in Matthew—will deny that he even knows him. Peter can't imagine that ever happening, but, of course, it does. It happens with Peter, just as it does with us. We may not say the words, since in our culture Jesus-piety is popular, but the disconnect between what he taught and how we live is just as direct a denial.

The amazing thing about this last meal is that we are all there: those who are distressed by our capacity for evil, those who betray that which we love, and those whose living denies any relationship with Jesus. We are all there, and all of us are offered a bit of bread and a taste of wine as a means of grace/forgiveness. Jesus doesn't offer it to the innocent, or the pious, or the strong, but to the guilty. Unless we can acknowledge that is who we are, or at least could be, I wonder if this feast is anything other than bread and wine.

The Church has called it a "sacrament," or a means of grace. For those of us hungering, thirsting and deeply distressed, it is a feast of grace to know that we are welcomed at the table hosted by the one we betrayed and denied.

Holy Week is the time in which the Church calls us to contemplate the deeper meanings of these historical events. We are called to do so with honesty and vulnerability. With each passing day, we draw closer to the mystery of pure love's suffering. It is offered to us all, even the Judases. The only limitation is our ability to be honest about our need for forgiveness and love. Even then, that only affects our ability to receive; nothing can impact God's willingness and capacity to give.

At the end of the evening meal, Jesus and his family of choice went out to a garden called Gethsemane to pray. There, Jesus wrestles with what he senses is about to happen. His time has run out. He longs for another way. In prayer, he asks God for another way, but, if this is how it must be, he is willing to do what must be done.

Jesus is rightly troubled, and he wants his disciples to pray with him and for him. But they can't seem to stay awake. Apparently, the heavy dinner and too much wine is stronger than their love … at least that must be how it felt to Jesus. For Jesus, the torture has already begun.

When they left the upper room Judas wasn't with them. He had gone to find the chief priest and collect his reward. In the quiet garden late at night, Judas comes, trailing soldiers with swords and clubs behind him. He kisses Jesus so they will know for sure which one to arrest. To the kiss Jesus says, "Friend, do what you are here to do." Even then Jesus called Judas friend. Who Judas was could not change who Jesus was.

In Matthew's version of this story one of the disciples draws a sword and cuts off the ear of one of those who had come to arrest Jesus. However, Jesus rebukes that disciple and says, "Put away your sword; because those who live by the sword also die by the sword." Then all the disciples flee.

Did they flee because they were afraid of being arrested too? That is a logical assumption I suppose, but they didn't arrest John's disciples when they arrested John. I can't help but wonder if they fled because it was only then that they realized that Jesus really wasn't going to be leading an armed rebellion to overthrow Rome and put them in power. Were they fleeing the reality that Jesus was serious about the kind of Realm he had come to create? Or did they just think he had failed?

Whatever the cause, Jesus was now alone. Utterly and completely alone, betrayed by one friend and abandoned by all the rest. Perhaps this, as much as the physical torture, was what Jesus had been praying to avoid. Next time we avoid people who fail, or even those who have made great mistakes, we should remember these disciples fleeing into the night leaving Jesus to face his enemies alone. Then, too, we should hear, "What you do to the least you do to me."

Matthew 27:11-54

Now Jesus stood before the governor; and the governor asked him, "Are you the King of the Jews?" Jesus said, "You say so." " But when he was accused by the chief priests and elders, he did not answer. Then Pilate said to him, "Do you not hear how many accusations they make against you?" But he gave him no answer, not even to a single charge, so that the governor was greatly amazed.

Now at the festival the governor was accustomed to release a prisoner for the crowd, anyone whom they wanted. At that time they had a notorious prisoner, called Jesus Barabbas. So after they had gathered, Pilate said to them, "Whom do you want me to release for you, Jesus Barabbas or Jesus who is called the Messiah?" For he realized that it was out of jealousy that they had handed him over. While he was sitting on the judgment seat, his wife sent word to him, "Have nothing to do with that innocent man, for today I have suffered a great deal because of a dream about him." Now the chief priests and the elders persuaded the crowds to ask for Barabbas and to have Jesus killed. The governor again said to them, "Which of the two do you want me to release for you?" And they said, "Barabbas." Pilate said to them, "Then what should I do with Jesus who is called the Messiah?" All of them said, "Let him be crucified!" Then he asked, "Why, what evil has he done?" But they shouted all the more, "Let him be crucified!"

So when Pilate saw that he could do nothing, but rather that a riot was beginning, he took some water and washed his hands before the crowd, saying, "I am innocent of this man's blood; see to it yourselves." Then the people as a whole answered, "His blood be on us and on our children!" So he released Barabbas for them; and after flogging Jesus, he handed him over to be crucified.

Then the soldiers of the governor took Jesus into the governor's headquarters, and they gathered the whole cohort around him. They stripped him and put a scarlet robe on him, and after twisting some thorns into a crown, they put it on his head. They put a reed in his right hand and knelt before him and mocked him, saying, "Hail, King of the Jews!" They spat on him, and took the reed and struck him on the head. After mocking him, they stripped him of the robe and put his own clothes on him. Then they led him away to crucify him.

As they went out, they came upon a man from Cyrene named Simon; they compelled this man to carry his cross. And when they came to a place called Golgotha (which means Place of a Skull), they offered him wine to drink, mixed with gall; but when he tasted it, he would not drink it. And when they had crucified him, they divided his clothes among themselves by casting lots; then they sat down there and kept watch over him. Over his head they put the charge against him, which read, "This is Jesus, the King of the Jews."

Then two bandits were crucified with him, one on his right and one on his left. Those who passed by derided him, shaking their heads and saying, "You who would destroy the temple and build it in three days, save yourself! If you are the Son of God, come down from the cross." In the same way the chief priests also, along with the scribes and elders, were mocking him, saying, "He saved others; he cannot save himself. He is the King of Israel; let him come down from the cross now, and we will believe in him. He trusts in God; let God deliver him now, if he wants to; for he said, 'I am God's Son.'" The bandits who were crucified with him also taunted him in the same way.

From noon on, darkness came over the whole land until three in the afternoon. And about three o'clock Jesus cried with a loud voice, "Eli, Eli, lema sabachthani?" that is, "My God, my God, why have you forsaken me?" When some of the bystanders heard it, they said, "This man is calling for Elijah." At once one of them ran and got a sponge, filled it with sour wine, put it on a stick, and gave it to him to drink. But the others said, "Wait, let us see whether Elijah will come to save him." Then Jesus cried again with a loud voice and breathed his last. At that moment the curtain of the temple was torn in two, from top to bottom. The earth shook, and the rocks were split. The tombs also were opened, and many bodies of the saints who had fallen asleep were raised. After this resurrection, they came out of the tombs and entered the holy city and appeared to many. Now when the centurion and those with him, who were keeping watch over Jesus, saw the earthquake and what took place, they were terrified and said, "Truly this man was God's Son!"

Matthew 28

The resurrection of Jesus as recounted in Matthew is told with great economy of words in only 10 short verses. Matthew closely follows the original ending of Mark, which was even shorter. Both of these versions star Mary Magdalene and the "other Mary" who Mark identifies as the mother of James and John.

Despite the fundamentalists' argument for inerrancy, a cursory reading of the resurrection stories in the four Gospels reveals that they are telling very different versions of the same story. For instance, Matthew says that, when the Marys found the tomb empty and heard that Jesus was alive, they ran to tell the disciples and, along the way, they ran into Jesus in person. In Mark the women flee the empty tomb, but "terror and amazement had seized them and they said nothing to anyone for they were afraid." (Mk. 16:8)

Luke and John give accounts of the story that are even more different. As a preacher, I always hated when the Easter reading was from Matthew or Mark. The story is so short and the details so few. Yet, the truth is that the more profound and transformational an experience is the less we are able to put it into words. Maybe that is the case with Matthew and Mark.

While many who grew up in fundamentalist churches feel a need to reconcile these four different accounts of the resurrection, I treasure their apparent conflicts. Clearly, in the wake of Jesus' death, different accounts circulated about what happened afterwards. The fact that the biblical writers didn't feel compelled to homogenize the stories and make them all say the same thing is a witness for the defense of the scripture. Police know that if four witnesses tell the exact same story in the exact same way, then they are not being completely truthful, or someone has shaped their experience of truth. Witnesses to transformational events see and hear things differently, and they sometimes even see and hear different things. We, who have had our lives transformed by the Living Christ, also bear different witness to that reality. This diversity of voices within the Church of Jesus Christ is further evidence of truth, rather than, as some would suggest, proof that our faith isn't valid since we don't agree. Conformity is artificial and contrived and doesn't serve Truth.

Matthew 28:1-10

So they left the tomb quickly with fear and great joy, and ran to tell his disciples.

Matthew 28:8

I think that is how Easter people live: with fear and great joy. The promise of resurrection doesn't take away the fear of death or of life's deaths, but it does allow us to pair that fear with great joy.

Whether you are convinced of the physical resurrection or understand the metaphor that resurrection offers us, we are people who believe that death does not have the final word on life. This conviction allows us to know joy even in the face of the worst life can do to us.

After one of the largest AIDS funerals at which I ever presided, many of us returned to the home of the deceased to have a meal with his partner. The survivor was also living with AIDS, and, in those days, the prognosis was pretty grim. As I drove from the cemetery to the house, I tried to think of what I could say to someone who had just buried the love of his life and was having to confront his own death as well. Although I tried to offer my best words of comfort at the funeral, I still expected to find a solemn gathering at the house afterwards.

When I walked in, I heard someone laughing hysterically. The laughter was so raucous that I initially thought someone was sobbing. What I found was a group of people closest to the deceased sharing funny stories and feeling the joy that came from knowing him. Through the stories of his life they were sharing, he was a source of great joy. Even though death had removed him physically from their lives, he was still with them and always would be.

Christians are people who refuse to let death have the final word, and, while we live with the fear and pain that is the common lot of all people, we also can live with joy because, for us, death is not the final word.

Matthew 28:11-15

This is a strange passage that occurs only in Matthew. It describes how the chief priests and elders paid a large sum of money to bribe the Roman soldiers guarding the tomb to say that the disciples had come in the night to steal the body of Jesus. Matthew concludes with the note, "And this story is still told among the Jews to this day."

Thirty years after Jesus was gone, when Matthew writes his Gospel, he notes that, when the Church tried to talk about the resurrection of Jesus, Jewish leaders explained it by saying that his body had been stolen in the night. Apparently, Roman soldiers backed up that story as well, though that is odd. For the soldiers to allow that to happen would mean they would be punished, even executed, for failing to do their job. So, was it the women who outsmarted the Roman soldiers and stole the body? Even the men who wrote these stories admitted that, except for John, the male disciples fled in fear.

Each of us must decide for ourselves what we believe about the physical resurrection of Jesus. Liberals tend to dismiss it as a metaphor. What is clear, though, is that those who wrote the Gospels believed it to be literally true. By the time some of the stories were written down, many of the eyewitnesses were dead. It would have been easy enough to put these stories in their mouths. The trouble is that many of those witnesses died because they insisted on telling these stories. So convinced were they that Jesus was alive, that they would die before they'd say otherwise. Few people have been willing to die for a lie. The conviction of Jesus' resurrection gave the disciples power they seemed to utterly lack before these events.

In addition, if the disciples had been smart enough to steal the body of Jesus even after the suspicious religious leaders put it under Roman guard, they would have been smart enough to synchronize their stories. The four different versions of the resurrection that the Gospels tell read just like four witness who saw the same thing but remembered it differently. This is not so much an argument for the physical resurrection of Jesus as it is a testimony to the conviction of those early witnesses that Jesus was alive. We may or may not believe it, but they obviously did. And that made all the difference in their lives.

Matthew 28:16-20

This passage begins, "Now the eleven disciples went to Galilee, to the mountain to which Jesus had directed them … " Even though the women were the first witnesses of the resurrection, the only disciples worth counting were men. Matthew notes that there were only 11 left. Judas is gone. He couldn't bear the guilt of his deeds, and he wasn't courageous enough to ask for forgiveness. Peter was still there, though, as were the other men who had abandoned Jesus.

On some unnamed, but prearranged, mountain Jesus comes to them one last time. He has one last piece of instruction: "Go therefore and make disciples of all nations, baptizing them in the name of the Father and the Son and the Holy Spirit."

In the book of Acts, we are told that converts were baptized in the name of Jesus. Here in Matthew, though, we find the only Trinitarian affirmation ever attributed to Jesus. This passage has greatly shaped not just the sacrament of baptism, but the theology that the Church regards as orthodoxy. We are monotheistic; that is we believe in one God. Here, however, Jesus gives that God three names.

It is worth noting also that this passage, which generally is referred to as the "Great Commission," sends them out to share the good news with all people. Matthew's Gospel seems to have been written primarily for Jewish readers, but, here at the end, even he acknowledges that Jesus was the ultimate includer.

After giving them a mission of inclusion, Jesus gives them the ultimate assurance. He scatters them across the globe, but it is with the final promise, "Lo, I am with you always to the end of the age."

Matthew began by identifying Jesus as the Emmanuel of which the prophets spoke. He even tells us what the name means: "God with us." He ends by reminding us that, even after the story of the physical life of Jesus ends, God is still with us. For those of us who must live without the physical Jesus, that is good news. In fact, you might say, when it is all said and done, that is THE good news/the gospel.

Mark

Today we begin a very quick journey through the shortest of the Gospels, the book of Mark. If you divide Mark into 105 sections, 93 of them occur in Matthew and 81 occur in Luke, which we will study next. Mark has 661 verses, and Matthew has 1,068. Matthew repeats 606 verses of Mark, 51 percent verbatim. There are only 24 verses in all of Mark that are not found in either Matthew or Luke.

What this means is that Mark was the first of the Gospels written, and both Matthew and Luke had copies of this work to guide them and shape their work. They have other sources as well, but the fact that they used so much of Mark is testimony to their own confidence in the reliability of Mark's witness.

We do not know who Mark was, but tradition holds that the author was a very young follower of Jesus. Or, perhaps more accurately, he was the son of an affluent woman who was an early disciple of Jesus. She is one of the Marys about which the Bible speaks and is said to have owned the home with the upper room in which Jesus and the disciples gathered.

In the book of Acts, we learn about a young disciple named Mark who was a protégé, and perhaps secretary, of Paul and a nephew of Paul's missionary colleague Barnabas. At one point in their travels, Mark became homesick and returned home. (Acts 13:13) When Paul prepared to leave on a later missionary journey, Barnabas wanted to take Mark along again, but Paul wouldn't hear of it. The two church leaders had a falling out over it and ended up going their separate ways. Paul took Silas, and Barnabas took Mark.

What happened between Mark and Paul after that is unknown, but when Paul writes to the Colossians some years later he is in prison and Mark is right there with him. In the book of 2 Timothy words attributed to Paul praise Mark as a most valued partner in the difficult work of spreading the gospel.

The fact that this is the Gospel on which two other Gospels depend is an important reminder that failure doesn't have to be fatal and, although we may disagree and even fall out with our sisters and brothers, that doesn't have to be permanent. Here is a model of the power of God to restore a person and a relationship.

Mark 1

Mark is clearly not a biography of Jesus. There are no birth stories in Mark and no genealogies. In this version, Jesus strides onto the scene fully grown and ready to go to work. There is a brief description of John the Baptist, complete with a quote from the prophecy of Isaiah that predicted his coming. Then, by verse nine, Jesus shows up to be baptized.

The reference to Isaiah with which Mark begins his Gospel leaves you with the impression that, like Matthew, Mark plans to present the story of Jesus as a fulfillment of the predictions of the Hebrew prophets. Such is not the case, however. In fact, Mark often explains the Jewish practices that we encounter. This makes it clear that his Gospel wasn't written for a primarily Jewish audience.

It is difficult to ascertain exactly to whom Mark is writing. He uses an economy of words. The story of the temptation of Jesus in the wilderness is dispatched in just two verses, and by verse 14 John the Baptist has been arrested and Jesus has gone to work. Perhaps it is this economy of words that caused Mark's Gospel to be neglected by the church. In the early Church almost all sermons and writings referenced Matthew or Luke. The neglect of Mark may have been the reason that the ending of the Gospel seems to have been lost.

A second-century historian named Papias was the first to offer an explanation for why Mark writes as he does. Papias suggested, and tradition has since held, that Mark was simply a collection of stories told, and sermons given, by Peter. It is impossible to know if this early analysis is correct. However, as the first Gospel written, current scholars seeking to uncover the "historic Jesus" pay close attention to Mark, and it has taken on more importance.

Scholars like Marcus Borg and John Dominic Crossan challenge us to distinguish between the historic Jesus and the Church's Christ. They do not allow us to accept one and reject the other, but ask us to know the difference. I have found that to be much more difficult than they believe it to be. However, it is important for us to remember that, often, the Jesus we encounter today is as much a product of the Church's teaching as history. That is why looking at a bare Gospel like Mark is so helpful.

Mark 6:3

Mark 6:1-6 tells the story of Jesus' rejection by the congregation in his hometown of Nazareth. Luke tells the story much more completely, but Mark has one interesting statement worth looking at. In Mark 6:3, when the crowd is discounting Jesus' authority, they cite his family connections. They name his brothers and mention his sisters and ask, "Isn't this the carpenter, the son of Mary?" That is what the older and most reliable manuscripts say. In later editions, and some lesser English translations, this verse says, "Isn't this the son of the carpenter and of Mary?"

The implication, of course, is that Mark is identifying Jesus as a carpenter, a manual laborer. Matthew and some later translations of Mark seem reluctant to identify Jesus as a common tradesman. In his brief account of the temptation story, Mark says that the Spirit *drove* Jesus into the wilderness. Matthew and Luke soften it to say that the Spirit *led* Jesus into the wilderness. Mark is the Gospel that tells of Jesus sighing, looking at the rich young ruler with love, being tired and needing rest, feeling pangs of hunger, and marveling at their unbelief. Mark wasn't afraid to show the very human side of Jesus. By the time Matthew and Luke came to write their Gospels, they seemed to feel a need to lessen the emphasis on Jesus' humanity.

Matthew and Luke also tell of Jesus using children to illustrate the proper attitude toward the Realm of God, but only Mark tells us how Jesus *took them into his arms*. (Mark 10:13-16) According to Mark, when the disciples get caught in a storm, they have to awaken Jesus who is *in the back of the boat asleep on a pillow*. Such details give us a powerful glimpse of the human Jesus. They also are evidence that Mark perhaps is recording many of the stories as they are told by an eyewitness. Neither Peter nor Mark seems to feel the need to sublimate Jesus' humanity.

Mark's witness is less to Jesus who is the Son of God and more to Jesus who is the Human One (Son of Man). Mark was the first Gospel written. With the passing of time, the Church seemed so determined to convince the world of Jesus' divinity that we were in grave danger of losing Jesus' humanity. That has a major spiritual impact, because, while I can worship the divine Christ, the human Jesus calls me to live as he did with compassion and forgiveness and as a servant.

With only 16 chapters, Mark is the shortest of the four Gospels. The story of the triumphant entry of Jesus into Jerusalem that begins the last week of his life is told at the beginning of chapter 11. It is almost as if Mark has rushed through the life of Jesus and spends one-third of his time describing the final week.

Mark is the only Gospel in which you find the statement that has been held by many to be the theological explanation for why Jesus died. This verse is offered just before the final act begins:

> *For the Human One came not to be served but to serve, and to give his life a ransom for many.*
>
> Mark 10:45

This verse becomes the cornerstone for what becomes known as the Ransom Theory of Atonement. Essentially, this earliest theory of what Jesus' death means holds that Adam and Eve sold the human soul to Satan and that Jesus came to redeem us, or buy us back. This was the Church's accepted understanding for the first millennium. In the 11th century, Anselm began the process of questioning this doctrine, and, subsequently, it has fallen out of favor in the West, though it is still considered true by the Orthodox faith.

Atonement basically refers to how God forgives our sin. There are a number of theories, and the Church has argued about it since the ink dried on Mark's parchment. Still, few Christians have ever actually given the matter much thought. So what does the crucifixion of Jesus mean to you and your life? Have your sins been so bad that an innocent person had to die to persuade God to forgive you? If God is omnipotent, who made the rule that someone had to pay for sin in order for God to be **able** to forgive? If someone actually died for you, doesn't that act deserve our grappling with what it means?

Ultimately, Mark thought the ending of Jesus' life was the most important thing. The Church historically has agreed, adopting the cross as its sacred sign. The challenge for us is to move beyond preachers' clichés to discover for ourselves what it means to us and for us.

Mark 16

The Gospel of Mark ends with an empty tomb. Actually, there are three endings to Mark. The most reliable ending is the first one in chapter 16, verse 8:

> *So they* (the three women) *went out and fled from the tomb, for <u>terror</u> and <u>amazement</u> had seized them; and they said nothing to anyone, for they were afraid.*

There is no appearance by Jesus, no affirmations of faith, no angelic choruses. The first and oldest description of the resurrection simply ends with an empty tomb. Then there is a shorter ending that was added later. The two sentences were clearly not written by Mark, as any reader can tell. There is also a third ending of about 11 verses in which Jesus does appear to the disciples in much the same way he did in the other Gospels. There is even a long verse or two in this segment that is in some ancient manuscripts, but not the most reliable. In short, the ending of Mark is a mess. Again, one is left to wonder how Biblical literalists explain which one of these endings qualifies as inerrant/infallible.

The most reliable version leaves us with witnesses who are too afraid to say anything to anyone about what they have seen. They are seized between terror and amazement, unable to say anything to anyone. That is how the story ends. Actually, Mark simply stops without an ending. That is why at least two attempts have been made to add one. We are uncomfortable with music that is unresolved.

Maybe that is one of the reasons Matthew and Luke felt they had to tell very similar stories, but with endings. What would Christianity have looked like if we had left Mark's Gospel as it was? Could we have lived with a missing body? Could we have believed that the Church, which rose up after Jesus, was the resurrected Jesus in the world? Would that be enough, or did we need an animated body to free us from our own fear of death?

Mark ends with an empty tomb. It is likely that the real ending got lost and others tried to provide one. What is unfortunate is that we have yet to realize that, regardless of what you believe about the resurrection of Jesus, the Body of Christ alive today must live in that tension between terror and amazement, and we must be the real ending to the Gospel.

Luke

After a very brief look at the Gospel of Mark, we come to Luke. We will spend a bit more time here because Luke has material that is not included in either Matthew or Mark. Luke is a favorite Gospel to many, though its radical message generally has been ignored.

Luke is known as the Gospel of the women. They star in many of the scenes of Jesus' life, and his birth is told through the eyes and experience of his mother, Mary. The acknowledgement of the importance and value of women to Jesus was one of the significant messages of Luke that the church ignored for centuries. Even today, women still are not ordained in the majority of the Christian Church. The Church's historical misogyny is a sin for which we will spend much of eternity repenting.

Luke is also the Gospel of the Gentiles. It historically has been assumed that Luke himself was perhaps the only non-Jewish writer in the entire Bible. It is clear from the stories that Jesus tells in Luke that his great value is the inclusion of the outsider in the family of God. Stories of good Samaritans and prodigal sons are found only in Luke.

Luke is well educated, and his Greek is perhaps the best in the New Testament. According to legend, Luke was a Greek physician. There is some textual evidence that the author did have, at least, some medical education. We are fortunate that such a well educated author wrote both this Gospel and the book of Acts, which records the history of the early Church.

Both volumes are addressed to Theophilus. It is uncertain whether this was an actual person or if the name, which means "God lover," is representative of the fact that Luke was trying to write to us all. I am convinced that if we took Luke's inclusive version of the Gospel more seriously the whole world is more likely to be God Lovers.

Luke 1:1-4

It is common today for books to have a preface as a way of preparing the reader for what is about to come. Luke's Gospel is the only one to use such a device. In it, he notes that "<u>many</u> have tried to set down an orderly account of the events." Scholars long to know what he meant by "many." We have Matthew and Mark's versions, but John's didn't come along until after Luke's. Two are not "many." Most scholars believe that, in addition to depending on Mark's version for information and structure, Matthew and Luke had a second shared resource known as Q.

So, what does it say about our understanding of scripture when we know that a number of Gospels have gone missing? Essentially, we have the synoptic Gospels—Matthew, Mark, and Luke—which tell basically the same story in the same order, with slight variations. And then there is John. How different might our faith be if suddenly we discovered four missing Gospels and they told a very different version of Jesus' life?

While that idea is interesting and should inform what we believe about the Bible being the "complete" story, the truth is Luke says that he is recording what he has heard from "eyewitnesses," and, ultimately, he is recording it as one of "us." Part of Acts is written in first person, which is the only way to respond to the story of Jesus.

Here in the Gospel of Luke we have a story told by someone who was originally an outsider, a Gentile. He obviously is sharing some of what he has heard that was meaningful to him. Now it is up to us to consider the stories and discover what is meaningful to us. Luke is great at retelling the parables of Jesus. Much of what is recorded as historical accounts in Luke is actually a parable of faith. Arguing about the historicity of this record may occupy Biblical scholars; however, we must read it as a testimony of what Luke found to be true for himself.

Luke's scholarship is the best, but that doesn't mean that he is a historian. If we are looking for facts when we read the scripture, we are in danger of missing the truth. Luke offers us a testimony of truth, not an account of historical facts. Therefore, we must read with the eyes of our spirit, not the left-brain training of Western education. As the prayer-book says, "Hear what the Spirit is saying to the Church."

Following the brief preface, Luke immediately tells a story that is not found anywhere else. It is not a story from the life of Jesus, but the story of the parents of John the Baptist. The Jews anticipated that, before the messiah came to establish the Reign of God, the prophet Elijah would return to prepare the way. John the Baptist was regarded by the early Church as the fulfillment of that expectation.

It would be interesting to ponder the Jewish understanding of reincarnation, but that will have to wait for another time. Luke begins his story by introducing us to a priest named Zechariah. Every Jewish male who was a direct descendant of Aaron—Moses' and Miriam's brother—was considered a priest. There were as many as 20,000 priests, so this story of Zechariah serving in the temple may be a record of the one and only time he got to do that in his life. As he was burning the incense offering as a symbol of the prayers of the people, an angel of the Lord appeared to him.

Luke has lots of angels, more in fact than the other Gospels combined. Of course, the word itself simply means "messenger," so we are left to wonder just exactly what it was that Luke meant. Is he simply saying that a messenger from God stepped up to Zechariah while he was alone in the Temple? This messenger identifies himself as Gabriel. A messenger by this name first appears in the book of Daniel. He is also named in the Qur'an as God's messenger to the prophet Mohammed, and he also makes an appearance in a sacred writing of the Baha'i faith.

Gabriel tells Zechariah that he and his wife, Elizabeth, will have a son. Zechariah asks how on earth this can be since both he and his wife are well along in years. The angel is a bit insulted by Zechariah's question. Although it seems logical to me, Gabriel reminds Zechariah that he is someone who stands in the presence of God. Since Zechariah did not believe this message, Gabriel informs him that he will be struck dumb until after the child is born. This seems to me to be an odd response. Why should Gabriel be so insecure? Maybe Zechariah's enforced silence wasn't about Gabriel's ego as much as it was to ensure that Zechariah wouldn't talk himself, and Elizabeth, out of their miracle. It is amazing how much power our words have over ourselves and others. When faith is required for nine months, silence may be the only solution.

Luke 1:26-37

In this passage, we find a record of what is known as "The Annunciation" or "announcement." Once more, it is Gabriel who is sent as God's messenger, but this time it is to a small town in Galilee rather than to the temple in Jerusalem. It is interesting that Luke is careful with the geography, or setting, of these two announcements. First, the conception of the forerunner is announced; then, six months later, Gabriel goes out to a village in the countryside to visit a young woman named Mary who was engaged but not married.

Again, this is the only place where this story is told. Gabriel says, "Greetings favored one." This story is well known in the church. It has been depicted by the greatest artists, and it is commemorated with feast days in the Roman Catholic and Orthodox Churches. Mary, of course, asks how she will bear a son since she has not had sex. Unlike his response to Zechariah, Gabriel is gentle with Mary and assures her that the Holy Spirit will come upon her and the child she bears will be called the Son of God.

Here we are left to decide if this is a record of history or a parable of faith. If Luke is recording the facts as they happened, we are left to assume that the source of this information had to be Mary herself since there were no other witnesses. We then are eavesdropping on a private spiritual experience, and, again, we are not reading a historical record. What we have is a story that is at least 60 years old told in the context of the hindsight of faith. Jesus has been gone for decades. The early Church worships him and has begun to venerate his mother.

Ironically, we might miss what seems to be Luke's original point. God is working through an old, unknown, unranked priest and his wife to prepare the way. Then God selects an unmarried young woman in an obscure village. While Zechariah got the first visit, it is really through the two women—who are distant relatives— that God does this most amazing work. Further, God is blessing the scandal of an unmarried woman who is pregnant by someone other than the man to whom she is engaged. The radical and revolutionary message of this story has been tamed by our art, feasts and Christmas cards. What Luke is telling us is that God is working through women—one scorned as barren, one scorned because of infidelity. Letting God's will be done in their lives didn't bring wealth or success, but these women are the very definition of faith: "Let it be done to me according to God's will."

Gabriel brought to Mary not only the news of her own pregnancy but also that of her cousin Elizabeth. Naturally, Mary leaves her home and goes to visit Elizabeth. When she arrives, Elizabeth immediately knows that something is going on with Mary. She explains that, the minute Mary greeted her, the child in her own womb leaped for joy. Luke then says that the Holy Spirit came upon Elizabeth who said, "Blessed are you among women and blessed is the fruit of your womb … "

This, of course, has become a part of the liturgy of the Church … or was it already a part of the worship of the early church when Luke included it here? Mary responds with a song, or psalm, known as "The Magnificat" because it begins "My soul magnifies the Lord."

This passage has become one of the great songs of the church. Because of that, we too often have missed the revolutionary message of the song that has been passed down to us from the earliest days of the Church. It reflects the inverse Reign of God that Jesus came proclaiming in which those on society's bottom rungs are blessed.

Of course, the Church has done to that message the same thing it did with Mary. This unwed, peasant, teenage girl was turned into the Queen of Heaven. In art, and in our minds, she has been transformed completely, and the meaning of Luke's story was completely perverted. In just such a way, when Christianity was made the official religion of the Empire, it was perverted to become the defender of the status quo. Far from "scattering the proud" or "bringing down the powerful" or "sending the rich away empty" the Church provides cover and support for those who exploit and neglect the poor and powerless.

Luke concludes that Mary stayed with Elizabeth for three months before returning to her own home. She stayed until Elizabeth gave birth, and then, with her own body beginning to show her pregnancy, she returned home where she would no doubt meet scorn. This journey to take the Christ of God into our bodies requires us all to move outside the status quo and to stand with the scorned. Luke doesn't want us to be surprised by that, so, in telling his story, that is how Jesus both begins and ends his life.

Luke 1:57-80

Luke goes to great lengths to describe the promise, conception, pregnancy and, now, the birth of John the Baptist. According to Luke, Elizabeth was in seclusion (except from Mary who stayed with her for three months) until John was born, but then all her neighbors and relatives celebrated with her. When the child was taken to be circumcised at eight days of age, everyone assumed he would be named Zechariah after his father, but his mother insisted that he was to be called John. The people who were there objected because none of their relatives had been named John. They tried to ask his father, but Zechariah was still suffering from angel-induced laryngitis. Still, he signaled for a writing tablet and wrote, "His name is John." (v. 63)

Zechariah immediately regained his voice and began to praise God. What follows in Luke 1:68-79 is called "The Song of Zechariah" or *Benedictus*. The song is in two parts. In the first, Zechariah praises God for keeping the covenant made with the house of David. This song, which was no doubt a part of the worship of the early Church by Luke's day, would have been premature for Zechariah to sing. Jesus, who is understood by Christians to be the fulfillment of God's promise, was still at least three months from being born.

In the second, Zechariah the priest addresses his son, telling him that he will be called a prophet of the Most High sent to prepare the way of the Lord:

> *By the tender mercy of our God,*
> *the dawn from on high will break upon us,*
> *to give light to those who sit in darkness and in the shadow of death,*
> *to guide our feet into the way of peace.*

John's role was to "guide our feet into the way of peace." That is how he prepared the way for the coming of the Lord. It seems to be a forgotten function. Perhaps if we were to walk more consistently in the way of peace—peace of mind, of heart, of relationships—we might be better prepared for the Lord to come to us.

The child grew and became strong in spirit, and he was in the wilderness until the day he appeared publicly to Israel.

With this sentence, Luke concludes the longest chapter in the Gospels. He seems to be saying that, like his mother, John spent a time in seclusion pregnant before he began his public ministry. To say "he grew and became strong" is a statement all parents hope to say about their children, but what does Luke mean by saying "he was in the wilderness?" Did his elderly parents, about whom nothing is ever said again, die and abandon him to be reared by wolves?

Luke has made a significant investment so that the reader understands and appreciates the importance of John the Baptist. In the other Gospels John simply appears on the scene fully grown. Without Luke, we'd be hard pressed to know just who he is and why he is important. In addition, we should note that John created his own movement, with disciples who were as devoted to John as Jesus' were to him. In the Book of Acts, Luke describes how Paul came to Ephesus and there discovered a group who were followers of John.

It is likely that the Church of which Luke was a part was confronted by two strands of faith. There are some who argue that Jesus was a disciple of John, having been baptized by him. Luke makes them cousins, though that fact is not substantiated anywhere else and some preeminent scholars doubt its historicity.

Perhaps what we have here is an attempt by Luke to tell the story of Jesus in a way that is palatable to those who still consider themselves followers of John. Maybe Luke was seeking to walk in the way of peace. At any rate, according to Luke, the early Church held John in high regard, but considered him a prophet who came out of the wilderness for the purpose of preparing people to hear Jesus.

John dies, but Jesus is resurrected and lives on in the life and ministry of the Church, which Paul calls "The Body of Christ." Still, the Church seems to struggle between the ministry of John, who called people to repentance and obedience, and the ministry of Jesus, who offers people transformation by accepting and being accepted by grace. It is a struggle each of us face, and, frankly, I think most of us end up in the wilderness with John.

Luke 2:1-7

And, so, we come to one of the most familiar passages in all of scripture. It is read each year at Christmas. Luke begins the story of the birth of Jesus by dating it. This birth occurred during the taxation census of the Roman Emperor Augustus, while Quirinius was governor of Syria. This double dating is typical in an age where there was not a common calendar.

Unfortunately, being educated does not ensure that you are correct. Matthew dates the birth of Jesus to the time of Herod and describes Herod's massacre of the children in Bethlehem. The trouble is one of these accounts is incorrect. If Herod was reigning in Judea, Quirinius would not have been the one collecting taxes because that was under Herod's authority.

New Testament scholar Raymond E. Brown notes that most historians believe that Luke is mistaken and doubts that a universal census ever actually occurred. Professor Brown is a brave man. He is challenging a story that has become a cultural cornerstone. The image of a very pregnant Mary making the journey to Bethlehem with Joseph, only to find a sold-out inn forcing her to give birth in a stable, is seared into our belief system as if written by fire from heaven. The magi and Herod have an only slightly lesser place. Yet now we are told that both cannot be true. Or perhaps more to the point, both cannot be factually accurate.

So, how do we decide which account is true? It is at this very point that courageous seekers of truth must no longer regard the Bible as a historical record and embrace it anew as a repository of truth. Which is more important factual accuracy or transformative truth? Honesty requires us to say that Luke was recording this story at least 60 years after the events. There were no photographers or biographers to record the events of Jesus birth. Now he is left to reconstruct the stories from legends, and what seems important is to retain the truth even if he doesn't know the facts.

And she gave birth to her firstborn son and wrapped him in bands of cloth, and laid him in a manger, because there was no place for them in the inn.

After all this buildup with angels and great canticles of faith, the birth of Jesus is described in one sentence. Just think of all the Christmas pageants this sentence has spawned, and all the holiday images:

- The "swaddling clothes," or bands of cloth, were a common way that newborns were clothed in that day. It was believed that keeping their limbs straight ensured they would not grow up crippled.
- From one word, "manger," an entire crèche-making industry was created. The word simply means "feeding trough," but every western human over the age of five has a clear image of the barn in which Jesus was supposedly born. All of this is born from one simple word.
- The innkeeper is second only to Judas as the archetype for Christian villains. Luke simply says there was no room in the inn. The truth, of course, is that if Mary and Joseph had been rich or powerful there would have been room somewhere for them, but they were not.

This verse even spawned a major theological divide in centuries past, as theologians debated just what Luke meant by "firstborn." The official doctrine of the Roman Catholic Church is that Mary was perpetually a virgin, living her whole life without a sexual relationship. "Firstborn" seems to imply that there were other children who were second and third born.

The Church has tried to sanitize this verse, making it a lovely event of sacred bliss. The truth is human birth is messy, and noisy, and painful, and the result of two people having sex. All of that has been hidden away, and Luke was a part of that conspiracy. After long descriptions, here at the birth, Luke takes pains to avoid depicting the human parts. Already, the Church is separating Jesus from the humanity he came to save. Perhaps we experience our redemption so poorly because we fail to embrace our own humanity. We are like Luke, pretending the messiness of life doesn't exist rather than being like Jesus, fully a part of life's noise and pain and messiness.

Luke 2:8-20

Here we have the second part of the Christmas story that is so artificial and yet so beloved. We all have permanently implanted images of angel choruses in the sky singing to freshly scrubbed shepherds on a beautiful rolling green hillside.

The entire scene is just a little too sweet and contrived. It has the feel of a mythological birth story for a Greek or Roman god. It seems out of sync with the idea of incarnation. It is like the president pretending to understand the plight of ordinary citizens. For the incarnation to really be meaningful, Jesus had to be FULLY human. Now, every parent feels that angels sing when their child is born, and that may be the true meaning of this scene.

Taken as a parable, though, Luke seems to be trying to communicate two things. First, while we have this idyllic and romanticized image of shepherds and sheep today, in that day it was a despised profession. They were dirty, un-bathed and ritually unclean, unable to worship in the temple. They also were considered shiftless and dishonest, grazing their sheep on other people's lands. Luke wants to tell us that, right from the start, Jesus came to the outcast and those at the margins. Later he will be scorned for hanging out with whores and tax-collecting thieves, but no one should be surprised. Just look who got the birth announcement.

The other connecting point, of course, was that King David was a shepherd. Of course, he was a "good shepherd," tending his father's sheep on his father's land as a kind of internship for someday managing his father's estate. Luke is reminding the reader that God has sent another shepherd-king who is born in Bethlehem. While this was especially meaningful to Jewish readers, Luke notes, through the angels, that this is "Good news of great joy for **ALL** people." So the shepherds rush off and find the baby, just as the angels had said. Luke concludes the birth story by noting that Mary kept all these things and pondered them in her heart. The implication, of course, is that Mary was his source of information, which would be necessary since she was the only one left … the trouble is mother's aren't the most accurate witnesses for their own children. Still, it is good to know that we have a heavenly Mother who tends to remember only the best about us.

After eight days had passed, it was time to circumcise the child; and he was called Jesus, the name given by the angel before he was conceived in the womb.

Like John the Baptist, Jesus was circumcised and named when he was eight days old. What I think is important is that the Bible acknowledges that Jesus had a penis.

Most of Christianity has functioned for 2,000 years as though Jesus was a genderless demi-god devoid of such human realities as genitals. I suspect there is hardly a church in America that has ever even mentioned Jesus' penis, but here it is, right in the second chapter of Luke. Even Luke only gives the circumcision of Jesus' penis a single line, though the purification ritual for his mother covers 17 verses. It is almost as if even Luke is a little embarrassed by Jesus' penis.

Okay, I'll quit, but my point was to force us to see Jesus in a new light and confront our own discomfort about thinking of him in normal, human, sexual terms. This discomfort is the other side of our investment in Mary being a virgin. It is both a symptom and source of the sex-negative attitude of the Church. Although human sexual expression is a private matter, the Church has created many layers of dysfunction around it:

- In 80 percent of the churches around the world women still cannot be ordained.
- The United Methodist Church wouldn't ordain me because of my sexuality, but they ordained a convicted murder that same year.
- Pat Robertson's at one time religious empire owned "The Family Channel," which aired the genocide of Native Americans, but would never show a program with a hint of sexuality.
- A recent Pew Research survey showed that the more often you go to church the more likely you are to support the use of torture and the more likely you are to oppose gay marriage.

Perhaps if Luke had been more comfortable with Jesus' penis the Church wouldn't be so driven by shame around human sexuality and our values would be more like Jesus'.

Luke 2:22-40

According to Jewish law, giving birth left a woman ritually unclean for seven days. She was to undergo ritual purification for 33 days if the child was a boy or twice as long if the child was a girl. (Lev. 12:1-5) This is so wrong on so many levels I can't even begin ... To not be outraged by the sexism of so much of religion is to fail to be filled with the spirit of Jesus who was always outraged by oppression.

Having gotten that out of my system ... I love these two stories that accompany Mary's purification. Luke alone tells any of this, and it is told through Mary's eyes. Despite the sexism of his day, for Luke, nothing was more important than Mary's witness. In these two Marian stories, an old man named Simeon affirms her belief that the child to whom she has given birth is special. In the second story, an elderly prophetess named Anna does the same.

Both of these older people believe the fulfillment of their life and devotion has come to pass in Jesus. Simeon says, "Lord now let your servant go in peace." It is a beautiful benediction on a life that has been well lived and now can be peacefully released.

Simeon's blessing of the child comes with words of warning to Mary that "a sword will pierce your own soul." While the text notes that the child's mother and father (as Joseph is always referred to) both were there, Simeon spoke to Mary. Luke is foreshadowing the pain that Mary will suffer as Jesus is rejected by his own people, tortured, and executed by the state.

After Simeon and Anna's blessings, Luke notes that, when the family had fulfilled all that was required by the law, they returned home to Galilee to the town of Nazareth. There is no flight to Egypt in Luke, but simply a trip home with the footnote that "the child grew and became strong, filled with wisdom and the favor of God was upon him." That is the desire of every parent for their child. It was all that Mary could ask for, at least for now.

Here we come to the end of material that is unique to Luke. He is the only one to even acknowledge that Jesus had teenage years. This story begins with the fact that the parents of Jesus went to Jerusalem every year for the Passover. It is as if the whole virgin birth story has been forgotten and Luke regards Joseph as Jesus' father with no footnotes. This story takes place in the 12th year of Jesus' life as they made their usual trip to Jerusalem.

The age was important because a Jewish boy became an adult at the age of 13, so Luke wants us to understand that Jesus was still just a boy. This was not his bar mitzvah but his last trip to Jerusalem as a kid. Even before he was an adult, Jesus was fascinated by the temple and the teachers, and, as a result, he gets accidentally left behind when Joseph and Mary head home.

Of course, they are panicked when they find him missing, but the explanation is valuable. They thought he was with the rest of the family. You see, unlike the American model of a nuclear family as the ideal, we see here that Jesus grew up in an extended family that routinely cared for him. When conservative churches talk about the "Biblical family," we are left to wonder if they never read the Bible. Extended families, clans and tribes are the models of the Bible, and we have abandoned them to our own destruction.

Although homosexual marriage is the great threat according to much of the Catholic and Protestant Church, it seems to me that the ideal is what is killing the family and damaging our kids. Nuclear families have been a nuclear disaster to family. Like almost the entire world, Jesus grew up in an extended family that also cared for him. It worked for him, but, for some reason, we think that a husband and wife and 2.4 kids locked in a gated suburb is the "ideal." I suppose it is, unless we want to rear healthy kids and build a healthy society.

Luke 2:48-52

I got so carried away yesterday about the idolatry of the nuclear family that I never got to Jesus being found. When Joseph and Mary discovered that he wasn't actually with the rest of the family, they returned to Jerusalem. Now, that was a big city, and at Passover it swelled by hundreds of thousands of people. A 12-year-old boy could have been anywhere, and it took three days before they finally found him. Imagine their fear and panic.

Luke tells us that when they found him, Jesus was in the temple listening to the teachers and asking them questions. The passage notes that people were astonished by his understanding and his answers. Frankly, I'd be astonished that a 12-year-old boy was voluntarily studying anything …

Mary and Joseph are naturally upset, and Mary scolds Jesus about how he has treated her and his father. He is surprised, just like a 12-year-old always seems to be by their parents' worry, so he says, "Did you not know that I would be in my Father's house?"

This entire story is told by Luke as a summary of the life of the young Jesus. Even at an early age, Jesus was fascinated by the things of God. To him, it was where he belonged. His parents were astonished by his response. We are not clear if this astonishment was that which is typical of the parents of pre-teen kids, or if they really were amazed at the young man Jesus was growing to be.

Luke notes that Jesus went home with them as a dutiful son. Then he adds, for a second time, that "Mary kept these things and pondered them in her heart." Some scholars believe that Luke is indicating that Mary was the source of the stories in these first two chapters. It is impossible to verify that, though most scholars doubt it. What is clear is that there was a different source for this material than for that which follows. At this point, Luke becomes a synoptic Gospel following the basic pattern of Mark and Matthew.

We leap from the Jesus of 12 to the 30-year-old Jesus being baptized by John. The first 20 verses of this chapter are a description of John the Baptist and his ministry. Luke has given extraordinary attention to John's birth, and, now, he gives the most attention of any writer to John's ministry.

The chapter begins with another attempt to date the events. Luke says it was the 15th year of the reign of Emperor Tiberius when Pilate was the governor and Herod was the king. He gives the names of other people who were also in power. This is the proper form for historical writing of his day, but it has proven to be of very little help in dating things. What Luke does do is introduce characters who will be important at the end of the story.

Luke describes the ministry of John calling people to repent and be baptized for forgiveness. He then quotes Isaiah 40:3-5. This passage is offered as proof that John was the fulfillment of a prophecy, and it then authorizes him as a prophet.

People were longing for a messiah who would rescue them from the oppression of Rome. They naturally thought that a passionate leader like John might be the messianic leader they needed. The prophet John makes it clear, though, that he is the one sent to prepare the way.

Luke ends this passage by telling how John had offended Herod by confronting him about his personal life. The result was that Herod had John thrown in prison. This seems like an odd way to end this passage since in the very next verse Jesus showed up to be baptized. Presumably Luke just couldn't resist telling how the story of John ended before introducing the real subject of the Gospel. Maybe it is a parable about how we all need to finish with secondary things and put them aside so we can focus fully on what is really important.

Luke 3:21-38

Each of the Gospels treats Jesus' baptism differently. After a 20-verse description of the ministry of John the Baptist, Luke doesn't even describe John baptizing Jesus. Luke simply says, "And when Jesus also had been baptized and was praying … " Luke's description is not of the baptism but of Jesus praying and what happens during that: the Spirit descending like a dove, a voice from heaven, God's affirmation of Jesus.

Prayer is a major theme for Luke, but it appears that something else is going on here. Apparently, the disciples of John who created a movement after his death insisted that John was the greater prophet because it was he who baptized Jesus, not the other way around. In Luke's description of the baptism, John's name isn't even mentioned. In Matthew and John's Gospels there is a statement by John the Baptist that he is unworthy to baptize Jesus. Luke takes another approach to making this point. In Luke, John is arrested in verse 20. If this was the only account, one might assume that Jesus is baptized after John's arrest since this is the order in Luke. The story doesn't say that, but it feels like a bit of misdirection.

It is ironic that Luke would do this since he then provides us with the genealogy of Jesus (vs. 23-38). Unlike Matthew, who only traces Jesus back to Abraham, Luke goes all the way back to Adam. This list of ancestors contains some real characters, including women, non-Jews, prostitutes and Joseph, who wasn't supposed to have had anything to do with this birth. The other thing about this passage is that here we have the only reference to Jesus' age as an adult.

Luke alone tells us that Jesus was about 30 when he was baptized, and tradition holds that his ministry then lasted about three years. We have been left to wonder why Jesus waited until he was 30 to begin his ministry, and what did he do before this time. The disappearance of Joseph from the scene has led some to suppose that Jesus, as the first-born, was responsible for providing for the family until all his siblings were old enough. While there is no evidence for this, it is probably meaningful to many of us who have had to make the choice between our dreams or family obligations. Jesus, too, may have delayed answering his call—as important as it was—to care for those he loved. There you have real family values.

Luke places the genealogy of Jesus between his baptism by John and his temptation in the wilderness. A casual reading of this passage might leave you with the impression that this story in Luke is just a repeat of the one in Matthew. However, there are some differences. Luke reverses the last two temptations, and the climax of Luke's version ends with Jesus being tempted to cast himself off the pinnacle of the Temple, the place where Luke began his Gospel.

Since there are no witnesses for these events, it might be tempting simply to dismiss them as fabrication of the early Church. That may well be; however, in light of Luke's efforts to convince us that Jesus is the Son of God, describing him struggling alone in the wilderness seems counterintuitive. While I don't know if this story actually happened, I do think it is true.

Jesus is baptized and affirmed as one who is beloved by God. He then struggles alone in a wilderness to figure out just what that means and how it shapes the way he lives. Every one of us has that same struggle. The way the story is told we might believe that Jesus wrestled with this for 40 days and nights, accepted that he was beloved of God, and went forth to do God's will. At the end of the story, Matthew says that Satan departed from Jesus. Luke, however, says that "the devil departed until an opportune time."

No, if Jesus was truly a Human One, he would struggle again with believing he was beloved, and he would grapple with what that meant for how he lived. While Luke and Matthew each describe three temptations, I am increasingly convinced that humankind only struggles with ONE temptation. It is the same temptation for every human great and small, rich and poor, young and old. Like Jesus, we struggle with truly believing we are absolutely, relentlessly and unconditionally beloved by God. Every other decision or struggle of our lives is simply a matter of deciding how to experience or express what we decided.

Liberating the Gospel

Luke 4:14-21

In the middle of a chapter, we move from the introduction to the content of Jesus' life. Both of those numbering systems are rather arbitrary, but, for the next five chapters, we will examine the public ministry of Jesus in Galilee.

What is interesting about Luke is that he wants us to understand that Jesus encountered opposition early on. This section begins:

> *Then Jesus, filled with the power of the Spirit, returned to Galilee, and a report about him spread through all the surrounding country. He began to teach in their synagogues and was praised by everyone.*
>
> Luke 4:14-15

Here we have life as we think is should be. Filled with the power of God, we are praised and appreciated by everyone. Jesus gets that experience for two whole verses. Then he makes the mistake of going home to Nazareth. There, as was his custom, he went to the synagogue on the Sabbath.

Now, if you are reading this, you probably gather for worship on a regular basis, but I am amazed by how many people do not. If the lake or the beach or being out too late or being irritated with the church doesn't get in the way, THEN they will attend. What Jesus models here is that being spiritual alone isn't enough.

It drives me crazy when I hear people say that they are spiritual but not religious. If you will forgive the crude analogy, what I want to say to them is, "Then you have discovered that masturbation is all the intimate physical contact you need?" To me, that is spirituality without religion. At the very least, we can say that solo spirituality practiced in solitude is not the spirituality of Jesus.

Despite the fact that Luke is a gentile, he begins his Gospel in the temple where Zechariah was serving. He describes Jesus as an infant being presented at the temple. Luke then gives us our only glimpse of Jesus as a boy as he is found lingering in the temple. Now Luke reminds us that it was Jesus' custom to go to the synagogue on the Sabbath. What I want to say to those who think they don't need regular, consistent worship is that I'm stunned how much more spiritual they must be than Jesus was. He seemed to think he needed it.

So, when Jesus showed up at his hometown synagogue, the people knew that he had been traveling around the region teaching because they handed him the scroll of the prophet Isaiah from which to read. He found the place where it was written, and then he read from Isaiah 61:1-2:

> *The Spirit of the Lord is upon me, because God has anointed me to bring good news to the poor, to proclaim release to the captives, recovery of sight to the blind, to let the oppressed go free, and to proclaim the year of the Lord's favor.*

He then told the congregation that this prophecy was being fulfilled in their presence. Isaiah had been putting words in the mouth of the Messiah, and Jesus is saying that these words were spoken about him and his mission.

This is a critical passage for Luke, and for us. Jesus could have chosen many different messianic prophecies to apply to himself, but he picked the one that expressed his understanding of who he was and how he thought those who were beloved should live.

If you compare this passage in Luke with the passage in Isaiah there are several discrepancies. The one that is most important is that Jesus stops too soon; he did not finish the passage. The next phrase says, *"And to proclaim the day of vengeance of our God."* According to Luke, Jesus left that out. Although the people oppressed by Rome were looking for an avenging messiah, by the time Luke was writing, the early Church had recognized that this was not whom Jesus was.

Today's Church too often has missed Jesus' omission. In much of the Church, the Christ who is worshipped comes to rescue the devout and abandon or punish those who don't properly believe. The nationalistic war god of Americanized Christianity would have read all of that passage in Isaiah and ended every speech with "God bless America."

This type of faith isn't new. Although Luke concludes by saying, "All spoke well of him and were amazed by his gracious words," tomorrow we will see that doesn't last.

Luke 4:23-30

Jesus did well with his hometown crowd when, in their midst, he claimed the mantle of the messiah who cared for the poor, the prisoners, the blind and the oppressed. They all spoke well of him, but, like most preachers, Jesus didn't know when to quit.

Jesus went on to offer two illustrations of the kind of messiah he felt he was called to be and of the kind of God he served. First, he talked about Elijah who helped the widow at Zarephath during a drought and famine. Then he reminded them of the story of how Elisha had healed the Syrian general Naaman, who had leprosy. When he finished, the people rose up and dragged him out of the synagogue to the edge of a cliff and tried to throw him off.

Now, I've had people react badly to sermons, but this is pretty dramatic. It seems almost impossible for the modern reader to appreciate what could have caused such anger. Well, impossible unless you were a part of the movement in the 1960s when some leaders tried to persuade their churches to welcome African-Americans into their churches; or unless you were among those involved in the fight to ordain women; or impossible to understand unless you have been a part of the movement to welcome lesbian, gay, bisexual and transgender people into full membership in the Church. Those have been bloody battles that have resulted in brave leaders getting thrown off cliffs.

Jesus told two stories in which God's blessings went to "them," "those people," "others," "outsiders." Never underestimate the anger that can be generated from people of faith when you try to genuinely include the outcast.

As a victim of that kind of excluding anger, I bear the scars, but integrity requires that I ask, "Where are my limits of inclusion?" Can I love the right-wing politician? How do I feel when the mentally ill disrupt my neat and pretty worship? How anxious am I to sit beside the homeless who haven't bathed in months? What about the child molester, can I offer them the hand of fellowship? Jesus almost got himself killed for taking inclusion too far … and then he called us—the resurrected body of Christ—to do the same. No wonder they tried to get rid of him.

Jesus was rejected by his hometown faith community after he tried to tell them that God's love wasn't for them alone. He then goes to Capernaum to continue his ministry there. What follows are three vignettes:

- Jesus casts out an unclean spirit who calls him the "Holy One of God."
- Jesus heals Peter's mother-in-law. This story is told in Mark and Matthew, but Luke uses medical terms to describe the fever from which she suffered.
- Jesus laid hands on the sick and cured them and then cast out demons who shout, "You are the Son of God."

Jesus then goes away to a deserted place to pray, but the crowds find him and try to persuade him to stay with them. However, Jesus insists that he needs to carry the good news throughout the region, so he moves on, preaching in synagogues throughout Judea. (Luke 4:44)

With an amazing economy of words, Luke describes an era in the life of Jesus following his baptism, but prior to calling the disciples. Although the stories are told in the other synoptic Gospels, they are not told in this setting. It is a bit odd that Luke has the healing of Simon Peter's mother-in-law in the fourth chapter when Simon isn't even introduced as a disciple until the fifth chapter.

For some reason, it is important to Luke for us to know that Jesus had a life and ministry before the disciples came along. Children often are surprised to realize that their parents actually had lives before they were born. Perhaps Luke, who wasn't one of the original disciples, is trying to make this point to those in the early Church who considered themselves disciples of a Disciple.

In our culture it is an exceptional person who can resist the axis perspective. That is, the attitude that all of life revolves around us. We all need to be reminded that there is a substantial amount of life beyond our little orbit. God was alive and at work before us and will be long after us. As insulting as it may be to our egos, the universe won't end when we do.

Luke 5

In the Gospel of Mark, which provided the pattern for much of Luke (and Matthew), the call of the disciples happens at the start of the story. Luke takes his time, though. He already has given us a significant amount of information about Jesus' birth, baptism, temptation and early ministry. Up until this point, it has been a solo act. Now Jesus calls his disciples against the background of a life that has been defined and a ministry that was begun without them.

Perhaps Luke did this because he knew that leaving everything and following Jesus would take more than Jesus simply calling his name. By the time Jesus calls the disciples in Luke, he has already established himself. His fame has spread, so Luke thinks it is more reasonable that fishermen and tax collectors might abandon their careers and families to follow Jesus.

Even with all this background, Luke still places the call of Peter, James and John against the background of a miraculous catch of fish. It was as if Jesus really needed to impress these fishers before Luke could imagine them making such a radical change in their lives. Maybe what we see lived out here is the author's own struggle. Luke is clearly the best educated of all the New Testament writers. Does that mean he is also sophisticated, successful and socially established? Maybe these are the factors that make him need to provide a context for the first disciples' willingness to leave their lives behind to follow Jesus.

When we are young, with few possessions and limited ties, we are much more willing to follow our "calling." With the passing of time, our roots grow deeper and that which we have has a stronger hold on us. The risk of change seems greater and the cost much higher. These are grown women and men who leave everything to follow Jesus. Familiarity with the story reduces the shock of such a decision for us, but not for Luke. The author struggles to explain why they did what they did. Maybe the explanation isn't really offered as much for us as for Luke himself. He will record teachings of Jesus about how hard it is for the rich and how there were those who could not make the leap. Here he describes those who could and did, but he goes to great pains to explain how it was possible. We always seem to need to explain why it is that others can make sacrifices that we don't make. It is human nature to justify our reluctance to follow Jesus when we are confronted by those who did or do.

This chapter begins with a conflict because the disciples harvested some grain on the Sabbath. The second story is about a conflict that occurred because Jesus healed a man with a withered hand on the Sabbath. The second story ends by describing how the religious leaders were furious and began "to discuss what they might do to Jesus." For Luke, the conflict that leads to the end began very early. In fact, this all occurs before verses 12-15 in which Jesus calls the twelve.

While Jesus has called people to be his disciple before this, Luke seems to be saying that, following these conflicts, Jesus names 12 select men to be his inner circle. Not only that, but this naming follows a night spent in prayer alone on the mountainside. This is no casual thing. According to Luke, it is a sacred promotion. Jesus called all his disciples around him, and, after seeking God, he designated 12 of them as apostles.

Luke is indicating that the conflict was a sign that the One sent from God would be rejected by the descendents of the 12 patriarchs. This rejection would lead to God replacing them with 12 apostles. Luke, who is a product of the early Church, gives us some insight into how the church came to understand the role of the original 12. The description of Jesus going up on a mountain to pray will be repeated at the end of the Gospel of Luke, just before Jesus ascends into heaven leaving the church and the work in the hands of his 12 direct descendants.

This theory of succession, first of the 12 patriarchs (tribal founders) of Israel and then of Jesus himself, is part of the reason that Luke alone describes how Judas is replaced. The word "apostle" simply means "one sent forth." It could be substituted for the word "ambassador" in many contexts. In the book of Acts, Luke refers to people other than the original 12 as apostles, so there is some debate over whether or not he understood the 12 as having been assigned to a specific office. What is clear, though, is that Luke understood the call to be issued against the background of conflict and risk, and that those who are called by Jesus have a responsibility to imitate him. We are called to do, as Jesus did, the work he described in the Synagogue in Nazareth: bring good news to the poor, work to free the prisoners, heal the sick, and relieve the oppressed. This work will be opposed, so we should just expect it, right from the start.

Luke 6:17-26

This section is parallel to Matthew's "Sermon on the Mount," though it is different in many ways. What happens on a mount in Matthew happens on a plain or "level place" in Luke. That difference is our first clue that what Luke understood to be the core teachings of Jesus differed greatly from Matthew's understanding.

In verses 20-26, Luke offers his own set of "beatitudes." While Matthew said "Blessed are the poor in spirit," Luke simply says, "Blessed are the poor." That two-word difference represents a huge theological shift. To the Jews of that day, where most were living in abject poverty and faced genuine hunger, being financially prosperous was considered a sign of God's blessing, if not God's approval. Matthew's Gospel was crafted for a Jewish audience, so talking about the blessings of poverty would have seemed laughable. Luke, however, is very clear throughout that he understood Jesus to be on the side of the poor and the marginalized. Luke has Jesus unapologetically saying that the poor are given a special place in the reign of God.

Unlike Matthew, Luke pairs his blessings with "woes," and he sees the rich as those who have received everything they are going to get. This is nothing new for Luke. Earlier, in the Magnificat, Mary sang about the God who sends the rich away empty. In fact, more than in all the other Gospels combined, Luke tries to warn us to exercise caution because with our wealth, comfort and security come great responsibilities and significant dangers.

There is a blessing to be found in poverty; we have a greater chance to recognize our utter dependence on God and God's provision. When we can provide for all our own needs we have a temporal security and comfort, but that is all we have. The spiritual connection that lasts eternally is denied us, because we don't even know it is missing or that we need it until it is too late. Latin American liberation theologian Gustavo Gutiérrez wrote:

> *God has a preferential love for the poor not because they are necessarily better than others, morally or religiously, but simply because they are poor and living in an inhuman situation that is contrary to God's will. The ultimate basis for the privileged position of the poor is not the poor themselves but in God, in the gratuitousness and universality of God's love.*

If love is the one true commandment of Jesus, then, here, Luke offers the specifics of how that is to be expressed. Being a disciple of Jesus would have been a whole lot easier if Jesus had simply left it at "Love!" Instead, we find Jesus telling us to love our enemies, even those who hate us. We are commanded to bless those who curse us and pray for those who abuse us. Further, he makes this the distinctive sign that we are one of his disciples. Anything less and we are acting like everyone else.

Frankly, I wish tithing was the distinguishing sign. As difficult as it may be to give away my money, it is even more difficult to give away my heart. Here Jesus is specifying that we are to give our hearts to those who broke it in the first place. It seems like spiritual masochism to me. I mean, think about the one person in your life who hurt you the most. Who is it that betrayed you? Who is it that tried to destroy you? Lied about you? Hurt the people closest to you? Who is it that still to this day would hurt you if they could? Got that person in mind? Now listen as Jesus tells you to love them, bless them, pray for them. Hear Jesus telling you that if you don't you are no different that they are. Ouch.

As I often say, "Everyone thinks forgiveness is a good idea, until they have someone to forgive." Many people think that the phrase "Forgive and Forget" is found in the Bible. It is not. In fact, Jesus teaches us that we have to forgive and *remember*. We are not called by Jesus to simply put our hurts behind us, or to put what happened out of our minds. No, we are to remember. We are to recognize that it wasn't a misunderstanding or an honest mistake. We need to recognize that we have an enemy who wants to hurt us, maybe even destroy us. Then, we are to love that enemy, bless them and pray for them.

Jesus says, "Blessed are you when people hated you, excluded you, reviled you, defamed you." He isn't saying that we need to rationalize or justify their harmful attitude, words or actions. He is saying that if we are blessed people we recognize the hurt and then we have an attitude toward them that doesn't come easily or naturally. Jesus isn't calling us to love a faceless enemy half a world away. Jesus is telling us that those who are disciples of his picture the person who personally hurt them the most and then we love them. If you think love is an easy commandment to keep then you haven't read Jesus' definition of whom we are to love.

Luke 6:37-45

Do not judge, and you will not be judged; do not condemn, and you will not be condemned. Forgive, and you will be forgiven; give, and it will be given to you. A good measure, pressed down, shaken together, running over, will be put into your lap; for the measure you give will be the measure you get back.

I suspect that every preacher or religious teacher has a different passage that she or he returns to again and again. Maybe everyone does. This is one of mine.

Ostensibly, these verses are about living generously and not being judgmental. However, taken as a whole, they are not instructions about what we should do; rather, Jesus is describing a way of being in the world. This teaching is common to almost every faith and every spiritual leader. Call it karma, "reaping what you sow" or "what goes around comes around," but almost everyone recognizes this as a basic principle of life. Then, almost everyone ignores it as a practice.

No one likes to be condemned/criticized by others, but we make an art out of being a critic. Do we not believe the truth of what Jesus said, or do we simply believe that we are exempt? Generosity is an increasingly rare quality, yet Jesus is crystal clear that the life that is open to give is also open to receive. Do we believe that we will be the first people to reap a harvest without sowing any seeds?

I love that beautiful phrase of Jesus, "Give and it will be given to you, good measure, pressed down, shaken together, and running over it will be poured into your lap." In a world where we are inundated with advertising, it is easy to be made to feel as though you don't have enough and therefore can't be generous. For most of us, that is largely an illusion, but, in a consumer-driven culture, resisting that illusion requires great spiritual strength.

Jesus says that the measure we use in our giving will be the same measure with which we receive. So, which is it for you? Is Jesus wrong, or are you the exception to that law of life that is taught by almost every faith? This teaching is so important that it should shape everything we say and do. It is the foundation for how we live.

For the next several chapters, Luke essentially retells stories told in Mark and Matthew. His emphasis is sometimes different, as he shows that Jesus is the Messiah, greater than the prophets (including John the Baptist). Then, in Luke 10, we encounter one of the most famous stories Jesus told: the Good Samaritan.

This story is told as the result of an expert in the religious law asking, "Teacher, what must I do to inherit eternal life." This is a strange question if you focus on the word "inherit." Children don't generally have to do anything to inherit what is theirs by birth. Perhaps Luke is trying to illustrate that this expert missed the point right from the start.

Jesus answers his question with a question about how this fellow understood the law. To his credit, he summarized it much as Jesus would have: Love God and love your neighbor. Jesus then simply said, "Do this and you will live." That simple exchange left the lawyer embarrassed, so he asks a follow-up question to try to prove he was smarter than Jesus: "Ah yes, but who is my neighbor?"

Maybe he had heard how Jesus almost had gotten himself thrown off a cliff in Nazareth for broadening the definition of neighbor too much. Was the lawyer counting on Jesus saying something that would alienate his listeners? If so, he may have gotten his wish, in that Jesus told a story that was far more radical than it sounds today.

In the story Jesus told, the hero is a member of a group that his listeners would have despised and rejected as being a part of the family of God. It would be like making a liberal lesbian a saint in a fundamentalist church or making Dick Cheney a hero in a liberal church. Jesus tells a story that is an affront to the values they held as a community.

There is a reason this story gets left out of Matthew and Mark's Gospels. There is also a reason it gets included in Luke's. Today the Church of Jesus Christ is divided into many camps on many issues. The bottom line then and now, though, is whether ours is a gospel of who is included or a gospel of who is excluded. Who really is our neighbor? And who isn't?

Luke 10:38-42

Martha, Martha, you are worried and distracted by many things; there is need of only one thing.

We could spend our entire week on the story of the Good Samaritan, but most of us have heard hundreds of sermons on that text. A couple more devotions are unlikely to persuade us to internalize Jesus' radical teachings found there …

What follows, at the end of chapter 10, is a very personal vignette about Jesus and Mary and Martha. Again, this story isn't really told anywhere else, but it gives us a glimpse into the life of Jesus. Here we find him dining with two women in a time when women were marginalized much like Samaritans.

The women are identified as "sisters," though some feminist theologians point out that women couples have been labeled that way throughout history. However, there is no way to discern that Mary and Martha had any relationship other than that of siblings. What I find most telling is how people react to the suggestion that this might be a story about Jesus eating with a lesbian couple. The fact that people react so strongly to this idea despite the preceding story just illustrates that, while we are all familiar with the story of the Good Samaritan, we still haven't done a very good job internalizing the truth is seeks to teach.

In this story, Mary and Martha do seem to be an old married couple. Martha was running about being a host while Mary simply wanted to sit at Jesus' feet and hear everything he had to say. Like many couples, they are opposite personalities. While Jesus appreciates Martha's hospitality, he affirms Mary's simply being present.

This story seems to be a reflection on the lawyer's question, "What must I do to inherit eternal life?" Martha was all about doing, and Jesus doesn't condemn her for that. He does however commend Mary for making a different choice. Of course, you would think from our culture that his response had been just the opposite. The way we live indicates that busyness and rushing about is a divinely sanctioned behavior pattern. The result is that, like Martha, we miss the one thing that Jesus says is needed. The interesting thing in this passage is that we are not told what that "one thing" is. The only clue offered is that being busy is not it.

In this chapter we find the heart of what Luke understood to be the teachings of Jesus. This chapter contains three stories, two of which are totally unique. The chapter begins with the story of the lost sheep and the shepherd who goes looking. No one is surprised that a shepherd goes looking for a lost sheep, but what is unique about this is that, according to Luke's version, the Divine Shepherd leaves the other 99 in the wilderness, thereby risking everything to find one that is lost.

The second story is revolutionary because it is a parable of how God is like a woman who is looking for a lost coin. Although the Church has used this story to illustrate God's passion for finding that which has been lost, seldom has it been pointed out that the woman represents God. This story was told in a day when a Pharisee might thank God that he had not been born a Gentile, a woman or a dog. This story is so radical that it is amazing that it has survived the sexism of the biblical editors.

The coin that was lost was a drachma, a silver coin equal to about a day's wages. While not an insignificant amount, it is not a fortune that has gone missing—valuable, but not worthy of panic. The woman sweeps her dirt floor, lights a lamp and searches carefully. When the woman finds the coin she calls her friends—woman friends the original says—and she has a party/celebration.

The joyful celebration is the point stressed by both these stories, a point that seems lost to the modern Church. Neither a sheep nor a coin can repent, so Jesus isn't calling sinners to repent. Rather, it appears that Jesus is calling the "righteous" to rejoice and celebrate when God (shepherd and woman) brings back into the fold one who was lost. Whether we rejoice or not depends on whether we think that people are a part of the Family of God by merit or by mercy. Anticipating the fact that we were likely to miss this point, Jesus tells one more story, his most famous of all.

Luke 15:11-32

Finally, this 15th chapter contains the most famous of all Jesus' stories: the parable of the Prodigal Son. Like the two stories preceding it, this one is about God's unconditional and relentless love for those who manage to get lost along the way. As we consider this renowned story with which we are all so familiar, I am struck by two surprising facts. First, why is this story only found in Luke? It is brilliantly told and appears to be original. The other fact that strikes me is how often Christians miss the story's point.

Just as in the preceding two stories, this one climaxes with a party. The father kills the fatted calf and celebrates that his son who was lost has come home. Of course, not everyone was happy with the younger son's return. A Sunday School teacher asked her eight-year-olds who in the story was most unhappy to see the Prodigal return. One wise fellow raised his hand and answered, "The fatted calf."

Almost as unhappy was the older brother. While millions of sermons have been preached on this parable, most focus on the interaction between the younger son and his father. It is a beautiful and graceful picture, and that alone makes the story powerful. However, Jesus didn't stop with the father's welcome. He goes on to recount the conversation between the father and the resentful dutiful brother.

That this is the real point of the parable is illustrated by the celebrations held by the shepherd and the woman. In each story, God rejoices, but Jesus knew that it was tough for the righteous to party hardy. Religion seems to leave us with a higher value for merit than mercy. The young son didn't deserve a party, but it was the father's nature. The older son grumbles about how he has been home all along serving faithfully, but the old man never threw a party for him.

It is at this moment that Jesus tries to make the point that few people of faith ever get: "Then the father said, 'My child you are always with me and **all that I have is yours.**'" We don't get it, or maybe we don't believe it. If we did, surely we could never begrudge anyone any love or mercy they might find. All that God has is yours; what is there to be envious, jealous or resentful for? Didn't you know? Haven't you believed that you are God's own child? It is all yours.

Luke 16:1-13

After filling chapter 15 with three beautiful stories of God's mercy-driven joy, Jesus then tells two stories that begin, "There was a rich man ... " The best-loved story of Jesus—the Prodigal Son—is followed by one that is almost beyond comprehension.

In this peculiar story, the rich man is firing his manager because he has been wasteful. Before he turns in his keys, though, the manager calls in all of the people who owe his boss money. He figures that he isn't strong enough for manual labor and he is too proud to beg, so he is going to make some friends before he is out of a job. He calls in the debtors and allows them simply to mark down how much they owe.

When the master discovers what the manager has done, he isn't angry, as you might expect, but he commends the manager for being shrewd. Jesus then goes on to say that the people of this world are shrewder in dealing with one another than people of the light. "I tell you, use worldly wealth to gain friends for yourselves, so that when it is gone, you will be welcomed into eternal dwellings."

This is truly odd. It has been suggested that the manager simply was eliminating his commission on the debts so that, rather than cheating his master, he actually was sacrificing his short-term income for a long-term benefit. Still, this is generally known as the "Parable of the Dishonest Manager," because it doesn't appear that he is the type to make a personal sacrifice. Apparently, we are not the first to struggle with understanding this parable, because it is followed by a couple of explanations that do not appear to have been originally attached to this story:

> *Whoever is faithful in a very little is faithful also in much; and whoever is dishonest in a very little is dishonest also in much. If then you have not been faithful with the dishonest wealth, who will entrust to you the true riches? And if you have not been faithful with what belongs to another, who will give you what is your own? No slave can serve two masters; for a slave will either hate the one and love the other, or be devoted to the one and despise the other. You cannot serve God and wealth.*

This is a collection of proverbs that were not original to Jesus, and, while they have some wisdom, they still don't explain this parable. What do you think it means?

Luke 16:19-31

After telling a parable that is incomprehensible, Luke then records another that is altogether too plain for comfort. Both stories begin "There was a rich man … " In this story, the two characters are the rich man and a beggar named Lazarus. The rich man dies and goes to torment, while Lazarus dies and goes to paradise. At this point, the story completely falls apart for most modern readers.

For us to proceed, it is vital that we have a bit more information. We know nothing about the rich man, not even his name. Oh, for centuries he was called Dives, but that is only a misinterpretation of the Latin word for "rich." We don't know how he got rich or just how rich he was, though he wears purple dresses in fine linen, and feasts sumptuously. That's really all we know: he was rich and lived well.

Then we meet Lazarus. Interestingly, he is the only character in all of Jesus' parables who is given a name. Apparently a name was all he had because he longed to fill himself with the crumbs that fell from the rich man's table. However, no one gave him anything. Actually, what he is longing for is the scraps of bread on which the rich man wiped his greasy fingers. Lazarus was covered with sores, which the dogs that ate the rich man's scraps would lick as they walked by.

Jesus paints a picture of one who is rich and one who is wretchedly poor. He doesn't tell us if one was a saint and the other a sinner. No deeds or attitudes or words are recorded about either. All we know is that one is rich and one is poor, and, of course, that one ends up in torment and the other in paradise. This is not a good story for modern readers. It would be even more difficult for original listeners who lived in day when people believed that the rich were blessed by God and the poor abandoned. Jesus takes that attitude and turns it on its head.

Imagine how unsettling this story might be to us if we lived in an age that made heroes of the rich and disdained the poor for their lack of effort or enterprise. Imagine how disturbing it would be if we lived in a time when our dogs were better fed than the poor outside our gates. Well, it is only a story … but where some are rich while others starve, the Dominion of God is nowhere to be found.

This story, found only in Luke, is well known to those who regularly attend Thanksgiving services in their local churches. It is, of course, the story about 10 lepers who are healed by Jesus. Only one of them returned to say thanks.

Preachers love to use this story to harangue congregations about living with ingratitude. That is certainly an important value, and I must confess that I have preached sermons about "Nine Ungrateful Turkeys." However, that really wasn't the point Luke had in mind when he included this story. Luke's point is found in the last part of verse 16. Luke describes the one healed leper returning to prostrate himself in gratitude at Jesus' feet. Then Luke adds, "And he was a Samaritan."

Luke's point seems to be that insiders often take the gifts of God for granted. People who have been on the outside seem to have a tenderness of heart that overflows with gratitude. Jesus sees the grateful man and asks, rhetorically, if there were not 10 originally. He then wonders if all 10 were not healed. No one answers, but Jesus lifts up the Samaritan and sends him on his way, saying that "his faith has made him whole."

Now, wait, weren't their 10? Weren't they all healed? Wasn't it Jesus who healed all 10? How was it, then, that the Samaritan's faith made him whole?

This may be purely semantics, but it also may be a profoundly important spiritual principle. You see, people who are physically healthy may be a far cry from being spiritually and emotionally whole. This Samaritan's gratitude, and his need to express it, spoke volumes about the kind of person he was. While Jesus healed all 10 lepers, the Samaritan's faith was what made him whole.

What did happen to the other nine ungrateful turkeys? Could it be that a few months later a spot developed on one leper's hand, and he panicked to think the leprosy might be returning? Perhaps he should go back and find the rabbi from Galilee. The leper suddenly recalls that he never even thanked the Master for healing him.

What about us? How many times have we been healed without giving thanks? Remember that cold that didn't turn into pneumonia? Remember that broken bone that healed? I suspect there are more than nine ungrateful turkeys …

Luke 17:20-21

The Reign of God is not coming with signs you can observe; nor can you say, "Look here it is!"' or "There it is." For, in fact, the Reign of God is within you.

This brief proverb is found only in Luke. It is followed by what might be considered an apocalyptic warning. Fundamentalism makes a great deal of fuss over the idea of the "second coming," but the profound truth of this passage is almost wholly ignored.

The Christian faith historically has emphasized the transcendence of God to the neglect of the imminence of God. Or to say that in plain language, for most of us, God is "out there" or "up there," but what Jesus is saying is that God is actually "in there."

Ponder for a moment what a different faith Christianity might be if we had taken this passage more seriously and spent more of our time seeking the realm of God within our hearts and less time looking for it elsewhere. Followers of Jesus have sought to create the Realm of God in our world—some by force, some by coercion, some by edict. Millions of goodhearted disciples have tried to build it with works of compassion and mercy and good deeds.

Is it possible that even the latter efforts might have been more effective if we had chosen a different starting point? Americans in particular seem to have a tough time being introspective, reflective and meditative. I'm not sure if our business and obsession with externals and appearances is cause or effect. What I mean is, would the culture we have built be different if our faith had better learned this truth from Luke 17?

Eastern religions do a better job of this than Christianity. Still, it should be noted that the impact on their culture hasn't really yielded significantly better results. Perhaps it is because Jesus isn't saying "The Realm of God is ONLY within you." It might be greatly helpful to start our search there, but it cannot end there. God is found in other people, in nature and in the world we are building together. While we seem to fall victim to either/or thinking, Jesus is constantly calling us to consider the one without neglecting the other. The Realm of God is within you, but don't be deluded into thinking you can contain it.

Luke ends this section of his Gospel with a random collection of stories and parables, most of which are shared with the other two synoptic Gospels. In chapter 19, he tells of the triumphant entry into Jerusalem that begins the last week of Jesus' life.

In 18:13, Jesus takes the disciples aside and says, "Look we are going up to Jerusalem." Jesus then passes through Jericho on his way to Jerusalem. There he heals the blind man in a story told in Matthew and Mark. Chapter 19 begins with the story of Jesus spotting Zacchaeus, the tax collector, up in a sycamore tree.

This story is well known but found only in Luke. Again, it is a story of amazing and radical inclusion. Of all the people pressing against him looking for help and healing, Jesus picks the worst identified sinner out of a tree and insists on having lunch with him.

Notice that Jesus doesn't preach to Zacchaeus or question him to see if he was ready to change his ways. Jesus just calls him down from the tree and says that he **MUST** stay with Zacchaeus. There is an amazing compulsion in Jesus' words. Jesus probably could have stayed anywhere, but something in his spirit forced him to stay with Zacchaeus.

What follows is a description of how all who saw this interchange began to grumble. The righteous didn't seem to like Jesus' choice of friends. It was almost as if they thought they had some claim on Jesus … as if they controlled where he stayed and with whom he socialized.

Not much seems to have changed. Luke's point has been missed completely. Of course, in the end, Zacchaeus's whole life is changed by this encounter, and he promises to Jesus that he will make complete restitution to any he has wronged. Notice this wasn't anything Jesus required. All Jesus required from Zacchaeus was a place to stay. That seemed to be enough. Jesus ends the story by saying that the Human One's purpose in coming was to seek **that which was lost.** Notice he isn't saying that Zacchaeus was lost. In fact, Jesus notes that he was "a son of Abraham." Jesus knew that what that meant had been lost to Zacchaeus, and, by simply honoring him, Jesus helped him find it. It is a strategy the Church might want to try. Zacchaeus isn't the only one who has lost what it means to be a daughter or son of God. Maybe if we could find that meaning we'd be secure enough to let Jesus love whomever he wants.

Luke 19:41-44

As Jesus came near and saw the city he wept over it saying, "If you, even you, had only recognized on this day the things that make for peace!"

I love this verse. Jesus is lamenting over Jerusalem. In an earlier lament following the death of John the Baptist, Jesus describes Herod, John's executioner, as a fox and himself as a mother hen. (Luke 13:31-35) Now the hen has deliberately come into the fox's lair and again he laments over the city of Jerusalem.

Most scholars believe this passage was written after the destruction of Jerusalem, 35 years or so after Jesus' death. It is written in such a way as to indicate that Jesus knew ahead of time what was going to happen. That is possible I suppose. An astute political observer might have predicted that the unrest in Palestine would ultimately result in an outbreak of violence, and it wouldn't require a prophet to predict that Rome would ruthlessly crush them. So, perhaps Jesus is making that kind of observation as he lament's Jerusalem's future. Or maybe Luke is reporting that Jesus was a prophet who could predict the future.

Regardless of the context, though, what I think is worth treasuring in this passage is that, right from the start, Jesus lamented that people of faith don't recognize *the things that make for peace.* Two questions leap from that statement: Why don't we, and what are they?

Both of those are questions too large for a 400-word devotion. Both are questions worthy of our prayerful contemplation:

1. Why is it that our faith doesn't call/compel us to be the world's peacemakers? Why is it that in the United States the more often you attend church the more likely you were to support the war in Iraq? Today Jesus would be lamenting over the Church that has bastardized his name.
2. What are the things that make for peace? And why, as people of faith, don't we readily know the answer to that question?

Pity the Christ who has spent the last 2,000 years lamenting over us.

In Luke, Jesus processes into Jerusalem, weeps over the city, and then goes almost immediately to the temple. Perhaps because he is a gentile, or perhaps because he is writing after the destruction of the temple, Luke tells a much shorter version of that episode than Matthew and Mark. For Luke the cleansing of the temple is not so much the event that set up Jesus' arrest as it is a prelude to the last set of teachings that Jesus offered.

In Luke, Jesus cleansed the temple and then spent the rest of his life there "teaching the people and telling the good news." (20:1) Jesus claimed the temple, and, of course, his claim is challenged immediately by the religious establishment who don't challenge what he is teaching, but question his credentials. "Tell us by what authority you are doing these things? Who gave you this authority?" (20:2)

In 1968, eight months before the Stonewall Riots launched the "gay rights movement," a former Pentecostal preacher named Troy Perry held a worship service in Los Angeles for lesbian, gay, bisexual and transgender people. That service gave birth to a denomination that was the first to welcome openly gay people back into the family of God.

Rev. Perry gave birth to a historic movement that changed, and is changing, the church of Jesus Christ. Four years later the United Church of Christ ordained the first openly gay man. This painfully slow, but inexorable, movement toward inclusion was possible because the spark was a Pentecostal minister, not a priest or pastor whose authority came from the religious establishment.

Troy Perry's authority came from the Holy Spirit. It never crossed his mind that he needed someone's permission to do what he did. Had he been a product of most mainline churches it never would have happened. Radical good news most often seems to come *despite* religious authority, not *through* it.

As a part of the religious establishment, that is something I need to remember. Perhaps what you need to remember is that you actually don't need anyone's permission to be a bearer of good news. The Holy Spirit in you is all that you need to speak courageously of the radically inclusive love of God. When the Bishop laid his hands on my head to ordain me in the Methodist Church he said, "Take thou authority … " What he didn't know was that I already had … and so should you.

Luke 20:27-40

Over the next two chapters, Luke records a rather random set of teachings by Jesus. Although I have tried, for the life of me, I can't uncover a common theme or any reason why these teachings are clustered here in the last week. None of the teachings are unique to Luke; they follow, almost exactly, Mark's pattern. In fact, in Luke 20:27-40, Luke recounts the attempt by the Sadducees to trip Jesus up on the topic of the resurrection. This is the only place in all of Luke where the Sadducees appear. Here the conflict is not between Jesus and the Sadducees so much as it appears to be an attempt to get Jesus to take sides. The Pharisees believed in the resurrection of the dead; the Sadducees did not.

Ironically, the Sadducees' view was the more orthodox, longer-held view in Judaism. Since Jesus often conflicted with the Pharisees, it may be surprising to find him taking their side here. Resurrection as **the** central tenant of the early faith became the deciding factor for Jewish theology from that era. Christians believed in resurrection as the Pharisees did, and Jews rejected the notion as the Sadducees did.

This is a much less clear division today. However, it is important to recognize that the idea of life-after-death is a much more modern concept in the way it is now popularly understood. The interesting contrast between how this story is told in Luke and how it is told in Mark is that in Luke it is very much a civil conversation between Jesus and the Sadducees. While they pose a bit of a riddle, there is no statement that they are trying to trick Jesus. Unlike Mark's version, here Jesus doesn't rebuke them or scold them; he simply offers an expanded view of how life after death follows different rules.

In the end, some of the scribes, who might or might not have been Sadducees, said to Jesus, "Teacher, you have spoken well." In both the title they give Jesus and the compliment, there is a recognition that, though they may not agree, the discussion has been worthwhile. All of which is to say that we all need to learn to be more like the Jesus of Luke and less like the Jesus of Mark. I am convinced that the reason it seems nearly impossible to have civil religious debates isn't so much that we feel strongly about our beliefs, but that we are secretly afraid we may be wrong. Here Jesus is able to talk civilly about the central tenant of the faith with those who disagree. It is a role model we'd do well to follow.

So what do good liberals do with these passages about the second coming? Personally, I like to ignore them if I can. I managed to do that in our journey through Matthew and Mark. Luke is the most educated and sophisticated of the synoptic Gospels, and that almost makes you hope that he will ignore these teachings, too, but he does not. In fact, it is what makes up the last set of teachings by Jesus before his arrest.

Luke doesn't shorten or soften this teaching either. In fact, though he follows Mark's outline pretty fastidiously, the changes Luke does make are interesting and not what we'd hope to see. For example, Luke omits Mark's statement that the Lord will cut short the days of suffering and inserts again a warning about false prophets who deny the coming apocalypse.

In the ways Luke frames these signs as precursors to the coming of the Human One, he is imitating the First Testament oracles. When the world falls apart, Luke says "Stand up, raise up your head, for your redemption is drawing near." He also warns against letting our lives get so entangled with worry and fear that this day of redemption takes us by surprise.

Frankly, having studied passages like this and the book of Revelation, I find myself struggling for a cogent explanation. What I do **not** believe is the kind of second coming apocalyptic theology that sold millions of copies in the "Left Behind" series. Trying to make these verses predictive of future historical events is crazy and crazy-making. The religion that results is alien to the person and personality of Jesus.

However, if we understand that all apocalyptic literature is by definition symbolic, and begin to think about our own apocalypses, then we can hear a word of promise. Into every life comes times that are overwhelmingly destructive when it seems everything is falling apart. To those times, Jesus says, "Don't let your fear and anxiety blind you to the possibilities that even in times like this God will send you a redeemer." If that is not what the "Second Coming" means, then I'm not sure I want to know what it does.

Luke 21:37-38

Every day he was teaching in the temple, and at night he would go out and spend the night on the Mount of Olives, as it was called. And all the people would get up early in the morning to listen to him in the temple.

Luke ends this section with a statement of conclusion. Just as Luke framed the triumphant entry and cleansing of the temple as Jesus claiming the place as his own, now he concludes that this is how he spent the rest of his life. He went out at night and slept under the stars on the Mount of Olives, but all day, every day, was spent in the temple teaching.

The temple was the embodiment of the Jewish faith. It was the nucleus around which family and faith circulated, ebbed and flowed. For the Christian, Jesus became all those things. Luke is very deliberately indicating that this wasn't accidental. Having predicted the destruction of the temple, Jesus offers himself as the temple that, although it will be destroyed, will rise again to live.

Luke offers us this amazing image of "all the people getting up early in the morning to listen to Jesus in the temple." Of course "all the people" wouldn't fit in the temple so this is obviously a bit of hyperbole by Luke, but what he is trying to say is that there was a deep and pervasive spiritual hunger that brought huge crowds to be taught by Jesus.

Having preached in large empty rooms at times, I do wonder if the difference today is that people aren't hungry, or that we aren't offering them the teachings of Jesus in a way that feeds. It is my conviction that who Jesus was/is and what he taught/teaches is still powerful and transformative. I also believe that people are more than hungry to experience the living God. That is what Jesus offered in the temple. They came in droves; they came early and stayed late because he offered them words of life.

That image is compelling. I'm left to wonder if we, too, might hear the words of life if we made that kind of effort. As a teacher/preacher, I'm left to wonder how I could do a better job offering spiritual food to a hungry people.

Luke 22:1-38

The Gospels are painfully brief and leave us longing to know more about Jesus, his life and teachings. All four of them give a large percentage of their time to the death and resurrection of Jesus, a period that only covered a few days. Some scholars believe that these stories were the first to be written down and passed along. Others have gone so far as to suggest that the final act in the life story of Jesus was memorized.

If you have a reference Bible you will note that nothing in the 22 nd chapter of Luke is wholly unique to this Gospel. The variations are fairly minor, but that is, perhaps, what makes them significant. Luke is highlighting standardized material. The story of the Passion of Jesus begins with a substantial narrative of the Last Supper.

Luke uses "The Feast of Unleavened Bread" and "The Passover" interchangeably, which only goes to prove that he was not a Jew. For his purpose, Jesus' death is linked to the death of the unblemished lamb that protected the Jews, and with the act of God to liberate the people from slavery. Much of the Church's theology that grew up around this idea uses Luke as the basis.

To me, the problem is not that the doctrine of sacrificial atonement is wrong; it is simply misaligned. To see Jesus as the innocent sacrifice for our salvation is one thing, but to see God as the randomly-slaying angel of death is quite another. When atonement (salvation) theology makes a monster of God, I believe we have missed the point. We do better to focus on the liberation components of this story. Jesus' life, death and resurrection are meant to set us free from the self-absorption, rage, despair and alienation that arise from our pervading fear. The root of our fear is that we are unloved and unlovely to the God of creation.

It is no accident that Jesus said that he would not leave us as orphans. That is the deepest human anxiety: that the One who created us does not love us and will not let us come home. If Jesus' life and death means anything at all, it is that the ultimate act of liberation is that everyone—even Judas—is welcomed at the table. When we fully understand and experience this, we are saved … not from the hands of the angel of death, but into the hands of the God of life.

Luke 22:21-38

Matthew and Mark both have Judas leaving to go out and betray Jesus before the institution of the Eucharist. In Luke it is explicit that Judas is a part of this special post-supper meal. In addition, Matthew and Mark have the argument about who is the greatest happening days before. Luke and John confess it was here at the last.

It is as if Luke is trying to remind us that the betrayal of the faith doesn't happen by those outside the inner circle, but by those inside whose pride and ambition get in the way. Michael Card's haunting song "Why" asks:

> *Why did it have to be a friend who chose to betray the Lord?*
> *Why did he use a kiss to show them? That's not what a kiss is for.*

Then he concisely answers:

> *Only a friend can betray a friend; A stranger has nothing to gain.*
> *And only a friend comes close enough to ever cause so much pain.*

That is the experience in Jesus' life that Luke is seeking to communicate to us. The Church has demonized Judas and rendered him somehow being beyond human. No one would ever name their dog Judas, but that doesn't mean that betrayal is banned from Christian community. Perhaps Luke had been a part of the Church long enough to know that it was perfectly possible for someone to rise from the communion table and go out and completely betray the teachings and values of Jesus. The image of the kiss seems a good reminder that, in the Church, our betrayal is often accompanied with a smile, sweet words and a warm embrace. These things do not make the knife in the back less painful or deadly, but they do seem to make the betrayer feel better about themselves.

Judas hadn't rejected the bread or cup that Jesus offered. He was there participating, just like us. Then, like us, he rose up and did what he had rationalized to be the right thing. His betrayal made perfect sense to Judas, just as ours seems perfectly reasonable to us. If it did not, how could we live as we do and then return each week to offer Jesus the kiss of our worship?

Luke 23:1-25

Luke's Gospel, more than the others, tries to help us understand the dilemma in which Pontius Pilate found himself. In Luke's version of the story, Pilate tries every possible means to set Jesus free, and, ultimately, Pilate simply "handed Jesus over as they wished."

According to Luke, all Pilate is guilty of is acquiescence. Perhaps to understand why it was important to Luke that Pilate gets off so lightly, we need to remember to whom Luke addresses this volume: "Most Excellent Theophilus." Perhaps he was a Roman official. In volume two of Luke's writing, the book of Acts, the apostle Paul is often rescued because of his Roman citizenship.

Perhaps Luke is trying to protect Pilate's reputation by describing how Pilate tried to free Jesus after finding him innocent, and then sent him to Herod, hoping Herod would take him off his hands. Pilate even offered to make Jesus the prisoner freed by the governor at Passover. None of that worked, and, in the end, Pilate simply acquiesced to what the crowd demanded. Luke may have wanted us to understand that Pilate really wasn't guilty ... but he was.

Human history is replete with evils that happened when people simply stood by in silent passivity and acquiesced. Could the Holocaust have ever happened if German citizens of faith had risen up to protest? Edmund Burke reminded us long ago that, "All that is required for evil to triumph is for good men [and women] to do nothing." Pilate knew Jesus was innocent. He announced his verdict to everyone, yet he lacked the courage, or energy, or will, or determination to do anything about it. Pilate was more concerned with his own position and reputation than he was with doing what was right for someone he did not know.

After the 20th person was exonerated in Dallas County alone, I decided that Texas should be renamed "Pilatesville." We, the good citizens, stand by as the most active death chamber in the world continues to kill our fellow citizens at a record pace, while, simultaneously, one of the largest counties in the state PROVES that our judicial system is corrupt and unjust. We don't administer the poisons in Huntsville; we just acquiesce by our silence. And Jesus is executed by the state again.

Luke 23:33-43

Luke assumes that the reader knows what a crucifixion is like and thus spares us the details. There are two unique elements in Luke's telling of Jesus' death that are both powerful and beautiful. The first is Jesus' brief prayer: "Abba, forgive them for they know not what they do." This defining sentence is found only in Luke 23:34, and even some of the most reliable ancient manuscripts omit it. No significant translators have left it out, though, because those who have read Jesus' other teachings about forgiveness find it entirely congruent with whom Jesus was.

The other element found only in Luke was the interchange between Jesus and the two who were crucified beside him. It is here we find the one thief asking Jesus to remember him and Jesus responding with the promise of paradise. What is meant by the promise is unknown. The word used by Jesus is a Persian word meaning "walled garden." It is a special intimate place to take a loved one.

Evangelical theology says that one was saved/forgiven/redeemed/heaven-bound while the other was lost/doomed/condemned/hell-bound. That may be, but it is not the only way to read the text. Jesus never replies negatively to the taunting thief. He does not rebuke him, or scorn him, or warn him of torments to come. All three of the men are enduring hell already. They are being physically tortured to death, condemned, naked, exposed in public. They are cut off from all comforts, from family and friends. They are alone, pinned like butterflies to wood, and left to die in the sun. Jesus doesn't warn the taunting thief of hell, because all three of them are already there.

Jesus does respond to the kind thief's plea: "Remember me." I'm not quite sure why we need to take the tender promise to one and make it into a win-lose scenario with God for the other. If the first prayer of Jesus has any meaning at all it was prayed for both thieves, the soldiers, the taunting crowds, the deserting disciples, and you and me as well. Promising one of the men paradise was a gift. The other thief was not condemned; in fact, he was forgiven because he "did not know what he was doing." The tragedy is that he never knew it. His bitterness, anger and self-justification all closed him off from experiencing the promise of Jesus to us all. It wasn't so much that he wouldn't be with Jesus after he died, but that he couldn't let himself know grace while he lived.

Luke 23:44-56

In recording the actual death of Jesus, Luke shares elements of both Matthew and Mark's account. Darkness descends, and the veil of the temple is torn in two. Then, Jesus breaths his last and commends his spirit into God's hands.

The centurion in charge of the execution pronounces Jesus innocent, and the crowds return back into the city, beating their breasts over what they had seen. Luke then notes that "all his acquaintances, including the women who had followed him from Galilee, stood at a distance, watching these things."

In all of the text, I think that last sentence is the saddest. At the moment in our lives when we want our loved ones closest, Jesus' stood at a distance out of fear. How awful. Many years ago, in the early days of AIDS, a young man lay dying in ICU. The hospital wouldn't let his partner in because he was not legally family. Finally, though, Frank couldn't stand it any longer. He rang the bell at the ICU, and, when the nurse came, he asked to be admitted. We all stood in the hall while she explained that the dying man's family had left strict instructions that no one was to see him. Then Frank said, "Well, then you'll have to have me arrested, because I am going to be with him." Still very calm, the nurse said she would have to call security if he tried to enter. Frank said, "Do what you must."

At that moment, a lesbian in the crowd stepped forward and said, "You better have a lot of security, because you are going to have to arrest us all, and then arrest everyone I can call to come down here. We don't all have to go in, but Frank does 'cause he is real family." The nurse was convinced by this formidable woman that letting Frank be with his lover as he died was the better part of valor.

For years, I have always wished that I had been the one with the presence of mind and courage that Frank's lesbian friend demonstrated that day. I suspect that the friends of Jesus probably spent the rest of their lives regretting standing at a safe distance while he was dying without them. Life is altogether too precious to live with those kinds of regrets. Rules are made to be broken, especially rules that get in the way of love.

John

For most of this book, we have been studying what are known as the "Synoptic Gospels." While this is not a term most of us know, it simply means that Matthew, Mark and Luke can be studied in parallel columns. It is believed that Matthew and Luke used Mark's Gospel as a guide when they were writing their own versions of the story. Though the Synoptic Gospels are very similar in their shared parts, each seems to emphasize what was important to them and their readers while telling the story.

John's Gospel is something else entirely. This Gospel is unique on many levels, though there are a few pieces it shares with the other three. Often when you see the four Gospel writers depicted in art they are represented by the four creatures described in Revelation 4:7. The winged lion stands for Matthew who depicts Jesus as the Messiah and the Lion of Judah; the winged human is used to represent Mark because in that Gospel Jesus is presented as the Human One (Son of Man); the winged ox is for Luke who described Jesus as a servant and sacrifice to make atonement for all humankind.

The eagle represents John's version of the life and teachings of Jesus, soaring, highly exalted image of Jesus. William Barclay, in his Bible commentary from half a century ago, points out that the eagle alone is able to look into the sun and not be dazzled. The eagle can see details from as far as 90 miles away. Certainly, John's Gospel dares to encounter the mysteries of the Christ, though the eagle became his symbol long before science discovered these zoological facts. In our study of John, we will encounter an exalted Christ who is clearly the incarnation of Divinity. Without the witness of the three preceding Gospels we might forget that Jesus considered each of us incarnations of the divine, daughters and sons of the Living God. Still, in an age when blasphemy is considered entertainment, John calls us to enter the holy presence of God and take off our shoes. It is an important call to a culture where almost nothing is sacred any more.

John

Having just journeyed through the Synoptic Gospels, which are more similar than different, perhaps we should begin with the ways in which John is different:

1. There is no birth narrative. Mark also lacks one, but John begins with a substantial theological statement about the incarnation of the Word/Logos.
2. There is no actual baptism of Jesus, though John the Baptist testifies about his experience when baptizing Jesus.
3. There is no wilderness temptation, not even a one-line reference as in Mark.
4. There is no institution of the Last Supper, though Jesus' final meal with his disciples is the context for a huge block of teachings found only in John.
5. This is the only Gospel in which Jesus washes his disciples' feet.
6. There is no ascension in John. He simply concludes with the statement that there were many more things to write about but if all of them were written the world itself could not contain the books.
7. In John, no one is healed of evil spirits, and there are no parables. Imagine what Christianity would be like without stories like the Prodigal Son.

Interestingly, the authors of Matthew and Luke had Mark to guide them, and they produced modified versions for their readers. They seem to take Mark as basic fact and put their own spin or texture on the truths that are communicated. For scholars, the most fascinating aspect of studying the Synoptics has been to examine the parts that make these three distinctive. So, what does that mean for John, since it is almost entirely distinctive from the other three?

Perhaps what we have is a model of the way much of life is lived. Most people seem to take what is given to them by their parents or society or tradition and modify it slightly. Each life is individual, but, from one generation to the next, values and lifestyles are generally more similar than different. Then there are those rare souls who find no need to repeat what others have said or done or felt. Like John, they want to supplement what others have offered, and they give us a unique view. We call these people visionaries, heroes, artists, mystic, crazy, schizophrenic, eccentric, etc. Perhaps they are all those things, but they are also those people who help us see the whole picture of life.

John

So who is the author of the fourth Gospel? Tradition and most conservative scholars hold that the author was John, son of Zebedee, who wrote it shortly before his death at the end of the first century. Most contemporary scholars dispute that. In fact, they suggest that the book actually was not written by any one person, but is a compilation of writings drawn mostly from a single "school" of disciples. They cite the fact that there are differences in the Greek style and grammar, there are breaks and inconsistencies in sequence, there are geographical and chronological "jumps" in the story, and that there are passages that are clearly out of context.

In that day, it was not at all uncommon to give a writing importance by attributing it to someone the readers would esteem. In that day, if the person who wrote something were a disciple of the line of John then assigning the authorship to him would have seemed the most honest thing to do. In addition, our modern minds define author as someone who is entirely the original source of every word. In that day, the author simply may have been responsible for editing together, or rewriting in an acceptable form, bits and pieces of stories and teachings that were considered meaningful, correct and accurate.

The Church long has believed that the Holy Spirit was involved in this process, which is why scripture is called "inspired" or "God-breathed." Fundamentalism is a fear-based faith, regardless of the religion, and acknowledging that we actually don't know who wrote most of the Bible seems to require too much faith for them. Liberals, on the other hand, at times seem to disregard traditions as meaningless, lest we be seen as unsophisticated and illiterate.

In my studies that seems to be the tension around many issues such as this. Could this book have been written by John the son of Zebedee? Possibly, but it seems unlikely. If it wasn't John who was it? No one knows actually. The identity of the author has great value, but the fact that it wasn't likely the fisherman who wrote it doesn't make the Gospel less valuable as a spiritual guide. On the other hand, people who honor the "authorship" of John are not illiterate fools either. Religion seems so prone to slide into either/or thinking. Authentic faith calls us to hold all matters loosely because we believe in the One God, and relinquish all claims to be the One.

John

So, mainline contemporary scholars generally don't believe that John the son of Zebedee was the author in the sense we use that word. However, it is still important to acknowledge that much of the Gospel is filled with knowledge and information that seems to rise from firsthand experience. It is possible that some of the source material may, in fact, have been written by a scribe disciple of one of the 12, perhaps John. There is a great deal of detail in John that is indicative of an eyewitness:

- In the story of the boy who shared his lunch with 5,000 others, John alone notes that the loaves were made of barley, indicating that the boy's lunch was the poorest of foods, but he was willing to share.
- John gives us the number of miles they had to row to get to shore the night they were caught in a storm.
- There were six stone water pots, each holding 20-30 gallons of water, which Jesus turned to wine.
- Only John describes the crown of thorns and how the smell filled the whole place when Mary broke open her vial of perfumed ointment for Jesus' feet.
- John tells us the exact weight of the spices the women brought to anoint the body of Jesus on Easter morning.

These unimportant details all are indicators that the source is describing their own experience of these events. While there are geographic "jumps" in the narrative, the source clearly knew the geography of the land and the layout of Jerusalem.

John is different in so many ways from the three Synoptic Gospels. Funny, isn't it, that we live in a culture where those who are different are often marginalized. We are uncomfortable with people who don't march in step. We dismiss those who have a different sense of style, and ridicule those whose value system serves a different master. The word "eccentric" is really a quaint way to diminish someone.

Yet here we have John, who tells the story of Jesus from a completely different perspective. His version is very different, yet there is internal evidence that he might have been closer to the actual events, and perhaps the truth, than the other sources of our faith. So, we let John in and admit him to the canon, but don't you push the limits of our tolerance …

John

We have spent this week getting ready to begin reading the Gospel of John. One more day of preparation should do. Before we start reading this great work, we should note that, since this was probably the last Gospel written, the author wrote in the midst of a Church that was trying to decide what was orthodox and what was heresy.

That has always been a major struggle of the Church. Unfortunately, truth is rarely black and white, and people of *faith* seem remarkably uncomfortable with grays. One of the most significant heresies to affect, and infect, Christian thought was called "Gnosticism." It essentially was the Greek thought that the physical is inferior to the spiritual, or that matter is evil but spirit is good. Of course, that means that God, who is the supreme good, is entirely spirit and has nothing to do with matter or the physical world. Ultimately, that means that creation is the product of a lesser god.

The trouble with that, of course, is that Jesus was a Jew, and Jews believe that the one true God is the source of creation and, in fact, that God pronounced the physical universe good, very good. Gnostics held that since Jesus was a physical being, born of a woman, he could not be divine. Or they taught that Jesus wasn't really human, but that God deigned to put on human flesh like a robe but careful observers would have noted that Jesus didn't leave footprints in the sand.

The early Church was quite insistent that Jesus was fully God and fully human. This concept is a paradox, but without it two problems arise. If Jesus were not fully God, then his message that we, too, are daughters and sons of God is hollow and without any basis. The other problem is that, if Jesus was not fully human, the implication is that there is something inferior and defective about being human.

John begins his Gospel insisting that the Gnostics were wrong. The remainder of what is written must be understood against the background of this argument. When the Church fails to understand this and resist modern Gnosticism we do terrible things like treat creation as without value, treat human sexuality as something to be ashamed of and hidden, treat women as inferior because they have less brute strength than men, disqualify women from the priesthood because of their physicality, insist on celibacy as if human sexuality damages the soul, and so on. Thank God we aren't Gnostics ... (sarcasm)

John 1:1

In the beginning was the Word and the Word was with God and the Word was God.

This is the first verse in one of the most amazing passages of the Bible. Regardless of whom the original author was, the thought and the use of language in this passage are remarkable. While we cannot study John verse by verse, spending this week looking at the prologue is probably a worthy effort.

The author deliberately mirrors the language with which the Torah/Bible opens: "In the beginning ... ." Of course, in Genesis the statement was "In the beginning **God** ... ." Here, John unequivocally equates the Word and God. Many would argue that John is the first in the Church to make claims for Jesus that he never made for himself.

To John, Jesus was the Word, or Logos, who was with God from the beginning and was, in fact, God of the beginning. The use of the word "logos," which is translated "word" in English Bibles, is an intriguing choice. So much has been written and said about the Greek word logos that it has moved into the culture and lost the nuance that made it the author's original choice.

In ordinary usage, the word logos referred to an instance of speaking: "sentence, saying, oration." It is never understood to mean "a word" in the grammatical sense. In modern English logos would be a verb. (That alone should be enough to keep us pondering and meditating for the day.) It is not about action or work, though, because the full meaning includes the inward intention of the communication. Think logic, reason, meaning.

Okay, if that didn't make you delete this meditation, let's try and figure out what this means to us. John is simply identifying with the logos who brought all creation into being. Modern Westerners tend to discount or dismiss words as marks on a page or vibrations on the air. The ancient mystics and indigenous peoples often knew better. George Lakoff (*Moral Politics*) has tried to teach us that what we say and how we say things frame issues and affect their outcomes. Our choices of what we say and how we say it ultimately may have much more power in creating our lives than we think. According to John, that has been so since the beginning.

John 1:1-3

*In the beginning was the Logos and the Logos was with God, and the Logos was
God. He was in the beginning with God. All things came into being through him and
without him not one thing came into being.*

John seems to intermingle the divine Logos and the human Jesus. That is why I left
the male pronouns in the verses above.

Nothing has been more challenging in our church than the issue of inclusive language. Those battles are ancient history now, but they rise again every
Christmas. Inevitably, someone will get up in arms over the fact that we have made
the familiar carols inclusive. They will insist that we have no right to change the
author's words, though we remind them that every week we do that with the Bible.

It is our highest value to ensure that all people feel fully included in the
family of God, so we would no more use gender-exclusive language in worship than
we would use racist language. For us, it is a matter of integrity since we have said,
"All are welcome here." The challenge, of course, is that the historic Jesus was a human male. Unfortunately, he couldn't be both, and he lived in a day when a woman
would have been discounted, no matter how many miracles she worked.

Even the word "God" is masculine, and people get apoplectic when you
use the word "Goddess," at least in the South. I love Virginia Mollenkott's solution
of always saying "God, she … " Always using male pronouns for God gives girls
the clear message that, unlike them, God is a he. It is a wonder any self-actualized
woman has remained in the Church. Our endemic sexism, which deifies the masculine without feminine balance, has nearly destroyed humankind with wars and the
rape of the environment, just to name a couple.

Unfortunately, there is a price to be paid for inclusion. I've survived the
wrath of the fundamentalists on this and other issues. However, the price of which
I speak is the danger that comes with implying that the *Logos* is **neither** male nor
female, rather than the fact that the *Logos* is **both!** This, of course, also goes back
to Genesis, where God created humankind in God's image, male and female. Like
God, we all are **both,** and embracing that is a critical act of incarnation.

John 1:1-4

In the beginning was the Logos and the Logos was with God, and the Logos was God. He was in the beginning with God. ***All*** *things came into being through him and without him not one thing came into being. What has come into being in him was life, and the life was the light of all people.*

Wow. I love that statement: "**All** things came into being through him and without him not one thing came into being." It is, of course, a reaffirmation that God is the source. That is a fact that we all too often forget.

The other side of that which gets forgotten is the "***ALL*** *things.*" In our judgments, we often act as if God was not the source of some things or some people. Now, I must admit that I have my doubts about things like mosquitoes, snakes and bell peppers. Those may have happened when God wasn't looking. However, the circle of life that has rippled outward for millennia would not have sustained anything that does not support and strengthen the circle.

John connects light and life a lot. In this passage, the life that emanates from the Logos is the light of **ALL** people. While John didn't understand that light was energy, he did know that when life is cut off from light it soon dies. Perhaps this ancient author understood better than we how being cut off from the source of life causes our spirits to wither and die.

Churches or communities of faith that forget the "**All**s" of the Gospel are seeking to cut people off from life. It is as unconscionable as taking beautiful plants and putting them in a closet where they quickly wither away. How different would the world be if we treated everything and everyone as if they had "come into being" through God? We call all that belongs to God "holy" and treat it with respect—like the "Holy Bible"—but now imagine a religion that treated every human as if she or he was holy.

The concept of *Logos* is that we are **ALL** the embodiment of the life and light that emanated from God. *Without "him" not one thing came into being.* Imagine a religion that worked to provide every human adequate nutrition, education and healthcare from the moment they arrive until the moment they depart because every human is holy. That would look very different from a religion where apparently only fetuses are holy.

John 1:5

The light shines in the darkness, and the darkness did not overcome it.

The King James Version (KJV) of this verse says: *The light shineth in the darkness and the darkness comprehended it not.* The true meaning falls in between "overcome" and "comprehend." The implication, of course, is that darkness, because it cannot understand light, seeks to extinguish it.

For John, logos, light and life are intimately connected. In his use of those terms, he never means just what they mean on the surface. Light, of course, is not merely the brightness by which we are able to see; there also is a sense of illumination. My personal interpretation of this would be: *The truth (logos) penetrates our flesh, bringing us illumination (light) that enlivens us (life).*

The darkness to which John refers is not the natural yin and yang of dawn and dusk, day and night. Rather, it is an inability to comprehend truth. It is a lack of illumination, understanding, receptivity. It is a refusal to take a concept, roll it around in your mind, and entertain the possibility of truth. Darkness is the refusal to be open to truth.

The late psychiatrist M. Scott Peck, in his book *People of the Lie,* talked about the darkness of people who lack the capacity to consider new facts or information, particularly about themselves. Our inability to see the other side, change our minds, grow in our understanding leaves us in the darkness. For this reason, I tend to favor the old KJV translation of this passage.

Darkness can never overcome light. In fact, the smallest light has the capacity to overcome darkness. The most moving part of the film version of "Harry Potter and the Half-Blood Prince" =is when the students and faculty of Hogwarts, though overwhelmed by grief, raise their wands to offer sufficient illumination to disperse the threatening clouds. Light always overcomes the darkness in our souls. The only limitation is our willingness to allow the light in. It requires that we simultaneously believe we are right without needing to pronounce the other wrong. It means we must be open to new truth and illumination without living as persons with no convictions. It requires an awful lot of maturity and grace. Maybe all this elevation of Jesus is simply John saying that he was the first one of God's daughters and sons to get it right.

This prologue interweaves the story of John with an explanation of the real meaning of the life of Jesus. After a few verses of a rather esoteric description of Jesus as the *Logos*, the author wants to provide a human witness to the truth of all this. Decades after his death, John the Baptist's influence remained. There were still believers who considered themselves disciples of John. It is important, right from the start, to both hear John's witness and to establish the superiority of the message and ministry of Jesus.

The writer says, "There was a man." Notice, Jesus was not referred to as a man; in fact, nowhere in the prologue is Jesus the man actually referred to. His name is not mentioned until 29 verses into this first chapter. In the prologue, the writer is trying to establish that Jesus was much more than "a man." John (the Baptist) is named and the purpose of his life made clear: "He came as a witness." To those who might still want to hold the Baptist in a more exalted position, the writer is explicit: "He himself was not the light, but he came to testify to the light."

Having put John in his proper context, the writer goes back to the Logos who was "the true light, which enlightens everyone coming into the world." The author is arguing here against those who might overly esteem John the Baptist, but this is also a clear statement to readers who live in a very polytheistic world.

By that day, the Roman Empire had declared that Caesar was a god. The Romans had no need or desire to make the world monotheistic, but insisted that Caesar be added to every religion's pantheon of gods. That was a problem for the Jews and even more of a problem for the Christians who were dispersed around the empire.

The importance of this passage is that it establishes that Jesus was not a deity separate from Yahweh, but rather was the true light come into the world. Much of the Gospel of John sounds exclusive and excluding to our ears, but he is struggling to hold Jesus up as God come to the world and, at the same time, retain the radical monotheism of the Jewish faith. It was a great struggle in the early Church to believe that Jesus was divine without believing Jesus was a deity. It required holding two opposing thoughts as true and accepting our inability to comprehend. Darkness never likes being unable to comprehend.

John 1:10-13

He was in the world, and the world came into being through him; yet the world did not know him. He came to what was his own, and his own people did not accept him. But to all who received him, who believed in his name, he gave power to become children of God, who were born, not of blood or of the will of the flesh or of the will of humans, but of God.

When I talk about the human Jesus, I try to avoid using pronouns as much as possible. There is no doubt he was a man, but if the incarnation has any meaning at all the important thing was not his gender but his humanity. Reading the passage above it appears that John was trying to use as many pronouns as possible. As I tried to make it inclusive, I discovered it was impossible, since John goes back and forth between talking about the human Jesus and talking about the divine Logos. That seems to be a deliberate literary strategy, and maybe it is a good theological strategy as well.

We tend to divide everything into "this and that," "up and down," "in and out," "good and bad," "heaven and earth," "human and divine." It is very frustrating to mortals when we can't categorize something. We rankle at ambiguity and uncertainty. That may have been what really got Jesus crucified. While the Gospel of John's agenda is to convince us that Jesus is the human incarnation of the divine Logos, Jesus seems to frustrate even John.

A naïve reading of the Gospels leaves us wondering if Jesus thought he was human or divine. They called him the son of God, and he kept calling them children of God. They called him divine, and he called himself the Human One (Son of Man). We might be tempted to say Jesus was this or that, but Jesus seems to insist that he is both and neither. Divinity and humanity were so blurred in Jesus that his own people didn't recognize him. I wonder if we do. We insist on lifting him up to a place we cannot attain. Perhaps Jesus serves us best as a mirror of who we are and who we might become. Was Jesus human or divine? The Church has always insisted that the right answer is both. Unfortunately, the point the Church seemed to miss is that we are all both human and divine. What wonders have been missed by the failure of our faith to call us to live out our divinity as daughters and sons of God? Perhaps that is what John meant by the "power to become."

And the Logos became flesh and dwelled among us, and we have seen his glory, the glory as of a father's only son, full of grace and truth.

Jewish society of Jesus' day was patrilineal. With conflicting views of what happened after death, the universally accepted understanding of eternal life was that your life continued in the lives of your children—in particular through the lives of your sons. Sons were the ones who were thought to carry on the blood line, the name, the identity, the history, the substance, the logos of the family.

While that is not how we understand life today, recognizing the historical context of this writing is the only way to appreciate what John was trying to say about Jesus.

In addition, in an age without social security and Medicare, the responsibility to care for aged parents fell first to the eldest son. They were not only their posterity after death, but their source of life before death. A family that had only one son faced a more precarious future than a family with many sons who lived to maturity and had sons of their own. In families such as Abraham and Sarah's, an extraordinary weight rested on the shoulders of an only son.

That is just a piece of what the original readers would have understood by this sentence in John's Gospel. What John is saying that they witnessed was the glory of a father's only son.

We already have talked about Gnosticism and the significance of John's insistence that the Logos **became** flesh. Jesus wasn't God dressed up like a human, but, as St. Athanasius taught, "In Jesus, God became human so that we might become divine." The doctrine of incarnation is linked to the doctrine of sanctification; that is the idea that God became human is connected to the idea that we are to become holy.

In Christmas, we celebrate one doctrine, but the Church, like most of us, has done little with the other. We embrace the incarnation, but neglect sanctification. I think that part of the reason the Church has so exalted Jesus is that it relieves us of the obligation to become like him. If he is the ONLY son (child), then I don't have to live like I am one too.

John 1:16-18

From Christ's fullness we have all received, grace upon grace. The law indeed was given through Moses; grace and truth came through Jesus Christ. No one has ever seen God. It is God the only Son, who is close to the Father's heart, who has made him known.

Leaving this passage with its gender-specific language was deliberate because the relationship that is described would be lost with more generic nouns and pronouns. That is the greatest risk with inclusive language. "Parent" just doesn't carry the emotional weight of mother or father. If we are not careful, the Spirit becomes an "it," and, by de-gendering Jesus, we are in danger of making gender a part of humanity that is not sanctified by the human experience of Jesus.

Having said all that, inclusive language is a justice issue for the Church. It is also a theological issue because for too long we have been out of balance in our understanding of God and appreciation for humankind. My point is that, like so many complex issues, when we simply fall into a rote, gender-neutral reading of scripture, we risk missing its richness and nuance.

This passage is a case in point. The image of "an only Son close to the Father's heart" has an intimacy that is lost when substituting "child" and "Parent." We also would lose the historical implications that we discussed yesterday. This truth must be acknowledged, while at the same time holding in tension the truth that God is both our Father and Mother. Though John was not free in his day to acknowledge this reality, it is a truth revealed in the total testimony of scripture. And, while Jesus was a human male, the incarnation means the "Word became flesh" not "the Word became Male."

The richness of John's writing is that it is multilayered and must be contemplated, not just exegeted or explained. On the one hand, John claims for Jesus pre-existent divinity, and then, in this passage, he describe Jesus as being unique as the result of his being close to the heart of God in an intimate familial way. This is the first time John mentions Jesus by name as he prepares to move from this theological foundation to a more biographical story. That is as it should be with us all. Our lives should be an outgrowth, an expression of our closeness to the very heart of the One who is our Heavenly Mother/Father.

Before we move on from this passage, there is another aspect we should note. In verse 16, John writes unambiguously about the grace that we **ALL** receive. In case we missed the generosity, he uses the phrase "grace upon grace." As far as I can tell, this is the only place in scripture that this exact phrase occurs. In fact, this is the only place John talks about grace, but he uses the word repeatedly because the life he is about to describe was a pure expression of God's grace.

If you are alone right now, I invite you to say it aloud a few times. Throughout the day, ponder exactly what you think John was trying to communicate to his readers and to you. There is a contemporary Christian song that says:

> *Grace upon grace, like the waves on the shore,*
> *Always enough, always more.*
> *Grace upon grace, like the waves on the shore,*
> *All that we need is ours from the Lord.*

Imagine yourself standing at the edge of the ocean and feeling the waves wash over your feet, relentlessly, unendingly washing over you. So it is with God: grace upon grace for ALL.

How tragic it is that the Church has spent so much time and energy putting up fences and deciding who is in and who is out when the Bible says through Jesus came grace for all—grace upon grace; no conditions, no limits, no exclusions, no exceptions. It has always been my suspicion that disciples of Jesus are so prone to placing limits on the grace of God because we have such limited experience of that grace ourselves.

Maybe my earlier illustration was wrong. So, close your eyes again and picture yourself at the ocean. Watch the waves as they wash on the shore repeatedly, relentlessly, unceasingly, grace upon grace. Now, let go of all that you hold on to and all that holds on to you, and plunge your whole self into those waves that emanate from the very heart of God, waves of grace upon grace. AMEN.

John 1:19-28

So, after beginning with an amazing theological treatise that has left the Church meditating for centuries, John now moves on to describe the life of one who expressed the Logos/Word of God in all that he did and said. For John, every act of Jesus was a "sign" that he was who John has just told us he was. Although we move on from this theological description, the rest of the Gospel must be understood as evidence that Jesus was and is the Logos of God.

John the Baptist has been referred to already, but now the Gospel moves to describe him and his ministry. The story begins with "the Jews"—by which John means the religious leaders—sending messengers from Jerusalem to ask John the Baptist just who he thinks he is. According to this account, the Baptist emphatically states that he is not the Messiah, but merely "a voice crying in the wilderness." John the Baptist describes himself as one who was unworthy to untie the sandals of the one who was coming.

This passage has less meaning today than it did to the original readers. Remember that when this was written there was a significant movement rivaling the early church that had sprung up around John the Baptist. Many scholars connect John the Baptist with the Qumran community responsible for some of the Dead Sea Scrolls and who believed that a prophet like Moses or Elijah would be the messiah. In this Gospel, John the Baptist explicitly denies being that prophet (John 1:21), but, in the synoptic Gospels, Jesus himself identifies the Baptist with Elijah (Matthew 11:14, 17:10-13, Mark 9:13). This is one of those contradictions that supposedly don't exist in the "inerrant" Bible.

In this passage, John the Baptist's humility and testimony are intended as much to speak to those who remained as his disciples in the first century as it was intended to speak to the Church. The author is arguing against faith in John as much as he is arguing for faith in Jesus. John wasn't the One and said so himself. According to the Gospel, to miss that is to worship the road sign and fail to follow the road. While that message may not be as relevant to our understanding of John the Baptist today, it seems to me that it is the perfect description of the Church today. Listen to the debates of any congregation or denomination and you will hear a people worshiping the sign and missing the path.

The next day John saw Jesus coming toward him and declared, "Behold the Lamb of God who takes away the sin of the world."

I love Quaker pastors and authors Philip Gulley and James Mulholland who have been courageous enough to assert that the Bible really means what it says in verses such as this one.

In their writings they insist that *If Grace is True* it is true for everyone. In their understanding of the Gospel, when John declared that Jesus was "the Lamb of God who took away the sin of the world" he meant just that. In the historical context of John's day, on the Day of Atonement the priests offered a sacrifice on behalf of the whole nation, not on behalf of each individual. John declares Jesus to be the lamb God gave to **take away the sin of the world.**

According to Gulley and Mulholland, evangelical Christianity has subjugated the work God did in Jesus to the will of the individual. John makes a clear, unambiguous statement about what God did for the whole world in Jesus. This work of God is not subject to our "acceptance." We may or may not experience the redeeming love of God expressed in Jesus, but our experience doesn't change the fact that, in Jesus, God took away the sins of the world.

There is much about this with which I may disagree, but I find it interesting that those who elevate the necessity of the individual's response to God's grace actually have a lower and diminished view of who Jesus was and what he accomplished. Insisting that we must each "accept Christ into our hearts" makes the work of Jesus subject to our control. Did Jesus **take away** the sin of the world or not? John seemed to think so, though most of modern Christianity does not.

The idolatry of individualism has had devastating consequences for our society. The fact that much of it is rooted in and supported by our faith is evidence that we might have done better believing what John said about Jesus rather than what preachers and priests have said. Just a thought …

John 1:35-42

The next day John again was standing with two of his disciples and as he watched Jesus walk by John exclaimed, "Behold the Lamb of God."

Yesterday, today and tomorrow's section from John begins with the words "The next day." They are written as if the Gospel writer was just hanging around for a few days watching. The first two days are spent watching John the Baptist; tomorrow John finally will be replaced as Jesus comes onto the stage.

The second chapter of John begins with the words, "On the third day there was a wedding." Just what that was the third day after is unknown because we've already had three "next days." I'm sure John is trying to make a point here, but I must confess that it eludes me.

"The next day, the next day, the next day, the third day." Often I look back at something I have written and realized that I have used the same phrase too many times without knowing it. Maybe that is what is happening with the writer, or maybe there is this sense that time moved all too quickly for Jesus. His life was too brief and had to be marked in days not years.

On this day, the event that was remembered was that two of the disciples of John the Baptist left to follow Jesus. One of the two was named Andrew, who then went and found his brother Peter. The next day Philip and Nathaniel will come to follow Jesus. Thus the author describes the collecting of Jesus' disciples. There is no calling fishers to leave their nets. If John was the only Gospel we had there'd be no clue as how these men made their living. In this account, that really isn't important. In this Gospel, Jesus is what is important, and people like John the Baptist and the disciples really serve only as witnesses to that importance.

John the Baptist repeats his witness that Jesus is the Lamb of God, so two of his own disciples leave him to follow Jesus. On these two days, Jesus does nothing but walk by; it is John who transfers his followers to Jesus. There is the sense that they "traded up" from the witness to the one witnessed to. Tick, tick, tick; the days are passing. For the author, there is no time to serve the secondary when Jesus walks in to give life meaning. Maybe we all need to hear that ticking clock as a reminder to focus on that which gives life meaning.

John begins naming Jesus as the Word/Logos of God. He also calls him the light of the world. John the Baptist is introduced to declare that Jesus is the Lamb of God. In this Gospel, John doesn't baptize Jesus, but he does describe how he saw the Spirit descending on Jesus like a dove. We then move to the witness of Andrew and another disciple of John who decided to follow Jesus. They call him Rabbi or teacher. Andrew then goes and finds his brother Peter, saying to him, "We have found the Messiah."

In today's reading, Jesus calls Philip, who then goes and finds Nathaniel and says to him, "We have found him about whom Moses and the prophets spoke, Jesus son of Joseph from Nazareth." Nathaniel replies with that famous line, "Can anything good come out of Nazareth?" Philip replies, "Come and see." Nathaniel does, and, when Jesus labels him an "Israelite in whom there is not deceit," Nathaniel asks how he knew this. Jesus tells him how he saw him when he was far away, standing under a fig tree just before Philip found him. To that Nathaniel proclaims that Jesus is "the Son of God" and a "King of Israel." Jesus replies and calls himself "the Human One (Son of Man)."

In just one chapter, the writer of the Gospel has Jesus do and say almost nothing, yet he manages to record almost all of the sacred titles for Jesus that must have been used in the early Church. It is an amazing literary feat and just part of what makes this first chapter so significant. These 10 titles define for us who Jesus is, but John is not through. For the rest of the Gospel, almost every action of Jesus will further define who he is in this divine context.

One of the interesting things in this account is that Jesus is identified to Nathaniel as the son of Joseph, but Nathaniel almost immediately calls Jesus the son of God. To John, Mary has no place in this defining of Jesus in the first chapter, but she is the co-star of the first episode in Jesus' ministry. It is interesting that in the exalted view of Jesus one of his own disciples trashes his hometown. Nathaniel has been accused of being prejudiced or perhaps classist in his disregard for Nazareth. Its inclusion here may be about that, or perhaps it is John seeking to remind us that Jesus really came from heaven, not some small town. The truth, of course, is that Jesus came from both. That is important to remember if we are to understand who he was. That is important to remember about ourselves, too. You, too, came from both.

John 2:1-12

This is one of my favorite stories in the entire Bible. I am grateful I have been able to preach on it every few years when it appears in the lectionary. Many people have missed those sermons because the reading happens right after the holidays and people haven't gotten back in the habit of coming to church. At least, that is my rationalization for why Christianity has missed this side of the personality of Jesus.

After the glorious, soaring description of who Jesus is, the second chapter of the Gospel of John begins with a story of Jesus attending a wedding feast, staying late enough that all the wine has been consumed, and then performing his first miracle: turning water into wine. This was not just any wine; it was the very best, so good that even those who were well along in their drinking noticed the improvement. And it was not just a couple of bottles; John describes six stone jars, each holding 20 to 30 gallons. That's 120-180 GALLONS of the best wine.

Where did that Jesus go? None of us grew up with a partying messiah or even a drinking savior. Jesus didn't turn water into Welch's grape juice. It wasn't non-fermented wine. It was more than 100 gallons of the good stuff. Why didn't someone tell me about this Jesus when I was younger? Like so many, my image of Jesus was Warner Sallman's dour sallow young Christ.

THIS Jesus would never party late and turn water into wine. But apparently John's would and did!

Oh, I understand about alcoholism and the dangers of substance abuse and addiction, but I also know that more people in this country die because of diet and overeating. It is also interesting to me that in countries like France and Italy where wine is served with good food rather than guilt, the rate of alcoholism is significantly lower … as is the rate of obesity.

How different our faith might be if we lived our lives as disciples of the one who celebrated life rather than this artificial Jesus who turns joy into shame.

I warned you yesterday that the miracle at the wedding feast at Cana is one of my favorite stories. I'm not quite ready to move on from it, so please bear with me.

First, we should consider that, following John's magnificent, soaring introduction, this is a strange miracle to offer as proof that Jesus was and is the Logos of God. It is a rather domestic miracle, really. One family was about to be embarrassed because the wine ran out too soon. Jesus' mother asks him to help. Some suggest that this request came not because she expected him to work a miracle, but because his having arrived at the wedding with these new disciples in tow was the reason they ran out of wine. That is an interesting theory, since so much of the Church has tried to convince us that disciples of Jesus don't drink alcohol.

Mary may not have expected Jesus to work a miracle, but she was fully confident that he could be depended on to do something. She told the servants to do whatever he said. This little tidbit indicates that Mary was either a wedding planner or that this was a family wedding.

At any rate, Jesus at first resists her request, saying that his time had not yet come. The implication is that he wasn't yet ready to show himself as a miracle worker, or maybe he wasn't ready to assume the role of the patriarch. Apparently, Joseph has died, and Jesus is the eldest son. Perhaps he was resisting taking on that role. The story ends by saying that, afterward, Jesus went down to Capernaum with his mother, his brothers and his disciples. Already, Jesus has his biological family and his family of choice.

None of us would be surprised if those two families created conflicting expectations. Those of us who are lesbian and gay know that we are one person with our biological family and a different person with our family of choice. For Jesus, his mother expected that he would do something. The other side of his life said it wasn't yet time for him to come out and start giving signs of who he really was. Interestingly, Jesus did what his mother said. Isn't that usually the way of it? Our biological bonds are so much stronger than we expect, or often wish to admit. Time and again, we end up doing what our mothers said, even long after we are gone from home. While some of those patterns may need to be broken, it is at least a little comforting to know that even Jesus was still doing what his mother said when he was 30.

John 2:13-25

This is one of the places where the Gospel of John is most different from the synoptic Gospels. The three of them place the cleansing of the temple at the end of the life of Jesus. John puts it here in the second chapter, right after the miracle at the wedding feast. In the other Gospels, this was one of the actions that got Jesus crucified. For John, it is a sign that, right from the start, Jesus confronted the Jewish religious leadership.

This is probably as good a place as any to address the fact that John's Gospel is regarded by many scholars as an anti-Semitic version of the life of Jesus. The three earlier Gospels were written in a time when Christianity was a movement primarily within Judaism when people saw themselves as followers of "the way" of a Jewish Rabbi named Jesus. In Mark, the first Gospel written, we hear Jesus saying, "Why do you call me good? There is none good but God." By the time we get to John's Gospel Jesus is the Divine Logos of God and "the Jews" are faulted for their rejection of him.

Hence, right from the start, John presents Jesus as being in confrontation with Judaism. The cleansing of the temple is not a closing act of one confronting the abuse of the poor, but a political act by which Jesus declares himself as One with authority over even the temple.

The same event is presented decades later to serve two very different purposes. You and I are left to decide which we accept as correct, or if there is a third understanding that perhaps even John and the Synoptics missed. To me, it is fascinating that in this Gospel, which presents the most exalted view of Jesus, one that evolved years after his life, Jesus' humanity still comes shining through.

The second chapter begins with Jesus celebrating a wedding at a great feast; it ends with an expression of Jesus' fury at religion's exclusion and abuse of the poor. Far from being a God dressed up like a human, Jesus is a human with the full range of human emotion. Here he helps people who are celebrating to continue to do so with the best wine, and he also rages at religious leaders who exclude and exploit the poor. The real Jesus of the Bible is anything but passive and uninvolved with life. Jesus is a human with great passion for life and living.

Chapter three of John tells the story of Jesus' late night visit from Nicodemus. John introduces him as a "leader of the Jews" who comes to Jesus by night. This is meant to imply more than the fact that Nicodemus arrived late in the day. When Nicodemus assists with the burial of Jesus, John again identifies him as "the one who came to Jesus by night." It could be assumed that Nicodemus was seeking to be a secret disciple of Jesus, but it also may be more than that.

Nicodemus addresses Jesus as "Rabbi" and then speaks in the plural, saying, "Rabbi, **we** know that you are a teacher come from God." It is possible that Nicodemus hasn't come on his own, but as an emissary of at least some of the Jewish religious leaders. He cites the signs that Jesus has done as the evidence of their conclusion about him. Now, while John keeps emphasizing the signs, throughout the Gospel Jesus pushes back against those who believe only because they have seen signs.

Jesus doesn't respond to Nicodemus' statement, but redirects the conversation with a non sequitur. It is one of the most often quoted, or misquoted, verses from the Gospel of John: "No one can see the Realm of God without being born from above." The King James Version says, "Except a man is born again he cannot see the Kingdom of God."

Much of the theology of the evangelical movement is based on this particular verse. Being "born again" referred to the event that happened when you "accepted Jesus into your heart." It was used synonymously with "conversion."

This is a good illustration of the challenges that result from translations. Jesus spoke to Nicodemus in Aramaic, or perhaps the more formal Hebrew. The Book of John, however, was written in Greek. In the Greek, John 3:3 says "you must be born *anōthen,"* a word that means BOTH "above" and "again" or "anew." There is no such double-meaning word in the language Jesus spoke nor in the language that we speak. Of course, the issue raised through this most critical passage for conservative Christians is the danger of making any verse or passage the litmus test for orthodoxy. Personally, I come closest to appreciating the inspiration of the Bible when I see these kinds of examples that make us keep taking it all by faith.

John 3:1-10

Do not be astonished that I said to you, "You must be born from above." The wind blows where it chooses, and you hear the sound of it, but you do not know where it comes from or where it goes. So it is with everyone who is born of the Spirit.

Fundamentalists love the part of this chapter that requires that we all be born again/from above, but they seem to miss Jesus' point about the Spirit being like the wind. Actually, I suspect we all miss this when it comes down to the fundamentals of our belief system. We like to feel that we are on solid ground, but Jesus seems to keep calling us to live our lives like a kite on a string, with God loosely holding on to the other end. Or, as Jesus said it, "The wind blows where it chooses … "

Nicodemus, trying to take Jesus' teaching literally, wondered how a person might enter into their mother's womb and be born a second time. This lesson about wind is Jesus' response to such literalism. It is what Jesus meant by telling us that we must be born of water and spirit.

Being born of water often has been treated as if it is a reference to baptism; however, in Jesus' day, the mother's water breaking was interpreted as humans being born out of the water of their mother's womb. Jesus quite likely could have been talking about how our lives are both physical and spiritual.

Here we again have a Greek word with multiple meanings. "Spirit," "wind," "breath" and "air" all are contained in the meaning of the Greek word *pneuma*. To this, Nicodemus, the legalist, again questions, "How can this be?" Jesus rebukes him for being a teacher yet being so narrow and literally minded.

Jesus' message has remained trapped by such thinking ever since. It is almost as though those of us who, like Nicodemus, are educated in our approach to the Bible need to control the message and impact by limiting it to what we were taught. Nicodemus came calling Jesus a teacher sent from God, but he couldn't escape the limits of what he always had thought to be true. Jesus repeatedly uses new images to try and free him, but there is scarce evidence of success. This makes me sad that we all grew up with acculturated Christianity. Where might the Spirit blow us if we could be free to hear and respond?

John 3:11-15

Very truly, I tell you, we speak of what we know and testify to what we have seen; yet you do not receive our testimony. If I have told you about earthly things and you do not believe, how can you believe if I tell you about heavenly things? No one has ascended into heaven except the one who descended from heaven, the Human One. And just as Moses lifted up the serpent in the wilderness, so must the Human One be lifted up, that whoever believes in him may have eternal life.

Here Jesus draws a parallel between his own life and a relatively obscure story from the life of Moses. The Moses story was problematic for rabbis of Jesus' day, and it is doubly so for us today. It is drawn from Numbers 21:4-9. According to the original narrator, the Hebrews, wandering in the wilderness, grumbled against Moses because of the quality of food they had to eat in that barren land. God apparently isn't fond of whiners and sent poisonous snakes to bite them … at least that is how the events were interpreted. Moses prays for the people, and, rather than just healing them, God instructs Moses to make a bronze serpent and put it on a pole. Anyone who looked at it would be healed. This is reputedly why the twisted serpent of the caduceus became a symbol of the medical community.

What you have, though, is the creation of a primitive talisman that is quite contradictory to the vehement Hebrew rejection of idolatry. In Jesus' day, the image of Caesar on a coin was forbidden. Using this illustration out of all the First Testament stories seems so strange that it actually may add veracity to this passage.

The idea that Jesus is the Human One who both ascended and descended from heaven is more of John's theologizing about the pre-existent Logos. At this point, no one can blame Nicodemus for being completely confused. The lack of flow, use of mixed metaphors, and incongruent transitions leave us wondering if Jesus was doing this deliberately or if John is just throwing everything into this passage and using Nicodemus as a convenient excuse. Again John uses a Greek word with double meaning: *hypsoō.* The word can mean "lifted up." like the snake on the pole, or "exalted." which is clearly what John is trying to do to Jesus. Nicodemus came calling him a "teacher sent from God." Jesus calls Nicodemus "a teacher of Israel." John is trying to make a clear distinction between the two roles, exalting one over the other. That doesn't ever seem to be Jesus' agenda, though.

John 3:16-21

For God so loved the world that he gave his only Son, so that everyone who believes in him may not perish but may have eternal life. Indeed, God did not send the Son into the world to condemn the world, but in order that the world might be saved through him.

This is, of course, one of the best known verses in all of scripture. What is interesting is that there is no way to determine if the author intended to imply that Jesus said these words about himself or if they are meant as theological commentary. Nicodemus is clearly no longer the audience, but has been forgotten completely.

This passage reflects a great deal about John's understanding of who Jesus is. There is no idea here that God loved Israel and sent Jesus to them. Rather, John alone has this expansive view that God loves **the world**. Yet John wants to be clear that, as he said explicitly at the end of the Gospel, "This is written so that you might believe and that believing you might have everlasting life." John is writing as an evangelist to persuade people to believe in Jesus. He has no doubt that God loves the whole world; however he is also clear of the need to believe.

This is another of those passages in which the author is clear that God sent Jesus to redeem, not condemn, the world. Yet humanity is still left with the response-ability, and that response determines our experience. God sent light, but we prefer the darkness. (John 3:19)

The reality, though, is that light dispels darkness, and, regardless of what we may prefer, unless we place limits on God's light/love, the darkness cannot stand against it. Our rejection is impotent in the presence of God's love, and our darkness is always subject to God's light. While I understand John's passion to convert the world to belief, I find it ironic that the Gospel with the most exalted view of who Christ is and what he did, still subjugates the effect to human will.

John 3:22-24

After this Jesus and his disciples went into the Judean countryside, and he spent some time there with them and baptized. John also was baptizing at Aenon near Salim because water was abundant there; and people kept coming and were being baptized—John, of course, had not yet been thrown into prison.

The Gospel of John differs from the synoptic Gospels in that John is clear that the ministry of Jesus and the ministry of John overlapped. In the synoptics Jesus' ministry begins following the arrest of John the Baptist. (Matthew 4:12) What is even odder is that, in this passage, John seems to pick an argument with himself. While there is some ambiguity in the English, the Greek makes it clear that the Gospel is saying that, while John and his disciples were busy baptizing in one part of the country, Jesus and his were doing the same thing in a different part.

The other Gospels leave baptizing to John and not to Jesus. In John 4:1-2, there is a reference to Jesus making and baptizing more disciples than John. Then there is this odd parenthetical comment that Jesus actually didn't personally do the baptizing.

What the author is trying to do is distinguish between the baptism of Jesus and the baptism of John, and to ensure that, while the reader should respect and admire John, we are clear that Jesus was superior in every way.

Even after both Jesus and John were long gone, there seemed to be a rivalry between the followers of the two that went on well into the second century. As the last Gospel written, John seems to be the most caught up in this ongoing debate. In the book of Acts we find Luke's record of how the two baptisms were distinguished in the early days of the Church. John doesn't seem to make a distinction, but seems to insist that John wasn't the only one baptizing and making disciples early on. A pastor I knew as a kid wrote in the front of his Bible, "Your job is to proclaim Jesus, not defend him." That might have been a good thing for John to remember. Although we are only three chapters into the book, I'm already a little weary of John's need to convince me of who Jesus is. Maybe it is just me, but I usually do better when someone simply introduces me to another person and lets me decide for myself what I think about them.

John 3:25-36

This passage begins by saying that a debate arose between John the Baptist's disciples and "a Jew" about the issue of purification. Although he then says nothing about that topic, John makes "a Jew" the antagonist in the story. Apparently this fellow is overtly trying to create tension or a sense of competition with John: "He [Jesus] is baptizing, and all are going to him."

This might be an innocent statement except that what follows is another lecture by John the Baptist that he is not the Messiah; in fact, he calls on his hearers to be his witnesses that he said that point blank. He identifies himself as "a friend of the bridegroom" who shares the bridegroom's joy. John goes on to say, "He must increase and I must decrease." He then goes on for several more verses, testifying to the importance of Jesus.

The writer of the Gospel is apparently obsessed with putting John the Baptist in his place. As uncomfortable as that makes me, it is important to understand that the author didn't really have me in mind when he was writing. That is one of the tough things about the Bible. We have elevated it to a place where it cannot be what it is.

What I mean by that is that we have such an exalted view of the Bible that we forget to whom the author was writing and what the original context was. Since there are very few modern followers of John the Baptist, the Gospel, which forces John repeatedly to be self-deprecating, feels almost abusive to us.

From all this effort, though, we can deduce that John was writing in the midst of a time and a community that was struggling. There was a time when the role of John rivaled the position of Jesus among those seeking to find what the Bible calls "the way." Because we were born into a culture where Christendom is so dominant, we seldom pause to consider times and places where that was not so. It is a healthy exercise to consider ancient debates and recognize how little what we have come to accept as "fact" really is. I wrote this week to a young person on Facebook that "there is often more real faith in atheism than in simply accepting what we've always been told."

The fourth chapter of John contains the amazing story about "The Woman at the Well." Before we get there, though, we must let John finish with John the Baptist. This chapter opens with Jesus learning that the Pharisees had heard that Jesus was attracting more followers than John. This apparently was the reason for Jesus leaving town.

It is an odd transition and seems like little more than an excuse to elevate Jesus over John one more time. Whatever the reason, Jesus leaves Judea and heads back into Galilee. John then notes, in verse 4, "But he had to go through Samaria." Perhaps the implied threat from the Pharisees was John's excuse for why Jesus has this encounter in Samaria.

The Samaritans, you may recall, were "half-breeds" disdained by proper and orthodox Jews. Jesus was neither of those things, but maybe John is protecting his reputation by giving Jesus an excuse for being in a place where no proper and orthodox Jewish Rabbi would ever go.

At any rate, Jesus ends up at Sychar (elsewhere known as Shechem) in Samaria near a well that tradition dates back to Jacob. When Jacob died, he left the land with this water source to Joseph, and, when Joseph died in Egypt, it was to this land that his body was eventually returned and was buried. The well, which reportedly exists to this day, is more than 150 feet deep. Getting water required a bucket and a long rope.

In a world where water is a matter of life and death, this well is a matter of history and legend. A traveler on foot, like Jesus was, likely would not have had a bucket or 150 feet of rope. They would have relied on the kindness and hospitality of others. John is very specific that Jesus ended up at this particular well, tired and alone, around noon. He is sitting there hot, tired, thirsty and alone. These are not characteristics we usually associate with Christ, but Jesus was all those things. Even Jesus has no access to the water until a woman who has lots of needs comes along, but she happens to have a bucket and 150 feet of rope. This woman needs Jesus, but, for the moment, Jesus needs her too. Have you ever wondered if there are times when Jesus may need you, and what you have and take for granted?

John 4:7-15

The story of the woman at the well is a popular, but often underappreciated, one. Back in Luke, when we talked about the story of the "Good Samaritan," we explored why there was such tension between Jews and Samaritans. Perhaps we should mention here the tension between Jewish teachers and women. This woman, who came to draw water at noon, is stunned that Jesus, a Jewish man, even would speak to her, a Samaritan woman.

Almost immediately, she becomes defensive. In part, it is because Jesus is nonchalantly wrecking the social barriers that defined who he was and who she was. This is a pattern for Jesus throughout the Gospels. It is remarkable that the Church that traces itself to his story seemed to miss that point for so many centuries, and still often doesn't get it today. Nontraditional or unconventional relationships don't bother atheists in our society too much, buts even now, religious people seem disturbed if arbitrary and totally artificial barriers are crossed.

One of the greatest joys of pastoring a mostly lesbian, gay, bisexual and transgender congregation is that, on a regular basis, I go to serve a person communion and have utterly no idea if the person is a man or a woman, transgender or heterosexual. At that point, I no longer can call them "brother" or "sister" but must call them friend. That felt inadequate to me for many years, until I remembered that the most tender moment in the Gospel of John may be when Jesus says to his disciples, "I no longer call you servant; I call you friend."

My transgender friends have a great struggle in a culture where everything must be either this or that. The Native Americans saw these as holy people because they helped us see life differently. So, too, people like Jesus, who fearlessly crossed arbitrary social standards and barriers, are holy people. They have the courage to build a bridge where others dig trenches and put a gate in a barbed wire fence. It didn't take a social scientist to know that this woman was drawing water in the middle of the day rather than the morning with the other women because she did not feel comfortable with them. They go on to talk about the many "husbands" she has had. Never does Jesus treat her with anything but respect, first asking her for a drink and then offering her, without condition, the Living Water of God's grace. Now, just where did the Church of THAT Jesus go???

We could, and probably should, spend weeks on the dialogue between Jesus and this unnamed Samaritan woman. You probably have heard as many sermons as I have on this text, though. It comes up in the lectionary every three years, and is a wonderful opportunity for the whole Church to hear a word of grace, liberation and hope.

I just love this woman and her courage, honesty and openness. She returns to her village to tell them about Jesus. Her witness says, "Come and see a man who told me everything I had ever done." Imagine that. Imagine being with someone who knew everything you've ever done. If you just sat for a moment and listed the five worst things you've ever done your ears would turn red and your face would burn and you'd hope that no one would ever find out and be able to tell the story of all you've ever done.

So what does that say about Jesus? Imagine the graceful tenderness with which he must have interacted with this woman to make THIS testimony the thing she goes through the streets shouting. Time and again, I've had people come into my office to talk to me about their problems. It seems that no matter how much I reassure them that they don't need to fear judgment from me, that meeting is often the last time I see them. Time and again, I have traced horrible rumors about me back to one of those people who came to see me and told me the truth about themselves.

Afterwards, I had to be out of their lives, or they had to destroy my credibility. For many years, I thought it was my fault, until a therapist explained to me that she discovered that the better job she did getting a client to be self-disclosing, the higher the likelihood was that the client would fire her.

What does it say about this woman that she encountered someone who knew everything she did and was but she didn't need to avoid them or discredit them? Instead, her witness brings the whole village to meet Jesus and trust their lives to him. What we have in this old story is a picture of TWO amazing people who model for us two of life's greatest challenges:

- Grace authentically and unconditionally given, and
- Grace authentically and unconditionally received.

Liberating the Gospel

John 5:1-9 by guest commentator Rev. Shelley Hamilton

Now in Jerusalem by the Sheep Gate there is a pool, called in Hebrew Beth-zatha, which has five porticoes. In these lay many invalids—blind, lame, and paralyzed. One man was there who had been ill for thirty-eight years. When Jesus saw him lying there and knew that he had been there a long time, he said to him, "Do you want to be made well?" The sick man answered him, "Sir, I have no one to put me into the pool when the water is stirred up; and while I am making my way, someone else steps down ahead of me." Jesus said to him, "Stand up, take your mat and walk." At once the man was made well, and he took up his mat and began to walk.

This passage from John is complex, and the question Jesus asks is important. The person in today's lesson has had his life grasped away from him. He had been ill for 38 years and was without friend, family or community. We don't know what his illness was, only that he was an invalid and had been for a long time. Perhaps darkness and fear captured him, causing emotional and spiritual paralysis. He couldn't get up and walk; he simply lay on his pallet day after day, waiting beside the pool of healing water. He hoped that someone would come along with enough compassion to help him into the water when it began to stir. The Bible doesn't say, but legend has it that an angel periodically would appear, reach into the water and stir it. In the movement of the water were healing powers, and whomever was fortunate enough to be lifted into the water would be healed.

"Do you want to be made well?" What a question for the man to consider. What a question for you and I to consider. What I believe Jesus really is asking is, "Do you want to be whole and all that means?" It isn't simply physical health Jesus is asking about; it's a much bigger question. **Wholeness, from a theological and spiritual perspective,** is more than *completeness* or fullness. Wholeness is a *reality* in which all parts are present in harmonious and right relationship with each other. For each of us to be whole individually, the community also must be whole. Jesus is asking, "Do you want what wholeness brings? Can you accept the freedom and responsibility of wholeness?" Jesus asks us the same question everyday. Do you want to be whole? Will you do your part to herald in the commonwealth, the dominion of God? Will you feed the hungry and visit the sick and incarcerated? Will you forgive as you have been forgiven?

"Do you want to be made well?" Why did Jesus even have to ask the question? Come on, Jesus! Of course he wanted to be healed! Why else would he be at that place filled with brokenness and disease? It was crowded and dirty, with so many sick people that I'm sure the place smelled bad as well, worse even than hospitals. I bet the guy wanted to be made well … and that Jesus knew it.

Jesus *watched* him lying there and *knew* he had been there a long time. Jesus *saw* him, really saw him. Looked at him. Jesus didn't avert his eyes, ignore him or pretend he wasn't there. Jesus looked deeply into his *soul*. I wonder how long it had been since that had happened, since someone had truly seen the man.

I'll bet there isn't a person reading this who doesn't know what it feels like to be invisible, to feel as though you don't exist. What a rush of excitement this guy must have felt when he realized that Jesus' eyes, voice, energy and questions were being directed at him. "Do you want to be made well?"

Jesus brushes aside the man's somewhat embarrassed and defensive answer and says with authority, "Take up your mat and walk." And the man did so. He picked up his pallet and walked.

It's such a big question Jesus is asking. What would "being made well" look like for this man? What would it look like for you?

Good question, and obviously one that, in some mystical way, the man answered in the affirmative. When Jesus told him to pick up his mat and walk he got up and walked. I'm sure he didn't really understand all the consequences of what had just happened to him, and I'm also sure that he understood whatever lay in the future for him he was ready to try. It had to be better than the last 38 years lying beside the pool of Bethesda.

Do you … Yes! You, do you want to be made well? And me? Yes, me too. Do *I* want to be made well? Do we as individuals and as a community of faith *want to be made well*?

What would we have to give up in order to completely experience wholeness, wellness, at-one-ment with God and Creation? Reflect on these things.

John 5:14   by guest commentator Rev. Shelley Hamilton

After the man who had been paralyzed for 38 years picks up his mat and walks, he has an encounter with the Pharisees. They are unimpressed with the healing; instead, they are concerned about the Sabbath rules having been broken. Then the scripture says "Later Jesus found him [the guy he had healed] in the temple and said to him, 'See, you have been made well! Go and sin no more, so that nothing worse may happen to you.'" Nothing worse. It seems to me there could not be much worse for this guy.

Most traditional views of this admonition from Jesus center on the importance of not sinning. They imply that the man's condition somehow occurred because of his "sinfulness." Christians have learned that sin is about action—something we do—and I suppose sometimes it is. It is important to understand, however, that the man's inability to walk had been healed instantly, but the change, growth, learning and transformation are just beginning. Healing is a lifelong process that requires relationship, community and accountability. Growing in grace and the knowledge of God isn't instant; it isn't something we can put in a microwave.

Jesus' statement appears even crueler then his original question. Tradition is inclined to blame the paralyzed man for his illness. I don't think Jesus is referring to any of the man's actions. Prophets throughout the ages have cried "Repent!", which simply means "return to God." I think Jesus is saying, "Listen, there are lots of things inside you inhibiting, no, barricading you from wholeness with God. Repent. Return to God." You see, Jesus understood all the anxieties of being human. He knew our propensity for denial and dishonesty, our unwillingness to be present in the moment, or to release our constant cravings. He knew how we become immobilized by our suffering. Jesus knew all about us; he was one of us.

He wasn't telling this man it was his fault he was paralyzed, and he wasn't even suggesting that the guy had made a poor choice by lying by the pool all those years. I think he was saying, "Look, you have a second chance; do something with it. Don't allow past brokenness and the pain it brings to separate you from God and the people of God. Don't allow it to prevent you from the fullest measure of God's grace and glory."

So, it really isn't as simple as saying, "Yes I want to be made well." No, not simple, but incredibly empowering and worth all it takes to get to wholeness.

The fifth chapter of John is becoming quite esoteric. After Jesus instructs the healed man to sin no more, the guy immediately shows up at the Pharisees' place and lets them know that Jesus is the one who healed him. Some think he betrayed Jesus by identifying him as the one who healed on the Sabbath. I think his mind simply was clouded from his experience. I don't think he intended to harm Jesus.

When the Pharisees accuse him, Jesus says, "My Abba God is still working, so I'm still working." Now this really annoys the Pharisees because they believe Jesus is holding himself up as equal with God. John, of course, describes Jesus' relationship to God with exalted language. John is letting us all know that, for him, Jesus and God are the same and that Jesus will sit in judgment of the living and the dead.

Verses 25-29 are what I would call examples of eschatology, meaning the end of days. Many of the writings in the Greek scriptures have to do with the end of days, final judgment and the resurrection of the dead. In the time after Jesus died, was resurrected and ascended, the early Christians believed that life as they knew it on earth was coming to a close. They expected Jesus to return any moment. The description John uses to talk about the resurrection and judgment reminds me of the apocalyptic writings of Daniel. However, many scholars believe that the reference to the dead in this passage means spiritually dead.

I don't think anyone really knows what these strange, otherworldly writings mean. However, I do know that John wants readers to know Jesus has a much greater status than John the Baptist and the Pharisees. In John's conviction, Jesus is equal with God and, in fact, is God. What's most important is Jesus' disregard for traditions and laws he doesn't consider relevant. Jesus is clear that, when the question pits law versus the wellbeing of humanity, the wellbeing of humanity is the appropriate choice to make.

Most of us understand how rules and laws can be perverted in order to oppress and destroy people. It is this fundamentalist rigidity Jesus pushes against and considers destructive to humans and our relationship to God and one another. One more thought: I don't believe Jesus condemns anyone, especially to an eternity of hell fire. I do believe he expects us to be accountable, responsible and compassionate, and if that means healing someone on the Sabbath, digging a hole for a neighbor's well, or any other kind and generous activity, do so with his, and God's, blessing.

John 5:25-29   by guest commentator Rev. Shelley Hamilton

Our verses for today are about *eschatological salvation*, or so say many Bible scholars and historians. That is to say that judgment and salvation will occur in the end times or, as I prefer, at the end of the age. I've been renewing my studies on the Gospel of John, which, by the way, is one of my favorite books in the Bible, and, to some degree, I also believe these writings are about what's going to happen at the close of the age. What I don't believe is that the world is coming to an end and that a savior will come charging in on a white horse wielding a sword of justice destroying everyone who doesn't believe. To say that we are approaching the end of an age is different than saying the world is coming to an end.

I'd like you to consider that, even in Jewish theological reflections, salvation is about wholeness—body, mind, soul, and, I would add, community. In other words, our salvation is approaching. It's very near us and around us and perhaps even just a bit within us. Even so, salvation is a process because its greatest task is healing, reconciling and returning. Our salvation has begun. It's a process, but it is not yet complete. The fullness of salvation remains in the future, now and still to come. You know, like the dominion of God. One of the things eschatology focuses on is the judgment that will occur at the end of days. Now, when most of us hear the word "judgment" we view it as unhelpful, exclusive, laden with condemnation. Those of us who are queer have had our fill of judgmental religious people. Part of the wonder and mystery of being human is our capacity to reason—an ability to think through our actions and decisions. I call this judgment.

Sometimes, in our zeal to break completely with the religious constraints of our past, we forget to observe the whole. Judgment can be used in positive and life-giving ways. If you ever have experienced an injustice, you likely were pleased when you were vindicated in some way. My parents tried to instill within me the ability to make good judgments and/or choices. All of us have been taught to look both ways before we cross the street, and that if we touch the flames in the fireplace we could be seriously hurt, and if we wandered into the deep end of the pool we could drown. They taught us to make appropriate judgments because they love us and want to protect us from hurt. Their efforts were intended to guide us, not confine us, just as the Sabbath and other laws in Jesus' day were intended to guide day-to-day behavior and not to condemn and oppress people (especially Jesus) as the

Pharisees did.

It is in this spirit of judgment that the Hebrew and Greek Bibles talk about God, who said, "No. Don't worship things of the world. Don't idolize money, people or statues. If you do, you'll be hurt because you separate yourself from God and God's people. Care for the impoverished and lonely. Be generous because generosity was extended to you. Don't steal or mess around with your neighbor's spouse or belongings."

The commandments are not intended to condemn us but to serve as a means of enjoying life and understanding boundaries and restraint. I read somewhere:

> *The opposite of judgment is not love. The opposite of judgment is indifference, and God is not indifferent about you.*

The first chapter of Romans teaches us that God's way is written on our hearts. All of us, whether we're Christian, Muslim, Hindu, Jewish or have no religion at all, are born with an innate understanding of what is right and wrong, good and bad. For me, this is an important part of what it means to be created in the image of God. We all have different ways of arriving at what we believe is right or wrong, and, I submit, God and Jesus don't really have to judge us. We do a pretty good job of that ourselves.

The remarkable thing is that, regardless of our standard for life, *hardly any of us really think we're good enough*, even by our own standards. Therefore, God doesn't have to judge us. We handle that pretty well on our own. Most of us recognize our lives are not what we would desire them to be, so we figure they aren't what God wants them to be. That's why I belong to a spiritual community: it's only in this context that I am able to remember that Jesus came not to condemn but to save.

John 5:30-47 by guest commentator Rev. Shelley Hamilton

In these last 17 verses of the fifth chapter of the Gospel of John, Jesus still is trying to soften the Pharisees' hearts. However, his words have a double meaning. He essentially is telling them, "Listen, I can see clearly that my words have no meaning for you. The things I do in God's name should be evidence enough for you. You must realize: apart from God I never could have healed the man who lay beside the pool of Beth-zatha. When I tell you who I am, I am only doing what God has asked of me. You reject my testimony because it is my testimony. But wait; I'll call other witnesses … ." The witnesses he appealed to were God, John and Moses.

Jesus points out that the Pharisees are spiritually blind and deaf. In the presence of the Incarnation of God, they could hear nothing but the sounds of their prejudice, fear and hatred. Rules and laws that even they weren't capable of following bound them spiritually.

Jesus also admonishes them because they search and study the scriptures. If they really understood the scriptures they would know what Jesus speaks is truth. We all are sometimes inclined to take liberties with how we interpret the scriptures, especially those of us who've been beaten up by them. The people to whom Jesus was speaking were no exception. Jesus, sadly, I think, accused them of not having the love of God within them. The wholeness that Jesus obviously shared with God was repugnant to them, and they loved the affirmation and limelight from human beings rather than listening to God. Jesus' life of humility, steadfastness, devotion, love and justice was an unbearable contradiction to the way they lived their lives and they way that they demanded that others live. No wonder they hated him.

Jesus is still a contradiction, even for Christians today. Clearly, the Savior of the world is unlike any Messiah for whom many have dreamed and longed. Unfortunately, many people still dream of and wait for a Messiah of war and retribution. Perhaps that is why violence continues to permeate our lives and world. Jesus kept stressing that he did nothing on his own—that the power, miracles, healing and love all came from God—and that he could only do what God did through him.

Personally, I don't know if Jesus was God, or if it even matters. What I do know and believe is that Jesus' primary role here on earth was to help us understand what it really means to be human and divine. God made us all to be like Jesus, and there's no turning back.

The feeding of the multitudes, told here, is the only sign or "miracle" of Jesus that occurs in all four of the Gospels. In both Matthew and Mark it actually appears twice. There obviously was something here the Gospel writers didn't want us to miss. In John the miracle is followed by Jesus' teaching about bread that goes on and on and on. At 71 verses, this is the longest chapter in any Gospel, and, for those of us who follow the lectionary when we preach, it seemed that we spent the whole summer in this chapter.

With six different stories of miraculous feedings in the Gospels, it is apparent that there were a number of versions of this event circulating at the time the authors wrote. Unlike Matthew's and Luke's, the version in John does not seem dependent on Mark's earlier telling. There are a number of details that are different.

According to John, it is Phillip to whom Jesus turns when he sees the need to feed the hungry crowd. This simply may be the result of where this event takes place. Philip was from Bethsaida (John 1:44) and would know the area. However, Philip also knew that all the bakeries in town didn't have enough bread to feed 5,000 people. Actually, what he says is that eight months of wages couldn't feed them all. John says that Jesus knew this and only asked as a sort of test.

I hate those kinds of questions. It drove me crazy when my father used to ask questions to which he already knew the answer. You expect it in school, but in life it isn't fun to be tested. Yet I wonder how often the questions with which we struggle are actually tests of who we are. I mean, fundamentalists of all stripes live as though they have all the answers to life's most profound questions. We liberals are supposed to be more comfortable with ambiguity and uncertainty. Perhaps the test comes with being aware of the places in which we still need to pretend we know, rather than living the questions.

Jesus asks Philip where they would find enough food to feed the hungry. Philip thinks in linear terms and calculates exactly how much it would cost. Perhaps the real test Jesus had in mind wasn't Philip's math skills, but his heart. He calculated the cost and then used it as a reason for why it would be a bad idea. I suspect that is why even today people are hungry in a world that has plenty. We first answer with our heads rather than our hearts.

John 6:8-14

As Jesus tried to find a way to feed the hungry people who had come to hear him, Philip responded that eight months of wages wouldn't be enough. The Bible doesn't say that Jesus rebukes this unhelpful accountant's response. Rather it offers another model for discipleship, Andrew. Rather than calculating why it couldn't be done, Andrew offered what he could find: a boy with five small barley loaves and two small fish. John's description makes it clear that all this boy had was small—barley rolls and two sardines. Even Andrew wonders how this little bit will help.

The point we always seem to miss when we look at this story is that Jesus takes what is offered to him and makes it enough. In a culture where "nothing succeeds like excess," we are prone to forget that God seems exceedingly fond of small things. In fact, I'm not sure God ever works through anything else. God uses a young boy to overcome giant threats. God whispers, never shouts. And seeds … they seem to be God's favorite tools. Time and again, God seems to plant the seed of a thought, a dream, or a possibility in someone's soul, and, the next thing you know, amazing things happen.

Jesus doesn't whip out his charge card to buy eight months of bread. He simply takes a small lunch that belonged to a little boy and he gives thanks. John clearly describes this story with the Eucharist in mind. Jesus took the bread, gave thanks to God, and distributed it to the people. It is a pattern that already was established for the spiritual feeding of the Church that has continued to this day.

It is funny that when we read this story we think about a literal miraculous multiplication of bread and fish. We take this feast literally, but the one we celebrate every Sunday is a spiritual feeding with a taste of grape and grain. My interpretation of this story always has been that the boy's faith in sharing what he had inspired everyone else to do the same, and there was more than enough. That interpretation tends to make my more conservative friends angry. They say I'm diminishing the miraculous power of the story. Actually, what I think I am doing is remembering how God works. The miracles in this world almost always are accomplished by little things—small deeds of compassion or kindness, or generosity or encouragement, or trust. The little boy was a hero, and so was the parent at home who packed his lunch and his soul with so much love and trust.

When Jesus realized they intended to come and make him king by force, he withdrew again to the mountain by himself.

This image of a mob seeking to make Jesus king by force is unique in the Gospels. There are vague hints that some of the disciples expected that this would be what happened, but this is the most explicit reference of the possibility. According to John, it was a fear that Jesus had, and he responded accordingly.

What is odd about this is that his withdrawal into the mountains might have delayed this prospect, but a brief absence wouldn't stop a movement of this magnitude. This statement follows the miraculous feeding and precedes a long teaching about Jesus being the bread of life, after which some of his followers fell away.

What John seems to be trying to say is that there was a profound hunger among the people. They thought Jesus could satisfy their physical longing, but Jesus was offering to meet their needs on a different level. They wanted a physical, political, military ruler. That wasn't the realm of God that Jesus came to bring. They wanted to force Jesus into a role that he had not come to play in human life.

I sometimes think that is true today. It seems that the Church has tried to force Jesus into a role that he did not come to play. Through the years, I have been asked to pray a blessing for feasts, the opening of shopping centers, the start of government meetings … for events and endeavors of all sorts. While I am grateful to be there, I always have been conscious that I have been called to be a disciple of one who came to bless the poor, the outcast, the marginalized and the excluded. It sometimes feels as if we are seeking to take Jesus by force and make him into the kind of messiah we want and need.

As people of faith, our charge is to seek God's will and God's way. Unfortunately, as a friend of mine used to say, "God created us in *his* image, and we promptly returned the favor."

John 6:25-34

Jesus withdrew after he sensed that people wanted to make him king by force. He couldn't hide forever, though, and they found him on the far side of the lake:

> *When they found him on the other side of the lake, they said to him, "Rabbi, when did you come here?" Jesus answered them, "Very truly, I tell you, you are looking for me, not because you saw signs, but because you ate your fill of the loaves. [27]Do not work for the food that perishes, but for the food that endures for eternal life, which the Human One will give you."*
>
> John 6:25-26

The long teaching that follows is based on the premise that crowds were looking for Jesus because of what he could give them physically. Jesus tries to change their appetites, but, if the attitude of modern Christians is any indication, he didn't succeed. Dr. Robin Meyers, in his book *Saving Jesus from the Church,* says, quite plainly, that if asked to identify the greatest problem of the world he would answer in one word: greed. I have thought a lot about that answer, and, increasingly, I am convinced he is on to something. I mean, which of our problems would not be resolved if it weren't for greed?

It seems to me the events of September 11, 2001 should have called a Christian nation to self-reflection and to confess that our greed has left too much of the world hopeless. When people watch their own children starve while they hear of a nation that acts as if it deserves to feed its pets better than much of the world can feed their children, we should not be surprised when resentment hardens to hatred and violence. Although nothing could justify what happened on that horrible day, using our wealth to wage unending war does not seem to be the best strategy. The actions of the terrorists were truly evil, but letting others starve because of our greed rather than our need is equally evil. More than 10 times as many children starve to death every day than people died in the attacks on 9/11. Greed makes terrorists of people who pretend Jesus came to bless us but has nothing to offer starving children who made the mistake of being born in the wrong country. Atheists may have an excuse. What is ours?

The miracle of feeding the 5,000 sets up an extensive and complex teaching. Jesus first reminds the disciples of the way God fed their ancestors with manna in the wilderness. He then says, "I am the bread of life."

This is one of many *egō eimi*, or "I am," sayings that we find in the Gospel of John: "Before Abraham was I am," "I am the way, the truth and the life," "I am the light of the world," "I am the good shepherd," "I am the resurrection and the life" etc. In this sixth chapter of John, Jesus twice says, "I am the Bread that came down from heaven."

Building on the first chapter's claim that Jesus was the pre-existent divine logos—the Word who was with God from the beginning and was, in fact, God of the beginning—John repeatedly connects Jesus to God's self-revelation to Moses in the wilderness. In this passage, he evokes the image of Moses as the provider of the manna; he then corrects that impression to remind them that God actually was the source. It was to Moses that God was revealed as "I am." John is seeking to make an unambiguous claim of divinity that devout Jews could not miss.

By saying "*I am* the bread of life," Jesus is claiming to be "the bread that gives life." Later, in verse 51, he says that he is the "living bread." While in Matthew and Luke Jesus quotes Deuteronomy, saying, "People do not live by bread alone," here he is claiming to be the "staff of life."

Until Dr. Atkins and his carb-free diet came along, few Westerners would have thought a meal complete unless it included bread in some form. For Middle Easterners, bread was a staple and a basic necessity for life. The Ancient Egyptians controlled its production as a means of controlling the population. In this phrase, Jesus is identifying himself as that which is necessary for life to exist. It is the same claim that John made for Jesus by calling him the logos, the word without which nothing could exist. While bread may be rejected by modern dieters, in a day when starvation was all too real and close, bread was that which satisfied hunger and sustained life.

In a land of epidemic obesity and opulent abundance, the closest we can come to understanding Jesus' claim is to imagine fasting for a day, only to walk into the kitchen and smell fresh bread baking. The visceral response our body might have to that smell is how the starving people of Jesus' day heard his words. God is that for which we hunger at the deepest level.

John 6:35

I am the bread of life. Whoever comes to me will never hunger. Whoever believes in me will never thirst.

We who have never known the threat of starvation can never appreciate what Jesus was saying, nor the impact this statement must have had. In the same way, as Americans, we have access to abundant and clean water, while Jesus spoke in a "dry and arid land" where travel consisted of moving from one source of water to another.

Our abundance is such a radical encumbrance to our comprehending what Jesus means that he may as well be speaking an unknown language. If we miss a meal our stomachs complain loudly and we proclaim that we are "starving." The truth is that starvation doesn't occur until the body is so deprived of nutrition that it begins to consume itself. It is unlikely that any of us actually have ever been "starving." Imagine what it would be like to watch your children begging you for bread, but you have no ability to provide it.

On September 11, 2001 there was a terrible tragedy. On that day, 35,615 men, women and children died an awful and needless death. They starved, and no one noticed. The next day the same thing happened, and it has continued to happen every day since. About 85 percent of the people who die needlessly every other second are children. They die from starvation or a lack of clean water. Imagine for a moment that you were their parent, grandparent, aunt or uncle and you could do nothing to save them.

The people who listened to Jesus were just a missed meal or two away from genuine hunger, and knew very keenly the danger of thirst in a dry and arid land. It was to this reality that Jesus offered himself as life-giving bread and the permanent answer to the dryness of thirst. Jesus offered to meet their most profound and aching longings. Because of their physical needs, they understood fully the implications of what he offered.

We who have many physical wants but few actual needs have a much tougher time comprehending what is offered to us. Our culture seeks to meet spiritual needs with material distractions, but the hunger and thirst returns. We get caught in a cycle of consumption that masks what is consuming us. Our starvation and thirst are no less real than theirs, just less apparent. In the end, they may have been the fortunate ones because at least they comprehended the gift that was offered to them.

Jesus said, "I am the bread of life." Then, verse 41 says, "The Jews began to complain about him." Statements like this have resulted in modern concerns about John's anti-Semitism. Although the author likely was Jewish himself, he generalizes his references in such a way that in later years his writings would be used to justify the distain and hatred that so many Christians held for Jews through the centuries.

That clearly was not his intent, but it is an important reminder that our attitudes and words can have powerful impact long after we are done with them. John is seeking to set up a defense of Jesus in a day when the majority of Jews still held that he was not the Messiah. His apologia sets up an entire religion to believe and say one thing, when there had never been that kind of monolithic belief in any race or religion. The "Jews" did not complain about Jesus. What probably happened was that some of the Jewish leaders were upset that Jesus made such claims of divinity.

Today, fundamentalist leaders get just as upset if anyone questions Jesus' unique divinity. Yet, the complete witness of the four Gospels is that Jesus was God's child and the incarnation of God's word. But Jesus tried to tell us that we are too, and then teach us how to live out of that reality.

John is trying to win people over to belief in Jesus. Today what might be needed is not so much an exalted image of who Jesus was/is, but a fuller understanding of who he tried to teach us we are.

Perhaps that is what upset the religious leaders most. After they begin to complain, they ask, "Isn't this the son of Joseph, whose father and mother we know?" You see, they wanted to emphasize that Jesus was just a human. They clearly had a dualistic view that humanity was down here and divinity was up there. Jesus' integration of his human and divine nature was very threatening. That still seems to be true about him and about us.

John 6:41-59

Jesus responded to the religious leaders who were questioning him and reminding him who his parents were by talking about people eating his flesh as the bread of life. This whole discourse seems to gross out modern readers. We have a visceral reaction to cannibalism. As Christianity spread, the Romans sought to undermine it with charges that Christians ate flesh and drowned infants (baptism).

It is interesting that outsiders had a much more dramatic and powerful view of our sacraments than we insiders do. This passage in John was clearly an attempt to let Jesus explain the Eucharist as it was understood in the early Church. While some Christians regard the meal as "only symbolic" and seem to have conspired to make it as boring and routine as possible, according to John, at least, it was a source of controversy and conflict from the very beginning.

Some scholars suggest that Jesus' words about eating his flesh reflected on the reality that, in that day, the flesh of animals sacrificed in the temple was actually consumed. Part of the animal was given to God, but part of it was given to the priest and, in some cases, to the worshipper who would make a feast for family and friends. In this way, everyone participated in sacrificial acts of gratitude and atonement. In many religions of that day the understanding was that, in the sacrifice, the god or goddess entered into the flesh of the animal and, therefore, when the worshipper consumed the meat, they were taking the deity into themselves. When they rose up from the feast, they believed that they went out into the world "god-filled."

This experience of a mystical sacred union was no doubt transferred to the early Church's understanding of the Eucharist. The bread and wine became a part of the believer's flesh, and thus they became the incarnation of Jesus. Christian's leave the sacrament "God-filled" and thus go forth to be the resurrected Body of Christ.

In this passage, John is not so much giving us a record of what Jesus said as an account of how Jesus' teachings had come to be understood decades later by the early Church. Today it seems the more literally a person claims to take these words, the less seriously we take them. Fundamentalists believe the Bible to be the infallible word of God, but take these words of Jesus as only symbolic. Given a choice, it seems taking the teaching seriously is much more important than taking the words literally. The problem is that most believers do neither.

In response to Jesus calling them to eat his flesh and drink his blood, verse 60 records that many of his disciples said, "This teaching is difficult; who can accept it?" Most modern readers would say, "This teaching is gross; who can stomach it?"

Greek Orthodox theology teaches that by taking on our flesh Jesus made human flesh holy. Thus, we who take his flesh into ours in the Eucharist are compelled to then live as new, holy and divine creations. Perhaps this is the part the early disciples found so difficult. As Shaw famously put it, "The Christian ideal has not been tried and found wanting; it has been found difficult and left untried."

Jesus is calling us to take his life into our life; to become the incarnation of the same Spirit that gave life to his flesh; to live fully and unreservedly as a daughter or son of the Living God; to give our flesh fully to a purpose greater than our own; to be a force for life, light and love in the world. Eat and drink Jesus; be nourished by his life and teachings so fully that your own body begins to forgive and love and give as freely and unconditionally as he did. Yes, THAT is a difficult teaching!

The Greek don't say that they found this teaching hard to understand, but they found it a tough teaching to obey ... so tough, in fact, that few of us do. Every tradition agrees that to be Christian is to be like Christ, but, in practice, we seem to work tirelessly to make Christ into *our* image. We make him into one who agrees with us, embodies our values, and advocates for our causes.

It is little wonder that Mahatma Gandhi said, "I like your Christ; I do not like your Christians. Your Christians are so unlike your Christ." I like that quote; I just don't like to think of how often he might have been talking about me.

John 6:66-71

We spent last week considering Jesus' teaching that arose after the miracle of the loaves and fishes. Crowds came looking for him, but Jesus knew their interest was aroused because he had fed them. He then teaches how he is the "bread of life" and that we are called to eat his flesh and consume his blood and thus become the incarnation of him in the world.

Many disciples found this teaching hard. Apparently, then as now, believers want a god who is like them; they do not want to be called to become like their God. Verse 66 begins by saying, "Because of this many of his disciples turned back and no longer went about with him."

I've often thought that what tells the truth about our religion is not what attracts us but what rebuffs us. That is, we all want to be loved by God, blessed by God, rewarded by God. On some level, improving our life attracts us to faith. But what challenges us so strongly that we are tempted to turn back? That may say more about our faith than anything else.

The trouble is that we don't take the claims of Jesus on our lives seriously enough to go away. Jesus calls us to "take up our cross and follow him." We don't refuse to do so; we simply turn the cross into jewelry or a decoration. Now, rather than a point of sacrifice in our lives, it is merely an ornament.

We hear the tough calls to forgive our enemies, go the extra mile, take the role of servant, be loving and kind. Rather than refuse to obey these commands, we make them into clichés. Needlepointed into cushions or painted on a plaque, the words of Jesus become safe and tame, and we can continue to pretend to be disciples.

I wonder if Jesus didn't prefer the honesty of those who turned back.

Jesus said, "Do you also wish to go away?" Simon Peter answered him, "To whom would we go Lord? You have the words of life."

What a beautiful and powerful affirmation. To whom would we go for words of life? I always have suspected Jesus would have suggested that, if we found life-giving words offered by another teacher, we should follow them. While his followers made other claims for him, the spirit of Jesus' teachings indicate that he saw his way as a path to God, not THE path to God.

Having said that, what has frustrated me with so many of my progressive friends is that they are so prone to chasing other paths before this one has been fully followed. The Cathedral of Hope recently hosted a Buddhist event. It was beautiful and moving to see so many people of a different faith share this space we consider holy. I find the path of Buddhism enlightening and intriguing. It is tempting to explore it, but then I remember that I can't.

I cannot follow Buddha, not because it would be wrong to do so, but because I am not yet a very good disciple of Jesus. Perhaps someday, or, if the Buddhists are right, perhaps in my next life, I will be able to give my heart and soul to another path. For now, though, Jesus still has a word for me, and in that word I still am finding life. There have been times when that has not been so, but, in all honesty, that had much more to do with me than with Jesus.

Simply reading, or hearing, or even memorizing the words of Jesus is not enough. In this sixth chapter of John, Jesus has gone on and on about how he is the bread of life. What I think that means is that discipleship involves taking the essence of the life and teachings of Jesus into my life. If words of Jesus become flesh again in me then his word will be the words of life for me. On that day, I may need to go to another, but, at the rate I'm growing, that day still seems far, far away.

John 7:1-13

This is one of the few Gospel passages that do not appear in the lectionary cycle. When I came to it today, it seemed unfamiliar. That may mean I've been preaching too long, or it may be a good reminder that I need to study for purposes other than sermon preparation.

In this story, Jesus is teaching in Galilee because the religious leaders in Judea were looking for an excuse to kill him. The time is the Jewish holiday called "the Feast of Booths." (Never heard of it? Maybe we all need to do more study.) This was one of the obligatory festivals that required every devout Jewish adult man who lived within 20 miles of Jerusalem to attend. It lasted eight days and commemorated the Hebrew's time in the wilderness.

Jesus was not planning to attend, but his brothers insisted that he should. Catholic scholars insist that the word "brother" means disciple, but most simply accept the word at face value. This makes the conversation interesting, because here we have Jesus' kin urging him to do something that was dangerous. As a way of explaining this, John notes that his own brothers did not yet believe in him. Jesus said, "I'm not going to this festival, because my time has not yet come."

That was that, and his brothers went without him. Then, in verse 10, we are told that, after his brothers went, Jesus also went, "not publicly, but as it were, secretly." We are then told what people were saying about him. It is as if he went in disguise to eavesdrop on people's conversations about him and discovered that the people were divided.

There has been some argument about whether Jesus deceived his brothers. Some suggest that he simply said that he was not going publicly, but that didn't preclude him from going privately. The whole debate about whether or not Jesus lied raises an important point. It seems that we are more comfortable entertaining the possibility that our savior was a liar, than to consider that what might have happened was that he simply changed his mind.

It is easy to see in our political leadership what an awful thing it is to create a dynamic in which people cannot change their minds. We might all be better off if the people we elect and follow were wise enough to change course. Resolve in the face of new information is hubris and never wisdom. Jesus knew that.

This passage also is not assigned to be read in church every three years. Reading through the first 36 verses of this chapter makes it clear why we avoid it.

As the story begins, Jesus makes the case for why he shouldn't and wouldn't go to Jerusalem for the Feast of Booths (Tabernacles). The leaders were looking for an excuse to kill him. His brothers insist that he should go be with his disciples, but he states emphatically that his time had not yet come. Then we are told that, after his brothers leave, Jesus goes in disguise. Now, in verse 14, we are told that, halfway through the eight-day festival, Jesus went up to the temple and began to publicly teach. (Now you see why we skip it.)

In verse 19, Jesus points to the good work he is doing and asks, "For which of these are you trying to kill me?" The crowd responds, "You have a demon. Who is trying to kill you?" There have been no obvious assassination attempts and so the people think he is a little strange. Then, just a few verses later, (v. 25) John writes, "Some of the people of Jerusalem were saying 'Is not this the man whom they are trying to kill?'" They go on to comment that since the authorities are letting him teach openly they must secretly know that he is the messiah.

Beyond illustrating that John chapter 7 is a mess, this chapter illustrates one of the things Jesus says in it: "Do not make your evaluation based on what is obvious, but seek to discern what is right." (v. 24) Taken as a chronological story, this chapter makes little sense. However, if we ignore what is obviously confusing, there may be a lesson to be gained.

That in itself seems an important lesson. It is why spiritual teachers so often use parables and paradox to entice their students to look beyond the surface. Ironically, it seems that the more education society has the less they are conscious that the facts and the truth are two different things. Our education system teaches us to value one and disdain the other. In that case, just skip John chapter 7 because the facts are a mess.

John 7:37-52

On the last day of the festival, the great day, while Jesus was standing there, he cried out, "Let anyone who is thirsty come to me, and let the one who believes in me drink. As the scripture has said, 'Out of the believer's heart shall flow rivers of living water.'" Now he said this about the Spirit, which believers in him were to receive; for as yet there was no Spirit, because Jesus was not yet glorified.

These two verses actually are the Pentecost reading for year A. In other words, these are probably the only two verses in this chapter that ever get read in church. This chapter is set around and during the eight-day Feast of Booths/Tabernacles. On the last day, Jesus offers to quench the thirst of any who will give him the chance. Jesus then goes on to quote the scripture that says, "Out of your belly shall flow rivers of living water."

It is important to understand that Jesus is calling us to quench our thirst from him, but that WE are the ones from whom the living water flows to the world. Now, the fascinating thing about this is that no one has a clue as to which scripture Jesus is referring. A thorough reading of the entire Hebrew Bible reveals that there is no such scripture there. Was Jesus simply mistaken? Did he remember wrong or misquote a text he thought he'd read? Or was he quoting from something he called scripture but that has been lost and we don't have it? Or was he quoting from some contemporary writer, or perhaps a person of another faith and applying that truth as scripture?

We actually don't know. All the questions and the fact that we have no answers raise fascinating issues about how we regard scripture and what we consider scripture. Is this verse sacred even though we don't know its origin? If it is then why is it we haven't taken it more seriously? We keep praying for the hungry and the spiritually thirsty, and I believe Jesus keeps saying "YOU are the fountain through which living water must flow."

More than anything else, this is what it means to live a spirit-filled life. It is not that we "have" the Spirit of life, but that the Spirit flows through us to others. Of course, the wonderful thing is that we get wet, too.

After Jesus spoke in the temple on the last day of the Feast of Tents, a conflict arose among his listeners:

> *Some said, "This is really the prophet." Others said, "This is the Messiah." But others asked, "Surely the Messiah does not come from Galilee, does he? Has not the scripture said that the Messiah is descended from David and comes from Bethlehem, the village where David lived?" So there was a division in the crowd because of him.*

This is interesting because John's Gospel, of course, didn't try to reconcile Jesus being a Galilean with the Bethlehem prophecy. Some commentaries suggest that John may not have known about the tradition that Jesus was born in Bethlehem but grew up in Nazareth. Neither cities are a part of John's story, but it would be hard to imagine that John did not know of Matthew or Luke's version of the birth.

Instead, John most likely is trying to make a point. The bottom line for him is that people don't know where Jesus is from. To John what is important is that Jesus is from God/Heaven. That is why he began his Gospel talking about the pre-existent *Logos,* or Word. John's primary point is still that "Jesus came to his own, but his own did not receive him."

What follows is an expression of frustration by the chief priests and Pharisees that the temple police did not arrest Jesus. Their excuse was that they had never heard anyone speak like this man. Nicodemus gives a tepid defense, not so much of Jesus, but that they were in danger of neglecting their own legal process. In turn, he is accused of being a secret disciple, which, ironically, he was.

The ultimate result is that while the people weren't unanimous in their support or understanding of Jesus as the other Gospels imply, they did recognize that he was something special.

It is a parable of sorts that from the very start people understood Jesus differently. In the end the strongest and most accurate witness came from the temple police who didn't pretend to understand, but knew that what Jesus had to say was worth hearing.

John 8:1-11

Today we come to one of the most beautiful and meaningful stories in the life of Jesus. Ironically, it also is one of the passages in the Gospel whose authenticity is most in doubt. Today we will deal with that and tomorrow with the content.

If you read from the King James Version of the Bible (which you shouldn't) you would never know that there is something different about this passage. Almost every modern version, deals with it differently. In the New Revised Standard Version of the Bible, which I use, the entire passage is double bracketed and footnoted. Other translations simply remove it altogether and add it as an addendum to John.

The trouble is the story of the woman taken in adultery is not found in the earliest manuscripts of the New Testament. Obviously, the older manuscripts are the most valuable, because they are the closest to the original writings. Of course, the originals don't exist anymore. This fact seems to be completely overlooked by those who claim that the Bible is the infallible, inerrant word of God. When pressed as to which version of the Bible is the perfect one, they will concede that the original writings by the original authors contain the perfect revelation. What does that mean when those documents no longer exist?

The Bible, as we have it today, is a compilation of various manuscripts that are copies of copies of copies, each copied by hand. The oldest of these manuscripts are called the Uncials because they were all written in capital letters, which, of course, presents its own translation challenges. They vary in their content, style and composition, and, ultimately, someone, somewhere has to make a decision about what will be in their version of the Bible. Never is that more apparent than with this chapter.

The manuscripts on which most of the New Testament is based date back to the fourth to sixth centuries. Make sure you get that. The OLDEST, most reliable manuscripts we have are copies made more than 300 years after the facts. This reality alone makes claims of infallibility foolish. No matter what the original autographs were, what we have today is imperfect at best.

All of that is not to diminish our respect for the Bible, but to say that the Bible itself is proof that God is still speaking. We don't have the originals, and in the best manuscripts this story of the woman taken in adultery is left out. However, the Spirit still speaks to the Church through it and to me. THAT is what makes it Holy Scripture, not its pedigree.

Yesterday we noted that the story of the woman taken in adultery was probably not original with the Gospel of John because it isn't in the oldest manuscripts or the earliest translations of the Bible. Jerome obviously was familiar with it because he included it in the Vulgate, the first Latin translation, which dates back to the early fifth century.

So why did he include it when it isn't to be found in most of the source documents he might have used? To me the answer appears in the story itself. It is a tender story of grace that obviously has spoken to people through the centuries. A lesser story would have been excised long ago or not included at all.

There is some evidence of this story as early as 100. So, it certainly could have been included, but it was not. Rather than wondering why Jerome included it, perhaps we might ask why the early Church fathers did not. Augustine offers a clue. He said that this story actually was removed by the early Church leaders because "some were of slight faith" as well as "to avoid scandal." Augustine seemed to think that, for the early leaders, the message of grace offered in this story was too potent to be trusted. Their fear was that if people really understood that Jesus offered such unconditional grace they might be more prone to sin.

As outrageous as the idea of editing out the acts of Jesus, it is apparent to the most casual observer that the Church often has edited out the grace of God. The only place where grace is rarer than Church is in the hearts of the righteous. While we sing of "Amazing Grace," in practice, in the hands of the Church, the unconditional love of God has lots of strings attached. It is no surprise that Jesus regarding with unconditional forgiveness a woman caught in the act of adultery is unpalatable to the Church.

Jesus doesn't demand that she come to confession, or repent, or promise to do better, or turn over a new leaf, or even acknowledge that she was guilty. Jesus simply refuses to condemn her, period. He couldn't be manipulated or coerced into condemning her, yet that has been the first response of his disciples to people caught in sin. No wonder they tried to cut this story out of the Bible.

John 8:2-11

When I read the story of the woman caught in adultery, I am left with several questions. First, how did they catch her? I mean there was no "National Enquirer" to stake out her house. My other question is, where was the man? Obviously, she wasn't having adultery alone.

The Biblical definition of adultery means that either she was having sex with a man who was not her husband or that she was with a man who was married to another woman. Men could have sex with other women, so long as they were not married. Hence it is possible that she was committing adultery, but the man was not. The law on this matter was largely designed to control the behavior of women. This was not so much about the morality of the act of sex as it was the need to maintain clear property and inheritance lines.

So they caught this woman in the middle of having sex, and they dragged her before Jesus. The Jewish law required her to be stoned to death, because, in addition to murder and idolatry, adultery was one of the three major laws. It is a trap for Jesus, because he either had to abdicate the rule of law or abandon his own principles that love and mercy were the highest value. If he condemned the woman to die he also would be in trouble with the Romans who said that no subjugated people would execute a citizen.

The religious leaders didn't really care so much about what this woman did behind closed doors, but they were using her to trap Jesus. They had no regard for her privacy or dignity, and cared nothing for her soul, since they had every reason to expect that he might condemn her to die. Their hope, of course, was, if he did, they could accuse him to the Romans. More importantly, the common people would lose faith in this rabbi who embraced them with mercy and grace.

The leaders expected Jesus to act as they would. He did not. He bent down and began to write in the sand, then said, "Let the one of you who is without sin cast the first stone." The crowd dispersed leaving him alone with the woman. "Is there no one to condemn you?" Jesus asked the woman. "No one," she said. "Then neither do I; go and sin no more."

Jesus refused to condemn this poor woman, but he did send her to live differently. That is how it is with grace. What I want to know is, what did Jesus write in the sand that dispersed the crowd that day?

It is called the story of the woman taken in adultery. I think it should be called the story of Jesus' radical grace. So powerful was the raw grace of Jesus in this encounter that it almost got left out of the Bible. So beautiful was this image of grace offered to one who was undeserving that the Church just hasn't been able to let it go.

That is the choice. Will we be people of radical, authentic, relentless grace, offered to those who clearly don't deserve it? Or will we be people who excise the grace of God from our story and demand that people live according to our prescribed rules for behavior?

When it comes to issues like this—sex and sexuality—the Church almost always has responded with rules and regulations. In one church where I least expected the congregation to be open and welcoming to lesbian, gay, bisexual and transgender people the pastor explained that the person responsible was one of their oldest and most conservative members. Apparently, on the day they had their congregational forum to decide what their policy would be, it appeared from the forum that the motion would fail. They wouldn't exclude lesbian or gay people, but neither would they take an affirmative and welcoming stand. Just when they were about to vote, an older woman stood up and said, "You know I'm not so sure about all this stuff about homosexuality. We didn't talk about these things in my day, and I'm still not convinced that it isn't a sin. The thing is, I've lived long enough to know that deciding that isn't my job. I say we fully welcome everyone and let God sort it all out later."

While it certainly wasn't an affirmation of LGBT folk, it was an affirmation of grace. I had a fundamentalist aunt who, in the midst of the worst of AIDS, once said at a family dinner, "Well, I don't approve of their lifestyle but … " Before she had a chance to finish her sentence, I said in a voice that rattled the china in the cabinet behind her, "And just which one of them asked you for your approval? When did God die and put you in charge of approving anyone?" She turned white, mostly from the volume and tone of my preacher's voice turned on her in a small room. It wasn't my best moment of grace, I suppose, but what I said is an important reminder to us all.

Jesus himself said to a woman caught in a major sexual sin, "Neither do I condemn you." How dare we ever presume an authority Jesus wouldn't take?

John 8:12-20

This is one of Jesus' more famous *egō eimi* (I am) statements: "I am the light of the world." John began the Gospel by making this claim for Jesus and explaining that John the Baptist was not the true light, but had been sent to bear witness to the true light who was the Logos of God. Here Jesus makes the claim for himself and couples with it the promise that those who "follow" him would never walk in darkness but would have the light of life.

As I read this again, I couldn't help but think of the bumper stickers that plead "Jesus save me from your followers." As a follower of Jesus, I am personally embarrassed by that, but, as an openly gay man, I understand the sentiment completely. So, what exactly does it mean for us, as progressive people of faith, to "follow Jesus"?

As I pondered this, I remembered that in my old Barclay Bible Commentaries—a classic series—there was an article on the Greek word that is translated here as "follow." Barclay says there are at least five understandings of how that word might be used:

1. A soldier follows his/her leader into battle. This, of course, implies absolute confidence in the leader because the soldier's own life is at stake.
2. It also is a word used to describe a slave attending her/his master. The implication is to surrender one's will and attend to the wishes of another who is in absolute authority over you.
3. A third meaning is to follow the advice of a wise counsel.
4. It also can be used to mean following the rules or laws. In this case, Jesus is seeking to persuade people to live out their lives in another "kingdom" under the rules of God that he came to reveal.
5. The other meaning is to comprehend, as when we hear an explanation of something and say "Oh, I follow you."

It is the latter description that speaks most clearly to me. As I seek to understand the life and teachings of Jesus, I periodically "see the light," and it gives me fuller life ... and, hopefully, it helps me avoid being one of those "followers of Jesus" from whom people feel the need to be rescued.

In this passage, Jesus twice refers to himself as "I am." Most English Bibles translate the phrase "I am he." The point is that, according to John, Jesus is making a clear claim to be the one they were seeking, the one sent from God.

Jesus says this in the context of telling his listeners that he was going away. While it is obvious that he is predicting his execution, some of his listeners wonder if he might be thinking about killing himself. As far as I know, this is the only place in the Gospel that talks about suicide. We sometimes think of suicide as a modern phenomenon in response to the social angst. However, history is replete with stories of people who lost hope and decided to end their lives.

The fact that people wonder if Jesus is contemplating suicide may be an indicator of how difficult a time he was having. People listened but did not hear. For centuries, God had called prophets to call, cajole and harass people into living more authentically spiritual lives. The prophets were almost universally ignored, persecuted and, in many cases, executed. Jesus was aware of that and anticipated that he would be treated similarly. While he accepted that reality, it no doubt left him sad.

No one who loves life and the people they share it with can face fully the end without sadness. As one who believed in resurrection, Jesus was not afraid of death, but saying goodbye has a certain sadness, no matter how joyous the journey on which you are departing. In this passage, Jesus tells them he is going someplace where they cannot follow. There must have been at least a touch of sadness in his voice because they do not wonder to what country he might be traveling, but they wonder if he is going to kill himself. (8:22)

Some might argue that Jesus was suicidal. He lived and acted in such a way that it was almost inevitable that the religious leaders would conspire with the government to execute him. Similarly, Dietrich Bonheoffer was suicidal because he had to know that resisting the Nazis would not extend his life. Dr. King was suicidal when faced with constant death threats as he continued to preach the gospel of liberation. Risking your life in a just cause might seem suicidal to outside observers. Heroes are those who chose the immediate danger over the slow poison of a safe life that is never fully lived. Jesus knew that was a place some could never go.

John 8:31-38

If you continue in my teachings, you are truly my disciples and you will know the truth and the truth will make you free.

This passage, which tells us how the truth sets us free, is a familiar one. What is interesting is that these verses are not a part of the lectionary reading—though they are an alternative reading for Reformation Sunday—so much of the Church never actually considers what this means.

So, what is the truth that sets us free, and what is it we are freed from? Actually, these were the questions with which Jesus' original listeners responded. They were insulted that he offered them a means for being set free. They respond by reminding him, "We are descendents of Abraham and have never been slaves to anyone. What do you mean by saying, 'You will be made free'?"

Now, what is interesting about this is that they claim to be descendents of Abraham, and Abraham's descendants spent many years as slaves in Egypt. In fact, the very identity of the Jews was that they were a people who had been liberated by God through the prophet Moses. Here Jesus is claiming to be a liberator like unto Moses, and their response is that they have no need of liberation.

It seems that, when we are ensnared in a belief system or lifestyle that keeps us trapped, our defense is to selectively remember our history. Jesus offers to set us free, but our response is to pretend we are not, and never have been, captivated by patterns, attitudes, values, relationships or systems that repress us. Like his listeners, we become indignant when anyone suggests that who we are and what we are doing might not be working.

Preachers like to tell a story about the only time the great Harry Houdini was locked in a jail cell that he couldn't get out of. Usually he was able to pick a lock within moments and get free. This time he worked for six hours with no success. Finally, he had to call his jailors to let him out. Imagine his shock to discover that he had been unable to unlock the cell because it had never been locked.

Let all the daughters and sons of Abraham and Sarah hear the truth that sets us free.

Jesus' listeners respond to his offer of freedom by insisting that Abraham was their father. Jesus offers them no quarter, though, and says, "If you were Abraham's children you would be doing what Abraham did, by now you are trying to kill me, a man who has told you the truth."

They wanted to live under the delusion that they were **entitled** to favor with God because of who their ancestor was. When Jesus challenged that idea, he made them so angry that they wanted to kill him.

We have seen this dynamic lived out in our own country of late in the response to any challenge to white privilege. While there have been lots of explanations for the great resistance to universal health care, ultimately, much of it is rooted in a sense of entitlement by those who already have health care. There are lots of issues that require significant work to create an equitable system, but those issues are not responsible for the anger, resentment and belligerence that the work on universal health care has created.

Every major western nation treats health care as a human right. In the U.S., though, it is the privilege of the rich, the well-employed, and the legal citizens. The anger and resistance comes from a sense of entitlement by those who have health care. It is as if they believe they are "children of Abraham," and having that belief challenged taps into a murderous rage.

That may sound harsh, but I believe letting people die when their lives might have been saved by adequate treatment or care is pretty murderous. This is especially true when the "haves" resist those who "have not" receiving care. What other than a demented sense of privilege could motivate supposedly Christian people from moving heaven and earth, and making whatever sacrifices needed, to ensure that the poorest and the youngest and the most vulnerable are cared for in the same way we are? Of course, every time I write an opinion piece or devotional like this I get the most murderous emails … from good Christian people.

John 8:48-50

The Jews answered Jesus, "Are we not right in saying that you are a Samaritan and have a demon?" Jesus answered, "I do not have a demon; but I honor my God, and you dishonor me. Yet I do not seek my own glory; there is one who seeks it and that one is the judge. Very truly, I tell you, whoever keeps my word will never see death." The Jews said to him, "Now we know that you have a demon. Abraham died, and so did the prophets; yet you say, 'Whoever keeps my word will never taste death.'"

In a recent conversation with someone I love very much, we got into a debate about health care. As my blood pressure began to rise, I realized that the conversation wasn't going far because we were speaking different languages and live in different worlds. They get their information from Fox News, and, for me, CNN is too conservative. They live in rural America, and the suburbs make me break out. As we talked, I had to remind myself that the person with whom I disagreed was just as compassionate and caring as me; we just saw the world differently.

That must have been a bit how Jesus felt as he tried to have spiritual conversations with the Jewish conservatives of his day. He was talking spirit; they were talking religion. He was talking about a *quality* of life that was eternal; they were talking about a *quantity* of life that ended in everyone's death.

What is disturbing about this dialogue in John 8 is how the religious leaders resort to labeling Jesus. They call him a "Samaritan" as a way of marginalizing him by lumping him in with a despised minority, even though everyone knew he was not born in Samaria. It would be like calling someone a lesbian just because she didn't fit the traditional expectations of femininity. They suggested he had a demon, which, today, is equivalent to calling someone a socialist or promiscuous. They are easy labels to apply and difficult to defend against.

I'd like to think that progressive people of faith don't do that so much, but … What we all must remember when we are tempted to diminish a person by labeling them is that these leaders did it to Jesus. Anytime we seek to diminish another, it might be good to remember that Jesus said, "What you do to the LEAST you do to me."

"Are you greater than our father Abraham, who died? The prophets also died. Who do you claim to be?" Jesus answered, "If I glorify myself, my glory is nothing. It is God who glorifies me, the one of whom you say, 'He is our God,' though you do not know him. But I know him; if I were to say that I do not know him, I would be a liar like you. But I do know him and I keep his word. Your ancestor Abraham rejoiced that he would see my day; he saw it and was glad." Then the Jews said to Jesus, "You are not yet fifty years old, and have you seen Abraham?" Jesus said to them, "Very truly, I tell you, before Abraham was, I am." So they picked up stones to throw at him, but Jesus hid himself and went out of the temple.

This passage is interesting on several levels. You will note that we did not inclusify the language. Frankly, I couldn't figure out how to do that without losing the intimacy between Jesus and God that was the point of what Jesus was saying. In this passage, Jesus messes with time. As we noted yesterday, he was speaking a different language from these religious leaders. They also seemed to be living on different planes of existence. We, of course, experience time as a linear thing, moving from one point to the next. That doesn't seem to be how Jesus was thinking in this passage.

The most intriguing *egō eimi* statement that Jesus makes is probably this one: "Before Abraham was *I am*."

So, tell the truth; if you were to encounter an unkempt person on the street who was talking like this you might think they had a demon … or at least a mental illness. This isn't how we think. Like them, what we hear Jesus saying is, "Before Abraham was, I was." That is how we talk and how we think. Apparently, it wasn't how Jesus thought. John is claiming for Jesus the same pre-existent deity that is described in the opening chapter. I'm not so sure that is what Jesus had in mind.

Eastern religions might suggest that Jesus was a spiritual being who was aware that true existence transcends time itself. Jesus was a great soul, aware that the elements of his existence were not created out of nothing at the moment of his birth, nor would they cease to exist upon his death. It would be many centuries before science would insist that matter is never really created nor destroyed, but merely transformed. Maybe Jesus is talking about all of this on another plane. We will never know, though, unless we seek to spend some time there with him.

John 8:53-59

Then the Jews said to Jesus, "You are not yet fifty years old, and have you seen Abraham?" Jesus said to them, "Very truly, I tell you, before Abraham was, I am." So they picked up stones to throw at him, but Jesus hid himself and went out of the temple.

I know we need to move on, but this passage has so much packed into it we need to look at two more things. First, notice that they say to Jesus, "You are not yet fifty years old." Much has been made of this in terms of seeking to determine how old Jesus was when he died. The general assumption is that he was 33. That is derived from the fact that we are told Jesus began his ministry when he was 30, and the Gospels record three visits to Jerusalem at Passover. Here, John's record says he is less than 50, not less than 35 or 40.

For the Jews of that day, 50 was considered old. Unlike today, that was an age of esteem, when people were considered wise. Perhaps more than talking about Jesus' age, the religious leaders are suggesting that Jesus hasn't lived long enough to offer to teach them. Youth or aged, both have their wisdom to offer, but each is dismissed too often by those in the middle. Would Jesus have been heard by his society had he lived beyond 50? We will never know because, like so many who sought to change things, he is violently killed by the religion and the state.

Apparently they tried to kill him that very day. They picked up stones to throw at him, but Jesus hid himself. Isn't that a fascinating image: Jesus hiding himself to avoid stoning. An old song about his crucifixion says, "He could have called ten thousand angels to destroy the world and set him free." Our image is that Jesus might have avoided his death but did not. Yet, here he is hiding.

I guess we should be glad that he hid; otherwise, there is much we treasure that he might not have had time to teach if he had died here in the eighth chapter. Besides, wouldn't it have been awful to have to wear a stone on a gold chain around your neck? Hmm ...

As Jesus walked along, he saw a man blind from birth. His disciples asked him, "Rabbi, who sinned, this man or his parents, that he was born blind?" Jesus answered, "Neither this man nor his parents sinned; he was born blind so that God's works might be revealed in him."

This is one of the great stories of the Bible, and John spends an entire chapter (41 verses) telling it. Because we all have heard many sermons and Sunday School lessons about the healing of the man born blind, we will spend only two days looking at it.

For many years, Bea Arthur played the character Maude on television. Maude's most famous line was when she looked at Walter and said, "God'll getcha for that." It always got a laugh because there was a cultural acknowledgement that her theology is widely, if subconsciously, shared. It doesn't matter how sophisticated and liberal we may be, when something really bad happens to us, we secretly wonder what we might have done to deserve such punishment.

That is the root of the disciples' question to Jesus. "Who sinned, this blind man or his parents?" In that day, it was a common theological assumption that God was the causal source of all things. When Jesus said, "Neither, " he was making a major shift in how we understand God. Long before medicine became a science illness and disease were as much a mystery as the stars above. The piety of that day attributed it all to God in a more immediate than ultimate way. Jesus said, "No illness doesn't come from God, but it does afford an opportunity for God to work."

Hopefully we all have heard sermons about how it is bad theology to think that God sends disease to punish. Hopefully our understanding of God is very different than the disciples' was that day. Hopefully Jesus' revelation of what God is really like has begun to seep into our soul and even our subconscious. Hopefully …

So, assuming you know God better than that, let me ask, would Jesus' answer have been different if the man was born blind because his father beat his mother when she was pregnant? Or if the mother had had an affair and contracted a venereal disease that caused his blindness? You see, God is not the source of disease, but neither does our faith exempt us from the law of consequences. Much of human suffering is the result of sin, our own or that of others.

John 9

The Pharisees are upset because Jesus healed the blind man on the Sabbath. First they challenge whether he had been actually blind at all. They call his parents as witnesses. The parents refuse to stand up for Jesus, or even for their own son for that matter, but they did confirm that he had been blind from birth. Twice they question the man himself. The second time they accuse Jesus of being a sinner because he did not live by their rules. In response to that, the formerly blind man utters one of the best known lines in the Gospel: "Whether he is a sinner or not I do not know. This I do know, once I was blind, but now I can see." (John 9:25)

This is an example we all must learn to follow. We don't have to get caught up in theological debates or disputes about what the Bible says or means. All we must do is bear witness boldly to the experience of our life. I have spent almost 30 years trying to persuade lesbian, gay, bisexual and transgender people of this. They have experienced God's love and grace, and no more proof is needed that you can be lesbian or gay and Christian.

In this response to his unwillingness to deny his own experience, the fundamentalists of that day put him out of the temple. What happens next, however, is a beautiful parable. The man is healed, but he is abandoned by his parents and then rejected by his own faith community. Alone now, Jesus seeks him out and comes to him.

Ironically, even there the Pharisees see and challenge them. Jesus tells the man that those who claim to see (know) so much are the ones who are actually blind. That is the great danger we who know so much face. We forget that at best our knowledge is partial, and we presume to judge others with our partial knowledge. Whenever we do that, we become the fundamentalists. Or, as the wise cartoon character Pogo put it, "We have met the enemy and s/he is us."

John 10:1-10

The first 18 verses of chapter 10 seem to record a blending of at least two different teachings of Jesus. There are two different *egō eimi* sayings: "*I am* the gate" and "*I am* the good shepherd." Of course, since a section of John 10 is read on the Sundays following Easter every year, most of us have heard the explanation of why these are not competing images.

Jesus' original image—declaring himself to be the gate—would have summoned immediately the image of a shepherd using his body to hem sheep in and protect them for the night. Guarding sheep from predators was much more effective if the sheep could be gathered into a pen or a canyon or a ravine with only one way in and one way out. The good shepherd literally would use his body as the gate to keep the sheep safe.

The passage begins by saying that anyone who does not enter the sheepfold by the gate is a thief. This passage has been used by Christian fundamentalists to insist that the only way to become a sheep of God's pasture is through Jesus. While I do not agree with that theology, it is true that some of the writers of the New Testament—including John—do make exclusive claims for Jesus. However, that is not what Jesus is saying here.

Jesus is not making a claim to be the exclusive way into the fold; rather, he was making the claim to be one who cares for his own sheep and is willing to lay down his life for them. Claims of exclusivity are dispelled by Jesus saying of the shepherd who serves as the gate, "His own know his voice and follow him." Again, his hearers would have been clear about what he meant. Several herds of sheep might share a fold for safety at night. Jesus as the gate would have laid his body down for them ALL. In the morning, the various herds were sorted easily because they each would follow the voice of their own shepherd. Notice Jesus isn't condemning other shepherds or claiming to lay his life down only for his herd. The thieves to whom he refers are those who try to use a shortcut, taking the sheep off without investing in the rhythm of their daily lives or risking anything for them.

Faith systems that promise only prosperity, health and happiness are thieves. The good shepherd is with us through the routines of life and the dangers and pains that come to us all. For that, there are no shortcuts.

John 10:10

The thief comes to kill, and steal and destroy. I came that you might have life and have it more abundantly.

Almost two decades ago, I wrote an essay based on this passage. It was turned into a pamphlet and thousands of copies were published and distributed. We were in the midst of the AIDS crisis, and all too many fundamentalist and TV preachers were proclaiming AIDS to be God's judgment visited upon the gay community. Of course, none of them ever bothered to explain what God had against heterosexuals in Africa … Using God to justify one's own prejudices has never been subject to standards of rationality.

Despite the idiocy of such statements, and the awful theology behind them, when you or a loved one is suffering it feels an awful lot like God is punishing you, or at least allowing you to be punished. That is probably why the pamphlet was so widely read. In the face of such hurtful statements, I simply tried to explain how Jesus divided life in verse 10. "*The thief* steals, kills and destroys." That which steals our life, kills our joy or destroys our community is never from God. Jesus did not come to take our joy away by burdening us with guilt or a new constricting rulebook. Rather, he came so we might have life, abundant and full.

Of course, dualism is dangerous theological ground. Life never can be divided neatly into "this or that," "good or bad," "black or white." We all have had experiences in which we thought something was a disaster or a tragedy, and it turned out to be the best thing that could have happened. We have discovered the most sacred moments of life in the midst of pain and disease. God is never more present than in the presence of death, which feels like the ultimate thief.

Still, I think Jesus was refuting theology that blithely says, "Everything happens for a reason," or "God is in control," or "All that happens is God's will." No, Jesus says that which steals life is not from God. AIDS was not from God, though, mercifully, I watched time and again as God came into the midst of that awful disease. Jesus wasn't advocating a dualistic view of life, but was simply trying to call us away from piety that tries to give bad things meaning by attributing them to God.

John 10:11-18

I am the good shepherd. The good shepherd lays down his life for his sheep.

No doubt, this passage was read by early Christians through the lens of Jesus' death. What Jesus was doing, though, was contrasting true shepherds with "hirelings." This passage makes me think about the difference between parents and babysitters. I also think of this passage whenever a pastor resigns in the midst of the congregation facing a difficult or challenging time. I must confess it is this image that has kept me from fleeing when circumstances sometimes were painful and difficult. Employees abandon the sheep when they are in distress, not shepherds. Hirelings can walk away because they were in it only for the money, or whatever ego satisfaction they got.

This is a principle that applies to more than parents or pastors. Many relationships end when times are tough. Divorces often follow the death of a child. Friendships often fail when one person is facing daunting challenges. To some extent, we all are conflict-adverse, and it often is tempting to walk away. Lifelong friendships are increasingly rare because a disagreement or a disappointment can cause two people to go their separate ways. We often have more and more people we call friends and fewer and fewer people with whom we share long-term significant relationships.

While there is a multiplicity of reasons for this, Jesus is suggesting that it is, in part, because we are not willing to make sacrifices, to lay down our lives. We are in relationships for what we can get out of them. When they stop "paying dividends" we tend to walk away. Jesus said that hired hands flee when times get tough because "they do not care for the sheep." What he might have said is, "Because they only care for themselves."

In a culture that trains us to "look out for number one," our instinct is to walk away from anything that doesn't "pay." I have had many people say they stopped going to church because they weren't getting anything out of it. I always want to ask what ever gave them the idea that that was what church is for. Eric Fromm said, "Immature love says, 'I love you because I need you.' Mature love says 'I need you because I love you.'"

ALL relationships must be about what we give, risk, lay down if they are authentic. Otherwise, we may as well hire friends, spouses or churches.

John 10:18

No one takes my life from me. I lay it down of my own accord.

Jesus' willingness to lay down his life for others distinguished him and permeated all he did and taught. It goes back to his teachings in the Sermon on the Mount. He called us away from an attitude of victimhood. Jesus was no one's victim. Regardless of what happened, he refused to accept that role.

In the Sermon on the Mount, he taught that when people struck us on one cheek we should turn the other. When someone took our shirt we should give them our coat. In our culture, that sounds simply like giving in to oppression and refusing to stand up for oneself. Those teachings might be understood that way without this verse from John. No one took Jesus' life. He laid it down. The result was the same, but Jesus wanted to be clear that he was no one's victim, not even God's. It is a matter of attitude. Another Jewish teacher, Holocaust survivor Victor Frankl, said, "Everything can be taken from a person but ... the last of the human freedoms: to choose one's attitude in any given set of circumstances, to choose one's own way."

Neither of these teachers were speaking theoretically from a life removed from pain and suffering. Both suffered greatly, but still refused to be anyone's victim. Charles Sykes, in his book *A Nation of Victims,* writes:

> *Something extraordinary is happening in American society. Criss-crossed by invisible trip wires of emotional, racial, sexual, and psychological grievance, American life is increasingly characterized by the plaintive insistence, I am a victim ... We want to be a pain-free, no-fault, no-guilt society. Frankly I think a little more personal guilt wouldn't hurt us at all.*

While, I do not agree with much of what Sykes contends, it is probably an important cultural corrective. Those of us who are disciples of Jesus are called to remember that, even when others slap us, we still get to choose how we respond, and that is the ultimate power of life.

Jesus said, "The sun shines on the just and the unjust." The same sun hardens clay and melts wax. Ultimately, just like Jesus, we get to choose which we will be.

John 10:19-42

This passage describes yet another conflict between Jesus and "the Jews." John insists on using this phrase instead of characterizing the conflict as being between Jesus and the Pharisees or Scribes or priests or religious leaders. It is a disconcerting choice of words. Whether or not it was John's intent, it sounds anti-Semitic. Like the other Gospel writers, John simply may have been describing the conflict that no doubt occurred as the result of Jesus challenging the authority of the religious leaders.

Unfortunately, the result of John's phrasing has been to give credence to a significant history of anti-Semitism in the Church. Clearly, "the Jews" didn't oppose Jesus since Jesus, his family and all of his original disciples were Jews. This very passage describes how Jesus fled from Jerusalem across the Jordan and how, there, many people came to hear him and believed in him. Those people were Jews.

The challenge, of course, is distinguishing between the actions of a powerful few and the attitudes of the general public. That is a challenge that exists today, too. Muslims get judged by the actions of a handful of desperate terrorists. Christians get judged by the words and actions of TV preachers. Republicans are all greedy selfish bigots. Democrats are fools who want to tax people to fund gigantic government bureaucracies.

We all know the dangers of such generalizations, yet we get caught up in them almost daily. The result is an increasingly fractured society that forgets that the darkest of us and the lightest of us, the richest of us and the poorest of us, all have more in common than we have distinctive. Our common humanity gets lost when we emphasize our differences.

The religious leaders in this passage demanded that Jesus speak plainly about whether or not he was the Messiah. He refused to do so because he was not the Messiah they were expecting. Instead, he suggested that they look at the evidence of how he lived his life and then judge for themselves. That seemed reasonable, but it challenged their confidence that they knew the answers. That made them so angry that they took up stones to kill him. Of course, in the end, their actions judged them just as Jesus asked to be judged by his actions.

Maybe our divisions would be reduced if, instead of debating, we let how we live and act be our only argument for what we believe.

John 11

The 11th chapter of John mostly tells a single story, though it does so in a way that raises a number of issues. The story of Jesus raising Lazarus from the dead is well known but little understood.

It begins by introducing the characters in the story: Lazarus, who never says a word, and Mary and Martha, his sisters. Mary is identified as "the one who anointed Jesus' feet with perfume and wiped them with her hair." Interestingly, in John, this story is told before that one. (12:3) It is unclear if the stories are simply put in the wrong order by a later editor, or if the story was so familiar that John simply referenced it before telling it.

Mary and Martha sent word to Jesus that their brother was ill. They don't ask for him to come to Bethany, but they do identify Lazarus as "the one whom you love." That is a very interesting phrase to use. If it had been read objectively in some other ancient writing than the Bible, scholars would hypothesize about the relationship that might have existed between the two men. Jesus loved Mary and Martha. We believe that Jesus loves us all. How was his love for Lazarus so different that it deserved to be commented upon by Lazarus's own sisters? "The ONE whom you love is ill." If someone sent me that message I would understand they were talking about the man with whom I have a special relationship. There are many men and women whom I love, but if they singled out one person as "the one" I'd know what they meant.

Now, I am not really suggesting that Lazarus and Jesus were gay lovers … but why not? Why is that so hard to imagine or, at least, to consider academically? If Jesus had been in love with a man would it have disqualified him from being the *Logos* sent from God? What if he had loved a woman? Is it homosexuality that makes this possibility so unreasonable? Or is it simply human love? If Jesus was fully human, wouldn't it be appropriate that he loved another person in the ways that we do? What would be wrong with that?

These questions don't say nearly as much about Jesus as they do about us and our faith and our need to "protect" Jesus' reputation by dehumanizing him. That is ironic since Jesus' favorite title for himself was "the Human One."

Mary and Martha send word to Jesus that the one whom he loved was ill. Jesus doesn't respond as we would have. If we had been told that our loved one was ill, we likely would have dropped everything and rushed off to check on them. That is what love does, isn't it?

Yes, it generally is, but let's be honest here. Our drama around times like this often arises as much from our need to be needed, to feel important, to feel as if we have some control over the situation. There is a cultural addiction to drama that often is the energizing force more than our compassion. Oh, yes, love makes us want to go and be with the ones we love in difficult times, but there are other dynamics involved as well. Rushing off in a panic when we can't do anything to help is often more about us than the ones we love.

Ironically, Jesus assures his disciples that the illness will not be fatal, though Lazarus does die eventually. John obviously is trying to indicate that Jesus knew all along that he was going to use this as an opportunity to demonstrate the power of God. A description of this event told with the knowledge of how this all turned out may make John's assumption logical. However, it seems cruel if Jesus simply hung out until Lazarus's illness killed him just so Jesus could make a point. Lazarus's pain and suffering were bad enough, but what about letting his sisters grieve for four days before Jesus showed up?

Taken literally, this story has lots of holes. However, if we read it as we would any of the spiritual parables Jesus told, we hear the truth without getting caught up in "facts" that may or may not be accurately recounted. Jesus somehow senses that the illness was more serious than he may have thought and that Lazarus has died. He decides to go to Bethany, but his disciples warn him that this is a dangerous decision that could cost him his life.

Sensing that Jesus is determined to go, Thomas speaks up faithfully, but cynically, as he encourages his fellow disciples, "Let us also go with him that we might die with him." (11:16) In the end, of course, they don't die with Jesus, but they didn't know that. So, they decide to go and be with him. Was it love that made them go?

John 11:17-27

Jesus said to her, "I am the resurrection and the life. Those who believe in me, even though they die, will live, and everyone who lives and believes in me will never die. Do you believe this?"

These words are a part of the funeral liturgy of several traditions. Martha has just said to Jesus, "If you had been here my brother would not have died." It has a tone of accusation, but maybe it was just an acknowledgement of another piece of her grief. She didn't think that Jesus should have been there. After all, even he couldn't be everywhere, but there is just the added sadness that something might have been done to save her brother.

Jesus assures Martha that her brother will rise again. Naturally, Martha assumes he is talking about resurrection of his soul, and she acknowledges that she believes that. Still, it is clear that the promise of a future resurrection isn't sufficient to ease the pain of her brother's absence in her life today.

Rather than engaging in a discussion about all that, Jesus gives what may be his most audacious *egō eimi* statement in the entire Gospel of John. To Martha and her grief, Jesus says "*I am* the resurrection and the life."

We read those words at funerals, but what on earth does that mean? It might have been clearer had this teaching not been attached to the physical resuscitation of Lazarus. Evangelicals claim—and I have witnessed it myself—that when people are spiritually dead and mired in sin, faith in Jesus has the power to resurrect them. Resurrection that comes when a soul reconnects with God through faith in Jesus makes sense to me. Perhaps, rather than a magical reanimation of a person who has been dead four days, we would do better to understand the story of Lazarus as a parable.

I suspect all of us have had times in our lives when we have felt dead spiritually, but our faith in Jesus brought us back to life. While Jesus has never shown up to physically raise one of our loved ones back to life, we all have known resurrections that have given our lives power, meaning and renewal.

Please forgive me if you take the story of Lazarus literally. I don't write these devotions just to upset you. For me, I believe we must bear witness to the power of Jesus to give us new life in this life, and I fear that witness is not strengthened by holding onto the magical thinking we learned as children in Sunday School.

After talking to Martha, Jesus calls for Mary. This is a scene of great grief. She comes out of the house with the other women who had come to join her in the weeping and wailing that was the Jewish method of grieving. Some of the funerals that I have conducted or attended in African-American churches have come closest to this ancient form of cathartic grieving.

Twice in this passage John describes Jesus as "greatly disturbed." This passage contains what is known as the shortest verse in the Bible: "Jesus wept." The "Trivial Pursuit" treatment of this verse has masked its profound beauty and meaning.

The Greek word translated "deeply disturbed" is *embrimasthai*. It is rarely used in the New Testament, and, in those other places, it implies a level of anger or sternness. Some have suggested that Jesus was irritated with all the grieving because it appears that they didn't believe his claim to be the resurrection and life. Perhaps, but Jesus himself joins them in weeping. The language indicates that this wasn't just a few tears trickling silently down his cheeks, but was demonstrable grieving. Eyewitnesses saw his grief and commented on how much he must have loved Lazarus.

Still, that doesn't mean Jesus wasn't angry. Oh, he wasn't angry at the grief-stricken sisters or other mourners. He was one of them. I understand fully how Jesus was feeling. Perhaps you do too. There are several elevators in the city of Dallas that I have struck with my fists after leaving a hospital room where a life all too young was coming to an end. At times I have been furious that the lack of health insurance had caused the disease to go too long untreated. There were other times when my anger was toward fundamentalist religion that kept families away from young men as they died of AIDS. Most of the time my anger was directed at disease and death itself.

Grief is often a mixture of anger and tears. To me that is the beauty of this passage. There are no glib clichés, no artificial piety, no stoic stiff upper lips. Jesus is feeling the same crazy mixture of anger, sadness, loss and resentment that come to us all at times like this. When I am faced with overwhelming grief, it helps to be able to talk to someone who understands because they have been there. Jesus has.

John 11:38-44

There is a part of me that wishes the story of Lazarus had ended in verse 38 with the statement that Jesus was deeply disturbed by his beloved friend's death. Up until this point, the story is an amazing picture of Jesus' humanity that redeems our own. The Gospel writer's thesis, though, is that it wasn't Jesus' humanity that got him killed. For John, what did Jesus in was the fact that he kept working "signs" to prove he was the *Logos* of God.

In the other Gospels, it was Jesus' cleansing of the temple and confronting religion's exploitation of the poor that brought about his demise. For John, raising Lazarus was the final straw. What the religious leaders and empire were determined to exterminate was Life itself.

So, in John's version of this story, Jesus grieved with Martha and Mary and then went out to the graveside, which is a perfectly normal part of the pattern of grieving. Jesus goes to weep at the graveside of the person the Bible described as "the one who he loved." What happens next certainly breaks the pattern of normalcy.

For John, it is a sign of Jesus' divinity. This moment—when Jesus orders the stone removed and calls Lazarus by name from the grave—has long been offered as one of the great miracles that Jesus worked. To me, the beautiful part of the story is spoiled by something that feels artificial and contrived.

Yet … somewhere Lazarus hears the voice of love calling his name and finds that even death can't separate them. Although I've never seen anyone come out of a cemetery grave, I have seen proof that, whether or not this actually happened, it is true. Love is more powerful than death. We all know that death might kill the body, but it does not kill the love. And we all have known people—perhaps ourselves—who have been called back from dead places by the voice of love. If our love is that powerful, just imagine the power of the love of the Human One. Just imagine if it had been your name Love called … actually, it has been. Love calls your name until you live again, even if it takes forever.

Jesus raised Lazarus from the dead. We never hear anything more about Lazarus, though one assumes he eventually grew old and died again. As any of us who have had close calls can attest, he probably treasured the days that were given him, but, sooner or later, we all must die.

In today's passage, we are given an unattractive picture of some of Mary's friends who ran to the Pharisees to tell them what Jesus had done. (vs. 45-46) What I could not uncover in my research is why the text says, "Many of the Jews who had come with Mary" believed, but some went to the Pharisees. It feels like something is missing here. Where is Martha? Or is it possible that Martha's sister is not who this verse refers to? Could it have been friends of Jesus' mother who went to the Pharisees?

Either way, it is an ugly moment of betrayal because the high priest calls a council, and, after some debate, they decide that their only recourse is to put Jesus to death. Did Mary's friends know that was what would happen when they carried their tale to the Pharisees? Perhaps, but I have never known a betrayer who saw herself that way. A betrayer almost always believes that he is working for the greater good. History may paint them in villainous colors, but their self portrait is almost always done in pastels. In fact, they look an awful lot like us.

As horrifying as the concept is, in truth, we all have the capacity to do the wrong thing for what we believe to be the right reasons. As a leader in an oppressed community, I have found myself feeling betrayed many times. I have tried to regard those folks as simply misguided, not really bad people. While I'd like to claim that my attitude arose from a place of spiritual maturity and grace, there is a much more base reality. They truth is I have never been betrayed when the betrayal didn't remind me of some action or attitude that belonged to me. We all have misjudged the actions of another. We all have thought we were on the moral high ground only to discover that we were wrong and the person we judged was actually the better incarnation of good.

So Jesus prays, "Abba, forgive them for they know not what they do." I wonder if Mary was able to pray that prayer for her friends. I find them the hardest people to forgive … almost as tough as asking them to forgive me.

John 12:1-11

John begins this chapter with Jesus returning to Bethany and the home of Mary, Martha and Lazarus. The scripture says that Martha served them and Mary took a pound of costly perfume made of nard and anointed Jesus feet and wiped them with her hair. John describes how the whole house was filled with the smell of the sweet perfume. It was as if he had been there to smell it and could still remember.

Judas objected to the extravagance, observing that the perfume was worth nearly a year's wages. He suggested that the money could have been used for the poor. It seems to me that he had a point. John says in a parenthetical aside that Judas wasn't really concerned about the poor, but he was a thief who kept the common purse and used to steal what was put into it.

I wonder how he knew that. It seems like John is just trying to make Judas look bad; after all, the author knew what Judas would do. Or could it be that Jesus, and maybe even the other disciples, knew all along that Judas was skimming money from them? Could it be that they knew, but Jesus wouldn't let them do anything about it? Maybe Jesus was hoping that Judas would be transformed by grace and by the love of the community of faith of which he was a part. It is fascinating that Judas was the trusted treasurer of the group.

We can't actually know if Judas was skimming money, but we do know that money was important to him—so important that he would betray Jesus. Jesus tells Judas to leave Mary alone because there would be many opportunities to do good for the poor but the chance to show her love and devotion to him would not come again. Jesus says that she is anointing him for burial. This, of course, is foreshadowing his impending death.

Again, all of this is written in retrospect, and treating it as a historical account is probably less valuable than asking what point John is trying to make. It may well be that the Church already was grappling with competing needs and values. Of course, the Church is called to care for the poor, but devotion to Jesus must remain at the heart of who we are if our service is to be more than humanistic charity.

The real betrayal of Jesus today may be to claim devotion but not care for the poor.

Jesus went to stay with Mary and Martha and Lazarus in Bethany, just a few miles outside Jerusalem. People heard eventually that he was there, and crowds began to gather. Interestingly, John notes that, in this case, the crowds also came to see Lazarus. It was as if he was the circus sideshow.

The chief priest decided that enough was enough. Not only would they put Jesus to death, but they would kill Lazarus, too. At that time, the high priests were Sadducees, and they didn't believe in the resurrection. So, John is suggesting that they were planning to get rid of the evidence.

I keep wondering what it would take for us to be such powerful evidence of Jesus' life and teaching that the powerbrokers would want to eliminate the evidence? It seems to me that the Church should advocate for the poor and the marginalized so powerfully, consistently and relentlessly that we are a threat to systems that keep people poor and disempowered.

The Sadducees were the wealthy who collaborated with the Romans. Lazarus was literally living proof of the power of Jesus and the validity of his teachings. That is really the whole point of the Gospel of John: these things were signs of the authority of Jesus. We who live under the authority of Jesus ought to be living signs today.

In the health care debate, there are some genuine issues of difference. However, it is incomprehensible to me that politicians blatantly playing to our self-interest worked with Christians. I mean, the opposition to universal health care was almost all rooted in the fact that what I HAVE might have to change, or I might have to pay more taxes for the poor to have health care. Low taxes have become the third sacrament in many churches, especially in the South.

I suspect if Christians started saying, "We are willing to pay a little more in taxes if it means the poor get health care," we would soon find the powers-that-be trying to get rid of us. The fact that we are NOT persecuted because of our relentless advocacy for those Jesus called "the least" indicts us all.

John 12:12-36

This is one of the few stories told in all four Gospels: Jesus' triumphant entry into Jerusalem. John says it happened "the next day." It is tough to tell if he meant the day after Jesus dined with Mary, Martha and Lazarus, or the day after the high priest decided both Jesus and Lazarus had to go.

At any rate, John is trying to make it clear that they didn't have to go hunt for Jesus out in the wilderness. Jesus came to them and in a most visible way. This time, the Pharisees are the ones who react. They suggest that nothing can be done because "the whole world is following him."

A parade certainly can give you that impression. Several years ago, we took our daughters and joined a march protesting immigration policies and attitudes toward those not born in this country. Every street for miles around downtown was filled with brown faces carrying signs, waving U.S. flags, and chanting peacefully. It looked like the whole city had turned out. Later we were told that more than a million people had participated in the march. My teenage daughters were confident that as a result of our efforts things would be different.

They were wrong. Oh, I know social transformation is incremental, and I've quoted Dr. King's statement about the arc of the moral universe a thousand times. Still, my point is that huge crowds don't change much. What this parade for Jesus showed was that you can turn out a crowd, but, when the time comes to put up or shut up, most people are too busy to do any more than shout.

Recently, I've looked at the constitutional amendment passed in Texas giving special rights to heterosexual taxpayers that are denied to lesbian and gay taxpayers. The percentage by which it passed was staggering, but a closer look shows that if the lesbian and gay community alone had voted the amendment would have been defeated. If our family and friends had voted it would have been crushingly defeated.

While I think marches, protests and parades have a purpose, my sentiment about them is about like the attitude expressed in a bumper sticker I saw recently. The driver obviously had grown tired of stickers that say, "Honk if you love Jesus." This one said "Tithe if you love Jesus … anyone can honk."

The part of this passage on which we often have heard sermons is where some Greek Jews who have come to Jerusalem for the Passover want to see Jesus. They approach Philip, who then found Andrew, and, together, they went to talk to Jesus for them. All of this seems to be little more than a complex setup for what feels like John's version of Jesus in Gethsemane.

What follows is a declaration by Jesus that his soul is troubled by the prospects of what is ahead. He asks rhetorically, "What should I say: Abba save me from this hour?" His conclusion, of course, is that his whole life has moved him toward this hour. Still, he doesn't have to celebrate it.

That seems to be a lesson lost on many moderns. Our approach seems to be "If it feels bad don't do it; if it tastes bad spit it out; if it is too heavy let someone else carry it." Convenience, ease, satisfaction and pleasure have become our supreme values. We don't "do" hard anymore. Whether it is parenting, or our jobs, or our church, or our relationships, it has become all about *how much we enjoy it.* We have forgotten that there are higher values in life than our own personal pleasure or satisfaction.

Jesus didn't enjoy being betrayed by his friend. Having everyone abandon him did not bring him personal satisfaction. It was not rewarding to be scourged. He did not relish being nailed to a cross. He understood that life really wasn't all about him and his good pleasure.

We have to wonder if these Greeks had come seeking Jesus for what they could get out of the relationship because in response to them Jesus said:

> *Very truly, I tell you, unless a grain of wheat falls into the earth and dies, it remains just a single grain; but if it dies, it bears much fruit. Those who love their life lose it, and those who hate their life in this world will keep it for eternal life.*

I doubt the Greek seekers really heard what Jesus said. Why should we think they did since, 2,000 years later, we sure haven't. The idea that discipleship might require sacrifice over satisfaction still evades us.

John 13:1-11

This chapter describes the third Passover that John talks about. From this, we assume that Jesus' ministry took place over a three-year period. There are other traditions that would differ, but that is the common assumption.

In Greek, John 13:1 is one very long run-on sentence. English translations usually divide the verse into two sentences, but it is like the writer is blurting it all out there, anxious to get this final act started. John begins by telling us that Jesus knew "the time had come for him to leave this world." In John's hands, it sounds like a mystical foreknowledge, but the truth is that any casual observer or reader would have drawn the same conclusion. The teacher was about to say, "Time's up. Put down your pens."

Jesus' awareness was important because the largest segment of his teachings, as reported in the Gospel of John, follows this knowledge. For 12 chapters, John deals with the signs Jesus offered as proof of his divine nature and the teachings that arose from those signs. Then, at the start of chapter 13, he announces that Jesus knew the end had come and celebrates one last Passover with his disciples. The teachings that will follow are to be regarded as the final words of Jesus—his dying words, if you will. The intent, of course, is to give them weight and significance.

John introduces this last meal by first noting that "the devil had already put it into the heart of Judas son of Simon Iscariot to betray Jesus." One wonders if John is seeking to blame Judas' actions on the devil. Is he seeking to ease Judas' guilt or justify the fact that he is still there with them? The phrasing of this sentence and its placement is significant.

It follows the statement that Jesus knew his time was up. It precedes the final family holiday meal together. John notes that the evil thought was in Judas' heart before the meal began as though this time could have, perhaps should have, dissuaded his actions.

We all have evil thoughts and intentions at one time or another. John is right; what should ultimately dissuade us is always love, connection and community. That is why any time a person or a group is made to be "the other" you can almost always count on evildoing and betrayal to follow.

In the synoptic Gospels the significance of this last Passover Meal is that it is considered the "institution" of the Lord's Supper/Holy Communion/the Eucharist. Yet in John, the last Gospel written, that is not the case. The impression the other Gospels give us is that the early Church re-enacted this last meal as a memorial. John tells the story of this meal differently, and then carefully recounts communion meals with Jesus that take place after his resurrection. For John, this is by no means the "Last Supper." The focus of this meal for John is Jesus washing his disciples' feet. This act of radical servanthood is done in a ritualistic and almost sacramental way. In fact, when Jesus finished this washing, he asked the disciples if they understood what he had done for them (v. 12), and then adds that they should do for one another what he has done for them.

I grew up in a small town in South Georgia that had the largest Primitive Baptist church in the world. That faith tradition practices foot washing as one of the rites of the church. Many congregations observe this ritual once a year on Maundy Thursday, though most re-enact the rest of this meal every Sunday.

In the text, when Jesus offers to wash Simon Peter's feet, he resists, and we seem to be disciples of Simon in many ways. We avoid washing the feet of others almost as much as we avoid allowing others to wash ours. Just as the bread and wine symbolize this meal, foot washing may be only a symbol, but I think it is a powerful one. Mostly, it is a powerful symbol of what is left out of the Church. Where is our sacrament of sacred servanthood and humility? I believe the Church would be a radically different institution if we had three sacraments instead of two.

While I do believe this text could be used to argue in favor of a sacramental act of humble service, that is not really the point. The point for us to ponder is how our failure to make servanthood sacred has left Christianity vulnerable to becoming the religion of the wealthy, the powerful and the defenders of the status quo. Could a church that knelt each week to wash the feet of others have ever oppressed women, enslaved Africans, exploited the poor, or excluded lesbians and gays? Would a foot-washing humility allow us to justify financial inequality? Could we hate those who washed our feet, if next week we might be washing theirs?

I don't know that foot washing should be a sacrament, but I know humility and service are sacred values the Church needs if it is to call itself the Body of Christ.

John 13:21-30

John says that, after washing his disciples' feet and instructing them to follow his example, Jesus was troubled in spirit because one of them would betray him. The word John uses to describe how Jesus felt recalls how Jesus responded in the face of Lazarus's death and his sisters' grief.

History has treated Judas as a caricature for all who are so greedy, wicked and self-absorbed that they would sell out for 30 pieces of silver. So horrifying is the idea that E.M. Forster said, "If I had to choose between betraying my country and betraying my friend, I hope I should have the guts to betray my country."

What Judas did was so terrible that he has become our culture's archetype for evil acts. We want to dismiss him as less than human, a person devoid of conscience. We think of him as some sort of sociopath. Who else could do such a horrible thing to the best person who ever lived?

Yet here is Jesus, deeply and profoundly troubled. This seems to imply that their relationship was not simply that of betrayer and betrayed. We all have known enough betrayal on some scale to know that when it comes from someone we hardly know or don't care about we might be bothered but not likely deeply troubled. Clearly, there is some emotional investment here and perhaps hope that it might all turn out differently.

John tries to give Jesus an out, saying that Judas had only been chosen "so that the scripture might be fulfilled" (v.18), but Jesus is clearly invested in Judas as a friend. This family feast ends with Jesus offering Judas a piece of the unleavened bread, saying, "What you are going to do, do quickly." Judas gets up from the table and John writes, "And it was night."

In a sexist story, a man asks a woman if she will sleep with him in exchange for a luxury trip around the world. She agrees. Then he says, "Will you sleep with me for $50?" Indignantly she asks, "What kind of woman do you think I am?" "Oh," he says, "We have established that. Now we are just negotiating the price."

Would you betray a friend for 30 pieces of silver? No? How much would it take?

After Judas has left, Jesus announces that the time has come for him to be glorified. It is in the context of all of this that John places what we must consider Jesus' most important words, his dying words:

> *I give you a new commandment, that you love one another. Just as I have loved you, you should love one another. By this will every-one know you are my disciples, if you have love for one another.*

In the Church year, the day before Good Friday is called Maundy Thursday. Many churches hold services that day or evening to commemorate the institution of Holy Communion. Some churches re-enact the supper and even include a foot washing. The services are usually sparsely attended, though. Larger crowds are drawn by Good Friday services, and even those pale in comparison to Easter.

Servanthood and sacrifice have little appeal for most of us. The promise of living forever attracts the crowds. Maybe that is as it is meant to be. After all, Jesus doesn't say, "By this shall all know you are my **fans**." Jesus isn't speaking to the thronging crowds on this night. He is talking to his disciples, to those who devote themselves to this teaching, not just those seeking his blessings. Jesus is talking to those who actually will be called upon to pay a price for their faith, not for those who want a faith that gives them a leg up on the competition.

Disciples … to YOU I give a new commandment, a new mandate. That is where we get the name Maundy Thursday. That was the day on which we were given a new command: Love one another. THAT is how they will know you are my disciples.

They won't be able to tell by whom you vote for, or what you do on Sunday mornings, or the bumper sticker on your car. Love is how they will know you are my disciple, not just my fan.

As I studied this passage, I couldn't help but notice that, although it clearly is connected to the act of foot washing, Jesus waited until after Judas left to give them this new mandate. Did he not want Judas to know the secret? Or did Jesus know that Judas was just about to offer them their biggest test?

John 13:36-38

Before Jesus' gave them their new mandate to love, Judas goes out into the night to betray him. Immediately afterwards, though, Jesus responds to Peter's declaration that he will follow him anywhere with the prediction that, before the morning comes, Peter will have denied him three times.

This story of Jesus predicting Peter's denial is told in all four Gospels. Including this embarrassing story about someone who became a hero for the early Church was clearly deliberate. It is part of the wonder of the scripture that it tells the stories that some of us might have edited out. Peter's denial is talked about in the same chapter as Judas's betrayal. While the two deeds might have differed in the severity of their consequences, the image we have is of two flawed and failing disciples whose stories had polar opposite endings.

That is the point of our faith. Any of us could end up like Judas if the price was right. All of us have acted like Peter in one way or another. The question now is how our stories endings will be written. That will not be determined by the seriousness of our misdeeds, or the depth of our flaws. Rather, the outcome is how fully we experience the grace and mercy of God.

According to legend, Judas recognized how terrible his crime was and, as a result, committed suicide. He never really understood that grace was unconditional love. Peter, on the other hand, hears the rooster crowing and goes out and weeps. His restoration was not magical or instantaneous, but it was ultimate.

The fact that this story is told here speaks to how the early Church obviously had preserved this story and told it universally. It was important to them that their eventual leader's failure didn't end with his denial. This story had to be saved and retold because it captures the power of the love and grace Jesus came to. So little of the synoptic is repeated in John, but this was a point he did not want us to miss.

When we consider how the Church has treated its failed leaders over the ages, it is apparent that, despite being in all four Gospels, it is still a story the Church needs to hear.

Jesus has just told them that he was going away. Peter declares that he will follow him wherever he goes, but Jesus says, "No, before the night is up you will deny me three times." Then Jesus says one of the favorite lines in the Gospel of John:

Do not let your hearts be troubled. Believe in God and believe in me.

I love the way this chapter begins so much that I quote it at almost every funeral. Of course, it follows with the promise that, *"In my Father's house are many rooms. If it were not so I would have told you. I go to prepare a place for you and if I go to prepare a place for you I will come again and receive you unto myself that where I am there you may be also."*

That promise is comforting in the face of death, I suppose, but the first verse is what gives this promise context. It is against the background of Peter's predictable failure that Jesus says "Do not let your hearts be troubled." Times of testing will come. You will know personal failures and shame, but don't despair. Believe. Believe in God, and believe in me. In other words, when the circumstances of your life cause you to lose self confidence, continue to have confidence in God and in the grace of God that Jesus came to bring you.

When you lose or fail so badly that you are filled with shame, it is easy to lose faith in yourself. Those times come to us all. What Jesus is saying is, when they come, don't lose faith in God, because, if Jesus' teachings mean anything at all, we can trust that God hasn't lost confidence in us. Our failure does not determine God's opinion of us or diminish God's love for us. In the face of failure, believe in the God who will never abandon you, even in death.

Soon Jesus will give them a new understanding of resurrection. What he is offering here is that, even in the face of terrible failures like denying Jesus, there is still life and a place for us in the family of God.

Despite my commitment to gender-balanced language, I have left the original language in Jesus' promise. Perhaps it is because I have known so many lesbian, gay, bisexual and transgender young people who have been kicked out of their homes by their fathers. Jesus is calling us to trust that nothing done to us or by us can cost us a place in our heavenly Father's house.

John 14:4-14

Jesus promises to go and prepare a place for the disciples whom he is about to leave. He concludes the promise by saying that they know the way to the place where he is going. Thomas doesn't think he knows this, though, and to his inquiry Jesus offers another *egō eimi* statement: "*I am the way, the truth, and the life.*" Thomas is looking for the way to where Jesus is going. Jesus tells him that he is the way.

The word used in Greek has a double meaning. "Way" can mean path, but it also can mean method or technique. This double meaning is part of what was intended when the early Christians called themselves "*People of the Way.*" This is a beautiful image for those of us who follow Jesus' life and teachings as more than just a belief system, but as a way of life and living. It might be helpful if, as modern disciples, we resumed calling ourselves **people of a way that leads to truth and life.**

Ironically, while this phrase by Jesus is powerful and helpful, what he is credited as saying next is not. "*I am the way, the truth, and the life. No one comes to God except through me.*" This last part has been used as a bludgeon by the Church against those who might seek God in another way.

So, what are we progressive and including people of faith to do with such an excluding statement?

We could simply reject it as out of character for Jesus. In so many places we find Jesus unwilling to turn others away that it seems unreasonable that he now makes a claim that he is the only narrow path by which people can come to the place God has prepared for them. It is congruent with John's vision and version of who Jesus is, but it sounds like he is putting words in Jesus' mouth.

On the other hand, many Christians have an equally exalted view of Jesus, but hold that Jesus' death and resurrection reconciled ALL people to God regardless of their faith. In this view, eternal life is a gift given by grace. Believing doesn't earn an unconditional gift, nor does disbelieving disqualify one from a free and unconditional gift. In this understanding, Jesus' redeeming work is the way all humans come into God's eternal presence.

There is much that could and should be said about these issues. In this short commentary, however, all I can say is that we must decide for ourselves what this passage means. In the end, our choice decides whom we believe God is, but, moreover, our choice may express who we really are.

Jesus says that he is the way for them to know God. To that, Philip asks, "Show us God, and we will be satisfied." Jesus replies, "Have I been with you all this time, Philip, and you still do not know me? Those who have seen me have seen God."

For John, Jesus was the Divine Logos/Word made flesh, or the physical expression of God. That was how the Gospel began, and, now, as Jesus' earthly life comes to an end, John takes every opportunity to cement that understanding in our minds. In this case, it comes at the cost of Philip saying something really dumb.

While it is not surprising that John wants to leave us with an elevated understanding of who Jesus is, what follows is a bit surprising. Jesus says, "I tell you, the one who believes in me will also do the works I do and, in fact, will do greater works than these, because I am going to my God." Given the exalted image of Jesus in John's Gospel, and all the signs that Jesus has done, this statement is pretty amazing. Jesus sees himself as an in-flesh revelation of God, but he says that his followers will be the same. In fact, we will be even more so. That this made it into the Gospel of John is amazing. That the Church has never really taken it seriously is disappointing.

Every Sunday, as I consecrate communion, I pray that God will pour out the Spirit on the gifts of grape and grain, and also upon us "that we may be the risen body of Christ doing your work in the world today." It is my conviction that this is who the Church is and our reason for existing. Our job is to do the work that Jesus did: heal the hurting, release the captives, proclaim good news to the oppressed. This is the work Jesus did. He had confidence that we would do it to an even greater extent than he did.

Once upon a time that might have been true. In every major city there are hospitals that were founded by churches. Most of them now belong to for-profit corporations, but once upon a time the Church believed it was responsible for caring for the sick. Now few churches even advocate for health care for the poor. Once upon a time the Church advocated for judicial and penal reform, but now pro-life means only anti-abortion, with little or no concern for the executions of souls Jesus calls us to redeem. Once upon a time the Church advocated for civil rights, but few churches think lesbian, gay, bisexual and transgender people deserve true equality.

Jesus obviously had a much higher view of us than we deserve. He thought we'd take his example seriously.

John 14:15-24

In light of Jesus' audacious statement that we would be able to do greater things than he did, he goes on to tell us how. While Jesus is preparing them for his physical departure, he also is promising them of his spiritual return in the person of the Holy Spirit.

Many of the churches we grew up in spent a lot of time talking about the second coming of Jesus. In verse 18, Jesus says plainly, "I will not leave you as orphans but I will come to you … " This is said in the context of Jesus promising the Spirit. A clear and fresh reading of John 14 would reveal to us that the giving of the Spirit was the fulfillment of Jesus' promised "second coming." The Church born out of that is the resurrected body of Christ.

Now, it is true that many of the epistles, and perhaps even the writer of Revelation, seem to have missed this reality. That should not surprise us. Any of us who lived through tumultuous times know that you do not appreciate fully what is happening, or what is happening to you, until time has passed and there is an opportunity for some historic context and perspective.

It is not surprising that early Christians trying to make sense of the fall of Jerusalem, the destruction of the temple, and the persecution of the Romans so longed for the physical presence of Jesus that they interpreted his words as a promise to physically return to be present with them and to set things right. There are later passages of scripture written in that context that seem to predict that event. However, here in John, Jesus does not agree with that understanding.

The promise is that we are not orphaned. Jesus said he would return, and, in the person of the Holy Spirit dwelling in and working through the resurrected Body of Christ, Jesus has returned. Adapting the words of others, Barack Obama said, "Change will not come if we wait for some other person or some other time. We are the ones we've been waiting for. We are the change that we seek." In essence, that is what Jesus meant when he said that we would do greater work than him and then promised not to abandon us but to return and live in us to empower us. We are the Christ that we seek.

I have said these things to you while I am still with you. But the Advocate, the Holy Spirit, whom God will send in my name, will teach you everything, and remind you of all that I have said to you. Peace I leave with you; my peace I give to you. I do not give to you as the world gives. Do not let your hearts be troubled, and do not let them be afraid. You heard me say to you, "I am going away, and I am coming to you." ... Rise; let us be on our way.

There is far too much in this great passage to unpack in this short space. I want you to read it, though, because it is so filled with promises. Jesus again is telling them (and us) not to let their hearts be troubled. It is a beautiful scene, especially since it ends with "Rise, let us be on our way." While there is no Gethsemane story in John, and there are three more chapters of teachings, it is clear that this was the original ending, or at least the beginning of the ending scenes of arrest, trial and death.

I have been privileged to know many saints who have come to the end of their journeys and made peace with the death that they faced. It is always a re-markable thing to watch as they comfort those who are to be left behind. I recall one sweet, gentle young man who was dying of AIDS though he was not yet 30. Nurses would leave his room sobbing, not because he was so sad, but because of his strength and the comfort he offererd to those grieving his passing. "It just isn't fair," they would say.

Death isn't fair, in one sense at least. If it were it certainly would not have claimed Jesus who was still a young man with so much good to do. In face of this reality, and the anxiety his disciples were feeling and would feel, Jesus is trying to comfort them. In another sense, death is the most equitable reality in life. It comes to the young and the old, the rich and the poor, the good and the bad. It even comes to Jesus. To those of us left to carry on, Jesus says, "*Peace I leave with you; my peace I give to you. I do not give it as the world gives. Do not let your hearts be troubled, and do not be afraid.*"

Jesus does not try to comfort us by denying the reality of death or by offer-ing us tricks for avoiding thinking about it. Rather, he refuses to be death's victim. The one who said, "If someone strikes you on one cheek offer them the other," again refuses to be anyone's victim, even Death's. Jesus says, "Rise, let us be on our way."

John 15:1-8

John chapter 14 ends with Jesus promising to send another comforter to be with us. I love the story about the seminarian who wrote a paper about how Jesus died to take away our guilt. Unfortunately, the student didn't proof his paper well. Instead of typing a "g" he typed a "q;" thus, the sentence said that "Jesus died to take away our quilt." The professor marked the sentence in red and wrote, "Fear not little one, for Jesus has given us a comforter instead."

I love that old joke because it is a good reminder that we haven't been left out in the cold spiritually. Having made that promise, Jesus ends chapter 14 with the words, "Rise, let us be on our way." It certainly sounds like the account at the end of the Last Supper in the other Gospels. When the supper was over, they rose up and went out to the garden of Gethsemane. What follows here, though, are three more chapters of teachings by Jesus.

Since each of the Gospels was written on several scrolls, and the chapter and verse numbers were not added until centuries later, it is quite possible that chapters 15, 16 and 17 are simply out of place. They do seem to belong together, but not necessarily as a teaching offered in the garden late at night after the disciples were full, had been drinking, and were very tired.

It is also possible, since John is not particularly concerned with sequence and timelines, that he placed these teachings here to give them added importance. The Church has attended to them because they come at the end between the Last Supper and Jesus' death. These would be final words, so surely what Jesus said in those moments would have been his most important teachings.

John 15 is the chapter in which Jesus tells us that he is the vine and we are the branches. It is a powerful image that deserves our meditation. Just as the sap of the vine flows through the branches to flower and bear fruit, so, too, this Spirit/Presence that Jesus would send to dwell in us flows from Jesus into and through us to bear fruit. In the end, you don't see or feel the sap/life flow. What you see is the fruit that is produced. The fruit of our lives is evidence of what flows through us.

For the third time in as many chapters, Jesus gives his disciples the commandment to love one another. In this chapter, the command is given against one of the most beautiful statements in the Bible, or in any literature. Jesus says:

> *No one has greater love than this, to lay down one's life for one's friends. You are my friends ... I no longer call you servants, but I call you my friends.*

Jesus goes on to remind them that they did not choose him; he chose them. What a powerful twofold reminder: You are a friend of Jesus, AND you are chosen! Wow. One wonders why we would ever have self-esteem problems if we honestly believed either of those things deep in our bones.

It has been my experience that the most dysfunctional people are those who don't feel chosen. Oh, they may act egotistical or even narcissistic, but the truth is they almost always are compensating for not feeling chosen. That is certainly the case in my own life. Never am I more likely to act less Christ-like than when I am feeling threatened or abandoned.

Perhaps that is the reason this teaching ended up where it did. John wanted to ensure that we got the message, so he placed it here as one of the last things Jesus said to his disciples and to us.

Verse 12 begins, "This is my commandment, that you love one another **as I have loved you.**" Verse 17 ends this paragraph with the words, "I am giving you these commands so that you may love one another." In between, Jesus tells them/us that we are chosen friends. Long before psychoanalysis was invented, Jesus obviously understood that our capacity to authentically love others is rooted in our own experience of being loved and valued. While he could not control how our parents might or might not have loved and affirmed us, he offered us his own love in the most tangible way possible. He called us chosen friends and then made it clear he was willing to die to prove that he meant it.

In the end, the "sin" Jesus died to redeem was our inability to believe that we are beloved by God. If we could get that right everything else might very well work itself out.

John 15:18-16:4

In this passage, Jesus warns that those who accept, experience and express the reality of being a child of God will be "hated" by those who do not. He says that this shouldn't surprise us since he himself was persecuted and hated. He ends by warning that they would be put out of their synagogues. (16:2)

John wrote this in a day when that was exactly what was happening to the disciples of Jesus. Early Christians continued to go to the temple and synagogues just as their parents had, and just as Jesus did. This created a conflict between the new faith that was being born and the old faith into which they had been born. Judaism and Christianity would come eventually to a parting of the ways, but Jesus initially was a faithful Jew who taught Jewish disciples to understand their faith differently. The loss of their community, tradition, history and place came as a painful shock to many of the followers of Jesus. Here, he is warning that this was to be expected since his way was rejected when he was alive. Again, this warning comes with a promise of the gift of an Advocate/Comforter.

During the three decades that I have been pastor to mostly lesbian and gay people, I have known hundreds of folks who have been rejected by the churches in which they grew up and were baptized. To them, it felt as though their family of faith had taken back their name, taken out a towel and dried off the water of their baptism. Talk about making someone feel un-chosen and friendless.

Ironically, Jesus said that this is what true disciples could expect. It probably should concern us that we so easily fit into the systems and communities that are a part of the status quo. I recently attended a dinner at which an organization was honored for caring for Palestinian children who were victims of the Israeli army. The speaker talked about the courage that it took to give them an award. I was struck by the fact that she didn't talk about the courage required to serve children in a war zone, but the courage to go against "accepted wisdom" and recognize a group that stood with those regarded by so much of the world as "the enemy." Perhaps Jesus is suggesting that our values and lifestyle should always put us outside the institutions of status quo. We are called to stand with those who also are outsiders. It is there, at the margins of society, that we most authentically encounter the Christ who was a persecuted outsider.

John 16:4-15

Jesus returns again to the theme of the promised Spirit who will come to be with them/us when he is no longer physically present. One of the amazing things he says is:

> *I still have many things to say to you, but you cannot bear them now,*
> *but when the Spirit comes the Spirit will guide you into all truth.*

We should spend some time pondering what Jesus meant by this. I don't know about you, but I just hate it when someone says that they have something to tell me but they can't tell me yet. I immediately start to worry about what it is that they can't tell me and why. Did the disciples do this?

What was it Jesus had to tell them that they "couldn't bear?" What truth was so startling, so strong, so amazing, so offensive that Jesus couldn't just say it? The Spirit's revelation is always a soft, gentle, gradual thing. Although we may have an "ah-ha" moment of revelation, it is the result of layers of preparation that gently moved us toward accepting the truth.

I'm not sure what it was the disciples couldn't bear, but, in my own life, I know that almost everything that I now believe is different from what I once believed. Today when I read authors that I read years ago, I understand what they wrote in a completely different way. I also find myself reading very different authors. Today I have almost no tolerance for the certitude and absolutes that I found so comforting when I was young.

Perhaps the disciples were in need of platitudes, assurances and directives. The day would come soon when the physical, tangible Jesus would be gone. They would not be left alone, but the revelation of the Spirit would come to the heart not to the mind. The words would be spoken in their souls not in their ears. When Jesus said something they would hear it clearly and take it in. He often spoke in parables and enigma so that they had to grapple with his meaning. This was good preparation for the day when the Spirit would blow gently across their souls and they would need all their faith to know if the leading they felt was divine or their own will.

Jesus still has much to say that we cannot bear. Only when we are still, quiet and ready to take the risk of changing our minds does the Spirit come telling us new and often disturbing truths.

John 16:16-33

Jesus continues to talk to his disciples about his impending departure. He acknowledges that it will be a painful time for them. He tries to reframe it as an opportunity for joy. That is a lifelong theme for Jesus. He tries consistently to teach us that pain and struggle are a part of the reality of living. Only the dead avoid it. Faith is not insurance against it. Disciples of Jesus do not get preferential treatment. When something bad happens, it is arrogant for us to raise our eyes to heaven and ask "Why me?" The answer always is, "Why not you?" Jesus said, "The rain falls on the just and the unjust."

If Jesus just left it there we would have no reason for faith. Instead what he says to his disciples, who are about to go through their own period of tribulation, was, "Think of it like a woman does the pain of childbirth." This, too, is a theme he has used elsewhere. In an apocalyptic passage Jesus describes the turmoil as "birth pangs."

Using this imagery, Jesus is not denying the pain. Few experiences of human pain are greater than that which a mother experiences in giving birth. Bishop Yvette Flunder says that, at those times, women are given a divine dispensation to cuss a blue streak because anything they may say is completely forgiven. I wonder if this is what Jesus had in mind here.

Seriously, is Jesus acknowledging that what we are feeling and how we may react to times of intense pain, suffering and loss is normal, understandable and forgiven? I often have talked with people in grief who say, "I know I shouldn't feel this way but … " I always try to say, "Don't 'should' on yourself. What you are feeling isn't right or wrong; it is simply real. It will pass, but pretending you aren't feeling it won't help it pass."

Jesus is saying to his disciples, "You are about to feel great pain, loss, grief and fear. Those feelings are real, normal and to be expected. They are not the end of the story, though. They are like birth pangs, because, for you, the pain will give birth to a resurrection."

When Jesus suffered and died most people didn't feel pain, or even notice. Only those who did knew the joy of resurrection.

This is the final chapter of John before Jesus is arrested. It is a 26-verse prayer. While it seems odd in our modern context, John is actually using a classic literary device for his day. Jewish literature often closes with a prayer of blessing. That was common for Mediterranean writings as well.

However, it is not unknown to us. I just read Cardinal Joseph Benardin's book *Gift of Peace*. In the last chapter he writes:

> As I write these final words, my heart is filled with joy. I am at peace. It is the first day of November, and fall is giving way to winter. Soon the trees will lose the vibrant colors of their leaves and snow will cover the ground. The earth will shut down, and people will race to and from their destinations bundled up for warmth. Chicago winters are harsh. It is a time of dying. But we know that spring will soon come with all its new life and wonder. It is quite clear that I will not be alive in the spring. But I will soon experience new life in a different way. Although I do not know what to expect in the afterlife, I do know that just as God has called me to serve him to the best of my ability throughout my life on earth, he is now calling me home.
>
> What I would like to leave behind is a simple prayer that each of you may find what I have found – God's special gift to us all: the gift of peace. When we are at peace, we find the freedom to be most fully who we are, even in the worst of times. We let go of what is nonessential and embrace what is essential. We empty ourselves so that God may more fully work within us. And we become instruments in the hands of the Lord.

In closing, he shares the Prayer of St. Francis: "Lord make me an instrument of your peace." As I read this, I understood what Jesus was doing with this prayer in John 17. In the face of the pain and tribulation that we all must face, Jesus wants to end his life commending us to God's care. He has absolute confidence that, whatever may come, that is enough to see us through.

John 17:1-5

Jesus begins his prayer with the kind of incredible statement to God that all of us hope we can make when we come to the end of life: ***"I have glorified you on earth by finishing the work that you gave me to do."*** Wow!

What an amazing thing to be able to pray just before you die. Of course, most of us don't know when our deaths will be, so it might be a good idea to consider our ability to pray that prayer at the end of every day. To live in such a way that our life glorifies God is the call of every life. To finish the work we have been given to do is the responsibility of every disciple of Jesus.

As the dean of an institution that calls itself a cathedral, I am constantly aware that the work we are called to do usually isn't finished in a single lifetime. Cathedrals historically have taken decades, even centuries, to build. No single individual is responsible for their construction. Both of those realities are healthy reminders.

While I cannot say what work God has given you to do, I know that we all are working as a part of a much larger effort. We are not just stone masons or carpenters; together, we all are building a cathedral. We are building the Realm of God "on earth as it is in heaven." We do that together, each of us doing our part.

Jesus also talked about how the Realm (Kingdom) of God was within us. That is in part what Bill Shore meant in his book *The Cathedral Within*. The subtitle of the book is "Transforming your life by giving something back." While self-help books have spawned a movement, few would argue that humanity has been improved substantially by spending billions of dollars on workshops, therapy and books. The paradoxical reality of what Jesus came to teach is that the help we need is almost always found in the help we give to others.

Humans are created in such a way that little is accomplished through self-help, but many a saint has been created by doing the work of Jesus. We are transformed best by giving something back. Let us live each moment so that on that day when we give our souls back to God we can say with Jesus, "I finished the work you gave me to do." Amen.

John 17:20-21

I ask not only on behalf of these, but also on behalf of those who will believe in me through their word, that they may all be one. As you, Abba, are in me and I am in you, may they also be in us, so that the world may believe that you have sent me.

The phrase "that they may all be one" in this part of Jesus' prayer is the motto of the United Church of Christ (UCC). It is also the theme of many ecumenical and uniting church movements. The "What we believe" section of the United Church of Christ's website offers this rational for why this verse is so important:

> **We believe the UCC is called to be a united and uniting church.** "That they may all be one." (John 17:21) "In essentials–unity, in nonessentials–diversity, in all things–charity,"

Ecumenism was an important movement in the first half of the last century. It was most fully expressed in the merger of a number of denominations. The UCC is the product of the merger of four disparate denominations. The result was a new denomination that was flexible and fluid enough to celebrate unity rather than conformity. That has been one strategy for answering Jesus' prayer. Unfortunately, this approach has happened simultaneously with the decline of mainline denominations.

The Roman Catholic Church and fundamentalist denominations take another approach. While the last two popes have co-operated much more with other churches, both have reiterated the view that Roman Catholicism is the true Church. Fundamentalism has used the threat of hell to coerce uniformity of belief and behavior. A strategy of conformity and coercion for answering Jesus' prayer is out of synch with modern values. Yet the Catholic Church and more fundamentalist churches have been the ones to show numerical growth.

This devotion is not about church growth, but the description of these two methods to answering Jesus' prayer is offered as a parable of two approaches we may take to life. The one that is filled with absolutes may allow us some security and success. The other requires maturity and for us to take responsibility for our own belief and behavior and allow others to do the same. We all secretly long sometimes for a pope to tell us what to believe, but I'm not sure that is what Jesus was praying for.

John 17:22-26

In this chapter Jesus has prayed for himself and his disciples. Now he expands the prayer to include those who would come to believe because of his disciples' witness.

Jesus prays that the first, second and subsequent generations of believers will know the love that he has known. This is the last phrase of Jesus' prayer before he is betrayed, arrested and executed. If we are looking for Jesus' last words to know what was really important to him, it seems to me that we need look no further.

The mission of the Risen Body of Christ should always and entirely be to help all people know that they are loved by God just as Jesus was. The Church has gotten so distracted by so many secondary things and forgotten what was really important to Jesus.

What follows these last verses in John is the death of Jesus. While many people believe that Jesus had to die so that God could love and forgive us, I don't believe that is true. Jesus did not have to die to persuade God to answer his prayer. Rather, Jesus was willing to lay down his own life to persuade us that we are loved by God and always have been.

What kind of monster would demand the death of an innocent man? God's love for us was never in question; as the Bible says, "God is love." What humankind always has had a tough time with is believing that that love was for them. To persuade us, Jesus was willing to die, and God allowed him to.

As I ponder all of this, I think there might be a number of circumstances under which I might be willing to lay down my life. However, I cannot conceive loving anyone so much that I would allow one of my children to die. That gives me pause to re-examine what I believe about God and the meaning of Jesus' death. In the end, perhaps it is that God has more confidence in life than I do. Perhaps God's love for us is so great that God could allow Jesus' death if that was what it took to save us from our despair and self-destructive belief that we were unloved. Faith in the resurrection of life may have been what gave God the strength to allow Jesus to lay down his life.

We who claim to be the Risen Body of Christ—the Church—ought to be willing to make any sacrifice to ensure that Jesus' death was not in vain. The ultimate perversion of Jesus' sacrifice is to use it to make ANYONE feel like they are outside God's love.

John 18:1-11

Chapter 18 begins "After Jesus had spoken these words." The implication is that the great prayer and the teachings of the preceding three chapters all took place in the upper room around the table of the Last Supper. This is, of course, a literary device, not a recounting of history. John rarely is concerned with history. He has left that to the Synoptic Gospels and resisted the temptation to repeat what can be found in them.

That is slightly different in chapters 18-20. While scholars believe these chapters were written by the same person, they are completely different in style. Now John will recount the facts of Jesus' death.

The other Gospels describe Jesus leaving the upper room for a garden. In Matthew and Mark, it is called Gethsemane, while Luke says that Jesus went out to the Mt. of Olives. John says it was a garden across the Kidron to which he and the disciples often went. All four likely are referring to the same place. For John, it is important that we understand this was a pattern that Jesus followed. That is how Judas knew where to find him.

Unlike the other three, John describes those who accompanied Judas as being both Roman soldiers and "Jewish officials." While this is consistent with John's anti-Jewish account, historians believe that the arresting parties were likely the temple police since it was highly unlikely for Roman soldiers to be placed under the authority of Jewish leaders.

John emphasizes that they came with torches and lanterns. It is his way of pointing out the artificial nature of their authority as they come to arrest "the light of the world." This distinction is an important reminder that we need to exercise care in what it is we allow to light our way. There are all too many artificial lights that lead to injustice, violence and betrayal. To be sure, any light that takes us to those ends is not the "true light sent from God."

John 18:1-14

According to John, a cohort of Roman and temple soldiers comes to arrest Jesus. When they appear out of the night with their torches and arms, Judas is with them. There is no kiss; for John, that would be entirely too passive for his Jesus who is the Divine Logos of creation. Jesus is still in charge. He rises to ask whom they seek. When they say "Jesus of Nazareth," Jesus replies with another *Egō eimi* statement. For one of the last times in John, Jesus says, "*I am* he."

Strangely, this exchange happens twice. Jesus' second "I am he" is so filled with divine power that the arresting crowd steps back and falls to the ground. While this seems like a kind of magical illustration of Jesus' divinity, every time I read it I think of those people in my life who have been a force of nature. Once, when a friend and I were fishing with my father in a dark cypress creek, my friend did something wrong. My father didn't say a word, but, when he turned and looked at my friend, this teenage boy was so terrified that he fell over backwards into the snake-infested water.

I've had teachers who could freeze an entire unruly class with just a withering glare or a sharp word. It isn't hard to imagine that the personal charisma of Jesus, who knew who he was, what he believed, and how he was called to live, had the power to cause armed thugs to step back and stumble over one another. John's intent with this story was to remind us of Jesus' divinity and of the fact that, even at the last minute, Jesus chose to let them take him and kill him. To me it speaks of the personal authority of a life that is integrated and focused. Jesus let himself be arrested because he believed that it ultimately served what he believed was God's will for his life. He was no one's victim.

In John's version, Simon Peter takes this as a sign that the revolution had begun. He pulls out a sword and strikes one of the servants. In this version, it is not just some unnamed villain Jesus is forced to heal; it is a man named Malchus.

Although I doubt it was John's intent, it seems an important reminder that the choice to do violence is made by a person with a family and a name, **AND** the target of the violence is a person with a family and a name. Those we execute or shoot in war, or blow up with unmanned drones, may indeed be villains, but they are also persons with a family and a name. In the end, healing them, not killing them, is Jesus' will.

John 18:19-27

This part of the 18th chapter of John seems to be a compilation of a couple of versions of the same stories. In 18:12-14, we are told about Jesus appearing before the Jewish authorities. That story is followed by Peter's denial of Jesus (18:15-18), which then is followed by a more detailed account of Jesus being questioned by the high priest. (18:19-27) That is followed by a description of Peter denying Jesus. (18:25-27)

As in the rest of John, the purpose of these passages is not so much to provide a historical and factual account of the events, but to teach the reader the spiritual truths behind all that transpired. For example, throughout John, we have heard Jesus use the phrase *egō eimi* or *"I am"*: "I am the bread of life," "I am the light of the world," "Before Abraham was I am." Even when they came to arrest Jesus, they ask if he is Jesus of Nazareth, and he responds *"Ego eimi."* It is John's continual reiteration of the opening poem in which he identifies Jesus as the preexistent divine *Logos*. "I am" is a historical reflection of God's self-identification to Moses out of the burning bush. Moses asked who he should tell people had sent him to do the work of liberation. God answered, "Tell them *I am* sent you."

In John's understanding, Jesus came calling disciples, liberating them, and then sending them to be liberators as the incarnation of that Word that became flesh to dwell among us. Now John tells the story of Peter's denial, not once but twice. It is as though John fears the reader will miss the point, and, by and large, we have. Preachers, authors and movie makers have focused on the failure and shame of Simon Peter. What we have missed is how Peter's denial is twice a play on the *egō eimi* claim of Jesus.

In John, Jesus identifies himself as "I am;" however, when asked if he is a disciple—a liberated liberator—Peter answers *ouk eimi:* "I am not."

This has been the problem with Christianity ever since. It is rare that we have failed to recognize the divine nature of Jesus; it is much more common that we have failed to recognize **our own.** Jesus' primary mission as the son of God was to convince us that we, too, are daughters and sons of God … and should not deny it by how we live and how we treat each other.

John 18:28-40

Jesus was taken from Caiaphas and the Jewish authorities to Pilate, the Roman governor. John wants us all to be clear that the Jews and the Romans shared responsibility for killing Jesus. Although it would be hard to disagree with that, when read in our modern context, John's writings sound anti-Semitic, and his words have certainly been used to justify anti-Semitism, I'm not so sure that was John's intent. Granted, he was a part of a time when the early Church felt oppressed and persecuted first by Jewish leaders and then by Roman officials. However, when seen in a larger context, I think John's message is true: the conflagration of religion and a militarized state was, and is, deadly to Jesus.

Americans have an easier time seeing the perils of co-mingling a military-state and religion when we look at fundamentalist Islamic countries. However, for minorities, women, lesbian, gay, bisexual and transgender people, and others, fundamentalist Christianity has had an oppressive effect on this country. You don't need me to cite examples, but it is always helpful to remember that, whether it is ancient Jewish authorities, radically fundamentalist Muslims, or right-wing televangelists and pastors, the compassion, inclusion and justice of Jesus is never well served when religion uses the state to advance their purposes.

So, maybe John wasn't being anti-Semitic or even anti-Roman. Maybe he was just inviting us to see what happens to Jesus in the hands of those in power. This is true whether the power is military, religious or economic. Jesus' truth has never suffered more than it has at the hands of the modern American religion: Capitalism. When the choice is between protecting profit or God's creation, Jesus almost always dies. If we have to decide between paying more taxes or health care for the poor, then Jesus and his values must go. We claim to follow Jesus, who was homeless, but turn our heads and hearts away from those sleeping on the streets. Our capitalistic values once again nail the homeless Jesus to the cross.

Was John anti-Semitic and anti-Roman? Is my rhetoric anti-American? Perhaps, or perhaps we both are simply calling people of faith to challenge their assumptions about the powers and principalities that rule our land. Judaism, Rome, America, Christianity and even Capitalism are not evil, per se. However, every time we defend their values over the values of compassion, mercy and justice, Jesus gets betrayed.

Jesus' trial before Pilate is staged as a one-act play with seven scenes. It begins outside between Pilate and "the Jews" (18:29-32), and then moves inside with just Pilate and Jesus. (18:33-38) Pilate goes back out to face "the Jews" and tell them what he has found. (18:38-40) He then has Jesus scourged in a scene between Jesus and the soldiers. (19:1-3) Jesus is returned to Pilate who brings him, pitiable and bleeding, back to "the Jews." And so it goes …

John does not want to let the Roman governor off the hook, showing him to be a person without integrity or courage, but it is clear in John's version of the story where the real blame lies. Again, this all can be understood as being anti-Semitic, but perhaps John's real intent was to show us that Jesus suffers more because of the dominant religion than because of the secular state. In fact, the point is that the dominant religion's manipulation and fear-mongering with the state is what ultimately drove Jesus' crucifixion. Pilate was complicit because he did what was popular and expedient, not what was right. Pilate decided on behalf of the majority, rather than stand with an innocent who was wrongfully accused.

Having watched religion manipulate the state in this country, Israel and Islamic nations, I'm not sure it is "the Jews" whom John is criticizing. Democracy is a great form of government, but the outcry of the religious and political right against "activist judges" has left the courts, like Pilate, afraid to stand against the tyranny of the majority. The mob rule of our day has made it acceptable for hundreds, if not thousands, of innocent people to spend years in prison and, perhaps, even be executed so that we can feel safe. The crowd cried out for security and revenge, and American jets rained destruction on innocents in two countries labeling them "collateral damage."

Crucifixion is a violent act of the State supported by a dominant fear-based religion. That was what John described. In his situation, the state was Rome and the dominant fear-based religion was Judaism. Would he write today about Iran, Iraq or Afghanistan? Or would it be closer to home?

Lest we feel a bit smug because we aren't supporters of violence, war or fear-based religion, mybe we should wonder just who would play Pilate in John's modern Gospel. Whose cowardly silence allows the crucifixion of innocents today?

John 19:16-37

This has been a heavy week. It is only fair, though, that we spend some seriously introspective time with the death of the innocent and compassionate.

This passage begins with the words, "Finally Pilate handed Jesus over to them to be crucified." The word "finally" is spoken as a soft defense of Pilate. He tried. He tried several times to find a way out of this for himself and Jesus. Oh, sure, John reports Pilate's cowardice born of self-preservation, but at least he tried, just not hard enough. We like to think that *trying* to do justice counts for something. We want to believe that *wanting* to do the right thing earns us some points. Oh, sure, in the end, we all have to "look out for number one," but we wanted it all to be different. Still, finally, in the end, we hand Jesus over and live pretty much like everyone else. It isn't our fault **they** crucified him. It isn't our fault the values of compassion and the vision of love he came to bring die on a hillside of practicality.

We've heard this story of Jesus' betrayal, denial, torture and death so often that it seems like a far away event of history with no antecedent in our own lives. Preachers told us that Jesus died for our sins as if that made it all worth it. Many of us believe that Jesus HAD to die so that God could forgive us, love us, reclaim us. What arrogance. It is as if we somehow had the power to keep God from loving, forgiving, reclaiming whomever God decided to love.

Dominant religion convinced us that we were so horrible the only way God could love us was for a compassionate and innocent soul to be betrayed, denied and tortured to death. Oh, I know some Biblical writers seemed to make us think that, but, in the end, I believe we have to choose between what we believe about the Bible and what we believe about God. We can't simply "hand over" our faith to what even the best preachers told us. We cannot simply acquiesce to what event the Bible tells us. Ultimately, we have to decide what is right.

As for me, I do not believe your sin or mine is so horrendous that it prevented God from loving us. I don't believe the most horrendous sins in the world have the power to change the nature of God. Ultimately, I believe God's nature is love. Jesus' death was the result of religion that couldn't trust that. Every time we support state-sponsored violence, or give our hearts over to fear, we hand over the God of love about whom Jesus came to teach, the God whose love Jesus was willing to die to convince us of.

In recounting the events of the crucifixion, John follows a pattern similar to the Synoptic Gospels, though there is one vignette that is unique to John. In this account alone, Jesus looks down from the cross and sees his mother. Standing beside her is "the disciple whom he loved." (John 19:28) Jesus appears to give his mother to this disciple's care and him to hers. Given the traditional understanding of Jesus' age at the time of his death, Mary may have been a woman in her mid-to-late 40s. Joseph was dead, and, as the eldest son, Jesus was responsible for his mother. Although Roman Catholics deny this, the Gospels seem to indicate that Mary had other children after Jesus. So it is strange that Jesus commends her to "the disciple whom he loved."

This phrase is used three times in the Gospel of John. In the end, it is used to identify the author of the Gospel. As a result, tradition has held that John, the author of this Gospel, was the beloved disciple who stood at the foot of the cross with Mary. It is a beautiful tradition, even if later scholars find it less than credible.

I have read this story most of my life, but, as the eldest son and a gay man with a partner whom I love, my reading is probably different now. I have younger brothers, but, if something were to happen to me, I can well see me saying to the man that I love, "Take care of my mother." Now, am I saying that Jesus and John were romantic partners? No, but I am saying that reading this passage through my own personal experience gives me a different understanding and feeling for this moment.

It often is said that we read the Bible through the lens of our own faith, experience and understanding. That is certainly true, but not always. As someone who grew up thinking there was something wrong with me because I am gay, it took a long, long time before I was able to read the scripture to that part of who I am. Today, I have no need to make Jesus and John romantic lovers; however, I also do not find anything wrong with that possibility. Ultimately, that may be the test of how much homophobia I cling to, or clings to me.

In the end, Jesus asked the disciple that he loved—whatever that means—to step in and care for his mother. It is a painfully tender human moment, an act of human love. It is also a more divine act than any miracle ever attributed to Jesus. If God is love then we are never closer to the divine than when we love, whatever the form that love takes. Perhaps Jesus wasn't taking care of Mary; maybe he was taking care of John.

John 19:28-30

---

*When Jesus knew that all was now **finished**, he said (in order to fulfill the scripture), "I am thirsty." A jar full of sour wine was standing there. So they put a sponge full of the wine on a branch of hyssop and held it to his mouth. When Jesus had received the wine, he said, "It is **finished**." Then he bowed his head and gave up his spirit.*

The Greek word that is translated "finished" twice in this passage might better be understood as "complete." It is the word of a painter who, after putting the final stroke on a canvas, steps back and beholds her masterpiece, and pronounces it, "Complete."

These are not the words of an innocent man being wrongly executed by the state. Rather, they are the words of one who has done absolutely everything in his power, given all he had to give, wrung out ever last drop of possibility, and now gives his spirit back to God.

Will it be enough? Will people actually change their minds about who God is? Will his disciples be able to carry the gospel—the good news—to people who consider that the way God regards them is bad news? Will his tortured death even be enough to convince people of how absolutely they are loved? Jesus didn't know. He couldn't know because the verdict is still out.

We still don't know if humankind is able to bear grace. A world that believed in a God of relentless and unconditional love would look very different from our world. Such a world would be free of the greed and competition that results in simultaneous epidemics of obesity and starvation. If even those who own the label Christian believed Jesus' message of good news, almost all wars would cease because our generosity and compassion would be an antidote to the resentment and hatred and fear that gives rise to violence between the haves and have-nots.

Perhaps more basically, the verdict is still out on our lives. Are you and I capable of genuinely allowing ourselves to be loved and accepted unconditionally with nothing to prove or disprove? What would the human life look like if it were lived by one who fully believed they were completely loved? So far, we have only Jesus as an example of such a life. Perhaps if you and I can move toward that ideal we, too, can come to the end, put on the finishing strokes, and proclaim, "Finished!"

With his last breath, Jesus declared his love for his own and for God was "complete." Wouldn't that be a great way for any of us to end our journey?

John then goes on to tell the familiar story of how the approach of sunset and Sabbath prompted the Jewish leaders to put an end to the crucifixion scene. Thus the Roman soldiers broke the legs of the two who were crucified with Jesus so they would be unable to push themselves upwards to breath. Suffocation. However, when they came to Jesus they saw he already appeared to be dead and thrust a spear in his side and blood and water flowed out.

This detail of the ending is not recounted in the Synoptic Gospels, so we might assume that John is offering this as a sacred sign of some truth. John quotes the First Testament scriptures as a prophecy that none of the Messiah's bones would be broken but he would be pierced in the side.

In Matthew's Gospel this convoluted fulfillment of scripture would be sufficient reason to report this story. That is not the case for John, however. John began by placing the life of Jesus in the larger context of the Creating Logos of God. Here the blood and water are no doubt a reminder by John of the sacraments of the rituals already held sacred by the time this Gospel was written. In the waters of baptism, we are joined to the life of Jesus, and, in the sacrament of the Eucharistic meal, we are nourished for the journey by the death (and, as we will see, resurrection) of Jesus.

It is also a reminder of the opening images of the Gospel in which John the Baptizer's role is to point to Jesus and proclaim, "Behold the lamb of God who takes away the sins of the world." (John 1:29) Here, Jesus is depicted clearly as the ultimate Passover lamb, sacrificed once and for all for the sins of the world. It would be arrogant of us to forget that, while we do not find sacrificial atonement appealing in our day, Jesus did not live in our day and John was not writing in or to our day. For John and for his readers, Jesus' sacrificial death, and the blood that was spilled that day, was the new sign of the "Passover of the Lord" and an invitation to a new exodus to true freedom and a new promised land.

John 19:38-42

So the lifeless body of Jesus is taken down from the cross. While the women have been the faithful ones, standing by Jesus even through the violence of his execution, John wants us to see the faces of two men. They are not the former fishermen Peter or James or John; they are two wealthy closet disciples of Jesus.

Joseph of Arimathea is named by all four Gospels as the man who went to Pilate to obtain permission to remove and bury Jesus' body. He was accompanied by Nicodemus who, earlier in the Gospel, visited Jesus at night, and to whom Jesus said, "You must be born again/from above." Both of these men were from the upper crust—wealthy, influential, religious insiders who secretly believed in Jesus but now come out of that closet to take the body of Jesus and bury it in style. Joseph gives a tomb, and Nicodemus brings enough spice to anoint ten bodies.

John clearly wants us to respect and admire the faith and courage of these two men, but I have to confess that I have a tough time. Oh, as always, we must acknowledge that we don't know the whole story. Jesus actually may have asked these closeted disciples not to use their power or influence to change the course of events. He may have told them that, despite their wealth and influence, as one of the Jewish Leaders, the events about to unfold were inevitable. John certainly doesn't want us to think badly of them. Perhaps they later became leaders in the early church … but still …

To have power but not use it to stop the abuse of an innocent person; or to have a voice and not raise it in the face of obvious injustice; or to claim to be a disciple of Jesus but only use your wealth for the corpse, sounds altogether like the putrid discipleship that passes as modern American Christianity. The American Church is powerful but utterly silent as drones bring silent death to Iraqi and Afghani children. The American Church has a significant voice, but it is rarely raised against the injustices done by a racist judicial system or prison industry. We American Christians spend our money to wrap the dead body of Jesus in beauty, but do not use our wealth to feed, clothe or educate God's poorest children.

I remain unpersuaded by John that Joseph and Nicodemus deserve my admiration for their postmortem courage and generosity. What I am convinced of, though, is that the death of Jesus obviously changed these two men, and my prayer is that it will continue to do the same for me.

Today we come to the resurrection of Jesus. It is unfortunate that, in both John's writing and in mine, chapter 19 ends with Jesus' burial and chapter 20 begins with the resurrection. In a very real sense, we need to sit with the death of hope for a while.

The tradition is three days, because, well, that is what Jesus said it would be. He used Jonah being in the belly of the well as a sign of how long it would take for resurrection to take hold. Of course, we all understand the story of Jonah and the whale to be a parable and analogy, a sacred metaphor, but we didn't take that to be Jesus' point. Instead, we take the three days so literally that we ignore the fact that in all the Gospels Jesus was only in the grave 40 hours or so, not the 72 hours that constitute three days. According to all four Gospels, Jesus died before sunset on Friday and rose before sunrise on Sunday.

To call it the third day technically would be accurate, I suppose. However, before we move to that third day, I'd like us to spend a moment with the second day. Crowds of people observe Good Friday, and even greater crowds celebrate Easter, but what about Saturday? As a preacher, I've always found it to be an odd day. Jesus is dead. It feels wrong somehow to go to a movie … Tomorrow will be a big day, but what about today?

If I was God, it would always be cold and gloomy and rainy on that Saturday. In our part of the world, though, nature usually has already thrown off the blanket of winter and is insisting that we notice the resplendent resurrection of spring. It is hard to sit at home in the dark when the world around is celebrating. The day after a tragic and violent death the loved ones sit in numb silence. The tears have run out, though they occasionally rise up and overwhelm us without warning. You can't sleep, but you wish you had never awakened.

The light of their world had gone out. All hope was gone. They didn't know what to believe anymore. Grief left them numb, deaf and dumb. They sat in silence.

Millions have known these Saturdays of utter grief. Most of us will know them sooner or later. While I don't know what John might have done differently in the Gospel, it seems he should have left a blank page for us to stare at for a day. Only those who have known the utter silence of Saturday can fully hear the angel of hope whisper out of the darkness of the third day.

John 20:1-10

There are four Gospel accounts of the resurrection and a fifth, the oldest, found in I Corinthians 15. While they share some things in common, they are striking in their differences. We shall look at the Corinthians account in the next volume of *Liberating Word*, but, as I read it today, I was struck by the author's description of Jesus appearing to "more than 500 brothers and sisters, most of whom are still alive."

John doesn't talk about this massive appearance. In fact, none of the Gospels do, but John's account is organized by appearances. The first is to Mary Magdalene. Other accounts have others present, but, for John, Mary was the one who got up early while it was still dark and discovered the empty tomb. She ran to fetch Simon Peter and the disciple whom Jesus loved. (There is that phrase again). Mary does use the plural in John—"we don't know where they have put him"—but John doesn't tell us who the "we" was.

Simon and the *beloved disciple* set out running to the tomb, which was out on the edge of town. We do not know whether it was because of his youth or because of his love, but, as John notes, the *beloved disciple* outruns Peter and gets to the tomb first. He looks in and finds it empty, but when Peter runs up he is true to character and busts right into the empty tomb. Peter notes the carefully arranged burial clothes. Finally the *beloved disciple* went in and saw the tomb empty. Neither of them knew what had happened but the *beloved disciple* "saw and believed."

The author is making the claim of being the first believer for the *beloved disciple*, though Mary will be the first to see the risen Christ according to this account. According to the account in I Corinthians the risen Christ appeared first to Cephas (Simon Peter). Hence, we have three claimants to being first.

What is so amazing is that the early Church felt no need to reconcile these various accounts. Unlike modern fundamentalists, there is no insistence on inerrancy or infallibility, no compulsion to make all the accounts balance like a budget. Instead, they heard all the witnesses gladly and allowed each of them to tell their story from their perspective.

Conformity and uniformity and compliance don't seem to be high values for people who have had an authentic experience with the God who is beyond anything our stories could ever capture or tell.

In most of the Christian Church (Roman Catholic, Eastern Orthodox, fundamentalist Protestant), women still are not deemed worthy to be pastors or priests. Nothing could be further from the testimony of the Gospels or the gospel. The four Gospels disagree about many of the details of the Resurrection narrative, but the one thing they are consistently clear about is that the first witnesses were the women disciples. Peter (whose descendent the Pope claims to be) ran to the tomb, but the risen Christ did not appear to him. The disciple Jesus loved was on the scene but saw no evidence of resurrection. According to John, it is to Mary alone that Jesus appears, and the risen Christ personally commissions her to be his first witness. Hers is the name he spoke, and it is she who says, "I have seen the Lord!"

In mainline Protestant churches, where soon a majority of pastors will be women, we are so accustomed to hearing the gospel proclaimed by a woman's voice that we sometimes fail to call sexism sin. We are prone to be silent when other traditions exclude women from their leadership, politely agreeing to disagree. The trouble with our silence is that it sanctions an insidious tradition that denigrates both women and the feminine. It also dismisses the witness of the gospel, which makes explicit Jesus' choice.

While this may seem tangential to this passage, it holds a crucial truth. The word of hope represented by the resurrection has, from the start, found as its most profound witnesses the voices of the oppressed and marginalized. While significant progress has been made in combating overt sexism during modern times, the fact that the Church remains a bastion of this prejudice is evidence that we still miss the point.

Resurrection not only speaks to those in our society who have been forced to the margins by the dominant culture and those who dominate culture, but the authentic witness of resurrection comes from those whose voices have been historically excluded, discounted or silenced. Mary, a woman from Magdala, was not allowed to own property or enter the inner courts of the temple, but all four Gospels name her as the first witness of resurrection. Perhaps if the Church took its own stories more seriously we might experience true resurrection more fully.

John 20:19-23

On the morning of the first day of the week, the risen Christ was revealed to Mary Magdalene, and she goes to tell the others, "I have seen the Lord." We are not told by John how the other disciples reacted to this witness. "Could it be true?" "Is Mary crazy?" "Why would she say such a thing?" "Wouldn't Jesus have come to us if he were alive?" We don't know what they thought or said.

Mary makes her discovery and tells her story Easter morning in verse 18. Then, in verse 19, John describes a completely different scene by noting that this takes place on the evening of that day.

The disciples are gathered behind locked doors "for fear of the Jews." Despite what might be identified as John's anti-Semitism, an atmosphere of fear is probably an accurate description. I sometimes wonder, though, if John misdiagnosed the source of the fear. In the darkness of early morning, they were bold enough to run to the empty tomb without being afraid of "the Jews." Now they cower behind locked doors. Are they afraid of the Jews, or are they afraid of the Risen Christ?

Resurrection, by-and-by, is a pleasant enough idea, but the idea that the Risen Christ is loosed among us is another story entirely. Did they doubt Mary's witness, or are they hiding because they believed her? Then, despite locked doors and sealed windows, on the evening of the first day of the week as they gathered together, "Jesus came and stood among them."

Twice Jesus greets them with the phrase "Peace be with you." That phrase has become a common greeting of the church, but, in that moment, Jesus obviously is speaking it to some troubled folks. To make this point, John records him saying it, showing them his hands and side, and then saying it again.

In the reality of faith, there is the disturbance that we feel in the face of fears and doubts, and there is the disturbance we feel in the challenging presence of the Risen Christ. Sometimes it is easier to grieve loss and death than it is to face the challenge to live again.

John 20:21-23

The second book of Luke, which is known as Acts, tells the story of the early Church beginning on the Day of Pentecost. That version has shaped how Christianity understands its birth. Mark and Matthew have no such story of the coming of the Spirit to the disciples, and, in one verse, we have the Gospel of John's total description of how that happened.

For John, there is no elaborate story of the coming of the spirit 50 days after the death of Jesus. Instead, what he describes is how the disciples learned to live with Jesus in a whole new way. When they gathered, he suddenly would be there with them. Even when they gathered in fear behind shuttered windows and locked doors, suddenly, the risen Christ was present.

In this verse, Christ blesses them and sends them out. Before they go, he breathes on them and says, "Receive the Holy Spirit," and apparently they did. There is no fire or mysterious other languages. Instead, Jesus breaths his Spirit on them in a manner reminiscent of Genesis in which God breathes into humanity and they became a living being. (Gen. 2:7) Here, Jesus breathes into his disciples, and they are empowered to spread divine forgiveness on the earth.

The verse about "forgiving" and "retaining" is complicated and even more convoluted in the original texts. It uses language that is otherwise foreign to John, and scholars have suggested that a separate writing from some other teaching has been inserted here. It reflects a passage found in Matthew in which Jesus said, "What you loose on earth is loosed in heaven and what you bind on earth is bound in heaven." There, too, that teaching is linked to Jesus' saying that "where two or more are gathered in my name, there am I in the midst of them."

Clearly the message is that when we gather together the risen Christ is among us, empowering us with his own spirit to do the work that he did. The passage implies a spiritual authority that the Church too often consigned to priests or, in our day, to therapists.

Jesus' presence empowers us to bring forgiveness to people. All that this means is unclear, but I often have seen that we have more power than we generally assume to set people free by pronouncing them forgiven. Conversely, by our shaming of others, we have bound them as well. If we are living with the breath of Jesus on our lips, I suppose we must ask, "Just whose sin would Jesus refuse to forgive?"

John 20:24-29

This passage about Jesus appearing to Thomas is quite well known since it is read every year on the Sundays following Easter. The preceding passage makes note of the fact that Thomas was missing when Jesus appeared that first night and, when they told him what had happened, he refused to believe without proof. It isn't until a week later that they again are gathered in the house, and, this time, Thomas is with them. Jesus appears again.

John offers us this pattern of the early disciples gathering on the first day of the week and Jesus coming to be with them. Jesus does not repeat the breathing exercise, even though Thomas missed it. What he does do is offer Thomas the signs that he said he needed in order to believe. All that Jesus ever did in John's Gospel was considered a sign, so it is not unusual that, even now, Jesus offers a skeptic a sign so that he might believe. Thomas' response—"My Lord and my God"—is the affirmation that the entire Gospel of John is seeking to illicit from every reader. In the book of Acts, "Jesus is Lord" is offered as the first and primary affirmation of faith in the early Church. John, however, began with his Logos poem arguing on behalf of the divinity of Jesus. Here, at the end, Thomas is the final witness to that divinity.

Thomas believes, but Jesus notes, "Because you have seen you have believed, but blessed are those who have not seen yet have come to believe." Writing as he is to those who live decades after the events, this affirmation was important to John. Those who have never seen Jesus are given a special blessing because they, too, have affirmed that Jesus is the incarnation of the Logos/Word of God and that he is the Lord of their life. In this verse, John's Gospel gets to the point of all he has written. Until now, every story and every teaching has been offered to illicit faith from his readers who never saw Jesus nor touched him. Thomas is called a doubter, but that word is not used by John. Rather, this event is described by John as the moment when Thomas went from unbelief to believing. That is John's purpose. He has written all of this that we, too, even though we have never seen Jesus in the flesh, might declare him to be our Lord and our God.

As for me, I believe there are many paths to God and many legitimate revelations for God. I have no need to dismiss or discount them and no need to argue with them. However, the better I have come to know Jesus, the more I affirm that THIS is the God I believe in.

John 20:30-31

Now Jesus did many other signs in the presence of his disciples, which are not written in this book. But these are written so that you may come to believe that Jesus is the Messiah, the Son of God, and that through believing you may have life in his name.

Here we come to the conclusion of the Gospel of John, but not to the end. In two short verses, John tells why he wrote this. The trouble, of course, is that there is another chapter and another appearance story to go.

There is also an addendum in Mark, but, unlike that Gospel, most scholars find John chapter 21 to be in a style and language consistent with the writing of the rest of the book. It also has a similar conclusion to these verses. You can read whole books that hypothesize about why John has two conclusions. I read five commentaries and found eight or nine different explanations. Frankly, I think they are all trying too hard.

In my own writings and preaching, there are times when I, too, have more than one conclusion. I often have finished a work, only to sleep and remember a story I should have told. The 21st chapter of John is essentially an epilogue that appears to have been added after John thought he was done.

In these verses, John leaves the role of storyteller and steps to the edge of the stage to look directly at the reader and explain explicitly what he has been trying to do. He again uses the word "signs," noting that Jesus did many others that were not written in this book. Perhaps he is referring to the miracles and teachings that one might find in one of the other Gospels, which had been written before this one. John no doubt knows of the existence of at least one of those Gospels but is not using it as a pattern, which is why this work is so different from the synoptics.

In fact, John tells us here why he has written. He isn't a biographer or a historian but an apologist writing **so that** the reader might come to believe that "Jesus is the Christ/Messiah, the Son of God." John offered 20 chapters of "signs" as proof.

Unlike modern bestselling authors, John made no money, so far as we know, from his writings. Rather, in this final verse, he tells us why he wrote and why we should believe. John is convinced that by believing we might find life in Jesus' name. Note he doesn't say "eternal life." For John, Jesus came that we might "have life and have it abundantly" starting now.

John 21:1-14

The final post-resurrection appearance that John describes is found in this, the last, chapter, following what appeared to be the conclusion of the book. It begins with the words, "After these things, Jesus showed himself again to the disciples by the sea of Tiberias." It generally is believed that this chapter was a later addition. The disagreement among scholars is over whether the addition was by the same author or a later editor. Nothing in the style or language precludes it from being the same source, and it is in all the oldest and most reliable manuscripts. So, there is no apparent reason to doubt this chapter's value to the gospel story.

What we have here is the story of one event/appearance told in two parts. The author tells us where the story happened: the sea of Tiberius, also known as the Lake Gennesaret and the Sea of Galilee. Then, the characters in the story are named: Simon Peter; Thomas, called the Twin; Nathanael of Cana in Galilee; the sons of Zebedee (James and John); and two other disciples. Seven all total, and, given the author's obsession with signs, we must assume the number is actually more important than the names. Seven means completion, and, with this sign, Jesus completes his ministry and the author completes the book.

Besides Jesus, Simon Peter is the major player in this story. It is Simon who, apparently out of the blue, declares that he is going fishing. Now, this is not a recreational fishing trip. The naming of these specific disciples is a reminder that fishing is what they were doing when Jesus first called most of them. It was their vocation in life away from which Jesus called them.

The fact that Simon announces he is ready to go back to his old life is important, not to mention that the others are so eager to join him. Perhaps this is why this story was told. The resurrection seems to us to be this cataclysmic event, as indisputable as the sunrise. However, the Gospels describe it with more ambiguity. Mary mistakes Jesus for the gardener. Two disciples walk all the way to Emmaus and don't recognize him. Thomas reflects their ambiguity, declaring that he needs to see the scars left from the crucifixion.

Even these first disciples seem to be uncertain and are required to exercise faith. These seven seem to think the fishing they know is more comfortable than the faith they are not sure of. Like us, it seems that, while God requires faith, they desired certainty.

John 21:1-14

Seven of the disciples went fishing. Then, just after daybreak, Jesus made an appearance walking along the shore. The disciple's boat is about 100 yards out in the lake—too far to recognize Jesus, but close enough to hear him when he asked if they'd caught anything. They had not, so he suggested they cast their nets on the other side. Then they caught so many that they could barely haul in the net.

This fishing story is almost identical to one told in Luke 5:1-11. The disciples' failure to recognize Jesus also is reflected in Luke 24:16, in which, describing the disciples who walked with Jesus to Emmaus, Luke wrote, "Their eyes were kept from recognizing Jesus." Those disciples' eyes were opened when Jesus gave thanks and broke the bread. Here in John, recognition comes when the fishers catch more than they can haul in. Far be it from me to spiritualize upon these stories, but it is an interesting contrast that, in one, recognition comes in the sacrament of gratitude (Eucharist), and, in the other, in a moment of abundant provision. Clearly, modern Christians are much more prone to recognize the hand of God when life abundantly blesses us than we are in humble gratitude for daily bread. The risen Christ is present for both if we only have eyes to see.

In John's story, "the disciple who Jesus loved" was the one who recognized Jesus, and he told Simon Peter. Peter, of course, sprang into action. Wrapping his outer garment around himself, Peter flung himself into the sea and swam to shore. The other disciples followed, dragging the nets, which were too full to lift into the boat.

Then they covered the 100 yards to shore, and the author notes that there were 153 fish in the nets. It has been argued that this level of detail is an indication that the author was an eyewitness, one of the seven fishers. However, it is more likely that the number held some symbolic significance to the author. It was "a sign." What exactly it was a sign of has been debated by the Church almost since the beginning. Augustine had a rather elaborate mathematical explanation, but the ancient Jerome simply explains that, in that day, they believed there were 153 different kinds of fish. Under Jesus' guidance, they caught them all.

This is a Pentecost moment in John. When describing that day, Luke has a long list of nations, some of which were long extinct. Both authors, writing to those prone to make the Church exclusive, remind us that, from the start, inclusion was the core value of Jesus.

John 21:12-25

When the disciples arrived on shore, pulling their inclusive catch of fish behind them, they discovered a charcoal fire burning already with fish and bread cooking on it. What a remarkable picture: the disciples come to shore to find the risen Christ has cooked them breakfast. Jesus tells them to bring some of the fish they have caught and, together, they will have a feast. It is difficult to tell if it is meant to be meaningful that Jesus doesn't just provide breakfast but also uses the fish they had caught. It may be just a device by which John again makes a point about the great number of fish that were caught. Then, verse 12 says:

> *Jesus said to them, "Come and have breakfast." Now none of the*
> *disciples dared to ask him "Who are you?" because they knew it*
> *was the Lord.*

Here, again, we have a strange statement about Jesus' appearance. The author is writing decades after these events took place, but even then there appeared to be some confusion and ambiguity of how they took place. More liberal theologians suggest that these are not literal appearances of the reanimated corpse of Jesus of Nazareth. Rather, in the days following his death, people came among the disciples offering them words of hope and encouragement, reminding them of whom Jesus had been. Hence the resurrected body of disciples became the Risen Body of Christ.

However, that isn't the author of John's understanding, because he describes the corpse of Jesus offering his scars as signs to Thomas. Yet, even John cannot escape that something different is going on here. "None of them dares ask him, 'Who are you'," but clearly they wanted to or there was some reason for them to. Beside the lake they had an encounter with the risen Christ, but it was clearly different from their encounters with the mortal Jesus by this same lake.

John says that this is the third resurrection appearance. Others are described in Luke and Matthew, but, in John, this is the third and final appearance. Here by the lake, doing the work they had done all their life, in the afterglow of success, they share a feast and Jesus is there. It is a rhythm of life and living into which we are all invited. Work, times with family and friends, feasting on good food … Jesus is present, making it all so beautiful and sacred.

In verse 13, John notes that "Jesus came and took bread and gave it to them and he did the same with the fish." It is almost a Eucharistic moment. If Jesus' last supper on the night of his death really had been his last, the Church likely would have commemorated that meal only once a year at Passover, or perhaps on Maundy Thursday. However, in the resurrection appearances in the Gospels, it seems that every time the disciples gathered and broke bread the risen Christ was there.

The church has made communion/Eucharist/the Lord's Supper so much about that last meal that it has lost the resurrection message of the feast. It is both a meal of promise and a meal of presence. "Where two or more are gathered I will be there," Jesus said. At the table, the people who have recognized they are all children of God gather. We are in communion with one another, with the saints who have gone before us and surround us as "a great cloud of witnesses," and with the Risen Christ.

There at the lake, the Risen Christ broke bread with the disciples. Then, Christ questions Simon Peter as their leader and the one who instigated this fishing trip, though perhaps he is questioning them all. "Simon son of John do you love me more than these?" There is great debate over what that question really means. Was Christ asking Peter if he loved him more than the other disciples loved him? Was Christ asking Peter if he loved him more than he loved his fisher friends? Or did Jesus point to the fish, the nets, the boat, the lake, the life Simon Peter had always known and ask Peter if he loved Christ above that life?

No one actually knows what the question means, but it is asked three times. Three times Peter affirms his love for Christ. Perhaps John doesn't want the reader's last memory of Peter to be his three-fold denial the night of Jesus' arrest. Without this story, one might assume that it was because of that denial that the risen Christ first appeared to Mary rather than to Peter. Here, the resurrected Christ resurrects Simon Peter by allowing him to affirm his love for him AND then assigning him a new vocation: "If you love me feed my sheep."

The Risen Christ comes to us in our work and love and times of feasting and restores us from the failures of our past. Then He assigns us His unfinished work to do. In John 10, Jesus describes himself as the "good shepherd." Now, to flawed and failed disciples for whom he laid down his life, the Risen Christ gives his life's work. To the life of Peter, and to you and me, has been given a divine mission and meaning.

John 21:20-25

So, after feeding Peter bread and fish, and reminding him that his life was to be more than fishing, Jesus ends by looking Peter in the eye and saying, at the end as he had at the beginning, "Follow me." It is the consummate call to us all. Our lives are to follow the teaching and the model of the life of Jesus.

It felt too much for Simon Peter. He spotted the "disciple whom Jesus loved," and asked, "What about him? What will he do?" Jesus replied, "What business is it of yours if I want him to live until I return? You follow me." There is so very much for disciples to learn from that exchange, but you don't need me to remind you of the lessons we all spend a lifetime learning. Comparison, deflection and projection have been the disciple's tools of evasion since the beginning.

The author goes on to say that, because of this statement by Jesus, the rumor went around that the "disciple Jesus loved" would not die until Christ returned. In the very next verse, the author identifies himself as that "disciple whom Jesus loved." This might have come as a shock to the original reader, but an effort clearly has been made all along to indicate that the author was an eyewitness of this account.

This Gospel wasn't written before the end of the first century, and, though it is possible that one of the original 12 wrote it, "the disciple whom Jesus loved" would have to have been a very young man who lived a long time. So, "the disciple whom Jesus loved" ends this story with a beautiful stroke of hyperbole that sounds just like something a loved one might write about a beloved:

> *But there are many other things that Jesus did; if every one of them were written down I suppose the world itself could not contain the books that would be written.*

Jesus lived only a short life, so this statement can be forgiven as an exaggeration of love or … Perhaps the author is thinking of the Risen Body of Christ made up of people from every tribe and tongue. If all the good the Body of Christ has done over the centuries was written down, one wonders if the whole world could hold the books. Perhaps John was thinking of Jesus … or perhaps he was thinking of YOU. What good have you done today in the name of Jesus that John might write down?

Acts

Tradition holds that the books of Luke and Acts were written by the same person. That person has been identified traditionally as Luke, a Gentile physician and early member of the Church. Although Luke appears in this second volume by name, and several passages are written in the first person as though he were a participant, Luke would not have known the historic Jesus. Again, traditionalists date the writing of the Gospel to somewhere between A.D. 64 and 72. More liberal scholars have argued against these traditions, but they have no more evidence to dispute them than the conservatives do to hold them up as facts. Suffice it to say that we don't know if tradition is true or not, and neither belief adds to or detracts from the importance and value of this work.

Almost all of what we know about the earliest Church is recorded here in Acts. It is regrettable that, unlike the Gospels, we don't have more than one voice telling the story and offering a different view. We have Acts and glimpses of corroborating and conflicting views in some of the Epistles. In the end, as with the life of Jesus, we must gather what information we can find, weigh its value and meaning, and, finally, make a judgment by faith.

The full title given to this book is usually "The Acts of the Apostles." Since the work didn't name itself, the title was assigned to it much later. The book begins with a story of the ascension of Jesus, and it ends when Paul is imprisoned in Rome. Again, tradition holds that Luke wrote this book during the two years that Paul spent in prison in Rome and that is therefore where the story ends. It also tells us that Luke himself died shortly after Paul did.

The story covers the first couple of decades of the movement we know as Christianity. What is reported is an evolution of early leadership. Simon Peter takes the initiative on the day of Pentecost, and he is the main character for several chapters. The last half of the story is told through the eyes of Paul. Some have suggested that the book should be called, more accurately, "The Acts of Peter and Paul." The truth is that most of history is a record of the acts of certain individuals. Have you ever thought about how your history would read if it only recorded your acts, not your thoughts or words?

Acts 1:1-5

The Church's understanding of the end of Jesus' earthly time and the beginning of the Church as the risen Body of Christ is based almost entirely on the narrative of Luke.

In Matthew, after a very brief resurrection account, Jesus appears on a mountain and commissions his disciples to go and make disciples and baptize them. He promises to be with them always. The end. Mark's Gospel ends so abruptly, and without any appearance of the risen Christ, that an additional ending was added that appears in most versions of the Bible. In John the transition from the physically-present Jesus to the spiritually-present risen Christ is told in a series of appearance stories. Time and again, the disciples gathered, often around food, and, suddenly, Christ was there. At one gathering behind closed doors, Jesus appears and breathes on them, and they receive the Holy Spirit.

This version of the giving of the Spirit is radically different from the one we will encounter from Luke in the book of Acts. Luke's version won the imagination of the Church and has come to be regarded as the factual version of what happened. In addition, Luke's version of the ultimate transition of Jesus also has been accepted as factual. The ascension is described only by Luke. Nothing like that happens in the other three Gospels. In John the conclusion is that Jesus' mysterious appearances simply ceased and the disciples got on with the work.

All of this is to say that, while the version of events we are about to study have been accepted as factual history, in the place where they overlap with the other Gospels, the story isn't nearly so black-and-white. The importance is to remind us that we are reading scripture, not a history textbook. Luke is recounting stories that he says right at the start have been "handed down." (Luke 1:2) The source of the stories, how he retells them, and which stories he chooses to tell all reflect the author's own faith and intent. Some of the stories may be an accurate factual recounting of events. Many will be spiritualized memories. Still others may be purely parables. Although written as history, we must "listen for the Word of God" here. Even if it were 100 percent accurate history, the value of this study still rests in allowing the Spirit to speak to our lives.

Acts 1:1-5

In the first book, Theophilus, I wrote about all that Jesus did and taught from the beginning until the day when he was taken up to heaven, after giving instructions through the Holy Spirit to the apostles whom he had chosen.

The Book of Acts begins with a reference to the author's "first book." This, of course, is a reference to the Gospel of Luke. Like that volume, Acts is addressed to "Theophilus." In Luke the apparent title "most excellent" is added, but that is absent here. The Greek term *"theo philus"* obviously means "God lover." Without the title in the first volume, this word no doubt would have been translated here "Christian Reader" or something similar. The phrase "most excellent" is used three times later in Acts (23:26, 24:3 and 26:25), and, each time, the author is referring to a high-ranking official.

Acts begins by defining the first volume as an account of what Jesus "did and taught" from his birth until his ascension. Although the text does not offer this, it could be said that the second volume—Acts—is an account of what Jesus "did and taught" through his disciples and theirs.

While the Book of Acts pretty carefully follows the sequence that can be found in Paul's major Epistles (Romans and I & II Corinthians), Luke doesn't make the assertion as Paul did that the Church is the Body of Christ. Since these Epistles clearly predate Acts, that is a remarkable omission. I believe the result of that omission has shaped the self-understanding of the church.

The reason Acts doesn't start with this idea is to be found in the various heresies that were being combated in that day. For early Christians, the physical body of Jesus was of critical importance because various Greek heresies considered our bodies inferior to our spirits. Hence John began insisting that the "Word BECAME flesh."

Had this conflict not been present, Luke might have described more fully how the Spirit of Jesus was resurrected in the lives of his disciples and theirs. While all too human, when the Church lives consistently with the Spirit of Jesus, we become the Risen Body of Christ. Perhaps we are the physical resurrection that Jesus promised. Perhaps we avoid that understanding because it is just too much responsibility.

Acts 1:3-8

Here we have the only Biblical account outside the Gospels of an event in Jesus' life. Luke retells, in a slightly different form, the story of Jesus' ascension. He begins with verse 3, which clearly assumes the reader is familiar with the Gospel of Luke. Unlike Mark, his primary source, Luke recounts that there were many stories of appearances over the course of 40 days, and, as far as he was concerned, they were "convincing proof." The word he uses is a strong one, translated by some as "irrefutable evidence." Regardless of how we may understand the physical resurrection of Jesus, or how the earliest Gospel (Mark) may have presented it, by the time Luke came to write, half-a-century later, it was established as historic fact in the minds of believers.

So, here we have the risen Christ with his disciples for the last time … again. Luke is telling this story again, but there already has been an account of tearful goodbyes from the cross. Jesus already has spoken last words at the supper. Now what we have is a kind of epilogue to his life and death. His last instructions conveniently set up the real story that Luke is telling here: the birth of the Church. Jesus said to them, "John baptized with water, but you will be baptized with the Holy Spirit not many days from now."(v. 5) That promise in Luke's account took place on the day of Pentecost. According to John, the risen Christ breathes upon them and says "Receive the Holy Spirit" and then sends them out to forgive sins.

Before rushing past the phrase "baptized with the Holy Spirit," we should note that many denominations (Pentecostals) and a major renewal movement of the church in the 1960s and 70s (Charismatic) focus much more heavily on this promise than mainline churches. For them, the "Baptism of the Holy Spirit" is a secondary spiritual experience in the life of believers accompanied by the "gifts of the Spirit," including speaking in tongues.

This all may seem like a total mystery to many of us, but it will come back again and again in Acts and in the writings of Paul. For now, suffice it to say that Jesus' last wish was for his disciples to be totally immersed/inundated/submerged in and with the same Spirit that controlled his life. Frankly, if that would happen to us I would be willing to tolerate us all speaking in tongues now and then.

If you ever have been a teacher who spent a semester teaching a lesson, only to have a student ask a question that revealed that they hadn't heard a word you said or, if you are a parent and had a teenager say or do something completely contrary to the values you have tried for years to instill in them, you will understand what Jesus must have felt in this moment.

He had just promised the disciples that God would baptize them with the Holy Spirit, the gift of God's self with and within us. They have no interest in that whatsoever. Their question is the same one they might have asked if they had just met Jesus 10 minutes prior. There is NO evidence in the question that all of his actions, his teachings, or even his death and resurrection had penetrated their understanding of what God was doing in the world or in their lives.

If a devout Jew, just off the street, had been introduced to Jesus and told that Jesus was the Christ/Messiah, he would have asked that very question: "Is now the time when God is going to violently or magically overthrow our oppressors (Rome) and reestablish the Reign of David and the power of Israel?" All of Jesus' work and teaching apparently was wasted. They still thought he was the political/ military savior. No wonder Jesus just took off … literally, according to Luke.

Jesus could not have been blamed if he had struck them all with lightning, but he had the patience of, well, God. Jesus simply trusts that the Spirit eventually will bring them around. So, with the patience of the God of evolution, Jesus doesn't try again to teach them about the Reign (Kingdom) of God, but simply says that God's timeframe is really not their concern.

I'm glad Jesus is patient because that thing about leaving the time of the outcome to God is a lesson we still don't seem to get. If the truth be told, most of us still are secretly hoping God will magically, or even violently (Iraq, Afghanistan, capital punishment, Guantanamo …), overthrow our enemies and reward us.

The spiritual power Jesus promised just doesn't seem enough, so, rather than letting the Spirit mold us into the image of Jesus who forgave his persecutors, and everyone else who crossed his path, we claim to be his disciples and secretly still follow the ways of the world. Or maybe I am the only Christian who is secretly satisfied when a drone kills a terrorist leader (a.k.a. "a child of God").

Acts 1:8-11

You will be my witnesses in Jerusalem, Judea, Samaria, and to the ends of the earth.

Jesus promises that disciples will receive power when the Holy Spirit comes into their lives. In the verse above, he doesn't tell them to go and be witnesses, but simply informs them that they will be. When our lives are filled with the presence of God, we can't help but be living witnesses. The other amazing thing in this passage is that Luke slips in the word "Samaria." It wasn't enough for Jesus to tell them they would be his witnesses to all the world. Luke had to make note that this included people and places for which they had great prejudice. Sending them to Samaria would have been unthinkable, given the mindset of their question about Jesus re-establishing the Davidic Kingdom. They never would have normally set foot in Samaria.

One evidence that we are under the influence of the Spirit of Jesus is that prejudices and barriers we long have held simply dissolve away. The Spirit seeks to convince us all that national borders, racial differences, sexual orientations, diverse language and beliefs are ALL a distant second to the fact that we are ALL God's children. The nationalism, sense of entitlement and privilege of ancient Israel could never hold a candle to the assumptions of most Americans: We think everyone should learn to speak OUR language. We take for granted the wealth and natural resources that we have. We resent, perhaps even hate, those who dare to cross our borders seeking a better life for their children.

To us they are "Samaritans" or, at best, secondary citizens of the Realm of God. They are "them" not "us." They are "others," outsiders to be regarded with suspicion and fear. That simple word, which, Jesus slipped in almost unnoticed, is a call to us all to examine our hearts and uncover who our Samaritans are. Who is it that we regard as "other" or "less than"? What are ways in which we live as though our race or religion or national origin entitles us to a more privileged lifestyle? Who is the Spirit calling us to include in our family that might never cross our mind? These are hard questions if we are willing to be honest. Asking the questions takes courage, and changing our attitudes and lifestyle takes spiritual and emotional power. That is why Jesus promised us the Spirit. The Spirit of Jesus isn't given to make us feel better about ourselves; the Spirit of Jesus is given to us that we might be changed into a Jesus able to love those who might otherwise never cross our minds.

We have spent a long time on the first 11 verses of Acts. In part, it was to lay a foundation for what is to come. In part, it was because I wanted to avoid this scripture. Frankly, I'm just never sure what to do with this story.

When we looked at it at the end of our study of the Gospel of Luke, I talked about how Luke and his readers lived in a three-story universe: feet on the flat earth, heaven above them, and the underworld below them. In such a world, the legend of Jesus ascending "up" into heaven makes sense; not so much when you know the world is round and Jerusalem is on the side of a spinning globe.

So, we have two choices in approaching this story. We can take it as a literal fact and believe, as Luke did, that Jesus took his disciples out on a hill and, as they watched, levitated into the clouds until he was out of their sight. Then two beings dressed in white robes suddenly came up to ask them at what they were staring. Then, without waiting for an answer, they told the disciples that this same Jesus they saw taken up into heaven would return to them someday.

Our other option is to ask what this story means for those of us who live in a post-magical world. We probably should begin with sufficient humility to acknowledge that, while science has explained much that was magical for the ancients, there is still much we do not know. It would be arrogance to declare, "That didn't happen." It also would be wrong to turn off our minds when we read scriptures such as this.

For me the best approach is to affirm that, while I don't know enough to declare the story to be fictional, neither do I believe in magic. So, holding that tension, what does the story mean? For me it means that, at a certain point, the Church's understanding shifted. No longer was the risen Christ the Jesus who had been crucified, but rather the resurrected Body of Christ was the Church. Women and men who followed the way of Jesus became empowered by the same Spirit that filled Jesus, and they witnessed to the whole world that Jesus was alive because he lived in them, loved through them, and helped and healed through them.

The same Jesus who went away came again to live in and through his disciples. Now our job is to let our lives be more and more shaped by that spirit of love and life.

Acts 1:12-14

After seeing Jesus for the last time, the disciples returned to Jerusalem, which was a Sabbath day's journey from the mountain. That would be about half-a-mile since travel on the Sabbath was strictly limited. They went back to the upper room, which had become their unofficial headquarters since they had the Passover meal with Jesus there.

What is fascinating about this passage is the list of people. Actually, it is just interesting that Luke offers a list at all. Rarely are the disciples all named. Of course, although Luke deserves kudos for mentioning the fact that women were a part of this first Church Council, even he doesn't name any of them but Mary.

Luke also notes that Jesus' brothers are present. They were not disciples of Jesus and, in fact, once came with Mary to try to get Jesus to give up his foolishness and go home. Perhaps after his death they recognized who he really was and now wanted to be a part of what came next. Luke mentions them because at least one of them will be important later in the book.

Ultimately, Luke tells us that there were about 120 identified disciples of Jesus. What follows this passage is the selection of Mathias to be the successor to Judas. For Luke's purpose here he is listing the 11 remaining disciples and including Jesus' family to offer evidence that this first council was valid and legitimate. That is important because their selection is never heard from again, and it would be easy to say that the real replacement for Judas was Paul who Jesus seems to choose for himself some time later.

After a time of prayer, Mathias was chosen by casting lots, which is a traditional form of decision making, but not a deeply spiritual one. Again, the magical thinking is that God controls the game of chance. As those of us who buy lottery tickets well know, God isn't in that business.

Did the disciples make a mistake? Perhaps, or perhaps we have insufficient data to know all that Mathias went on to accomplish. In the end, they made a decision and moved on. One truth in this may be that, after we have authentically prayed about something, sometimes we just have to decide and move on and trust that if we've made the wrong choice God's work will not come to an end. Indecision sometimes does more harm than poor decisions.

In those days Peter stood up among the believers ...

With this sentence, Luke describes Peter as the de facto leader of the believers in the absence of Jesus. The way the sentence begins is meant to indicate that this didn't take place on the same day that Jesus departed but during the 10 days between the ascension and the day of Pentecost. Luke puts the number of believers gathered at about 120 people. The first item of business was replacing Judas. The number 12 was important in this still-Jewish body. There were 12 patriarchs and, therefore, 12 tribes. The Gospels all talk about the disciples who sometimes number 70 and sometimes 120, but they are clear in depicting the inner circle as 12 men.

Peter begins talking about how the scripture was fulfilled by Judas betraying Jesus. Luke puts into Peter's mouth a strange description of how Judas used the money he was paid to buy a field. Judas then "fell headlong, he burst open in the middle and all his bowels gushed out." If that sentence makes no sense, don't worry; it makes no sense in the original either. Did Judas fall in the field? Luke or Peter goes on to identify the field as *Hakeldama* or the "Field of Blood."

Matthew's version of Judas' death was quite different (27:3) from how Luke/Peter tells the story. According to Matthew, Judas saw Jesus' arrest and what was going to happen to him, and he repented. Judas took the 30 pieces of silver back to the chief priests and threw it down in the temple. He then went out and hanged himself.

Matthew rehabilitates Judas a bit, but Luke leaves him completely without hope. The Psalm Peter quotes says, "Let his homestead be desolate and let no one live in it." Then he says, "Let another take his position of overseer."

The term "overseer" is translated in some denominations as "superintendent" and in others as "bishop." All of us can translate accurately what it means to have the final words spoken about you be without redemption or hope. Judas was to be replaced as though he never existed. I've done funerals where I struggled to find something good or kind to say about the deceased. Here, his fellow disciples have nothing positive to say about Judas. They describe his death in graphic terms because they think he deserved it. There is nothing kind to say except ...

The last time Jesus saw Judas, he kissed him. Even as Judas betrayed him, Jesus kissed him.

Acts 1:21-26

They cast lots for them and the lot fell on Matthias.

As a pastor, I probably have spent more time in cemeteries than most folks. I actually like to walk around and look at the tombstones, wondering about the dash between the date of birth and the date of death. What does that little mark represent?

I think about my grandparents' graves. They were some of the most important and beloved people in my life. I will remember them as long as I live, but then what? My children didn't really know them. They could never find their graves to stand and remember who they were and all they did in their lives. My grandparents all would be more than 100 now, so all their friends are gone. When my cousins and I are gone, Nadel and Bill, and Frank and Anna will be gone, too. Someday it will be my turn to be among those remembered only as a dash between two dates.

Matthias got me thinking about all this. You see, you just read the only place where he was remembered. Luke tells the story of his selection, which was made by simply casting lots. Matthias won, and a man named Justus lost. Both apparently were qualified because they had been eyewitnesses to the resurrection of Jesus. No other qualifications were listed, but it came down to these two.

It has been argued that they picked badly because, after this, Matthias is never heard from again. Luke doesn't mention him. The Apostle Paul makes long lists of people, but Matthias is not among them. There are no reliable legends handed down about what he did or how he died. Apparently, though, they wouldn't have fared any better with Justus, because he, too, was mentioned here and then forgotten.

Some suggest that they were such a bust as apostles that Jesus himself later chose Paul to be the 12th apostle. However, I think Matthias was one of those dash people. We may not know what he did with his life, where he went, or whom he loved to the Lord. This story may be his dash—that place where he is remembered.

I am the oldest son of the oldest son, so I was fortunate to know my grandparents even when I was well grown. Today, I see them all the time in my parents and brothers and cousins. My children may never have met them, but they, too, have heard their voices and felt their love. Who their father is today is an expression of people who were, and are, much more than a dash on a tombstone in South Georgia. Don't dismiss Matthias as a dash; he was probably someone's spiritual grandparent.

Pentecost

The beginning of Acts chapter two is one of the most important stories in the Christian Church. Luke tells how the disciples got the Spirit in a much more dramatic fashion than John, who simply talked about Jesus breathing on them. This story of the Day of Pentecost is told here and only here, but it is what all Christians have come to believe about the birth of the Church.

Pentecost was a Jewish holiday also known as the Feast of Weeks, or Harvest. It falls seven weeks (a week of weeks) after Passover. So, like Passover or Easter, it is a movable feast for both Jews and Christians. It is no longer such a major festival for Jews because, after their diaspora, when the temple and Jerusalem were destroyed, harvest time changed in meaning. Pentecost, as the name implies, fell 50 days after Passover. Most Christian traditions hold that Jesus was executed at Passover. Now, 50 days have passed, and it is another holiday. Although it was not as big a holiday as Passover, Jews from all over still came to Jerusalem for the festival. It was one of three holy days when Jewish males who lived within walking distance of Jerusalem were supposed to come to the city.

As the crowds built in the city, the disciples probably were reliving the tragic and traumatic events that took place at the last festival, 50 days earlier. Perhaps it was this fear that caused them all to gather in the large upper room where they had been for the Passover feast with Jesus. Maybe it was just a holiday, and they had come to think of one another as family. Luke simply says that, when the Day of Pentecost came, they were all together in one place. We will look at what happened on that day in the next lesson; for now, though, it is important for us to understand the setting. It is a historic holiday they had celebrated all their lives with their families. Now they are together with their new family.

The upper room where they were gathered had begun to feel like home. It was the site of their last supper with Jesus before his death, but it was also the place where they gathered in fear afterwards. It was the place where they found the risen Christ among them. It was home base, but it had become a holy place where they connected to one another and to God.

God certainly can be found any place, but it is true that, when we gather in sacred places with people who are our spiritual family, there is a sacred wind that often blows through. I feel sorry for those who miss that gentle, divine caress.

Acts 2:1-5

When the Day of Pentecost had come, they were all together in one place. And suddenly from heaven there came a sound like the rush of a violent wind, and it filled the entire house where they were sitting.

The sound of rushing, violent wind is the first sign of the Holy Spirit that Luke offers us. In Greek, the same word can be translated wind, breath or spirit. So, perhaps it was the sound of violent breath. Wind makes more sense, I guess, since the sound of it filled the entire house where 120 people had gathered. Actually, Luke is careful not to confuse the Spirit with the wind. Notice that what "came from heaven" that day was neither wind nor breath but a sound. It was "a sound LIKE the rush of a violent wind." The sound is what filled the house, not the wind.

It is a fine distinction, I suppose, unless, of course, you have found yourself recently being blown by the rush of a violent wind. Luke is using words sparingly to describe this momentous event, so we probably should pay attention. Next came fire, so it is probably a good thing that it was just the sound of wind and not wind itself.

Except, it wasn't actually fire. Luke writes, "Divided tongues, as of fire, appeared among them and a tongue rested on each of them." It is unclear just what Luke is trying to describe. Was it fire or not? Toward the beginning of the Gospel of Luke, John the Baptist said that, while he baptized them with water, the One for whom he was preparing the way would baptize them with the Holy Spirit and with fire. Clearly, Luke wants us to understand that this is the fulfillment of John's promise about Jesus.

Ezekiel has a vision of a valley of dry bones, dead until the breath of the Spirit is breathed into them. The Bible begins with the image of God breathing into clay so that humanity might come to life.

Here, in just a couple of verses, Luke calls together the great imagery of the Bible to say that something of earth-changing historic significance happened in that upper room on the Jewish holy day of Pentecost. Wind and fire represent the work that God was doing that day to give birth to a new people.

We are descendents of the people of Pentecost. Like them, our lives are meant to be enlivened by the Spirit. Too often, though, it seems we are all wind and very little fire.

Acts 2:1-13

All of them were filed with the Holy Spirit and began to speak in other languages, as the Spirit gave them authority.

The wind and fire were signs of the coming of the Holy Spirit. Now these scared and scattered disciples give voice to what is happening to them. Again, what this phrase means is just as much a mystery as the wind and the fire.

The stir of all this apparently drew a crowd. Luke observes that there were Jews from every nation gathered in Jerusalem. This could be a factual statement since it was Pentecost and Jews had come from all over. However, Luke says, "There were devout Jews from every nation under heaven." This isn't just a crowd of people from all over. Luke is saying they were all gathered there for this great gift of our self-giving God.

Luke goes on to list a sampling of those who were gathered. Since this passage is read each year in most churches, we all have had to endure the list and the mispronouncing of the names of these scattered nations. So odd are the names that we miss the point that Luke is trying to make.

Among the nationalities he listed as represented that day were Parthians and Medes, nations that had ceased to exist centuries before Luke wrote this story. What he is trying to say is that the Spirit gathered into one family women and men from every nation, every language, every land, AND every time. The Spirit, who is not limited to our time and space, is the God of all the living and the dead, the God of the then and the now.

Luke is offering us an ultimately inclusive vision of the Church to which God gave birth. We who are so prone to draw lines between us have completely missed this vision of God's all-including Spirit. All people of "every nation under heaven" are included in this Pentecost picture of the family of God. Every person heard God speaking to them in their own language.

How amazing that God doesn't require us to learn English or expect us to adjust who we are. God's Spirit comes to speak in our own language. Notice God is speaking through Christians not in the language of the Christians, but in the language of the people God is calling Christians to love.

Acts 2:11-13

The sound of wind, tongues like fire, disciples speaking about God's deeds of power in languages they apparently didn't know—these are the signs Luke offers of the drama and mystery we call Pentecost. Luke's description is careful, but often missed, even by progressives' tendency to read the Bible like history rather than mystery. Luke doesn't say there was wind, but a "SOUND like the rush of a violent wind." He doesn't say there was fire, but "tongues AS OF fire." Then Luke describes the disciples speaking other languages "as the Spirit gave them the ability." Did the Spirit give them the power to speak or the power to speak a language they didn't know? In the end, the listeners seem to think the real miracle was not in the speaking but in their hearing: "In our own language we hear them speaking about God's deeds of power."

In this carefully-worded description, Luke leaves the widest possible path for understanding, interpretation and perception. He isn't recording what happened so much as he is recording the impressions that were left on those who reported what that day had been like. Again gathered in the upper room, perhaps fearing for their lives, but fearing even more that Jesus had left them, something suddenly came upon these women and men, and they were transformed, empowered and emboldened.

We so often focus on the wind and fire and tongues that Luke cannot describe, let alone explain, and we miss the real miracle of the day. All these "signs" were described with great brevity because Luke wants us to realize that, at a certain point, something happened that filled these disciples with such power that the rest of the book of Acts will be required to describe their deeds.

Some of those who saw the disciples—NOT the wind or fire—asked, "What does this mean?" Others sneered and said, "They are filled with new wine." What they saw was a boldness and confidence that was so unexpected that they had to assume it was artificially induced. It is the kind of cynicism that we liberals too often convey when others express passion and exuberance about their faith. Is it possible that there are human events we cannot fully explain, like Luke the author and intellectual experienced? Our call is simply to respect the experience of others and wonder what it all means, rather than slip into the arrogance of criticism and derision. THAT attitude is never of the Spirit.

One of the other hats I wear is training leaders of new and renewing churches. In that capacity, I really struggle with discerning which leadership abilities are gifts/ talents and which are skills. Some people are frequently described as "born leaders," but I wonder if that is ever really true. Some folks seem to have innate abilities that enhance their leadership capabilities, but it seems to me that in other settings those abilities are seen as liabilities.

If you will forgive a personal example, there are some who have called me a "natural born leader." That is something I would dispute, since I am, by nature, actually an introvert. However, as my parents discovered when I was quite young, much to their dismay, I am, by nature, quite stubborn (determined). While some regard that as a gift, my parents certainly didn't see it that way when I was six. I became painfully aware of this because my youngest daughter apparently inherited a double dose of her father's "gift," and the fact that she is alive today is evidence that there is really only one law in parenting: "Thou shalt not kill." Today, I admire her determination and the person she is growing into, but when she was six her stubbornness drove me crazy.

So, on the day of Pentecost, the impetuous, gaffe-prone, loudmouth, boastful disciple stood up to lead. Were we left only with the Gospel, and not the book of Acts, we might think Simon Peter was a completely inept disciple of Jesus. Yet here, under the influence of the Spirit, those traits we judged earlier as liabilities become assets.

In the face of sneering and derision, and in the midst of a time of transition and transformation, Peter is the one who rises to the occasion. In front of a great crowd that had gathered, he dares to take charge of the situation and speaks with authority. He interprets scripture he has known since boyhood, but which probably had never before made sense. He addresses the scorn of the crowd directly: "We can't be drunk because it is only 9:00 in the morning."

None of us need sneering critics to point out our faults, weaknesses and failures. We try to hide them and deny them, but we know. Peter's face had been red more times than he could recount, but suddenly, on the Day of Pentecost, at 9:00 in the morning, the Spirit took all that Peter had thought was bad about him and used it. The possibility ought to make Pentecostals of us all.

Acts

And it will come to pass in the last days, God declares, that I will pour out my Spirit upon all flesh ...

This passage from Joel provides the backdrop for the rest of what Luke writes. Acts recounts God's Spirit being poured out on people from every tribe—young, old, male, female, slave and free. In Luke's hands, Peter said that none of this should surprise us.

To understand the importance of this amazingly inclusive passage, we need to keep in mind that Luke is writing in the wake of the first great conflict in the early Church. So far everyone in the story has been Jewish. The early Church regarded Jesus as the Jewish Messiah. The pivotal question for the early disciples was the shift from being a Jewish sub-sect, like the Pharisees or Sadducees, to being an inclusive movement. Luke will describe in detail how this happened, but, here, he sets the stage with how the beginnings of the movement were understood.

Peter is a Jew speaking to Jews quoting a Jewish prophet. However, of all the words of the First Testament, these are among the most inclusive. The promise is that the Spirit would be poured out upon all flesh. No statement could be more including. THIS, Peter says, is the real sign that God has broken into history.

Some believe inclusion is a peripheral issue, but, for Christianity, it is the defining issue. It is unfortunate that the Church has not taken its own history more seriously. What part of the word "all" don't we get? We who have been included by this radical gift of the Spirit act as though God's presence is our exclusive possession. We took a radically including act of God and turned it into a religion that drew boundaries and barriers for who was in and who was out. Every act of exclusion, cynicism and derision of another is a willful negation of what God did, first in Jesus and then on the Day of Pentecost. From this point on, Luke will describe how God intervened in, and through, fragile people like Peter, to draw the circle large enough to include everyone. Joel/Peter offers a specific list—young/old, male/female, slave/free—just in case we miss what "all" means. The story of Acts will show how hard the early Church found it to change their minds about who was included. The history of the Church has shown that while they succeeded we too often have failed.

God's gift of the Spirit (God's self) is for all; tragically our Heavenly Parent still hasn't taught us to share.

After quoting five verses from Joel chapter 2, Simon Peter goes on to preach his very first sermon. Actually, there are a number of sermons in the book of Acts. In this one, Peter tries to make the case to the Jews gathered there that Jesus was the One sent from God, the one for whom they had been looking. He begins with the statement that this fact was confirmed by God with deeds of power, wonders and signs that God did through Jesus. This statement reflects Luke's Christology (understanding of who Jesus was) and is in sharp contrast to the understanding in John's Gospel.

John understood the work Jesus did as a sign that Jesus was the divine, pre-existent Logos/Word. In Acts, Peter is saying that God did the work through Jesus as a sign that he was the Christ sent from God. While the differences might seem subtle to us, there will be centuries of debates over this issue. Church councils will gather to fight over the outcome, and the debate will embroil empires and rulers. For now, though, Peter simply is trying to persuade his listeners that they had been mistaken about Jesus and wrongly executed him.

Peter goes on to say, in verse 24, "**But,** God raised him up having freed him from death because it was impossible for him to be held in its power." That three-letter word that begins this verse is one of my favorites. Peter is saying, "You thought you had the last word on Jesus, BUT …" Beyond their misjudgment and wrongful execution of Jesus, though, Peter is offering a word of ultimate hope. Death seems like the final word of life, BUT …

Actually, I suppose the point is two three-letter words: "But God …" When we are tempted to despair, those are the two words we must remember: "But God …" All is never lost if we are people of faith. We may not, and perhaps should not, know how it will ultimately all come out. After all, that is why we call it faith, but God … may have other ideas.

It is also a strong argument against arrogance. Modern Western thinking and education presume to know all the answers, "but God …" There are still mysteries and wonders—concepts like eternity and infinity—that cannot be tamed by our intellect. Whenever we are tempted to make final judgments or pronouncements about our lives or another's life, remember these two words from Acts 2:24 and whisper, at least to yourself, after the final word, "But God …" may yet have something different to say about this.

Acts 2:25-36

In the midst of making a full-throated declaration that Jesus is the Davidic Messiah promised by God, Peter sums up what happened on Pentecost by saying, "Having received from God the promise of the Holy Spirit, Jesus has poured out this that you both see and hear." Quoting from various Psalms and, frankly, taking most of it out of its historic context, Peter (Luke) completely reframes the Jewish understanding of one of the core covenants of their identity.

While most of us grew up with Luke's (Peter's) understanding of this, that certainly wasn't the case then. In fact, all of the birth narratives at the beginning of the Gospel of Luke have been building to this point. Luke begins with the claim that Jesus was born in Bethlehem because he was "of the house and lineage of David." Here, in Peter's sermon, we have the first complete claim that Jesus is the fulfillment of God's promise to the Jews that David's throne would be established forever. Peter talks about Jesus risen, exalted and seated on a throne at the very right hand of God. This reigning Christ is a common image for the Church, institutionalized in our creeds, but Luke is describing the first time this claim was made. It was a very different image for the listening Jews to comprehend.

After centuries of living under the oppression of Rome, Greece, the Babylonians and Persians, the Jews were expecting God to send a Messiah to overthrow their oppressors and restore the nation to its glory days when David was king and they were the military power in the region. This was what they thought of when they heard these ancient promises in their scripture. This is how they understood power to be exercised. Now, Peter is reframing a basic cultural understanding and claiming that Jesus, who had come and gone without overthrowing Rome, was actually the Davidic ruler God had promised. Beyond the throne of Herod, or even of Caesar, this Jesus they had crucified now reigned from the right hand of God.

I don't fully know what happened on the Day of Pentecost, but I know something did. I know that because humans aren't prone to give up old ways of thinking or established systems of belief without some dramatic reason. We don't even question what we have long believed unless there is some crisis or intervention.

Was Simon Peter that persuasive? What is required for you to make significant shifts in what you believe about God? Sometimes I wonder if a mighty wind and fire isn't required for all of us to open our minds to new ways of believing. "But God …"

In the rural Methodist churches where I began my ministry when I was just 19, it was the custom to give an invitation at the end of every service. The idea was that someone might be present who wanted to join the church by "profession of faith or transfer of membership." It was a very odd practice since, in those small congregations, everyone knew everyone else and no one new had joined them in decades. Still, it was what was done, and I'd caused enough trouble without tinkering with that tradition. Then, one Sunday toward the end of my second and final year with them, someone actually responded to the invitation. I had no idea what to do. No one had ever done that before, and no one had told me how to handle someone old enough to be my grandfather who finally had decided he wanted to be a Christian.

My preaching professor, Fred Craddock, likes to say that we preachers live with two fears: What do we do if no one responds, and what do we do if they do? The latter happens so rarely in the Church that it probably holds more fear. I can't help but wonder if the courage it took Peter to stand up and speak that day for the first time wasn't less than the terror he felt thinking that people actually might respond to the message.

When the people heard that they might actually have executed the Messiah, the Son of David, they were "cut to the heart." The Church has called this response "conviction." They felt convicted that what they had done was wrong. Regardless of the subject, that feeling is the beginning of wisdom. For a scientist to pursue a new line of thinking, she first must be able to acknowledge that what she was taught, what she had always believed to be true, is wrong. There is great resistance to that awareness. Some of us seem incapable of it, as though we somehow are less of a human if we admit we've been wrong.

Gandhi once was assailed by one of his opponents because Gandhi took a different stand on an issue than he once had. "Just last month you said something completely different," his critic shouted. "Yes," said the wise man, "but I have learned some things since then." Peter's listeners learned some things, and their response was as miraculous as anything else that had happened on that amazing day of Pentecost. They asked, "What should we do?" Acknowledging an error is most rare. Asking what we need to do differently is rarer still. So rare, in fact, that it is proof that the Spirit still is working miracles.

Acts 2:37-42

When the people listening to Peter recognized that they had been party to killing the Messiah, they wanted to know immediately what they should do. Peter's response has become formulaic, so much so that it clearly was a part of the phraseology of the early Church. "Repent and be baptized in the name of Jesus Christ," he said, "so that your sins may be forgiven and you will receive the gift of the Holy Spirit."

Frankly, I think Luke assumed this is what Peter said because by the time he came to write Acts that is what was being said. At that moment, though, none of this process or theology had been worked out. How could Peter know God would give them the Spirit? Because, in this account, all of this happened within a short amount of time, Peter might have assumed that the Spirit was given only to those who knew Jesus before he was gone, or that you had to be inside the upper room to get the Spirit, or that you had to have seen the risen Christ, or any one of a thousand things.

While what Luke wrote made perfect sense at the time he wrote it, on the first day of the Church's existence, there probably were a lot more questions than answers. Frankly, 2,000 years later, there still are. Unfortunately, the Church tends to forget that **faith** is about living with the questions rather than pretending to have all knowledge.

This account in Acts says that 3,000 people were added to the Church that day. That is hard to comprehend. Even the logistics of that seems challenging. For example, where did they find enough water to baptize 3,000 people? (v. 41) Still, if we remember that what we are reading is not history but a spiritual teaching, we can see that something happened to so change the core group of disciples that people wanted to join them. That IS factual.

Querulous, self-absorbed, thick-headed people were so transformed that hundreds, and then thousands, of people wanted what they had found. There was something about their faith that was so winsome and life-giving that they very rapidly gave birth to a movement that swept the western world.

In the absence of their charismatic leader and wonder-worker, these scared and scattered men and women attracted crowds of people who "devoted themselves to the apostles' teaching and fellowship, to the breaking of bread and the prayers." (v. 42) I'm left wondering where that attractiveness went.

Acts 2:43-47

If I were pope of all the Church of Jesus Christ, I'd require every Christian, everywhere, to read this passage over and over until they understand what Christianity is really supposed to look like. This was a snapshot of the Church before it became the protector and defender of the status quo. Empires and emperors couldn't kill with lions or swords the movement Jesus started, but Constantine killed it quite effectively by making it the state religion.

What was a movement of grace, generosity, inclusion and compassion devoted to the Way of Jesus became an institution and an instrument of the Empire. In most churches, if a pastor was to recommend the above lifestyle as the model for a Christian economic system, they would be called a socialist or communist. Although communism became more abusive than the style of governance it sought to replace, the Bible describes the early Church as disciples of Jesus who held "all things in common."

So, what would that look like? What would be the spiritual reality of that kind of lifestyle and value system? Communities have tried periodically to live this way, but the flaws of humans always seem to creep in and destroy the idea. Still, it is incumbent upon us to learn what we have lost since the Church was born. When you look at how Christendom has evolved from those days, it seems that we have "gained the whole world and lost our own souls." Today, few of us eat our food "with glad and generous hearts, praising God and having the goodwill of all people." (v. 46)

The community was in awe of the power in that original body of believers. It wasn't the power of influencing voters, or building great buildings, or protecting a comfortable lifestyle. It was a spiritual power that grew out of knowing Jesus intimately and having your life changed from within by the Spirit. It was expressed by compassion, trust, joy and generosity.

These days, I am considered a church-growth consultant. I am embarrassed to say that this early Church probably didn't follow any of my prescriptions, but was so powerful and joyfully winsome that people beat a path to join them, were forever changed, and went out and changed their world.

Acts 3:1-4:4

We spent an awful long time in the second chapter of Acts looking at various aspects of the Day of Pentecost, Peter's sermon, and the community's response. The entire third chapter, and part of the fourth, is taken up with a single story. This is a well-known account of Peter and John healing a lame beggar outside the temple gate.

The transition from the wonderful description of the attractiveness of the early Church to this miracle is quite abrupt. Still, there is continuity as well. Here, we have a story told as evidence of the power that came on the apostles at Pentecost. Peter and John are still devoutly practicing Jews, so they head to the temple for evening prayers. The beggar asks them for money, but Peter replies, "Silver and gold we do not have, but what we do have we give to you. In the name of Jesus Christ of Nazareth rise up and walk." (v. 6)

One of my favorite stories happened centuries later, but is a powerful, though perhaps apocryphal, commentary on this event. According to legend, the pope was giving Francis of Assisi, who had taken a vow of poverty, a tour of the Vatican. Regaling his guest with the astounding art and beauty, the pope said, "As you can see my son, the Church can no longer say 'Silver and gold we do not have.'" The barefooted monk replied, "Neither, your Holiness, can we say 'Rise up and walk.'"

Just as Christians must read the Gospels with humility and acknowledge how far our lives are from the model of Jesus, so the Church ought to read the book of Acts in a posture of grief and repentance. Even if we try and demythologize stories such as this one, there is ample evidence that the early movement that rose up after the life of Jesus had a spiritual power that the modern Church lacks. Francis may well have hit the nail on the head because the power of his life lay in his own humility and refusal to live by the value system of the world he inhabited.

Peter and John lifted up a fellow human who was hurting, estranged and impoverished. Immediately, the healed man accompanied them into the temple where he joined them in prayer and worship. The healing of this man created quite a stir, and people came running to see what had happened, giving Peter a chance to "preach" his second sermon.

Is it possible that, today, people might be just as drawn by our faith if they found us healing the poor, sick and estranged? That image of people running toward Peter and John to learn about their faith calls me to examine my own.

While Peter and John were speaking to the crowds who were attracted by the healed beggar, the leaders of the temple came to see what was going on. Since they had been responsible for Jesus being wrongly executed, you might guess that they weren't happy to find two of his disciples hanging out on their turf telling people what an evil thing they had done. Luke notes that, along with the priests and the Captain of the Temple, the Sadducees didn't believe in the resurrection of the dead.

Luke simply says they were annoyed, so they had Peter and John arrested until the next day. Then he notes that the number of those who believed as a result of this sermon was 5,000. (I guess Peter's sermons got better because the numbers went from 3,000 to 5,000.) What are we to make of these numbers? If Peter's preaching was that powerful, it seems that this would have been all that was needed to convert the entire city.

This is the first story where the religious/institutional authorities try to silence voices that challenge what they did or said. Peter and John won't be the last Christians arrested for speaking in a challenging way what they believed to be the truth. Writing during a time of on-going persecution, Luke may have been trying to say that lots of people respond when disciples of Jesus raise their voices in defense of the poor, the sick and the marginalized.

Henry David Thoreau was thrown in jail because of a stand he took on what he believed was a matter of conscience (a poll tax). That evening, he was visited by his friend Ralph Waldo Emerson who asked, "Henry, what are you doing in there?" To which Thoreau fired back, "Waldo, the question is what are you doing out there?"

Criticized for civil disobedience, Dr. Martin Luther King, Jr. reminded us in his *Letter from a Birmingham Jail* that, for people of convictions who follow Jesus, it is sometimes more wrong to be outside than inside. Peter and John went to jail for healing a poor sick child of God and then having the temerity to speak a word of hope that contradicted the religious power brokers.

The question for us to grapple with is this: What are we willing to be jailed for? Are there people for whom we should be willing to raise our voices so loudly and persistently that the only way to silence us would be to jail us? The question I suppose is, "What are we doing out here … when Jesus is in there?"

Acts 4:5-12

Peter and John spent the night in jail, not because they healed a lame beggar who sat outside the temple gate, but because they had the temerity to speak up about something the powerbrokers wanted silenced. It seems little has changed with powerbrokers, religious bullies and protectors of the status quo. Today, they do not throw their opponents in jail, because they are too securely entrenched and in control to feel that threatened. Now, they control the media, so they are able to imprison the voices that challenge in a cell of silence. When that fails, the powerbrokers unleash a wave of false information, or confusing spin, making their opponents look foolish, uninformed or unpatriotic.

Peter and John probably would prefer the night in jail. The next morning, these very ordinary working men were dragged before the council to be questioned: "By what authority or in whose name did you do this?" This what? This healing? Or this resistance to their control? Peter says, "... if we are questioned today because of a good deed done to someone who was sick and are asked how this man has been healed, let it be known to all of you and to all the people of Israel that this man is standing before you in good health by the name of Jesus Christ of Nazareth, whom you crucified, whom God raised from the dead."

The text then notes that those to whom Peter spoke recognized that Peter and John were uneducated people, as well as companions of Jesus. They were amazed by their boldness. They were amazed that ordinary people without standing or education could stand up and speak their own truth. The council orders these commoners to be silent, but Peter and John say that they cannot. They are compelled to speak out of their own experience and reality.

Since they had committed no transgression of the law, all the council could do was threaten them and let them go. It would be nice to proclaim boldly that anyone who stands up for the poor and the sick, and speaks up in the name of Jesus will pass through unharmed. Some seem to make that claim, but they forget that Jesus was not spared. In fact, Peter will lose his life ultimately for his bold witness. No, they did not speak up for those who are without voice because they had divine protection. They stood up and spoke out because it was right. That was once reason enough.

Peter and John were released from jail, and they returned to their friends to report what had happened. When they did, a spontaneous worship service broke out. So powerful was the subsequent prayer meeting that Luke writes:

> *When they had prayed the place in which they were gathered was*
> *shaken and they were all filled with the Holy Spirit.*

v. 31

Peter and John were filled with the Holy Spirit when they were on trial, and, now, as the community gathers to worship and pray, they are filled with the Spirit. Luke is seeking to make the point that Pentecost was not a one-time event at which the Spirit came and that was that. The Book of Acts is an account of a people who were continuously in communion with God's presence. Luke presents a rhythm of the Spirit here. It isn't just that God is present when we are caring for the sick or speaking boldly for justice; the Spirit also is present in our times of worship and devotion.

Too often the Church has made the mistake of forgetting one part of this or the other. There have been great movements of personal piety when the Church has invested all its energy in worship and devotion and holiness. Conversely, others have believed the faith to be about following the example of Jesus in feeding the hungry, caring for the poor and healing the sick. Neither understanding is wrong; it is just incomplete.

In Acts, we find this rhythm between personal spirituality and doing justice. One nourishes the other. The Holy Spirit/God's presence fills us when we gather as a people to worship and pray. The Holy Spirit also fills us when we are scattered to do the work of Jesus. Just as the Church forgets the rhythmic breathing in and out of the Spirit/breath of God, so we, too, are prone to give our energy to one or the other and seldom find the balance.

In that, we may discover why the early Christian's lives were marked with a spiritual power and boldness that seems absent from our lives today. So, are you forgetting to breathe in deeply, or neglecting to breathe out? Doing one without the other soon becomes impossible, and eventually you do neither.

Acts 4:32-37

Now the whole group of those who believed were of one heart and soul, and no one claimed private ownership of any possessions, but everything they owned was held in common. With great power the apostles gave their testimony to the resurrection of the Lord Jesus, and great grace was upon them all. There was not a needy person among them, for as many as owned lands or houses sold them and brought the proceeds of what was sold. They laid it at the apostles' feet, and it was distributed to each as any had need. There was a Levite, a native of Cyprus, Joseph, to whom the apostles gave the name Barnabas (which means "son of encouragement"). He sold a field that belonged to him, then brought the money, and laid it at the apostles' feet.

It has long seemed critical to me that we get people of faith to read this passage. It is an amazing description of how the early Church functioned in its day-to-day life. *"There was not a needy person among them."* How did they manage that? By this time, thousands had come to faith, so it wasn't that it was such a small intimate group that everyone's needs were met.

This description includes the corporate experience of the larger group, as well as giving us a specific example of one person. This passage is the first to introduce an individual who apparently joined the Church rather than followed Jesus. Joseph was a Levite from Cyprus. The apostles nicknamed him Barnabas, apparently because of his encouraging nature. Barnabas will be heard from again; for now, it seems his nature, generosity and willingness to submit his life to the teachings of the apostles are the incarnation of how the early community functioned. As we will see in the next chapter, all is not perfection, but Luke wants to give us a beautiful picture of people who lived out of communal caring, compassion, encouragement and trust. They didn't claim possessions as their own, but understood that they were stewards of them for the good of the larger body and of the work God was doing.

Encouragement, generosity, sharing, caring and trusting are the descriptors of the early Church because those traits describe the early Christians like Barnabas. It is tempting to rage against the excess and abuses of the modern Church. The truth is that, just as the early Church was an expression of the individuals who formed that community, today we have the Church we deserve … or at least the one that is created with each of us as cells of the body.

Acts 5:1-11

This passage is one of the most vivid, strangest and, frankly, disconcerting in the entire Bible. Acts chapter 5 begins with the word "but." It is a word of transition meant to contrast what comes after with the gracious description of the early Church and Barnabas, the generous "son of encouragement."

This story of Ananias and Sapphira presents us preachers with a conflicting set of values. On the one hand, it is the perfect illustration for Stewardship Sunday since these two are struck dead because they pretended to be generous like Barnabas, but secretly kept part of the proceeds of their land sale for themselves. Anyone who has ever tried to raise money for a church or nonprofit would love it if they could threaten donors who are much less generous than they pretend to be. If God had just kept this practice up, the Church never would have any financial problems. My partner swears that our congregation became significantly less generous after I told them that I really didn't believe in hell. Some people need negative consequences to motivate their spirituality. Maybe that is what this story is doing.

The trouble is I just don't believe in a God who kills people—even despicable ones—who pretend to be more generous than they really are. Heck, if God struck dead people of faith who pretend to be generous, or compassionate, or kind, or just, there would be few of us left, and, frankly, I wouldn't be one of them. So, what are we to make of this story?

Well, although I'd like to make it a story to motivate tithing, it is actually a story about integrity. When Peter confronts them about the real selling price of the land, he is careful to say that the land was theirs to do with as they pleased. Even after it was sold, the proceeds were theirs to use as they choose. However, the issue was that they **pretended** to give all the proceeds to the church. The pretense, distortions and deception were much worse than simple greed.

While I do not believe that God struck Sapphira and Ananias dead, those attitudes can be spiritually deadly. Honesty, vulnerability and integrity are essential for our own spiritual vitality. Barnabas and Ananias/Sapphira were of the same class: land owners. They were a part of the beginnings of something God was doing. In Luke's description, one was filled with the Spirit and one with Satan. While this dualism may be artificial for us, the truth is that each of us decides each day if we give our wills to life or death. Fear not; God won't strike you dead. God won't need to.

Acts 5:12-42

After a brief negative aside to kill off Ananias and Sapphira for their duplicity, Luke goes back to the story of the successes of the early disciples, especially Peter. They kept meeting and teaching at the temple under Solomon's Portico. Luke says that everyone held them in high esteem, but they didn't dare join them. Still, they managed to create enough of a stir to get themselves arrested again. Somehow, though, the prison doors were mysteriously opened, and the apostles went right back the next day to preaching and teaching. When the religious rulers found them, they were furious and wanted to kill them.

> *... an old Pharisee named Gamaliel stepped forward and offered a very great bit of wisdom. He said to the other leaders, "I tell leave these people alone because if this is a human undertaking it will fail, but if this is of God you will not be able to overthrow them. In that case you may even be found fighting against God."*

His wisdom prevailed, but, just for good measure, they had them flogged before they were released. They might be doing God's work, but they had insulted the powerbrokers. They didn't care who they worked for; that wasn't going to pass.

Over the years I have thought about Gamaliel's wisdom many times. So often I have wanted to take on preachers or teachers with whom I disagreed. Sometimes I manage to remember Gamaliel's advice and let God sort it all out. It has been helpful in dealing with individuals, too. I can't tell you how often someone has come to me with advice or a wise word about what I should or shouldn't do with my life. There have been times when I knew the wisdom was right or wrong, but there have been many times when I just had to sit and wait and see what came of that course or that person.

It is tempting to believe that we have all knowledge and wisdom. The religious leaders in this passage were deeply convinced that they were right and needed to deal with this matter forcefully. We've all been there. One of the greatest challenges in life is living with deep values and convictions, while at the same time allowing for the possibility that we just MIGHT be wrong. Once again, it is critical to leave room for God. We must remember there is only one God ... and we are not the One.

This fascinating passage begins with the Greek Jews complaining that their widows were being neglected in the daily distribution of food while the Hebrew widows were being cared for. There are many informative things about that. First, the early Church had assets with which to help the poor. This is one of the first indications that the Church was changing from a movement of Jesus' followers into a more organized institution. Also, the early Church made caring for the vulnerable a seminal expression of what it means to follow Jesus. They don't just gather to worship, pray and make converts. They organized a social justice program to address the need of the marginalized. The other thing I find interesting is also a bit disturbing. Prejudice and favoritism already had crept into the Church. It is unclear if the disfavor is with immigrants or simply that people who spoke Hebrew were treated more favorably than those who spoke Greek. In the end, it might simply have been a communication problem.

The outcome is that the apostles express frustration that presiding over these kinds of things is taking up more and more of their time. They call together the whole community and propose a solution. They invite them to pick seven people from among them to manage things. They suggest that these men (unfortunately) were to be people of "good standing, full of the Holy Spirit and of wisdom." They are chosen and named. Then the apostles lay their hands on them and pray for them.

The next verse says, "The word of God continued to spread; the number of the disciples increased greatly in Jerusalem, and a great many of the priests became obedient to the faith." This picture of success seems linked to how the Church responded to a conflict by finding people who could ensure that the ministry of compassion and caring was carried out effectively.

Too often today's Church acts as though the paid staff/pastors are the ones called to do ministry, while everyone else is called to volunteer occasionally. The truth is that, for the Church to be the Body of Christ, we all must find and answer our vocation. Each of us has a role to play. Those who taught were overwhelmed by trying to do it all, and the result was that some of those most in need got neglected. They didn't call the ministry off because there wasn't enough time; they called out others who could share the ministry. The world produces enough food to feed every person, so why are people hungry? God calls enough people to care for the needs of the world, so why are people hungry?

Acts 6:8-16

In the list of those who were chosen by the community, one person stands out. Luke noted that Stephen was "a person full of faith and the Holy Spirit." This description is a foreshadowing of what is to come. Today's reading begins, "Stephen, full of grace and power, did great wonders and signs among the people." The story will continue through chapter eight. In part, this is a sign of its importance, but it is also a sample story of what hundreds would experience over the decades to come. The other reason that this story gets more time than the Day of Pentecost, or any event, is that Luke brings to a close the Jerusalem picture of the early Church. This event will result in the disciples being scattered across the world.

Luke wants us to be clear that what follows is not Stephen's fault. He was a good man, and his goodness was expressed by how he lived his life, full of grace and power. I wonder what it would look like to have that description applied to our lives today. I also wonder if people who live with grace and power might find life much more challenging than we might imagine. Gandhi, King and Romero all might have had those adjectives applied to their lives, and they all were assassinated.

Hence this story is important for Luke because Stephen is, of course, the first martyr of the early Church. The early disciples hid in fear following the execution of Jesus, but it is a second generation of disciples that ultimately proves that their fears were justified. He does so not by being caught out of hiding, but by living with power and grace, and because he spoke with great boldness about Jesus and his faith.

According to Luke, a group from the "Freedman" synagogue began to challenge Stephen's bold preaching. The name implies that they once had been slaves who now are free. This may seem ironic that these formerly oppressed people are now the ones who take offense at Stephen for exercising his freedom of speech and religion. If you find this surprising you obviously have never worked closely with formerly oppressed people. It is staggering to me that any lesbian, gay, bisexual or transgender person could be prejudiced. It is disappointing that so much of the opposition to civil rights for LGBT people comes from people of color. It has been reported that the Equal Rights Amendment, which would have ensured equality for women, ultimately was defeated by women. Oppression, in whatever form, infects our souls and often gets expressed more toward our sisters and brothers than our oppressors. Wonder how this dynamic gets lived out in your life.

Stephen's opponents from the Synagogue of the Freedmen argue with him, but, apparently, Stephen got the upper hand. As so often happens, when logic and dialogue didn't win out, they made the attack personal. They began to spread rumors that Stephen was speaking against Moses and God. They even recruited false witnesses, until Stephen got summoned before the council to give an account of himself.

When the council asks if the accusations against Stephen were true, Luke writes that they noted that he had the face of an angel. (6:15) What follows is what is called the longest sermon in the entire New Testament. For the next 53 verses in chapter 7, Stephen lectures these religious leaders on the history of Israel, what the scriptures say and mean, and how Jesus was the fulfillment of all they taught. Not only did they fail to recognize the meaning of their own history, Stephen concludes that they are "stiff-necked people" who are opposing the very Holy Spirit of God.

As you might imagine, they were not pleased. If you read Stephen's sermon, you probably would shrug your shoulders because, for us, it doesn't really contain great words of wisdom or advice. However, many scholars consider this to be a critical document in the evolution of the early Church.

You will recall that the disciples and the others have been regarded as a group of Jewish people who believed that Jesus was the Messiah, but otherwise embraced the same Jewish faith into which Jesus was born and of which he was considered a rabbi (teacher). The cross-examination of Stephen begins with the leaders asking if the accusations were true. Stephen simply could have said, "No. I have never spoken against God or Moses." It then would have been a case of his word against theirs.

What he does instead is begin retelling important pieces of Israel's history and giving it completely different meaning. When he is done, the faith they had held for centuries had been completely reframed, and they didn't like it at all.

None of us do. I can't tell you how many enemies I have made over the years this way. I rarely deny the truth, or what someone believes, because that would be arrogant. However, shifting or reframing how a person understands their faith is no less antagonizing. What has disturbed me most, though, is that many people ultimately come to embrace a new understanding, but they never seem to forgive the person who forced it on them. Actually, there is something else that bothers me even more, and that is how often I've resented those who have done the same to me.

Acts 7:54-8:1

This passage describes how Stephen became the Church's first martyr. His sermon made the religious leaders so furious that they were willing to break the law and risk the wrath of Rome. You will recall in the Gospels how careful the religious leaders were to enlist Pilate in the execution of Jesus. They were clear that Roman law prohibited any but Rome from imposing the death penalty. This was precisely the reason. Stephen had done nothing wrong, but he infuriated the wrong people. The final straw was not his insulting them, but declaring that he could see heaven and, there, Jesus standing at the right hand of God. That picture of one they had executed was more than they could bear, so they dragged him out of the city and stoned him.

Luke notes a strange detail that foreshadows what is to come. The witnesses to Stephen's murder laid their cloaks at the feet of a man named Saul, who, Luke later notes, approved of Stephen's execution. As Stephen is dying, he cries out with a loud voice, "Lord Jesus receive my Spirit. … Lord do not hold this sin against them." This prayer, of course, is a clear reflection of the prayer of grace and forgiveness that Jesus prayed as he was unjustly executed: "Abba, forgive them."

This is the holy of holies. Stephen hasn't had years to work through his anger and resentment. When their stones cut him to the heart, what flowed out was what he was full of: "grace and power." He prays not for mercy on his own soul, nor for those he loves but will now leave behind. He prays for those who are murdering him with their own hands. What power is in such a prayer of pure grace?

I know this is a classic preacher's technique, but I can't help myself. When Stephen looks up into heaven, he sees Jesus *standing* at the right hand of God. This is an odd thing, because it was noted earlier in Acts that Jesus is "*seated* at the right hand of God." Some may say that, symbolically, Jesus is standing in honor of this servant Stephen who is dying with such amazing grace. To me, though, what is symbolized in this parabolic vision is that Jesus stood so that he might see clearly for whom his servant Stephen was praying. Luke notes that Saul was standing there, and perhaps it was on that day that Jesus said, "I must go to him in answer to my beloved Stephen's prayer." Hence, Jesus returns to earth and, on a deserted Damascus road, Jesus encounters Saul again. That day, in answer to Stephen's prayer of forgiveness, Saul becomes the Apostle Paul. Stephen's life and ministry was all too short, but his prayer continues to be answered.

Acts 8:1-8

Following Stephen's murder, a severe persecution of the Church breaks out. Everyone but the apostles are scattered across the countryside. There is no indication in this passage that the people who scattered for safety were cowards, but Luke does note that the apostles stayed. They, of course, were the ones in greatest danger, but perhaps by this point their reputation left them with some measure of protection. As we will see later in history, the fact that they had been with Jesus would not keep them from being arrested and, ultimately, executed. What it may say is that those who accomplish great things with their lives almost always have to stand firm at times and live with almost irrational courage.

Luke notes that Stephen was buried and that there was a great outpouring of grief. This was just not a random death; it struck deeply at the very heart of the Church. Stephen had been one of the seven chosen. He is one of the few people in the Bible against whom not a single negative word is spoken. He was one of the good.

Against that, Luke writes, "But Saul was ravaging the church by entering house after house; dragging off both men and women." While later Luke and Paul become co-workers, he wants to ensure that NO mistake is made. Saul was bad, very bad. The word translated "ravaged" in the New Revised Standard Version of the Bible implies savagery and, perhaps, even sadism. The ugliness of Saul's soul is deliberately contrasted to the beautiful and beloved soul of Stephen.

As with any good storyteller, Luke is trying to let us get inside the feelings that were a part of this time in the history of the Church. Luke is, of course, setting up our surprise when Saul actually becomes a Christian. Perhaps he also is trying to remind us that the life that authentically encounters the love of God in Christ can be genuinely changed.

Saul's cruelty is not rooted in the fact that he is a godless man. Ironically, as he later would write, he was the most devout of the devout. What we see here is how religion can crowd from our lives all grace, tolerance, patience and compassion. I am certain that none of us believe that is true about how we live or how we treat others, but I am also certain that Saul didn't think that was true about him either. The challenge is that living with the vulnerable, heart-exposed tenderness and grace of Stephen can kill us, and, from that fate, we are prone to flee behind the façade of cynicism, superficiality or even religion. Stephen or Saul? Who is your role model today?

Acts 8:4-25

Earlier, in Acts 6, Luke described the election of the next eight leaders of the church, who often are referred to as "deacons." That term is not found in the text, and different denominations have interpreted this office quite differently. According to Acts, these were leaders selected to ensure that the poor and vulnerable were cared for; however, the subsequent narrative shows them to be much more.

Certain widows were neglected, so the apostles instructed the Church to select seven competent people to oversee that ministry. That work for which they were chosen is never mentioned again. Perhaps they did it exceedingly well, or maybe Luke was just using a literary device to explain where this second generation of leaders came from. At any rate, the very next story was about one of the deacons whose name was Stephen. He, of course, became the first martyr of the new Church. It is a powerful story about a person who, while not one of the original disciples referred to as apostles, was still a person of great courage and spiritual power.

Luke uses the religious mob's murder of Stephen to introduce two important themes in the history of the Church. First we learn that a person named Saul, whom we have never heard of until now, "approved of their killing him." Then we learn that Saul led a season of persecution. This is beginning of the Diaspora, or dispersion, of the Church across the Roman Empire. Until this time, the Church had been a sub-cult of Judaism whose worship still centered around the temple in Jerusalem. One wonders how long that might have lasted if this time of persecution hadn't come. Would Christianity have remained simply another way of understanding the Jewish faith? Luke will return to this evolution again in a few chapters.

Having introduced these major pieces of information, Luke turns to the life of one of the other "deacons" elected to care for the widows, Philip. At this point, a reader might assume Luke is simply going to tell the story of each of the deacons in turn, but that is not the case. We actually know nothing about the other five. Perhaps they were not successful as deacons, or maybe they simply did what they had been asked to do and faithfully cared for the poor and the vulnerable. It is important to remember that, for every person whose name we know in history, there are legions whose accomplishments were not recorded, but who made all the difference. They make up the cells of the Body of Christ and are the true strength and health for the body, not the organs whose names we know.

This passage begins, "Now those who were scattered went from place to place *proclaiming the word*." This verse is the description of how the persecution of the Church was the wind that scattered the seeds of the Word across the world. While it would be terrible theology to suggest that the persecution was the will of God so the word of hope could spread, it is a good reminder that every time of testing carries in its bosom the seeds of new possibilities. If we can synchronize our hearts with the heart of God/Life, we greatly increase the possibility of "all things working together for our good." (Romans 8:28) Following this very important verse, Luke gives an illustration from the life of the second deacon who was named. "Philip went down to the city of Samaria and proclaimed the Messiah to them."

One might assume that, since Samaria was just one of the regions of Palestine, Philip wasn't scattered very far, but, to the first-century Jewish mind, he may as well have become a missionary to the Taliban in Bora Bora. In fact, that is not a bad way for us to understand just how radical this story is. Every sermon on the parable of the "good Samaritan" or the Samaritan woman at the well has described the profound enmity between Jews and Samaritans. One might be tempted to believe that, since he was not a Jew, Luke didn't get how deeply this hatred ran; otherwise this would not have been the first story of inclusion that he told. Of all the places that the scattered seeds of the Word might have landed, this might have been the unlikeliest.

Yet, it isn't an accident that the story of the Good Samaritan is found only in the Gospel of Luke. This story of Philip isn't an accident. Luke begins the book of Acts with Jesus' last commission that they would be his witnesses in "Jerusalem, in all Judea and Samaria, and to the ends of the earth." (Acts 1:8) It is hard for us to comprehend the radical nature of this casual inclusion of Samaria. It would be like an evangelical church casually including lesbian and gay people as a matter of course, or a Roman Catholic Bishop routinely including women in the list of priests of the Church. Perhaps it would be like us including people like Karl Rove, Dick Cheney or Pat Robertson as people who are anointed by God, too.

Everybody thinks inclusion is a core value of the Christian faith. We think that right up until we are called to include someone we don't want in. I remember the day a man who had been convicted of child molestation called to ask if it would be okay if he attended our church ... Philip went to Samaria; would I?

Acts 8:9-13

Philip's ministry in Samaria was met with great success. Crowds gathered to hear him, and they believed him when he said that Jesus the Messiah had come. The Samaritans who were Jews cut off from Jerusalem and the temple were very messianic in their faith. That is, they actively anticipated the coming of one who would save them from their circumstances.

This passage describes the deeds of power that accompanied Philip's ministry. People were healed and delivered from unclean spirits "so that there was great joy in the city." These people, expecting a political or military leader to change their circumstances, had an encounter with the Spirit of Life that changed them in the circumstances of their lives. That ultimately became the identity of the Church. Jesus, and faith in Jesus, does not change our situation, but it changes us in our situation.

In the midst of this passage is a strange little story about a man named Simon who is called "Simon the Great" by the Samaritans because he apparently had some power with which they were impressed. Luke says that he practiced magic; hence, he is referred to later in history as Simon Magnus. Luke seems to offer two pictures of men with power. Ultimately, though, Simon comes to believe as well. He is baptized and stays with Philip, amazed by all that is taking place.

Eventually the apostles in Jerusalem got word about what was taking place in Samaria, and they sent Peter and John to check it out. They come and lay hands on the new believers, and they received the Holy Spirit. When Simon saw all of this, he actually offered Peter money to teach him how to do such amazing things. Although Simon had become a Christian, he still practiced magical thinking.

Peter is incensed and tells him that he hopes his money perishes with him. He denounces him and calls him to repentance, telling him that he is "in the gall of bitterness and the chains of wickedness." (8:23) Strong stuff, though I'm really not sure what it means. Simon responds by asking Peter to pray for him. Thus the story ends.

We don't know what happened to Simon from there, but we do know that he is not the last believer to practice magical thinking and be attracted to faith by power and what can be gained. He also is not the end of the line of apparently sincere people who believe that the presence of God can be bought, earned or somehow acquired. I'm not sure what "the gall of bitterness" really is, but it doesn't sound like something for which we should strive.

Acts 8:26-40

Peter and John return to Jerusalem with news about how the new believers in Samaria have received the Holy Spirit, and Philip moves on. He is instructed by an "angel" of the Lord to go south along the road from Jerusalem to Gaza. I wonder what would happen if an angel told us to do that today. You see, that road is blocked because the nation of Israel has put up checkpoints on one side, and Egypt has put them up on the other. The Palestinians who live in Gaza have been isolated there.

The dynamics of the conflict between the modern nation of Israel and the people who lived there before Israel was formed in 1948 fills the headlines. Many of us hold views that have been shaped by hearing only one side of the story. Fundamentalist Christians ironically promote modern Israel, since much of conservative Christianity has been historically anti-Semitic. Even today it is not so much the Jews that are supported as the Biblical Israel, rooted largely in how fundamentalists interpret the book of Revelation and the events they believe will take place in Israel.

The media's presentation of the Palestinian-Israeli conflict also has been mostly one-sided. Hence, almost all U.S. policies have favored Israel and neglected the plight of the indigenous Palestinians. Both sides of every conflict have strengths and weaknesses, but, in this case, no honest attempt has been made to hear both sides. The result in the Arab world has been great resentment toward America.

So, if Philip was a modern Jew, what possibly could motivate him to take the road south out of Jerusalem to Gaza? That idea is as ridiculous and dangerous as Philip including Samaritans in his family of faith. Such radical inclusivity required Philip to be someone who could look at things from both sides, to be someone who could see things through the eyes of others. This will serve him well, because, on the Gaza road, he encounters another person that will stretch his vision of who should be included in the family of God. Along the road, Philip encounters a man who was a eunuch servant of Queen Candace of Ethiopia. This explains why Philip is the patron saint of the 40 million-member Ethiopian Orthodox Church. Philip is their patron saint because, when he was on the road and saw this strange, foreign, person of color, he sensed the Spirit urging him to go to the Ethiopian, AND HE DID.

I believe the Spirit often urges us to open ourselves up to someone we normally wouldn't, but we ignore those gentle nudges. If we didn't, there is no telling whose patron saint we might be.

Acts 8:26-40

We cannot leave the story of Philip without noting that not only is he the patron saint of the Ethiopian Church, but he also might deserve to be the patron saint of the lesbian, gay, bisexual and transgender Church. What we have in this story is the first known example of someone of a different sexuality being deliberately included in the early Church.

Philip's teaching leads to the conversion and baptism of a eunuch who was the treasurer of Candace, the Queen of Ethiopia. This man apparently had been to Jerusalem to worship and was reading the book of Isaiah as he traveled home. We are not told why he had been to Jerusalem to worship. Perhaps he was just curious and wanted to visit one of the great ancient worship centers of his day. He came as a pilgrim, but we know from the story he doesn't really understand what he is reading.

There is much to be said about this passage, but nothing more important than for us to recall that the eunuch was someone who, because of his sexuality, would have been excluded and marginalized, shut out of the inner courts of the temple. In Matthew 19, Jesus talks about three types of eunuchs: those who were born eunuchs (lesbian or gay?), those who were made eunuchs (castrated), and those who chose to be eunuchs for the sake of the Realm of God (celibate).

We actually don't know which "type" of eunuch this Ethiopian was, though many scholars have suggested he was gay. Castrated men still have a sex drive, and, therefore, the eunuchs who worked closely with women of the royal family were usually gay, lest they rape or become sexual with the queen or princesses.

What is clear, however, is that the book of Deuteronomy (23:1) specified that, because of their sexuality, eunuchs were not allowed to be a part of worshipping communities. Isaiah (56:4) predicts that there will come a day when God will give to eunuchs a special place in the household of God. What we have in this passage in Luke is the fulfillment of that promise in Isaiah. Those who have been excluded from the family because of their sexuality are now included by a deliberate and conscious move by the Holy Spirit, and by the responsive faithfulness of Philip.

First, Philip is sent by God to the hated Samaritans, and then to the excluded eunuchs. What an amazing person Philip must have been to be so open to a new word from God and to be able to open his heart to those shut out by other religious folks. Maybe Philip should be the patron saint of us all.

Acts 9:1-9

Acts 9 marks the end of the first section of the book and the story of the birth of the new Church. In this chapter, we hear the story of the conversion of Saul of Tarsus who becomes the legendary apostle Paul. Soon the story of Acts becomes the story of Paul, with occasional vignettes of the apostles and other early leaders.

Paul will shape much of the rest of the New Testament. He is the author of a good deal of it, and credited as the author of still more. In the end, the New Testament may be shaped more by Paul than by Jesus. That is not always a good thing. Although Paul, like Jesus, saw himself as a Jew working to transform Judaism, in the end, he is largely responsible for the Church breaking away from its Jewish heritage and becoming a separate religious movement. Luke already has hinted at the importance of Paul by describing his role as a persecutor of the early Church. This part of the story might have been left out, but the Bible is a remarkably frank and honest book. Paul himself repeatedly acknowledges his crimes against the early Christians.

In chapter nine we leave the story of Philip and the deacons. It begins:

> *Meanwhile Saul, still breathing threats and murder against the disciples of the Lord, went to the high priest and asked for letters to the synagogues at Damascus, so that if he found any who belonged to the Way ... he might bring them bound to Jerusalem.*

There are several important things to note about this passage. First, in those days, people who believed in Jesus were not called Christians, or even the Church; they were people of "the Way." In the beginning, discipleship was not seen as a religion or a set of beliefs but as a Way of living. It seems a worthy goal to work to return to that reality today. The other thing that Luke is doing in this passage is trying to establish in our minds just how bad a person Saul was. He didn't just respond passively to the Apostles when they did something; he aggressively sought out people of the Way and dragged them back to Jerusalem to be punished.

Saul saw himself as a protector of the faith. He isn't the first or last to take on that role, but one in a long line of those who believe they know the truth and that those who think differently aren't just wrong, but are threats and enemies. Luke is clear that such an attitude has no place in the hearts of people of the Way.

Acts 9:3-9

Having secured his arrest warrants, Saul sets out for Damascus. What follows is the most famous conversion story in history:

> *Now as Saul was going along and approaching Damascus, sud-*
> *denly a light from heaven flashed around him. He fell to the*
> *ground and heard a voice saying to him, "Saul, Saul, why do you*
> *persecute me?" He asked, "Who are you, Lord?" The reply came,*
> *"I am Jesus, whom you are persecuting. But get up and enter the*
> *city, and you will be told what you are to do." ... Saul got up from*
> *the ground, and though his eyes were open, he could see nothing.*

Some have suggested that lightning struck so close to Saul that it knocked him unconscious and temporarily blinded him. As he approached Damascus, he passed through an area where the warm air of the plains meets the cool air of the mountains. Violent electrical storms are a frequent occurrence there. No doubt others had experienced them, but none had experienced such radical transformation.

What is clear is that, metaphorically, Saul was "struck by lightning." From this moment on, his life is forever changed. (Brushes with death do tend to focus one's attention.) He is transformed from persecuting people of the Way to being the principal teacher of the Way. The tragic truth is that all of us have opportunities when we are called to reconsider who we are, the values we hold, and the way we treat other people, but few of us emerge from those times as different people. Jesus said, "The rain falls on the just and the unjust." Ultimately, it is up to us whether the storms lead to growth or we just get wet. Saul's response to this dramatic event was to spend three days in darkness, fasting and praying. All too often when lightning strikes us or near us our response is to ask, "Why me?" as if we have been victimized.

I do not believe that God strikes us down, but I do believe that, if our hearts are tender and our souls responsive, God can speak in those moments when our attention is focused. For that to happen, though, we must be willing to set aside all other distractions and listen for that still, small voice. If we had been Saul, we probably would have wondered for a moment what this meant and then got right back to living life as we always had.

The Lord said to [Ananias], "Get up and go to the street called Straight, and at the house of Judas look for a man of Tarsus named Saul. At this moment he is praying, and he has seen in a vision a man named Ananias come in and lay his hands on him so that he might regain his sight." But Ananias answered, "Lord, I have heard from many about this man, how much evil he has done to your saints in Jerusalem; and here he has authority from the chief priests to bind all who invoke your name." But the Lord said to him, "Go, for he is an instrument whom I have chosen to bring my name before Gentiles and kings and before the people of Israel; I myself will show him how much he must suffer for the sake of my name." So Ananias went ...

Saul got up from the ground and was led by his companions into the city of Damascus. Then, in this passage, we meet a disciple of the Way that we have never heard about before and will never hear from again, Ananias. He is in a city about a week's journey from Jerusalem, perhaps sent into exile by the persecution of the Church led by Saul, and, as he prays, the Lord tells him to get up and go to Saul.

Saul was on his way to Damascus to arrest Ananias. No doubt Ananias knew what had happened to Stephen, so God is calling him to walk literally into the lion's den … and he does. What an amazing soul to obey so courageously an inner urging of the Spirit.

Ananias was a soul to whom God could speak. He wasn't one of the original 12. There is no indication that he was in the upper room on the Day of Pentecost. When the Church came to elect seven leaders/deacons, he was not one of the chosen. Yet, here he is willing to be an instrument in the hands of the Spirit to minister to an enemy who ultimately would be the most powerful witness Christianity ever had.

I can't help but wonder how many disciples in Damascus God also called that day, but to no avail. Perhaps Ananias was the only one. God called him not because he was great or famous, but because he was willing. Ananias was willing to do the toughest thing people of the Way are ever called to do: genuinely love our enemies and do good for those who hurt us. Just think for a moment about someone who has wounded you deeply and deliberately. What would it take for God to persuade you to go to them, lay your hands on them, and pray for them?

Acts 9:20-25

Saul's conversion to the Way (Christianity) was a momentous event. Never shy and retiring, Saul spends "several days" with the disciples in Damascus. He then goes to the local synagogue and begins doing the very thing that he had been trying to arrest Christians for just a short while before. People in the synagogue naturally were confused by this sudden and dramatic change of direction.

The Church has a word for such a change: *metanoia*. It most often is translated in the Bible to mean "repentance," which is unfortunate. Repentance has gotten a really bad reputation because of how it has been used as a weapon. The truth is it is a powerful word of hope and grace. *Metanoia* is the great promise of faith. It says that there is, in fact, hope that our lives can change direction, that we can turn things around. On a daily basis, the word means that it, is in fact, possible that the gentle breath of the Spirit might lead us to have a change of heart or mind. It is a hopeful word. Without it I am wasting my time writing these words and you are wasting yours reading them. The promise of the Spirit is that we can, in fact, change.

Saul's change was dramatic because it happened so quickly, but if we are honest we all could identify ways in which we have changed. I grew up a fundamentalist Christian in the South, but, now, on a daily basis, I am labeled a heretical liberal by my former colleagues. Time and again, people from high school find and befriend me on Facebook, only to "deFace" me a few days later after I have posted something they consider unorthodox or too liberal for their taste. They no doubt feel betrayed by the change that has taken place in the person they thought they knew.

So, too, the people Saul encountered at the synagogue were skeptical at first, but soon turned hostile. You may have encountered that kind of hostility, too. So violent was their response to Saul that they wanted to kill him in order to silence him. They might have succeeded, but some good Christians put him in a basket and, in the dead of night, lowered him over the city wall.

Think about those holding the rope gently lowering the basket. Just a few days before Saul had been a threat to them and their family. Now his life was literally in their hands. He was fortunate that those bearing the weight genuinely believed in the hope of *metanoia*.

Your church may not be the most liberal, but imagine walking into the sanctuary to see Dick Cheney, Karl Rove or Donald Rumsfeld sitting on the front row. That probably doesn't do this passage justice … Imagine a member of Hamas showing up at a synagogue in Tel Aviv. The tension would be incredible, and that is just how it felt the day that Saul showed up for church in Jerusalem.

He tried to join the disciples there, but they wanted nothing to do with him. They were afraid and distrustful. Sure the red and black banner outside said, "No matter who you are, or where you are on life's journey, you are welcome here." Still, you can take that too far, can't you? The disciples felt that welcoming Saul was a step too far. Only Barnabas was willing to take a chance on Saul. You may remember meeting Barnabas a few chapters ago. Barnabas listened to Saul tell his story of meeting Jesus on the road to Damascus. He then went to the disciples and told them the story. Because of the witness of Barnabas, they accepted Saul, who almost immediately went to work as a witness there in Jerusalem.

God bless Barnabas. May his tribe increase! The Church today is in desperate need of women and men who are willing to engage others, believe in them, and then stand as their friends with them before skeptics. The Church also needs people who have the credibility of Barnabas. They weren't sure of Saul, but they were sure of Barnabas. If Barnabas vouched for Saul then that was enough. Imagine the power of such a witness. Barnabas had lived his life in such a way that others were willing to risk their lives on nothing more than his word. Where are the Barnabas souls today?

When you go to get a loan, if your credit is bad, someone can sign for you. In doing so, they vouch for your reliability. They also stand behind your debt. They gamble their own finances and credit and credibility on you and your word. All of us have had people in our lives who did that for us. It may have been a loan, or a job that a friend helped you get. Perhaps someone introduced you to those they were close to and thus you became their friend.

I must admit that this is a risky thing. People default on loans, turn out to be bad employees, betray friendships. Barnabas no doubt knew this, but he resisted the lure of cynicism and took a chance. He stood for Saul, and the world was never the same. Saul changed the world, but he got his chance to do that because Barnabas took a chance on him. You and I are called to be Barnabas in this world.

Acts 9:32-43

Luke shifts scenes very quickly here. He has been focusing on Paul, but, now, the spotlight shifts back to Peter and a couple of miracles that he worked. The leading men of Acts are Peter then Paul, then back to Peter and, finally, back to Paul. Along the way, there are a number of co-stars including Stephen and Barnabas, but most of the story is a record of the lives and acts of these two leaders. Of course, we understand how it is when history is written. We know the names and stories of Churchill and Roosevelt and Hitler and Mussolini, but the truth is the Second World War was a tragic history of millions of people whose names we will never know. While Peter and Paul were probably important and impactful leaders, the truth is the story of the early Church is largely the story of millions of people whose names we will never know.

Few of us will ever be the leading women and men about whom the history of our day is written, but the truth is we are the ones who make up the story. Each day we faithfully live largely unremarkable lives. We don't like to think of ourselves as "ordinary," but the truth is most of us are. We go to work, love our family and friends, do a little good when we can, as little harm as we can, and our time on this planet passes all too quickly, and we are gone. We are not stars or heroes or saints. We are the people.

It is tempting to dismiss our role as insignificant and unimportant, but that is not the same thing as ordinary. We have only to think of the millions of cells that make up our body. Because there are so many and because they go about their days functioning as they were designed to, we can call them ordinary. However, their role is not insignificant or unimportant. One has only to think of what happens to the body when one of these cells becomes cancerous. Our bodies are healthy and strong because of the amazingly effective functioning of millions and millions of cells. Thinking of ourselves as the cells that make up the Body of Christ might help us to see that, while we may be ordinary, our lives are not unimportant. The last verse of that old African-American gospel hymn "Balm in Gilead" says, "If you cannot preach like Peter, if you cannot pray like Paul, You can tell the love of Jesus and say, 'He died for all.'"

We may not be the star in the story of the Church of Jesus Christ in our day, but there is something for us to do. Doing it makes the body healthy and strong. Failing to do it may have greater consequences than we can imagine.

The entire 10th chapter of Acts tells a single story. It is the story of how Peter witnessed to a man named Cornelius who became a Christian. It seems a fairly ordinary story to consume 1/28th of the entire book of Acts. No miracle takes place. No huge crowd is converted. No one dies. We have no idea what happened to Cornelius or his family after this. It is the story of the conversion of a single family, but there must be something important here for Luke to give it so much time and attention.

Actually, this story is a turning point in the life of the early Church. Until this point, the Church has been simply a Jewish sect who believed that Jesus was the messiah and that he rose from the dead. Everyone who has come to faith thus far was apparently Jewish. The Samaritans were considered defective half-breeds by many of the Jewish leaders, and the Ethiopian eunuch was a marginalized proselyte, but they were all Jewish believers of a Jewish rabbi named Jesus.

In Cornelius, we have the first convert who is a Gentile with no connection to Judaism. Furthermore, Cornelius is a Roman Centurion, a leader in the army that occupied and oppressed Israel. Accepting such a person as a member of the Way would require a complete paradigm shift for the other believers. It was not just that he was from outside the faith, and that he was of a different faith. It was almost as though he was of a different species.

Tradition says that Luke is the only Gentile author in the Bible. This chapter is critically important to him, but he recognizes that telling this story carefully and fully is vital. Luke begins with Cornelius. He tells us who he is, but then adds that he was a "devout man who feared God." Since he is clearly a Gentile, it is unclear what this means exactly, but Luke wants us to see Cornelius sympathetically. He goes on to add that Cornelius gave alms to the poor and prayed constantly.

In the early 1980s, the president of the Southern Baptist Convention said that God did not hear the prayers of Jews. While rarely is such religious prejudice expressed so blatantly, there is a sense of superiority that permeates many religious hearts. We all are too prone to think that, because we believe our faith is right, the faith of others is wrong. Luke sets the stage to make an argument of inclusion to those who couldn't imagine God including others in the family with them. No wonder he dedicated an entire chapter to Cornelius. Even today it seems almost impossible for devout people to remember the difference between "right" and "right for me."

Acts 10:1-48

Luke introduces Cornelius as somebody we will like. To his original readers, that was no small feat since he was a military leader of an oppressing army. However, Luke says Cornelius was a devout, prayerful, compassionate and generous person. One afternoon, Cornelius was praying and saw a vision in which an angel (messenger) of the Lord told him to send a delegation over to Joppa to a man named Simon who would introduce Cornelius to the God to whom he had been praying.

In the meantime, Simon had his own vision. Around noon the next day, he went up to the roof to pray and fell asleep. Actually, Luke is much kinder, writing that Simon fell into a trance. Luke notes that Simon is hungry, so he dreams about food. The trouble is the food he dreams about is not kosher. When a voice commands Simon Peter to get up and eat, he protests that he has never eaten anything that is profane or unclean. To this, the heavenly voice replies, "What God has made clean you must not call profane." This was repeated three times. Like most of us, Simon was a slow learner, especially when it came to changing a lifetime of beliefs.

While he was still pondering just what the vision meant, the men from Cornelius' house arrive. The Spirit nudges Peter that he was to go with these men, and, to his credit, he does. It is easy to make fun of Peter needing to see the same vision three times, but I wonder how often the Spirit has nudged us to do something that wasn't on our agenda so we completely missed the prompt.

Cornelius tells Peter about the vision that he had, and Peter responds by saying, "I truly understand that God shows no partiality." While that statement might seem obvious, for people whose core identity was as the "chosen people," Peter's statement is revolutionary. Heck, while we Americans pretend to value egalitarianism, we live in every way as though we are God's chosen people who deserve to exploit the planet and live extravagantly while half the world lives in abject poverty. Peter's words are powerfully prophetic, and, were he to preach that in America today, he would find few followers because we all like to feel like we are God's secret favorite.

When Cornelius and his household believed and received the Holy Spirit into their lives, Simon had to argue with the "circumcised (Jewish) believers" for their right to be baptized. If you think this has changed you didn't read the story of the pastor of a large nationally known Methodist church who was fired a couple of years ago for baptizing a baby … whose parents were two gay men.

In any account of the birth of something new, almost every event is critical. In an account as concise as Acts, Luke must choose with care the stories he tells. It is logical to assume that they are chosen because they had greater significance than the event itself. That is certainly true about the story of the conversion of Cornelius and his family. In the previous chapter, we read how God spoke to Cornelius and then how God spoke to Peter through a vision commanding him to eat things that had been traditionally regarded as unclean by devout Jews. Peter told Cornelius and his family the good news about Jesus, and they believed. Just so there could be no doubt that this was God's work, not Peter's, the Spirit fell on this family of Gentiles in the same way that the Spirit fell on the original disciples.

Chapter 11 begins with the disciples in Jerusalem summoning Peter to explain just what he was thinking when he baptized Gentiles into what had been a Jewish movement. As momentous as Peter's including action was, what follows is just as critical. The disciples react badly, "criticizing Peter saying, 'Why did you go to uncircumcised men and eat with them?'" Of course, they weren't really concerned about the condition of Cornelius' penis, but circumcision was for the Jews what baptism eventually became for the Christians. Circumcision was the mark or sign of being Jewish. In the sexist culture of that day, women were Jewish by birth or by marriage, but men were marked as Jewish through a painful and vulnerable ritual. Modern Christians hardly can comprehend the significance of circumcision to the Jews … unless you imagine that, in their minds, Peter should have taken a flint knife and, without anesthesia, circumcised Cornelius BEFORE he baptized him.

This confrontation between Peter and the original Jerusalem disciples was the deciding point for this issue. Did people have to convert to Judaism before they could be people of the Way? It was a logical conclusion since Jesus was born a Jew, was circumcised at eight days, and spent his life teaching as a Jewish rabbi. How could one be a disciple of a Jewish rabbi without joining the religion of the rabbi?

This is the biggest moment in the life of the young Church. Two thousand years later, it is difficult for us to comprehend how momentous this decision was or how difficult. We liberals advocate for unconditional inclusion but often without adequately wrestling with the consequences. This would forever change who the Church was, and they took this change seriously.

Acts 11:1-18

The Church summons Peter to give an accounting for eating with Gentiles. It is funny, but nothing is said about his preaching the Gospel to them and then baptizing them. The disciples understood breaking bread together as a sacred act for both the host and the guests. It was a sharing of more than food, and the Jews were careful with whom they shared this experience.

Peter defends his actions by simply telling the story, which Luke recounts in complete detail. For us, it is boring to reread a story that we just read, but Luke obviously was making a case for inclusion. By the time the book of Acts is written, decades after Jesus' ministry, you would think this issue would have been resolved. As we will see later, even Peter can't resolve it in just this one experience.

So, from verses 4-17, Peter simply retells the story of how he ended up at Cornelius' house. He concludes by reporting that "if then God gave them the same gift that God gave us when we believed in the Lord Jesus Christ, who was I to hinder God?" He has a point. It is a point the Church seems to often miss even today.

I find it interesting that Peter talks about God giving them the same gift the original disciples received "when we believed in the Lord Jesus Christ." Since he is talking about the gift of the Spirit, is Peter saying that they didn't really believe until that day in the upper room? That is an interesting proposition.

The Synoptic Gospels tell the story of Peter's declaration to Jesus: "You are the Christ, the Son of the Living God." The trouble was Peter didn't really know what that meant. In the very next verse, he rebukes Jesus for suggesting that his message and ministry will cost him his life. "That will never be," Peter declared. Obviously, he missed the mark on that prediction, and it was because he still didn't understand who Jesus really was and what he really was trying to accomplish.

Like Peter, the disciples' faith had been so shaped by what they had been told and taught all their lives that they simply could not believe in who Jesus was, apparently, even after he died. That didn't happen until they experienced the risen Christ in the person of the Holy Spirit. When the Spirit came into their lives, they believed in a way that they never had before, perhaps in a way they never could before.

The world longs for an experience with the living God … not so much to know more about God. Like with Peter, intellectual knowledge just isn't enough to transform our lives.

So, Peter defends eating with Gentiles by retelling the story of how hard God had to work to get him there. Then he defends baptizing them by reporting that God gave the Gentiles the same gift that God had given them. Then the text says about the original disciples, "When they heard this they were silenced."

I have seen that happen only on rare occasions: A crowd of folks or a group of people who always have believed a certain thing, or taken a certain position, or assumed a certain thing was true until they heard someone tell their story, and their arguments are silenced. It is often a powerful and moving moment when people actually change their minds. It also is remarkably rare.

What might have happened that day was that the disciples sat there listening to Peter's long story waiting impatiently to refute his points and make their case again. This seems to be what passes for listening to those with whom we disagree. Taking turns arguing is not dialogue.

To the disciples' credit, they called Peter on the carpet to rebuke him. That by itself is an interesting dynamic since Peter is the nominal leader and spokesman for the group. Then they actually listen to Peter, trusting his heart even if they might not have initially agreed with his actions. Against a lifetime of culture and religious teaching, they actually consider that God might be doing something different or that they might—just possibly—not know the full mind of God. They listened with their hearts, suspending judgment until their brother had told his story. Then they were silent, pondering the possibility that they were wrong.

This posture allowed them to then "praise God saying, 'Then God has given even to the Gentiles the repentance that leads to life.'" I love that phrase: "repentance that leads to life." We liberals tend to avoid the word "repentance" because it so often has been used as a cudgel against us and others. The truth is repentance is the best part of the good news. Repentance holds up for us the possibility that we can hear new things or hear things in a new way and change our minds, or our lives, or our direction.

After Peter's story, the original disciples were happy that even Gentiles could turn their lives around and move toward life. I am happy that I can, too.

Acts 11:19-30

This passage has a number of interesting points. It begins with a description of how "the persecution that took place over Stephen" (Saul was the leader) had a good side, too. The believers were scattered as far as Phoenicia, Cyprus and Antioch, but the text notes that "they spoke the word to no one except the Jews." However, there were some people who came to Antioch and preached the good news to the Greeks. In this picture, we see the evolution of the Church. First, Philip took the Gospel to the Samaritans—outsiders who were half-Jews. Then Peter went to Cornelius and his household. They were Gentiles, but it was Cornelius who sent for Peter. In this text, we find for the first time the disciples preaching deliberately to Gentiles in Antioch. This is a movement to inclusion that revolutionized the Way. It might not have been so, but the response among the Greeks was great. So great, in fact, they had to send for help.

Fortunately, the help came in the form of Barnabas. He has been a hero of the story before, but, this time, Luke says of him "he was a good man, full of the Holy Spirit and of faith." One of the first things Barnabas does is send for Saul. This act of welcome, inclusion and support was typical of Barnabas. Saul comes to Antioch, and he and Barnabas spend an entire year studying and teaching together.

Antioch was a major city, one of the three or four in the Roman Empire in that day. Under the ministry of Barnabas and Saul, the Church grew rapidly. Then Luke notes, "It was in Antioch that the disciples were first called 'Christians'." I'm not sure how that is important, unless you are playing Biblical Trivial Pursuit, but it is interesting that several decades passed before the term "Christian" came to be used. Until then, the followers of Jesus were known as "people of the Way." I wonder if that is something worth reclaiming. So often the values and lifestyles of those of us called Christians today are something Barnabas would never recognize. Barnabas was a man of generosity whom we first met as someone who sold his land and gave the money to the Church. He is a tenderhearted soul who took in people who were once his enemies, like Saul who even had Barnabas's friends arrested and one killed. Barnabas was not a Christian; he was a person of the Way.

This passage ends talking about a severe famine that struck Judea. The believers in Antioch took up a collection and sent it to the believers there with two men they trusted: Barnabas and Saul. One person of the Way who had taught the other the Way going as ambassadors of compassion … which should always be the Way.

Acts 11:27-30

The People of the Way first were called Christians in Antioch. That could be just a historical footnote, but the truth is it was in Antioch that the believers actually became the Church as we know it. Until this point, the movement was largely a growing number of Jews who believed that Jesus was the long-awaited Messiah from the household of David. Now, here in Antioch, non-Jewish believers begin to make up the bulk of the group. It is no accident that it was in this diverse and divergent body that Barnabas decided to include Saul and disciple him. They spent an entire year there, studying and teaching. Then, a prophet stood up one day and told them about the famine that was taking place in Jerusalem. Luke, as a way of dating these events, notes that this was during the reign of Claudius. Claudius ruled from 41 to 54. In this context, he officially annexed Judea into the Roman Empire—the prelude to the ultimate destruction of Jerusalem and scattering of both Jews and Christians.

Antioch is important because it was a deliberately inclusive church. They didn't wait until Gentiles came and asked to join them; they deliberately shared the story of Jesus with people whom the Jewish Church had assumed would have no interest and no place in the new community of The Way. The other thing they did that would model the evolving Church was they took an offering for the church in Palestine, which was suffering under the famine.

This passage also distinguishes two, or maybe even three, types of leaders in the early Church. There are prophets who speak to the people on behalf of the Spirit; there are the elders who apparently give spiritual leadership and guidance to the church; and there are the apostles who were revered still as those who actually knew Jesus firsthand.

In Antioch, the church acted like church. They gathered for study and nourishment to hear the word from God; they scattered to share the good news they had discovered; and they sacrificed their own goods and comfort to assist those in need. It isn't a bad pattern for the Church today.

It probably isn't a bad pattern for us either. In a consumerist world, we sometimes are tempted to think we can write a check to do our spiritual duty. However, generosity that is not linked to spiritual community and spiritual grounding can become just a way to buy off our conscience. Generosity that grows from devotion helps the giver and receiver.

Acts 12:1-5

In the seventh chapter of Acts, Luke describes the killing of Stephen in some detail. In this chapter, we find a record of the second known martyrdom of the early Church. King "Herod had James, the brother of John, killed with a sword." That is the sum total of the story. It is all we know, which is pretty amazing when you consider that this is the death of one of Jesus' first followers and a member of his intimate inner circle. James and John were the two brothers who were sons of Zebedee the fisherman. Jesus called them early on, and, along with Peter, they were among the inner circle for events such as on the Mount of Transfiguration.

James's death around 44 A.D. is the first of the 12. According to legend, all but his brother John are martyred ultimately, and John lived to be an old man in prison. His remains are supposedly at Santiago de Compostela in Galicia, Spain, which is considered the third holiest town in Roman Catholicism. This legend is highly implausible, but it nonetheless had a major cultural impact. The cult of St. James came to replace several deeply rooted pagan cults, and St. James, who never left Jerusalem, became the patron Saint of Spain. In the next sentence Luke says that, when Herod saw how his murder of James pleased the Jewish leaders, he proceeded to have Peter arrested.

I want us to ponder the dynamics of what just happened. For just a moment, picture religious leaders pleased by the murder of anyone, even a religious enemy or heretic. Envision the pious smiles on the face of priests. It is reprehensible and almost incomprehensible. Yet, capital punishment and military fervor flourish because they have religious support in America. In fact, the higher the percentage of church attendance is in a community the greater the support for state executions and war.

It is much more complicated than bloodthirsty churchgoers, but it is also worth wondering how much good going to church is doing us, and how much bad. The cultural piety that demands satisfaction by revenge and death is deeply rooted in the cultural religion of Americana. Challenging it requires great courage. It has become orthodoxy in places like the South and will remain so unless we—who are disciples of One who was executed by the state and who is called the Prince of Peace—speak up. If you are reading this in a more progressive place, you are not without responsibility. Your heart must break with God's for religion that has gone so badly astray that it gives its blessing on any state killing.

Herod had Peter arrested. Everyone expected that, like James, he would be executed very soon. Herod handed him over to four squads of soldiers to guard him. His intent was to bring Peter out to the people at the Passover, which was just beginning. Luke notes that, while Peter was in prison, the church prayed fervently to God for him.

A miracle happens and someone breaks Peter out. This someone is called an angel, and I suppose that is what I'd call someone who broke me out of prison. Peter thought he was having a vision. It wasn't until he was out that he "came to himself." He went immediately to Mary's house. Mary is identified as Mark's mother, and the assumption is that her house is where the upper room was. This is the first time Mark's name is mentioned, but it is mentioned as if the reader knew who he was and would therefore know who Mary was and what house he was talking about.

Luke also notes that when Peter arrived he discovered many other people gathered praying for him. There is a funny scene that follows, which we will look at tomorrow. For now, though, I want to call our attention to the fact that, according to the story, God sent an angel to rescue Peter but let James get killed.

What is that about? Did God love Peter more than James? Was Peter's survival more important than James'? Was it that the church was praying for Peter and God answered their prayers, but James death happened so quickly they didn't have time to pray? Did God answer one set of prayers but not another? Ultimately, Peter is executed, at least according to legend, but not this time. So why would God send an angel to save him once but not twice?

These are all questions we need to ponder because our failure to do so leads to our making inane comments about how God works, answers prayers, and intervenes in human life, or does not. How do you think John and his family must have felt when they saw Peter walk in that night? Of course they were happy and relieved, but it had to have been tinged with sadness that their brother had not been rescued.

Every time something so good happens that we are tempted to thank God and call it a miracle, we should think of James and Peter. For every tumor that comes back benign, there is someone, somewhere, weeping because their loved one just died of cancer. Life is complex, convoluted, multi-faceted, difficult and mysterious. Prayer that doesn't take all of that into consideration is trite and, sometimes, callused and insulting.

Acts 12:12-19

Peter is rescued by "an angel," and he returns immediately to Mary's house where many people are gathered to pray. Luke notes that, when Peter knocked on the outer gate, a maid named Rhoda came to answer. When she heard that it was Peter, she was so overwhelmed that she forgot to let him in but left him standing outside waiting while she ran to tell everyone else.

Now, that scene is funny enough to be in a sitcom, but what I find even more amusing is that, when they hear her news, they responded by telling her that she was out of her mind. Don't you love it?

This is like the case in which a church was praying for a neighborhood bar to be closed. They "called down fire from heaven on that den of sin." When lightning struck the bar and burned it to the ground, the owner sued the local church. They swore in court that they had nothing to do with the bar burning. The judge said, "Well this is a fine mess. Here I have a church that doesn't believe in the power of their prayers, and a bar owner who does."

Poor Peter, newly escaped from jail, is left standing outside on the street because those inside praying didn't have any confidence in their own prayers. Luke notes, "Meanwhile Peter continued knocking," and, when they finally opened the door, they were amazed. Peter had to shush them lest their commotion attract the attention of the guards.

He tells them to go and tell the news to James and the brothers, while he goes to stay somewhere else. Just reading this at face value is confusing because the chapter begins with James being executed. The James to whom Peter refers here is not one of the 12 but James the brother of Jesus, who was becoming the leader of the church in Jerusalem. James was not a disciple of Jesus, but I Corinthians 15:7 seems to indicate that the early Church believed that the risen Christ made a special appearance to James. That may be, but it also may be that James couldn't quite buy that this brother he had grown up with was the Messiah. Perhaps it took seeing that Jesus was willing to die for what he taught. Giving your life to faith that differs from that of the majority has the power to transform even the most cynical.

People often ask me how to witness to their family about Jesus, or peace, or justice. My answer comes from James. Give your life to and for what you say you believe, and then your words have the power of life—your life and Jesus'.

The next morning, when the guards discovered that Peter had escaped somehow, there was a huge commotion. Herod went and searched the prison himself, which seems odd, but, after questioning the guards, he had them all executed. That was a common practice with jailors who allowed a prisoner to escape, but it also speaks to the utter sadism of Herod.

He then leaves Jerusalem, perhaps out of embarrassment, and goes to Caesarea. What follows is one of the most bizarre stories in the Bible. Herod is struck down and dies of a terrible disease in which worms eat his body. For those who had suffered under Herod, or who had friends like James executed, Herod's death was good news. They gave God the credit for striking him down.

While this is certainly tempting, it leaves us with many questions: If God was going to kill him, why didn't God do it before he killed James rather than after? If God strikes down evil rulers, why did God let Hitler live so long, or Stalin, or …?" Although it is tempting to attribute the destruction of evil people to God, we need to be careful because it creates a capricious God who kills Herod for killing a Jew named John, but allows Hitler to live long enough to kill six million Jews of many names.

In addition, do we really believe in a God who manages life with death and disease? As this week ends, you may be wondering what you actually CAN say about God. The truth is theologians have warned us that ANYTHING we say about God is heresy. By that they mean whenever we seek to contain God in the limits of our words we, by definition, fail.

Perhaps the lesson we need to embrace is that the more simple, or simplistic, our explanation of events becomes the greater the danger that we say terrible or foolish things about God. Luke gives God credit for striking down Herod, and you may believe that, too. However, we should not accept even the Bible's conclusions without being careful about the implications. If God is responsible for Herod's death then God also has to be given responsibility for letting others live too long.

For me, God is the God of life and light. We humans don't seem to need much help with death and darkness.

Acts 12:24-25

This chapter began with the execution of James, the brother of John. Then, the largest section described the arrest and amazing liberation of Peter, and it includes a bizarre description of the death of Herod. After all that, Luke says **"But** the word of God continued to advance and gain adherents." The implication seems to be that, regardless of what the government did, or what happened to the core leadership, or even what happened when governments failed, God continued to have a power and effectiveness.

Luke's final report is about Barnabas and Saul. The text that the New Revised Standard Version of the Bible relied upon says that Barnabas and Saul returned *to* Jerusalem, bringing with them John Mark. However, other texts say that they arrived *from* Jerusalem. Although it may seem arrogant to disagree with the prevailing scholars on this, it makes no sense to see Barnabas and Saul coming into Jerusalem. In fact, since the next chapter begins with Barnabas and Saul and Mark in Antioch, it is likely that this verse belongs there.

The church at Antioch took up an offering for the church in Jerusalem, which was suffering under the effects of a famine. Saul and Barnabas were entrusted with the offering and brought it to Jerusalem. While there, they encountered young John Mark. Apparently, he was a part of the company of disciples who met regularly in the upper room of his mother's house. Tradition holds that this is the Mark who wrote the Gospel by that name. Other legends contend that Mark was very young when Jesus died and that, when the soldiers came to arrest Jesus in Gethsemane, his mother sent him to run and warn him. Mark alone tells the story of a young man who was almost caught in the garden. He escaped only because, when they grabbed him, he literally ran out of his robes, fleeing the scene naked.

Barnabas had taken Saul in when no one else would have anything to do with him; now he is taking young Mark along to mentor him. This fact will be important later, but, for now, it gives us a clue about the kind of person Barnabas was and the kind of leadership that was present in the early Church. Mentoring another person is how Jesus led, and now it is how Barnabas leads. We, too, should seek opportunities to mentor those who are young or outcast, for thus the world is changed.

Now in the church at Antioch there were prophets and teachers: Barnabas, Simeon who was called Niger, Lucius of Cyrene, Manaen a member of the court of Herod the ruler, and Saul. While they were worshipping the Lord and fasting, the Holy Spirit said, "Set apart for me Barnabas and Saul for the work to which I have called them." Then after fasting and praying they laid their hands on them and sent them off.

The church in Antioch seems to be taking the lead from the church in Jerusalem, which is undergoing a time of hardship and persecution. We see from these verses that there were prophets (plural) and teachers (also plural) in the church at Antioch. Apparently, prophets went around from church to church preaching, while the teachers' role was to train and educate the church where they were. Several names are offered, though we aren't told if the list is prophets, teachers or both.

The list of leaders is quite diverse and includes at least one African, as well as a member of the court of King Herod. One is named Saul, and one named Simeon. Lucius is from Cyrene, which you may recall from one of the Gospel's stories of Jesus' crucifixion. Simon of Cyrene was compelled to carry the cross of Jesus after the loss of blood caused Jesus to collapse. There is a quaint tradition that suggests that Simon was transformed by that encounter and ended up as a teacher of the church in Antioch. It is a beautiful legend, with little to support it. However, of true beauty is the early Church's ability to make leaders of people who were quite different.

We see in Antioch a second generation of the Church. The devotion of this group is amazing. A prophet speaks to them and tells them what they think is the will of God. These folks don't simply follow blindly; they fast and they pray to discern if this word of God rings true for them. Only then do they lay hands on Barnabas and Saul, a former deadly enemy, consecrating them as missionaries and church planters.

The Church needs women and men who dare to speak a word of vision and direction from God, but that word needs confirmation by the people. They may not be gifted preachers or teachers, but they have the same Spirit and can practice spiritual discernment. That is an ancient gift that is missing from the modern Church. It requires us to be still and listen, and that seems to take a miracle for most of us.

Acts 13:4-16

Barnabas and Saul set out on their missionary journey to Cyprus. They take John Mark along to assist them. What is interesting in this story is that, for some reason, Luke makes a major shift in the dynamics of the story. It happens without any explanation or introduction. Saul becomes Paul, and "Barnabas and Saul" become "Paul and Barnabas." The story doesn't comment on the name change, nor does it attempt to explain why, from this day forward, Paul gets first billing and Barnabas becomes a supporting character.

When they encounter opposition from a local magician who doesn't want one of his clients to become a Christian, it is Saul who takes charge and works his first miracle, which seems a lot like magic, though he credits God with striking the magician temporarily blind.

Verse 13 begins, *"Paul and his companions set sail from Paphos and came to Perga in Pamphilia. John however left them and returned to Jerusalem."* From this point on, the book of Acts, and most of the rest of the New Testament, becomes about the life and teachings of Paul. He took a backseat and was discipled by Barnabas for a couple of years. Now, his strong gifts come to the fore, and he takes a leading role as an apostle. Barnabas is never referred to by that title, but Paul is destined to be a principal leader and shaper of this new faith that is spreading like fire across the Roman Empire.

Luke simply notes that John Mark went back to Jerusalem. There is no explanation in this passage as to why, but it becomes an important issue later. Perhaps Mark saw the change in dynamics that Luke simply reports and didn't like that Paul was suddenly the leader and his longtime friend and mentor Barnabas was not. Such changes are tough, especially for the young.

It also may be that he simply got homesick, but he bailed on the mission before the job was finished. Whatever the reason, and we don't want to be too harsh on him, it is important to note that starting well is good, but finishing strong is vital.

There are many disciples who answer the call, but drop out when it becomes difficult. G. K. Chesterton famously said, "The Christian ideal has not been tried and found wanting; it has been found difficult and left untried." There are parts of the ideal each of us have found difficult, so we returned to our comfort zones. Perhaps, we should reserve judging Mark.

... but they went on from Perga and came to Antioch in Pisidia. And on the Sabbath day they went into the synagogue and sat down. After the reading of the law and the prophets, the officials of the synagogue sent them a message, saying, "Brothers, if you have any word of exhortation for the people, give it." So Paul stood up and with a gesture began to speak.

Tomorrow we will look at the only sermon of Paul's of which we have a record, but, today, I don't want to pass over this brief transition passage. Luke doesn't say anything about the journey from Perga to Antioch in Pisidia, only that Paul and Barnabas went from one place to the other. What goes unmentioned is that this was one of the most arduous and dangerous journeys they will make. First, there is the climb. On foot, they had to ascend 3,600 feet to the plateau on which Pisidian Antioch was built. In addition, the road from where they were to where they were going was dangerous because the narrow passes made it the perfect place to be attacked.

Pisidian Antioch was an important city in that day, and Paul and Barnabas obviously decided that they needed to hear the good news. However, this is early in the missionary days of the Church, and there were lots of places that needed the Gospel. Except for the importance of the city, there is no hint about why they decided to go there. What is important, though, is that they did. They didn't make a different choice simply because this one was difficult or dangerous. So, when was the last time you did something truly challenging because of your faith? When did you follow the Spirit into a place that was risky and perhaps costly? When did you last take the more difficult road because you believed it was the way you were supposed to go? Barnabas and Paul went to Pisidian Antioch. They could have taken an easier, safer, better traveled road. Which choice would you have made?

Paul later writes a letter to the churches they established in this region. It is the book we know as Galatians. In it, he mentions that he was sick when he first came to them. It has been said that Paul caught malaria when he was in the low-lying Pamphylia. The resulting headaches may be what he later refers to as his "thorn in the flesh." Although we cannot know what was wrong with him, we do know that he made this challenging journey while he was sick. A lesser man or woman would have just stayed home, I suspect. Are we lesser disciples?

Liberating the Gospel

Acts 13:16-41

Exhausted from the journey, and apparently not feeling well, Barnabas and Paul went to the synagogue on the Sabbath. It was their habit, their discipline, their practicing of faith. Like Jesus, it was their custom. There, the leaders asked them if they had a word from the Lord for them. Paul couldn't resist the invitation, and, sick or not, he delivers one of the longest sermons in the Bible.

Of course, what we have is Luke's reconstruction of this sermon. It is very similar to the one Peter delivered on the day of Pentecost. He sets the coming of Jesus in the context of the history of God's work through, and with, Israel. He begins with their slavery in Egypt; then their deliverance; their taking the Promised Land; the last prophet/judge, Samuel; and the first king, Saul. Of course, he talks about David and how Jesus was the fulfillment of God's promise through David. Paul is clear that Jesus was the one the prophets foretold, but those who lived in Jerusalem did not recognize him and executed him. Paul notes that no charge brought against Jesus merited the death penalty, but the religious leaders demanded that Pilate put Jesus to death. Paul then goes on to talk about the resurrection and what it means.

Ultimately, his point is found in verse 38, when Paul says that, through this Jesus, forgiveness has come to the people and everyone who believes is set free. These really are the two sides of the Gospel coin. Forgiveness has come to us all, but experiencing the liberation of someone who is forgiven comes through faith.

So much of the theology we heard growing up made it seem that we could only be God's child if we believed. The truth is that every human is a child of God; we did not create ourselves or give ourselves life. We are God's children, but, frankly, we haven't lived like we believe that. Jesus came to show us what the life of grace can look like. Living free from guilt and shame is an experience few of us have ever seen in parents, pastors, teachers or friends. That is why we must receive for ourselves by faith. Then, moment by moment, we must renew our belief that we really are the forgiven. Jesus was willing to die to convince us that we are loved and that experiencing that love can resurrect us to the true life for which we were intended.

Paul told the people in Antioch that good news, and many were moved to faith. Everywhere, then and now, people are desperate to be invited to live as those who are Loved. What they need is someone to tell them of this Love ... someone who dares to believe it for themselves.

I have always loved the perspective of the bishop who assumed he was a success as a minister and a Christian and said, "Everywhere the early disciples went there were riots or they got stoned or were thrown in jail. Everywhere I go they serve tea."

So, Paul preaches his first sermon on the first missionary journey for which he got top billing. This passage says, "They talked to them and tried to persuade them to *abide in the grace of God* ." I love that phrase and that image of what Christian teaching and preaching ought to be all about. The Church does not impart grace because it is a free, unconditional gift from God. What the Church can and should do is invite and encourage people to live their lives abiding in the grace of God. What would a life lived fully in the grace of God look like? What would a person look like who lived a life fully and consistently that was anointed by the unconditional love, approval and favor of God?

Well, I believe it would look a lot like Jesus, and, as his disciples, that ought to be our only goal. We get caught up and distracted by so many things, but our only obsession ought to be to *abide in the grace of God,* knowing that all other things will take care of themselves.

This simple message of grace should have been received with glad hearts, but the religious leaders of Antioch were not amused. If grace was all it was about, then what about all their rituals, rules and restrictions? The sufficiency of grace alone seemed to be a critique of religion whose mission is to control the thoughts and behavior of people. That was true then and now. Ultimately, the Jewish religious leaders attacked Paul and Barnabas and their message. As a result, the missionaries take their message to the Gentiles in the city. This citation is another transition point in the Church. Luke is using this story as the pivotal point in the evolution of the Way of Jesus moving outside of Judaism and into the larger culture. For Luke, the Jewish religious leaders rejected the message of grace, so they took it to the Gentiles.

The established religion didn't give up easily, though. As the Gentiles began to join the Way, the establishment leaders stirred up the people, and they began to persecute Paul and Barnabas. Finally, it got so bad that they were forced to "shake the dust off their sandals" and move on to Iconium. Whenever faith challenges the status quo it causes trouble. Our question ought to be do we want to live out a faith that causes trouble, or one where people simply want to serve tea?

Acts 14:1-7

When Paul and Barnabas arrive in Iconium they follow their established pattern. Start at the local synagogue, many people believe and join the Way. This disturbs the religious leaders who stir up people against the disciples. The city is divided, and their success led to more than people running them out of town. They hatched a plot to stone them. Fortunately, they got word of the plan and fled the city.

Some scholars suggest that the growing opposition and threat of violence were because Barnabas and Paul were getting further away from "civilization." This seems to me to be the thinking of urban elites who only appreciate the civilization they know. Perhaps, as the status quo and power-keepers feel threatened, they are increasingly willing to use force, and even violence, to maintain the homeostasis that keeps them in control. This is a fear-based response that increases as fear increases. Our temptation is to see the power-keepers as "them," never "us." While it is true that some of us have known marginalization because of our sexuality, gender or race, most of us reading this are Americans, and, to the majority of the world, we are the power-keepers who use religion to justify the status quo of privilege that we enjoy.

Perhaps enough time has passed for us to honestly consider how privileged America reacted to the tragic events of September 11, 2001. The shock and horror had not even sunk in fully before we were seeking people with whom to go to war. Yes, we were grief-stricken for the loss of those precious 3,000 lives, but a stronger and more enduring emotion was outrage. So strong was the emotion that we invaded not one but two countries, killing tens of thousands more innocent children of God than died on 9/11. There has been little grief over that, though, because those lives were "them" not us. We have reserved our grief for the hero-soldiers whom we sent to kill and, if need be, to die to protect our privileged way of life.

Contrast that to the response of black South Africans after the end of apartheid. Most of the world expected bloodshed in revenge for tens of thousands of lives lost and decades of cruel oppression. Instead, the longsuffering oppressed created a "truth and reconciliation" process to bring redemption and healing. Perhaps only the oppressed can truly follow the Way of Jesus. Maybe this is what Jesus meant by saying it was "easier for a camel to go through the eye of a needle than for the wealthy to know the Reign of God." May we Americans who are wealthy by the world's standards hear what the scriptures have to say to us today.

Paul and Barnabas went to the ancient city of Lystra. There, they again preached and drew great crowds. One member of the crowd who came every day was a man who was lame. Paul saw the man's great faith and told him to stand. When he was healed, the people were amazed. So amazed, in fact, they called Paul and Barnabas gods. They called Paul "Zeus" because, as Luke notes, Paul had become the spokesperson for the two missionaries. They called Barnabas "Hermes." The reason is rooted in the mythology of the place. For centuries, a story had been passed down that these two gods long ago visited the city in disguise but found no hospitality. Eventually, two citizens did welcome them, so, when the gods destroyed the rest of the city, they were spared. They lived long lives, and, when they died, they were turned into the two great trees that stood at the entrance to the temple.

The people of Lystra were determined not to make the same mistake twice. When they saw Paul work a miracle, they immediately welcomed the gods back to their city. While some of us might be honored to be treated like gods, Paul and Barnabas were horrified. Paul argued vociferously that they were just mortal men like them. Apparently, he succeeded in convincing them that they had learned the wrong lesson because, shortly after that, some people from the synagogue in Iconium came to town and told people of all the trouble Paul and Barnabas had stirred up there. The people soon took up stones and, this time, succeeded in striking down Paul. Thinking they had killed him, they dragged his body out of the city lest the Romans find out what they had done.

However, Paul was not killed, only dazed. When he awoke, he got up and went right back into the city. I'm not sure if this is a story about Paul's courage or about his stupidity. At any rate, they didn't have to stone him twice. The next day, he and Barnabas moved on. Paul doesn't ask God to destroy them, as Zeus had done. Paul is, after all, a disciple of Jesus, so he simply moves on. I suppose there are times when we wish we worshipped a god like Zeus, especially when we have been mistreated and abused. Some Biblical writers were prone to interpret certain natural disasters as the vengeance of God. Then Jesus came along, teaching us to turn the other cheek, and, even when he was put to the ultimate test, that is exactly what he did. It is what Paul did, too. So, today, when someone stones you, get up, face them with courage—but without any hint of vengeance—and move on.

Acts 14:21-28

Paul and Barnabas move on to Derbe, where they convinced a considerable number of people to become disciples. They returned to Lystra, where Paul had been stoned, and then on to Antioch in Pisidia. They backtracked to reinforce the work they had done in these cities. He began by reminding them that faith was not insurance against affliction, but that affliction is one way in which we experience the Realm of God.

Perhaps Paul and Barnabas discovered that, when testing came, these new Christians became unstable, because, in each church, they selected elders. After fasting, they prayed for them and offered these new leaders to the Lord. They followed this pattern in all the churches they had established as they retraced their steps.

Eventually, they sailed home to Antioch and arrived at the church that had commissioned them and sent them out. They were able to report with great joy the success this congregation's faith in them had wrought. They all rejoiced that the Church had spread beyond the original boundaries of their expectations. The multitudes in various cities who came to faith were mostly Gentiles. What had started out as a movement within Judaism now had moved on to the larger population.

Paul and Barnabas didn't force these new believers to become Jews as they were, but they were able to let the Spirit work through them in completely new ways. When they came back to the church at Antioch and reported this, the news was received with joy. This wasn't going as they had planned, but who were they to expect God to follow their plans? Maybe they remembered that Jesus said that the Spirit was like the wind. We don't know from where it is coming, and we don't know where it is headed.

This passage ends by noting that Paul and Barnabas stayed with the disciples of Antioch for a long time. This was their home church, and, here, they recharged their batteries and renewed their strength. I am writing this on a plane on which the flight attendant moments ago reminded us to put on our mask first and then assist others. That spiritual wisdom is needed in the Church as well.

Christians breathe in as we gather to worship and study and care for one another. We breathe out as we scatter to serve and give and share. This rhythm is not only wise, it is critical. These missionaries were effective because they remembered that. My prayer is that this devotion is one of the ways you breathe in each day.

This chapter of Acts records the first real crisis in the early Church, which arose from the success of Paul and Barnabas. The result was a conflict between the younger missionary church in Antioch and the original congregation in Jerusalem, where most of the original disciples still lived. They were Jews who had come to faith following a Jewish rabbi named Jesus. When they heard of the exponential growth coming out of the church at Antioch, the mother church sent representatives to see what was going on. They found that most of the growth was taking place, not among the Jews, but among the Gentiles. The representatives of the establishment began to insist that Gentile converts had to be circumcised, going so far as to say, "Unless you are circumcised you cannot be saved."

Of course, this made no sense at all to the leaders in Antioch who knew that these uncircumcised Gentiles WERE saved. What we have is a classic church conflict between correct theology and experiential reality. In practice, the spiritual experiences of the circumcised Jewish Christians and the uncircumcised Gentile Christians were the same. Despite their personal experience, Paul and Barnabas (who both were circumcised Jewish Christians) were able to see the validity of the experience of others. That trait is quite rare. Even today, the overwhelming majority of the Church seems to have a singular understanding of how God works based entirely on how God worked in their own lives.

The dispute became so heated that the church at Antioch decided to send Paul and Barnabas to Jerusalem to resolve the matter once and for all. When Paul and Barnabas arrive, they are received with welcome arms in Jerusalem. However, Luke says that soon some of the believers who had been Pharisees rose and spoke against them, insisting that, when people became Christian, they should "keep the Law of Moses." While we may not appreciate it today, this was the most dangerous and critical moment in the life of the Church. Such conflicts will come again, but, at this point, it might have been fatal to the movement if the wrong choice was made. Of course, the conservative established church thought it would be fatal if they abandoned the religion of Jesus: Judaism. It is a strong and logical argument. Fortunately, the leaders of the church invested more faith in how the Spirit was acting rather than in how the Spirit was supposed to act. Don't you just hate it when God doesn't conform to our theology?

Acts 15:6-12

The Christians who had been Pharisees, and some of the stricter Jews, insisted that, for someone to become a Christian, they first had to be circumcised in obedience to the Law of Moses. Paul, who had become the main missionary to the Gentiles, insisted that was not the case. Of course, the women who were members and leaders in the early Church might have watched this argument with some amusement. The law that long had excluded them now posed quite a quandary for the men.

The decision will be made by a council of church leaders. This is a pattern that will continue for centuries, until a hierarchy eventually develops and leaders begin to act more like monarchs. In this council, one might assume that Simon Peter was the first among equals, but that apparently is not the case. Still, he was a person of great influence, so he stood to speak. He stakes his claim as the first missionary to the Gentiles and recounts his own experience and how the Spirit had fallen upon Cornelius, the Roman Centurion, and his family. Peter then says:

> *Now therefore why are you putting God to the test by placing on the neck of the disciples a yoke that neither our ancestors nor we have been able to bear? On the contrary, we believe that we will be saved through the grace of the Lord Jesus, just as they will.*

Peter is acknowledging, for one of the first times in the Bible, that the Jewish law had evolved into a burden that the average person was simply unable to bear. This wasn't about whether or not male converts would be circumcised, but about whether those new to faith would be required to keep the same set of rules that Jesus and the first disciples had kept, and apparently were still keeping.

It was a complex question, and, while Peter is the first to articulate that salvation is a gift of grace, the Church continues to wrestle to this day with the tension between law and grace. While it might be easy to say that the Gentiles need not be circumcised, do they have to keep other laws, like the Ten Commandments? Then, as now, the Church had a tough time trusting grace. Is it enough? We say it is … until someone acts in ways we find offensive or sinful. So, if Christians need to obey the laws, which ones? Who decides? Who decides for you? How do you decide? Things really haven't changed that much, have they?

Acts 15:13-21

Peter stands up before the council of leaders and speaks against placing the burden of the full Jewish law on new Gentile believers. Then, Luke notes, everyone was silent while Barnabas and Paul spoke about all the amazing work God had done among the Gentiles.

While it may just be happenstance, it is interesting that this is the first time in several chapters that Barnabas' name is listed first … and it's the last. Perhaps Paul was wise enough to allow Barnabas to take the lead here among those who had known him and his ministry for so long. While Paul was clearly the more articulate and, as a former Pharisee, had a convincing argument to make, what is true now was true then: in the end, relationships trump logic, experience and oratorical skills.

After Peter's words, and Barnabas and Paul had spoken, the true leader of the Jerusalem church spoke up. James, the brother of Jesus, was the one who spoke for the council. He quotes the scripture and then says, "Therefore I have reached the decision that we should not trouble those Gentiles who are turning to God but should write to them that they should abstain from things polluted by idols and from fornication." Reading this, one might assume that James made this decision on everyone's behalf; however, the original text is much more nuanced. He essentially is stating his own opinion/conclusion, not issuing an edict like a modern pope or bishop. He lists a couple laws that he thinks everyone should keep. Some texts include the prohibition from eating animals that had been strangled, and from eating blood.

It was an interesting redaction of the Jewish law. Eating food that had been offered to an idol has no context for us in our day, but, in that day, it was food that might otherwise have gone to waste in an age of great scarcity. This issue will arise again in Paul's writings. As for fornication, James is advocating for chastity. Interestingly, he doesn't talk about adultery, perhaps because the way in which law was lived out was more punitive to women than men.

James was the voice that carried the day. According to legend, it was his deep piety and devotion that were the source of his influence, not the fact that he was Jesus' brother. He was not a disciple while Jesus lived, but, apparently, when he came to faith, he came all the way. It is said that, when he died, they discovered that his knees were like a camel's from all the time he spent on them in prayer. Our deep desire should be to have leaders of such authentic devotion … and to become such people ourselves.

Acts 15:22-35

So, after listening carefully to the issue, the council of church leaders chooses Judas, called Barsabas, and Silas to accompany Paul and Barnabas back to Antioch to deliver their judgment. If Paul and Barnabas had returned alone their enemies might have doubted their story.

What we find in this chapter is the first "epistle" in the New Testament. It is written from, "The believers, both apostles and elders to the believers of Gentile origin in both Antioch and Syria and Cilicia." The letter goes on to disavow those who had arrived earlier and created the controversy in the first place. They clearly were speaking on their own and not representing the leadership. The letter notes that they decided unanimously on this course of action.

This is surprising because, clearly, it was a controversial decision about which they had strong disagreements rooted in centuries of tradition and core values. As I read this, I longed for this kind of Spirit in the Church today. For many years, in one congregation where I was pastor, the governing board worked very hard never to take a vote, but to do everything by consensus. The guiding value was that, unlike secular organizations, as much as possible, we should seek to avoid win/lose scenarios. Ironically, a member was publically critical about our "circumventing the democratic process." The early Church makes no claims to be a democracy; instead, it sought to be a community that discerned the will of God rather than voted to have their own will win the issue.

There is a profound need in the Christian Church, and in our lives as individual Christians, to spend less time debating and more time silently praying. If we listened to God more and our own voices less, we might have a much greater chance to reach a consensus or find a third way.

Ultimately, we all need to remember that the "decider" for the Church is not the will of the majority, but the will of God. If culture is any evidence, God's will and the will of the majority are often quite different. God's vote is ALWAYS cast for the poor, the marginalized and the powerless. Majority rule really has no place in the Church. God should rule, and we should pray until, to the best of our ability, we discern the will of God. What would it look like if our churches never voted but listened to one another to hear what we believed was God's will? What would our lives look like if we lived by discernment rather than decisions?

Acts 15:36-41

The delegation from Jerusalem delivered their message and then stayed for a while, helping out and strengthening the church. They had not come as authorities from on high, but as fellow ministers on the journey. After a while, Paul decided it was time to hit the road again, so he asked Barnabas if he wanted to go and revisit the churches they had founded. Barnabas was ready, but he wanted to take John Mark with them as well. Paul didn't want Mark to go since, on the last journey, Mark had "deserted" them in Pamphylia. A sharp disagreement arose between the two, and, in the end, Barnabas took Mark and went one way while Paul took Silas and went another.

It is ironic that the Church could reach a consensus over a profoundly divisive issue, but, here, two leaders and longtime friends part ways. Every sermon and Bible study I have ever heard (or, for that matter, taught) about this incident makes a hero out of Barnabas because he gave Mark another chance, and, in the end, Mark proved to be an effective disciple. It was the same spirit in Barnabas that allowed him to take in Paul when no other Christian really trusted that his conversion was legitimate. It is why Barnabas early on was called "son of encouragement."

Is it possible, though, that Paul had a point? The trip he was suggesting was the very one that they had taken the first time. If the course had been too much for Mark last time, what would make this one different? It was a physically challenging trip and at least one leg of it was quite dangerous. Paul wanted someone he could depend on, someone who could carry their weight, someone who wouldn't be more of a liability than an asset. This trip wasn't really about Paul or Barnabas or Mark; it was about the people they were going to serve. Paul isn't suggesting that Mark is a bad person, or that he doesn't have anything to contribute; he was concluding, from personal experience, that this trip wasn't a good match for Mark.

While we all admire Barnabas' faith and encouragement, a good deal of damage has been done in the Church by the inability of good, tenderhearted people to say, "No." How many ministries and, for that matter, churches have suffered greatly under leaders who should have been told no? How many people have suffered in positions for which they were ill-suited because people refused to be lovingly firm? In the end, Barnabas took Mark, but they took a much easier course. We will never know who was right about this, but we do know that God used both to spread the Gospel twice as fast.

Acts 16:1-5

After a three-to-five year absence, Paul returned to the neighboring towns of Derbe and Lystra. So successful was Paul in converting these cities that, two centuries later, the Roman Emperor Diocletian had Derbe destroyed and buried. Many of the residents fled to France, taking the church with them.

It was during the first missionary visit to Lystra that people mistook Paul and Barnabas for Zeus and Hermes. It also was here that Paul was stoned and left for dead. This time, he returns to find the church they had established flourishing. Of note, he meets a young man named Timothy and makes him his disciple. While nothing sexual is implied, this was an age and a region where older men often took young men under their wings as students or apprentices. Were this any text other than the Bible, we would discuss just what kind of relationship Paul had with Timothy. Again, there is nothing to indicate that it was sexual, but it is enlightening to know that the Church's sex-negative attitude is what keeps this conversation from ever happening. In any other Greek text from that day, we at least would consider this possibility, but I'm not sure that even I am brave enough to say any more.

Interestingly, Timothy's mother was Jewish and his father was Greek. Because of his father, Timothy apparently was not circumcised as an infant. The text says that Paul decided that needed to be done. Some translations indicate that Paul actually did the circumcision. The challenging thing is that Paul has just fought the conservatives in the Church to win the right for Gentile Christians not to have to be circumcised. The text says that it is because Timothy's mother was Jewish that Paul thought he needed to perform this ritual for the sake of his work among Jewish Christians. This is interesting because Timothy is the product of a mixed marriage, and even circumcision would not win him acceptance among orthodox Jews of that day.

Paul's discipleship of Timothy will continue and will find its way into other New Testament books as well. Paul will even make mention of Timothy's mother and grandmother. Timothy will accompany Paul as a missionary, be his emissary, and, in the end, accompany Paul to Rome for his execution. When Paul wrote to the Corinthians, he called Timothy a "beloved son." Life is forever changed for Paul, for Timothy, and for the Church by the relationship that is born on Paul's second visit to Lystra. The first time he is stoned. This time he finds a young friend and disciple for life. If I'd been Paul, I'm not sure I'd have gone back to see what God had in store.

This story begins with the strange contention that the Holy Spirit wouldn't allow Paul and Silas to preach in "Asia." It is an explanation as to why they went east rather than west to preach the Gospel. Interestingly, Luke explicitly refers to the Holy Spirit as "the spirit of Jesus." This is the only place that phrase is used, but it is an important clue about how the early Church understood the Holy Spirit. When they were "filled with the Spirit," they were filled with the Spirit of Jesus. Hence, they understood that Pentecost was the second coming of Jesus in the person of the Spirit. The Spirit of Jesus filled their lives, and, together, they became the Body of Christ.

Much of the Church looks for the "second coming" of Christ and forgets that we are called to BE the second coming of Jesus. We who are filled with the Spirit of Jesus should be doing the things he did: feeding the hungry, including the excluded, healing the hurting, reconciling the alienated and marginalized to God, and challenging the oppression of religion.

Under the influence of the Spirit of Jesus, Paul had a dream in which a man in Macedonia pleaded with him to come over there and help them. Just as the door to Asia closed, another door swung wide open. Paul "immediately" left for Macedonia. That prompt response is an important reminder.

We have a new puppy in our house, and, yesterday, he somehow became convinced that the person he was looking for was behind a closed door. That wasn't true, but, as he sat outside whining, I wondered just how often I have done that. Whining and barking outside a closed door that I thought had cut me off from what I wanted/needed. In the meantime, if I'd just turned around, or been more open to other possibilities, I might have heard a still small voice calling me down a better path. Why do we become so fixated on the half-empty part of the glass that we die of dehydration while a half-full glass sits before us?

Acts 16:11-40

In this passage, there is a dramatic shift. Verse 6 begins, "We set sail from Troas and took a straight course to Samothrace." The pronouns shift from "they" to "we." While the writing style is much the same, the story is now told in first person. The implication, of course, is that Luke has become a part of the traveling band of missionaries.

They land on the peninsula and then head directly to Philippi. It was a significant Roman city, but, here, the pattern for ministry begins to shift again. In Philippi, there were few Jewish citizens. Ten adult Jewish men were required to start a synagogue, but, at Philippi, the Jews worship at a special spot down by the river. In this setting, most of the missionary efforts will have to be made to people of other religions who don't know anything about a rabbi from Galilee.

At the river, they encounter Lydia, a well-to-do Jewish woman and a merchant selling purple dye or cloth. She became the first European convert to Christianity, and her home became the home-base for the missionaries and, eventually, the church.

Ironically, Paul's second encounter in this record is with a young woman who was a slave and made money for her master by telling fortunes. She recognized Paul and Silas as representatives of "the Most High God" and began to announce it loudly to the whole town. She probably wasn't exactly the kind of publicist that the missionaries wanted, but she got them lots of attention ... and trouble.

After a while, Paul got so annoyed with her that he cast a demon out of her, and she lost her ability to tell fortunes. When her owner realized he had lost a source of income, he had Paul and Silas arrested. Then, as now, compassion was a crime if it interferes with profit. Don't believe me? Just try violating prescription patents to save the lives of millions of Africans by giving them cheap medication.

Acts 16:19-40

The owner of the slave girl managed to get Paul and Silas arrested, beaten and thrown in jail. Now, imagine how you would feel at the end of that very bad day. Stripped in public and beaten with rods, then shackled hand and foot, and thrown in a nasty dark and dank cell. What a pity party would have ensued for most of us, especially considering that all of this had been done to them because they helped a poor, possessed slave girl.

Not Paul and Silas, though. The familiar text says, "And at midnight Paul and Silas prayed and sang praises to God, and the prisoners were listening to them."(16:25) Later in life, Paul will write, "If we live we live unto the Lord and if we die we die unto the Lord. Whether therefore we live or we die, we are the Lord's." (Romans 14:8) In this story, we see that attitude toward life lived out. No self-pity, no cynical resignation, no resentment or bitterness, and no depression.

Years later, Paul will write a letter to the church that gets established here in Philippi. It is the book in the Bible that we know as Philippians. In Philippians 4:1 Paul wrote, "… for I have learned in whatever circumstances I find myself, I can be content." Such talk might ring hollow to some, but those to whom he wrote the letter knew that it was true. Regardless of the unfair abuse, Paul found a place within himself to be at peace, not because of the circumstances, but despite them.

As they prayed and sang, an earthquake occurred that actually sprang open the prison doors. When the jailer discovered this, he began to commit suicide because, as we saw earlier, he would have been executed for allowing prisoners to escape. Paul stopped him just in the nick of time. Of course, if Paul had been quiet they all could have escaped, but Paul was more concerned for the jailors' wellbeing. As a result, this man became a Christian. Paul baptized him and his whole family.

I can't help but wonder how many people might follow Jesus if they saw more followers of Jesus who cared more about them than they did themselves. It makes a powerful witness because it happens so seldom.

Acts 16:35-40

The next day, the magistrates decide that they had been a bit harsh and hasty, so they sent word to the jailer to let the missionaries go. The trouble was Paul refused. He said, "Absolutely not. They had us beaten in public and thrown in jail and now they want to release us in secret?" As a result, Paul extracted an apology from them for the injustice that had been committed.

While that may sound silly, it restored their integrity, and the integrity of the church they would leave behind. There is a great need today for the spirit that filled Paul. Too many of us are simply silent or compliant in the face of inequity and injustice.

I regularly embarrass my family by speaking up and confronting businesses that take advantage of people. Recently, I closed a bank account, but I first demanded to see the manager. In the lobby, in front of witnesses, I explained—using my preacher's voice, of course—that I was ashamed that his bank was practicing usury. When he made the mistake of asking what I meant, I lectured him on the immorality of manipulating accounts to assure that, if someone was overdrawn, they bounced the maximum number of checks and charged the greatest amount of penalty. By clearing the largest check, they may be able to bounce half a dozen small checks, when they could have chosen to honor the small checks and bounce only the largest. The result of this deliberate manipulation further impoverishes the very poorest.

Now, I haven't bounced a check in my life, but that didn't excuse me from using my voice to speak up on behalf of those who have no voice. Most people in Paul's shoes would have left prison as quickly as possible, just glad to have the matter behind them. Not Paul, though. He wasn't leaving until those in power recognized they had committed an injustice. Left unchallenged, practices like this continue to crush those who cannot defend themselves.

When we are silent about injustice we are co-conspirators of injustice.

Having given birth to the church in Philippi, the missionaries moved on to Thessalonica. There, too, their preaching was met with a positive response and with resistance. Paul and Silas preached in the synagogue, and many Jews believed in Jesus. An even greater number of Greeks believed, and Luke notes that a significant number of the leading women of the city came to believe. From the very beginning, women responded to the message of Jesus. Because of the sexism of that day (and this), their stories were not told. We have to read between the lines, but there is overwhelming evidence that Christianity became established because of the support of first-century women.

In Thessalonica, some Jewish leaders didn't like what Paul was saying, so they used a political argument to stir up trouble against him. They reported that the missionaries were claiming that Jesus was a king, but Roman law had established that there was no king but Caesar. It is, of course, the argument used against Jesus. The duplicity of the religious right defending the status quo by manipulating the government to serve their purposes is nothing new.

They couldn't find Paul and Silas and ended up dragging some of the new believers into court. Among them was a man named Jason. They demanded that he tell them where they were, but he apparently really didn't know. He had simply offered them his home as a gathering place.

What is worth our attention is the description of Paul and Silas that the religious leaders use: "These people who have been turning the world upside down have come here also." Regardless of how the accusation is couched, the thing that religious people then and now seem to fear most is having their world turned upside down. When will we learn that this is how the Spirit always works, blowing through our lives and scattering our neat stacks of beliefs and certainties everywhere?

Acts 17:16-34

At last, Paul's journey brings him to Athens. He left Silas and Timothy behind in the cities they had passed through so they could shore up the churches that had been planted there. When he got to Athens, though, Paul found the city overwhelming and sent for his friends to come and help him. Athens had passed its prime and was no longer the most important city in the West. Still, it was the cultural and educational center and was the largest city Paul had ever visited.

As was his custom, he went to the local synagogue and started his work there. He also soon discovered that a city who trafficked in ideas offered many opportunities for him to proclaim the truth as he understood it. Paul's sermon on Mars Hill was a major shift and has been called the first act of the modern Church.

He was not talking to Jews, and the typical resistance from Jewish leaders to which he was accustomed was completely absent. What he encountered was similar to the experience of early missionaries to India. No one really resisted the proclamation that Jesus was divine; rather, they just acquiesced that Jesus was just one more God they had not heard about before. There were shrines and temples and statues to hundreds of gods scattered all over the city. Athens was a Roman province, so they knew that even Caesar claimed to be the incarnation of a deity. So, what's one more? Ho hum.

This is not unlike the response of society to the modern Church. Just one more thing competing for people's time and attention. Nothing bad, but ho hum. Paul's words were initially dismissed as "babble." (17:18) He discovered that he would have to find a different, more creative way to connect with people who were busy and well educated and erudite. Their glasses were already too full for him to offer them anything more. He might have given up and gone on to places where people were thirsty. What he did, though, was offer them a new glass.

Paul was brought before the Areopagus on Mars Hill, which is the same court that tried and sentenced Socrates centuries before. Now that the city was under Roman rule, their only real power was to decide who could and could not teach in the city. Paul was in no danger, but the Gospel was.

Paul began his defense by using their starting point rather than his own. He affirmed just how broadly religious they were, noting that they even had an altar to "the Unknown God." Then, using an understanding they already held, Paul built his argument from there. Essentially, he said, he had come to tell them about this unknown God.

Having established a rapport with his listeners, Paul moves directly to the Hebrew God by describing this "unknown" God as the one who created everything that is and, from a single ancestor, created all of them. This message, direct from Genesis, connects them all together as family rather than the "us vs. them" approach of so many witnesses. Paul famously describes this unknown God as "the one in whom we live and move and have our being."

Paul is not describing a distant God who sends lightning and thunder from mountains in the sky, nor is he describing a deity who comes in disguise and moves among us. Rather, Paul is turning all religion on its head—God doesn't live with us; rather, we live IN God. Even today, if the Church were to take seriously Paul's description of God, we would need to rewrite our theology and reorder our worship.

The truth is that, by and large, Christians still live in a three-story universe with heaven above and hell below. What would today be like if you spent every moment as if Paul was right?

God is the One in whom we live.

God is the One in whom we move.

God is the One in whom we have our very being.

Wow.

Acts 17:28-34

After telling the sages on Mars Hill that this unknown God was the one who created us all, he goes on to point out that this unknown God didn't fling creation into existence, but continued to be one with creation and one with us. This God is the One in whom we live, and move, and have our being.

Paul then goes on to speak to them about the resurrection of the dead. Some of his listeners scoffed at him, but others were intrigued and insisted that he return and talk to them again. That of course is the preacher's dream: to have people want to listen to her again or to know more from him.

So, Paul left with some hope, even if he did not feel like he had accomplished much. Still, Luke notes that there were some who were convinced, including Dionysius the Areopagite and a woman named Damarius as well as others. Dionysius was one of the 30 or so members of the court who heard Paul that day. He didn't need to hear anymore. Something in Paul's words rang true to him, and he took them into his heart and was changed.

We don't know who Damarius was. In that day, the average Athenian woman would not have been present in a crowd of strange men. The implication, of course, is that she is one of the less respectable women, or perhaps she was simply more courageous or willing to disregard the opinions of others. Either way, she is one more example of how the Church's early appeal was equally to those at the center of power and those on the margins of society.

Luke wanted us to know that, while huge numbers of people were not converted in Athens, a powerful man and a marginalized woman were left behind as the nucleus of what ultimately became the Athenian church. Luke names them because, though they may mean little to us, they obviously were the ones who made the Gospel a reality in the place where they lived.

While his visit to Athens was important it was not marked with incredible success, and the next chapter finds Paul moving on to the Greek coastal city of Corinth. The city had existed for 6,000 years by the time Paul visited. It is about 50 miles south of Athens, and was once a powerful city-state until the Romans destroyed it around 147 BC. By the time Paul visited, it was a significant provincial capital for the Romans. Paul stays in Corinth for a long time and will later return for about three months. Eventually, his letters to the church at Corinth will become books of the New Testament.

Here in Corinth, Paul meets Aquila and Priscilla who become dear friends and colleagues. Paul will praise them in other writings, and they became the most famous couple in the New Testament. They are mentioned seven times, and five of those times Priscilla's name is listed first. She was obviously a significant leader in the early missionary days of the Church. She is a Jewish Christian from Rome, and so important was she that some traditions credit her with being the author of the book of Hebrews.

Paul worked with Priscilla and Aquila as a fellow tentmaker. With money in short supply, Paul fell back on an old vocation to pay his expenses. Today that willingness to do secular work so that you can be in ministry is rare among young and new ministers. It is virtually unheard of among more mature pastors, and, as you might imagine, people who have obtained as much fame as Paul and know such success cannot conceive that they would have to do manual labor so that they might be able to do ministry. This is not said as a criticism of modern pastors (of which I am one) but rather to help us appreciate Paul, who he was and what he did.

The phrase "tent-making ministry" is taken from this story. It simply means working a secular job to pay your expenses so you can do ministry. The truth of the matter is this is what we ALL are called to do. The work most of us do is sacred because we can be God's missionary there and because it affords us the opportunity to support other ministries and give our lives to them. How different sewing the seams of a tent must look when you see it as a tool for being a minister of the living God. You may be a Christian minister cleverly disguised as a copy writer, or computer programmer, or … It is an ancient and noble tradition.

Acts 18:18-28

Chapter 18 ends with Paul and his partners—Silas, Timothy and Priscilla and her husband Aquila—planting churches in Ephesus, Galatia, Phrygia and, eventually, Corinth. In Ephesus, we meet Apollos who becomes a chief missionary and preacher. All of these places and people will be heard from again in Paul's epistles that comprise much of the New Testament. Without reading these stories in Acts, there would be little context for reading those letters. The ironic thing is that the writing of the letters probably came first. Luke, having read those letters, is now trying to explain to us who these people are and why Paul wrote to the Galatians, Ephesians and Corinthians.

In these verses, Christianity is referred to as "The Way of the Lord" and "The Way of God." Priscilla and Aquila were the ones who explained The Way of God to Apollos. It is unfortunate that preachers and teachers have given up that approach to the Christian faith. The Church has fought and divided and split many times over doctrine and theology. What a different thing Christianity might be, and what different people we Christians might be, if we simply had understood that we were people of "The Way of Jesus."

Living as Jesus lived, and treating people as Jesus did, are only vaguely and distantly related to the religious industry known as Christianity. There have been times when people have genuinely sought to recover the way of Jesus, but they have been short lived. I can remember as a child seeing the Jesus people who grew their hair long, dressed simply, and talked a lot about peace and love. Then they grew up to be stockbrokers, CEOs, bankers and lawyers. The Way of Power and The Way of Money seemed too powerfully alluring.

So, is it too late for us? As we read through the book of Acts, one of the things that strike me is that people like Paul, or Barnabas, or Aquila all were successful established adults who gave up their way of life and living to authentically follow the Way of Jesus. If they could do it, so can we. The question is why don't we?

The 19th chapter of Acts is largely a description of Paul's time in the city of Ephesus. It is probably the place in his ministry where he stayed the longest. Always an itinerant, it is surprising that Paul probably spent three years in one place.

Ephesus was a major Greek, and later Roman, city located about half-way down the western coast of what is Turkey today. It was renowned for the Temple of Artemis, which was build around 500 years before Paul's visit and is one of the Seven Wonders of the Ancient World. Ironically, the temple was destroyed approximately 400 years after Paul by a Christian mob lead by John Chrysostom, Archbishop of Constantinople.

Paul writes his famous epistle to the church at Ephesus. It is one of the seven churches mentioned in the book of Revelation. Legend has it that the Gospel of John was written out of the Christian community in Ephesus and that Paul wrote his letter to the Corinthians from there. Mary, the mother of Jesus, was reputed to have spent her last years there, and a church there was built in her honor. A house about four miles out of town has long been said to have been her last residence.

When Paul and his company first arrive in Ephesus, they find a small band of about a dozen disciples already there. They were surprised and ask them if they had received the Holy Spirit after they believed. The implication is that receiving the Spirit was a sign that accompanied coming to faith. The Ephesian disciples said that they didn't even know that the Holy Spirit existed.

This spiritual state would make them fit right in with most modern churches. Their faith had all been intellectual. They had no actual experience of the presence of God in their lives. Theirs was a faith of mental *assent*, but not spiritual *ascent*.

Paul then asked them then what their baptism had meant, and they explained that they had experienced only the baptism of John for repentance, not the baptism of Jesus for forgiveness. Paul explained to them the next step of their faith, and they believed and were baptized in the name of Jesus and received the Holy Spirit in the same way the first believers had on Pentecost.

This story leaves me wondering if we in the modern Church might not have stopped too soon in our faith process.

Acts 19:8-41

Paul taught in the synagogue in Ephesus for three months. Eventually, a group there began to "speak evil of the Way." He and the disciples then moved on and used the hall of a local philosophy teacher named Tyrannus where Paul taught for the next two years. While he had critics who were quite vocal, Paul's work in Ephesus went well, some would say too well.

Being a Greek city, there was great tolerance in Ephesus for different religions and different gods and goddesses. The principal deity of the city, though, was the goddess Artemis/Diana. The Way was tolerated by the folks in the city until so many people began abandoning the worship of Artemis and joining the Way that it cut into the profit of the local merchants. A silversmith named Demetrius fomented a riot by stirring up the merchants whose livelihoods might have been threatened. Of course, he frames the issue in pious terms as though he was concerned about the honor of the goddess, not his own profit. People got all worked up, and they dragged some of the disciples out of the theater where they were preaching. The trouble was the mob was unclear what it was that they were supposed to be so outraged about. Luke writes that "some were shouting one thing and some were shouting another." This continued until a magistrate of the city brought order and insisted that, if Paul and company had committed any crime, it should be handled by the courts, not a mob.

In our day, we often have seen mobs gather to protest. Recently, there have been huge protests about taxes. The irony is that the tax rate for most Americans is the lowest in decades, and it is lower than almost any industrialized nation. Taxes were not raised to finance the wars we are waging, but money was borrowed to do that. There were few protests against that borrowing, but put forth the idea that taxes might have to increase to provide health care for all and, suddenly, those who have health care took to the streets.

The truth is that, whenever the Way of Jesus is taken, it inevitably will come into conflict with capitalism, the true religion of America. The fact that the conflicts are so few is an indictment of the Church and says that we are not living into the Way of Jesus. Who we are, how we live, and the values for which we advocate should cause those whose chief value is profit to riot. Instead, they comfortably fill our pews, and we are cowered into silence, lest the Way of Jesus offend them … and their giving. Where is Paul when we need him?

Acts 20:1-6

After the riot in Ephesus, Paul knew that is was dangerous to lead a movement that threatened people's pocketbooks. He decided that, after two years, it was time for him to get out of town. He made some short trips and stirred up trouble in other places, and then he returned to Ephesus where he called the elders of the Church together and made an impassioned farewell speech. It is an emotional good-bye because Paul says that, unlike other churches he had planted, he was not coming back to check on them.

In this parting speech, Paul encouraged them to care for those in need, "remember the words of the Lord Jesus, for he himself said, 'It is more blessed to give than to receive.'" This quote is fascinating because, if taken seriously, it shifts our very way of being in the world. It also is interesting because these are among the few red letters in the Bible after the first chapter of Acts.

The Gospels contain the words of Jesus, and those words often are printed in red. However, after the ascension of Jesus in Acts chapter 1, the red letters essentially end. Here in Acts Luke quotes Paul quoting Jesus. That simply doesn't happen anywhere else in the book of Acts. Paul also very rarely quotes Jesus directly in any of this writings that make up much of the rest of the New Testament.

The other fascinating thing to me is that Luke records these red letters here, but they are nowhere to be found in the Gospel of Luke, nor are they found in any of the other Gospels. This is the only place they are found in the Bible. Paul didn't know Jesus firsthand, so it may well be that these words are taken from another account of the life of Jesus that Paul had but that has been lost to us.

Finally, I find it interesting that, if Luke records Paul quoting Jesus only once, this is the quote. Clearly, this was much more than just a quaint religious cliché to be quoted at the time of taking an offering. In the context of the early Church, it was a way of living and the core of a value system that believed God was more interested in blessing what we give than in blessing what we get. What would a society look like whose supreme value is philanthropy, not consumption?

As one who lives in a city where the chief recreational activity is shopping, this verse calls us to a greater shift than we imagine. Maybe that is why it got left out of the Gospels. Maybe it was a shift so radical that Luke buried it here in the 20th chapter of Acts where no one would think to look for red letters.

Acts 21:1-16

This passage is mostly a travelogue. It is written in first person, so Luke apparently was traveling with Paul again. The story is almost annoying in its detail. You wonder why some of the ink was wasted to tell us of each of their stops along the way to Jerusalem. Twice Paul is warned that he shouldn't go to Jerusalem. In one prophecy, he is told specifically that he will be arrested by the Jewish leaders and handed over to the Romans. No one needed reminding that this was what happened to Jesus.

Paul also didn't need reminding that, like Jesus, you can't make your decisions based on fear of what might happen. Paul was determined, so the other disciple decided to stay quiet and pray for him. What a strange strategy; so strange that it rarely has been followed by disciples since. Most Christians seem to believe that they know the will of God, and they are determined to force that will to happen. It is rare to find a disciple willing to say their piece and then trust the matter to prayer.

This passage concludes in verse 16 by telling us that they spent the night in Caesarea with a disciple named Mnason who was from Cyprus. I love this verse because, other than that Mnason was from Cyprus, the only fact we are told about him is that he was "a long-term disciple."

Every time I read this verse I think about those elderly women and men who used to fill the country churches I pastored as a young man. I started preaching when I was only 19. What on earth did I have to say to people who had been going to that church for most of a century? Yet, every Sunday without fail, they were there. Many of them had lived hard lives and had known a great deal of heartache, but they had not abandoned the faith. The young people had moved on from those farming crossroads, yet here were men and women who gathered week after week to worship and to study. Like Mnason, they were long-term disciples.

One Sunday, I watched as a woman who could have been my grandmother's mother struggled up the steps of that little country church. What on earth could I say in my sermon that Aunt Mary needed to hear? As I greeted her that day, I said how glad I was to see her. She said, "I wouldn't miss it. I've prayed for all our young preachers before you and I have to be here to pray for you, too." She hadn't come to hear my sermon; she'd come to pray for me. Aunt Mary has been dead for at least 20 years now, but, every now and then, I can still feel her praying. My prayer is for God to give us more of those long-term saints … and, someday, make us one, too.

Acts 21:17-26

After his many adventures in Greece, Paul returns to Jerusalem. He has been gone for at least three years, but word of his work had spread—true words and false words. His first act is to meet with Steven and the elders to give a complete report. They were excited about all the good things that had been happening, but they were also concerned. Rumors had spread that Paul had been teaching the Jews that they no longer needed to obey the law. While it was true that Paul taught the new Gentile Christians that salvation did not come though obedience to the law, he had not tried to persuade Jewish believers to abandon their traditions. The elders, leadership and original leaders, and even Paul himself, all were Jewish. A natural tension was beginning to arise because the overwhelming majority of the new converts were not.

Several times in my ministry, I have been the pastor of a church that grew. New members eventually outnumbered the old. For several years, though, the longtime members held all the power, made all the decisions, and set the agenda. The longtime members welcomed the newcomers because they brought new life and hope for a future. Still, they found it difficult to change how things had always been done. The new folks arrived with great enthusiasm and excitement, but little regard for tradition. It is a challenging dynamic to navigate. The issues are much more subtle and complex than I have just described; as a result, there are misunderstandings.

So, too, when Paul arrived back in Jerusalem, the elders are very happy to hear about what Paul is doing, but it is easy to see how the fine line he was walking led to misunderstandings and rumors. As a result, the elders sought a compromise, and Paul agreed. He and four other believers would submit to the rite of purification. In doing this publically, everyone would see that he hadn't abandoned his heritage and traditions and he still obeyed the Jewish law. The trouble was the issue was complicated and didn't lend itself to simplistic symbolic acts. This compromise ended badly, as we will see tomorrow. For today, our lesson might be to remember that:

1. We shouldn't be surprised when good deeds get misconstrued or distorted;
2. Rumors can be dealt with only directly and with the truth; and
3. Life is more complex than sound bites or bumper stickers. Conflicts must be resolved in community with direct communication. Even then, change is tough.

Acts 21:27-36

To combat the rumors about him, Paul agreed to join four other believers in the rite of purification. Just as the seven days were almost complete, Paul goes to the temple where some folks recognize him and stir up the crowd against him. They accuse Paul of daring to bring Greeks into the temple to defile it. That seems like a blatant lie, but the truth is Paul was bringing Greeks into faith in a way that many Jews believe defiled their traditions and their way of life.

The rumors and accusations were rooted in some truth because they were rooted in people's fear of losing something they valued. They were also afraid that, if what Paul said was true, what they believed was wrong. Few people, especially religious people, seem to have the capacity to believe they are right without having to prove that all who disagree with them are wrong. Fundamentalists, whether liberal or conservative, need to buttress their own insecurity by attacking others.

Paul is physically attacked and dragged out of the temple. Such a commotion ensued that the Romans soon show up to keep the peace. They arrest Paul, since he is obviously the source of the trouble, and try to sort it all out back at the barracks. While this isn't the first time something like this happened to Paul, the fallout from this one changes everything.

After Paul is arrested, he offers his defense to the crowd in Hebrew. It is a long retelling of his own personal testimony. Toward the end, he starts another riot, so the Roman guards decide to scourge him to get the truth. Apparently, their Hebrew wasn't good enough to understand what Paul had said to the crowd. In those barbaric days, people with no faith thought nothing of using physical pain to coerce a prisoner to tell them what they wanted to hear. Of course, WE would never stoop to such barbarism or tolerate it from our elected government …

In the end, Paul stops them by reminding them that he is a Roman citizen who has been convicted of nothing. These soldiers might have been un-churched barbarians, but even they would not use torture to coerce a fellow citizen to confess …

Asserting his Roman citizenship stops the guards from torturing Paul, but it doesn't get him set free. What he gets, though, is a hearing. Even faithless barbarians don't believe in holding people indefinitely without charging them or giving them a trial by which they might prove their innocence. Apparently, only "Christian" nations like the United States do that.

Acts 23:1-11

The Romans had no idea what to do with Paul, so they called the Jewish council together to discover what the issue was. What takes place is an amazing bit of drama. Paul notices that the council is made up of Sadducees and Pharisees, so he pits the two against one another. As Luke explains, the Sadducees don't believe in angels or the spirit or resurrection. The Pharisees believe in all three.

Paul begins his defense by saying that he is a Pharisee and the son of a Pharisee and his only crime was to proclaim "the hope of the resurrection." This infuriates the Sadducees but forces the Pharisees to come to his defense. Soon, there was such a ruckus between the two groups that the Romans had to take Paul back to the barracks for his safety. Since he was a Roman citizen, they were obligated to protect him.

Then, in verse 11, Luke writes, "That night the Lord stood near Paul and said, 'Keep up your courage! For just as you have testified for me in Jerusalem, so you must bear witness for me in Rome.'" Paul had declared to the folks back in Ephesus that he was going back to Jerusalem, but then he wanted to make his way to Rome, the capital of the world. This is a classic case of needing to be specific in what you wish for. Paul wanted to go to Rome, but not necessarily as a prisoner.

The next day a group of men decided that the best way to deal with Paul was to kill him. Some 40 of them conspired to have the Romans bring him back to the council where they could attack him. Paul's nephew, his sister's son, heard about the plot and reported it to the Roman Tribune. The tribune couldn't let a Roman citizen be assassinated in his care, so he got two centurions to put together 200 soldiers and 20 horsemen to escort Paul out of town. He sent Paul to Felix the Governor, a successor to Pontius Pilate.

Paul must have thought it was an awful lot of fuss for a simple preacher. It wasn't that Paul had any power, but the message he preached challenged everything the Jews believed. Soon, it would challenge the Romans, too. Calling people to reconsider beliefs in which they are deeply invested is a dangerous business. People will try to stop you with rumors first, and, if they can't assassinate your reputation, there is no telling what they will do to stop you.

Liberating the Gospel

Acts 23:26-24:27

Felix was hated by the Jews. His wife was the daughter of Herod Agrippa, and she had been married to another minor king until Felix seduced her. A riot occurred as the result of a conflict between the Jews and Greeks in Caesarea. Felix took the side of the Greeks, allowing his soldiers to ransack the homes of prominent Jewish citizens. After they complained about him to the emperor, he eventually was recalled.

During this time, though, Felix kept Paul in jail for two years, hoping to curry favor with the Jewish leaders. He is neither the first nor last politician to condone injustice because it was the politically popular thing to do. While democracy is a great form of government, ruling by popular opinion often leads to the oppression of those who are not the majority and to injustice for those who are out of favor with the majority.

Felix was succeeded as governor by Porcius Festus. He tried to get off on the right foot with his Jewish subjects by offering to hold a trial for Paul in Jerusalem. The plot to assassinate Paul was still in the works, so, in order to prevent this, Paul exercises his right as a Roman citizen and appeals his case to the emperor. Festus has no choice but to send him to Rome.

Several days later, King Herod Agrippa and his wife arrive in Caesarea to welcome Festus into his new job. Festus tells them about Paul and his exchange with the Jewish leaders and Agrippa wants to meet Paul himself. So, the next day, Paul is brought before Festus and Agrippa, and he is asked again to make his case. Luke records yet another long passage of testimony from Paul. At one point, Felix interrupts and suggests that too much learning has made Paul mad.

Agrippa, however, is a Jew and knows the context of all Paul is saying. He asks Paul if he is trying to convert him to Christianity. Paul said that it is his desire that all who hear him become as he is, except without the chains.

In the old King James Version of this story, Agrippa is reported to have said, "Almost thou persuadest me to become a Christian." More modern and accurate translations do not indicate that Agrippa goes quite that far. What he does do, though, is tell Festus that Paul isn't guilty of anything. He then adds, "If he had not appealed to the Emperor, he could have been set free."

Paul used his Roman citizenship to protect himself, but, in the end, it keeps him imprisoned. I'm sure there is a sermon illustration in there somewhere …

And so we come to the last of Luke's stories. It is one of my favorites, at least in Acts. Luke is a great storyteller. Were he not a Biblical writer, he would have gained renown similar to Homer, Dante or Shakespeare. His stories, including the Good Samaritan and the Prodigal Son, have shaped Western culture and defined Christianity.

This last story isn't nearly as well known, but it has almost as many lessons within it. Although it appears in the lectionary, and I have preached from this passage many times, it is a challenge because the story is so long and is woven so tightly together. Like the other passages in Acts that are written in the first person, the details almost overwhelm us. Before we unpack them, let me summarize the story and the setting.

Upon returning to Jerusalem, the elders ask Paul to undergo the rite of ritual purification because rumors have accused him of betraying his heritage and teaching Jewish believers that they need not keep the law. As he was doing this, a mob in the temple attacks him, and he has to be rescued by the Roman authorities. They arrest him and hold him for more than two years. He faces trial before both Roman and Jewish rulers. At one point, they threaten to flog him to determine the truth. To avoid this government-sanctioned torture, Paul asserts his right as a Roman citizen and insists that he be allowed to appeal his case to Caesar.

When he is questioned by King Agrippa, he says to the Roman governor Festus that Paul was clearly innocent of any crime and could be released, except for the fact that he has appealed to the emperor. As a result, they have no choice but to send him on his way to Rome. This final story in Acts is the account of Paul's last missionary journey.

As they set off for Italy, Paul and some other prisoners are placed in the custody of a Roman Centurion named Julius. Since Paul was clearly innocent, Julius treats him kindly. Luke and another friend named Aristarchus were allowed to accompany Paul. This was risky because, though Paul is innocent, the outcome is anything but certain. It is a remarkable thing to have friends accompany you when you are under accusation and your reputation has been maligned. If you have people like that in your life, then, like Paul, you are most blessed. Pause and think of who those people are in your life and give thanks for them. Now, pause and think of who might count you as that kind of friend. Which list is longer?

Acts 27:9-20

Luke describes in great detail the fits and starts by which Paul's journey to Rome began. He notes that so much time had been lost that the weather made the journey dangerous. By now it was November, and, with the tiny ships of that day, sailing was suspended until spring. Julius was in a hurry, though, and the ship's captain thought the weather would hold. Paul strenuously warns against setting sail. The fact that he had any voice in this at all is telling. No doubt Paul was the most experienced traveler on the ship, but, nonetheless, the centurion heeded the advice of the ship's captain rather than the prisoner.

They soon sailed headlong into a terrible northeaster that threatened to break the boat apart. The sailors knew they were in serious trouble. They had no choice but to furl the sails and let the wind drive them. As the storm grew worse, they threw overboard some of the cargo that was the real purpose for the journey. With that gone, there would be no profit or payoff for this journey. Still, their only choice was their money or their life.

Luke notes that days passed without them seeing the sun or stars, and, ultimately, "all hope of our being saved was at last abandoned." It isn't a statement of cynical pessimism but a realistic assessment of the situation. The ship would not survive and, hence, neither would they. Notice that the statement is not tentative or conditional. A terminal diagnosis has been pronounced. "All hope was abandoned." Now what? Do they simply accept their fate and sit down prepared to die? We all have faced a terminal diagnosis for ourselves or those we love. The truth is none of us get out of this life alive. How we live with that reality is the ultimate test we all face.

The week before writing this, a dear, longtime friend died. Her death came far too quickly and long before those of us who loved her were ready. She knew for just a couple of months that she had a terminal diagnosis. As I cast around trying to deal with her passing, a quote came to mind that I used many years ago at the funeral of a young man who died of AIDS just before his 30th birthday. I remember the quote but not the source: "Death is more universal than life. Everyone dies, but not everyone lives." It brought me comfort to know that, although my friend died all too soon, she was someone who truly lived. I'm not sure if the sailors could say that, but Paul certainly could. He had crammed all the life he could into all the time he had, so he faced the end very differently. The question is will we?

So, after many days on a small ship, in a storm-tossed sea, Paul, Luke, Aristarchus, Julius the Centurion, the captain and all the sailors had done all they could and all hope was lost. Then the prisoner takes charge. Rather than tell the story let me let you read it just as Luke tells it:

> *Since they had been without food for a long time, Paul then stood up among them and said, "Men, you should have listened to me and not have set sail from Crete and thereby avoided this damage and loss. I urge you now to keep up your courage, for there will be no loss of life among you, but only of the ship. For last night there stood by me an angel of the God to whom I belong and whom I worship, and he said, 'Do not be afraid, Paul; you must stand before the emperor; and indeed, God has granted safety to all those who are sailing with you.' So keep up your courage, men, for I have faith in God that it will be exactly as I have been told. But we will have to run aground on some island."*

Paul can't resist saying, "I told you so," but then he encourages them from his own reservoir of faith. In his time of prayer, he received assurance that he would survive this and ultimately stand before the emperor.

This seemed to help, but, after 14 days had passed, during the night the sailors sensed that they were being blown against land. They lowered four anchors and prayed for day. Then, under the pretext of lowering more anchors, the sailors tried to make their escape in the lifeboat. Paul recognized what they were doing and warned the centurion that if the sailors abandoned ship all would be lost. The centurion had his soldiers cut the ropes and the boat fell into the sea. Now they really were literally stuck in the same boat. Then Luke writes:

> *Just before daybreak, Paul urged all of them to take some food, saying, "Today is the fourteenth day that you have been in suspense and remaining without food, having eaten nothing. Therefore I urge you to take some food, for it will help you survive; for*

none of you will lose a hair from your heads." After he had said this, he took bread; and giving thanks to God in the presence of all, he broke it and began to eat. Then all of them were encouraged and took food for themselves. (We were in all two hundred and seventy-six persons in the ship.) After they had satisfied their hunger, they lightened the ship by throwing the wheat into the sea.

This is an amazing scene. Paul the prisoner presides over a Eucharistic-like meal. An old preacher once described the three most amazing acts of gratitude: Jesus, in the face of torture and execution by the state, takes bread and wine and gives thanks. Pilgrims, having lost much of their family, and facing another harsh New England winter, gather with Native Americans to give thanks. And Paul, a prisoner on his way to a Roman jail, in the midst of a storm, gathers with his captors and gives thanks. There we have the essence of true faith: Gratitude that trusts God even in the midst of life's storms.

After giving thanks, Paul fed everyone on board, and, as day broke, they saw a bay on the coast of Malta that looked promising. As they made to sail into it, though, the ship struck a reef and began to break apart. Soon they were all in the sea—prisoners, soldiers and sailors. Fortunately, Paul had kept all the sailors on board long enough that they were now close enough to swim to shore. Those who couldn't swim held onto pieces of the ship, and they all made it safely, just as Paul had promised.

Now, if that wasn't enough drama for one day, as they build a fire to warm and dry themselves, Paul picks up some wood and a snake bites his hand. He shakes the snake off into the fire, but everyone watching decides he must really be guilty because, though he survived the shipwreck, he was going to die of snakebite. Of course, that doesn't happen, so some of the natives decide he must be a god. It apparently never occurred to them that some snakes aren't poisonous. Still, it made a good impression, so they spent three months on the island and were offered gracious hospitality. Paul is able to preach and minister until it is safe once again to resume the journey.

After all this, the ending of the book of Acts is very anticlimactic. Ultimately, Paul arrives in Rome where he is allowed to live and work, preach and teach, for two years while awaiting his appointment with Caesar. Luke never tells us what happens when that time comes, and tradition holds that much of Paul's writings came from this time. To modern readers, it seems exceedingly disappointing that Acts doesn't tell us how the story turned out. Here we have journeyed with Paul for years, but we don't know if he lived or died. There are numerous traditions about that. Most hold that he was released ultimately, only to be rearrested and beheaded later by the notorious Emperor Nero. Luke doesn't tell us that, though. Why?

Perhaps it was because Luke understood that this really wasn't Paul's story. Luke set out before Bethlehem to tell how this Jesus got from Galilee to Rome. In the first volume (the Gospel of Luke) the story is of the physical journey of Jesus of Nazareth. In this second volume, he has been telling us how the risen body of Christ—the Church—traveled to the very heart of what was then the known world. Faithful servants like Peter, and Steven, and Barnabas, and Lydia, and Aquila and Priscilla, and, ultimately, Paul became the incarnation of the Spirit of Jesus.

Perhaps Luke stops the story because he knows that faithful servants like you are still writing it.

Hope for Peace & Justice (H4PJ) is a 501(c)3 non-profit organization that is equipping progressive people of faith to be champions for peace and justice. Founded in 2004 by the Cathedral of Hope, H4PJ is led by the Rev. Michael S. Piazza, a longtime social justice advocate who has been a leading progressive voice for more than 20 years.

HOPE
FOR PEACE & JUSTICE
h4pj.org

Religious dialogue is so dominated by conservative churches, denominations and para-church organizations that the average American is left believing that radical conservative views are the only ones held by spiritual people.

In recent years, it has become apparent that there is a need for an organization that will speak to the values and views that are held by progressive people of faith and give voice to those views in our national dialogue. Seeking justice for the marginalized and advocating for peace have been, and continue to be, values deeply rooted in the tradition of Judaism, the history of Christianity and the authenticity of Islam.

The Progressive Church has a long and noble history of engaging the political system around issues of peace and justice. From the fight for the abolition of slavery to the modern civil rights struggle, churches, synagogues and mosques have worked for justice. In that tradition, Hope for Peace & Justice was formed to be a vocal force for those of progressive faith and ideology. To accomplish this mission, H4PJ has taken a three-fold approach:

- **The Center for Progressive Renewal** is dedicated to supporting the birth of new liberal and progressive Christian congregations and strengthening existing progressive churches. In a time when much of the culture in America leans toward progressive values in areas such as civil rights, environmental concerns, peace and human liberation, churches that espouse these values are in danger of extinction. There is a real danger that the growth of fundamentalism will redefine the Christian faith as a nationalistic, militaristic, exclusionary system of belief. We find that prospect unacceptable.

- **Art for Peace & Justice** is our principle strategy to create a cultural orientation/bias toward peace and justice using the arts to educate, enlighten and inspire. Through partnerships with artists and arts organizations, Art4PJ seeks to create a shift in values away from war and violence toward peace with justice.
- **Peace House Dallas** is bringing together peace and justice organizations to create a world-class coalition for peace and justice programming and advocacy housed in Dallas, Texas. Resident partners include the Dallas Peace Center, the United Nations Association, Maryknoll Mission Education, Peacemakers Incorporated, The Center for Progressive Renewal, Art for Peace & Justice and Hope for Peace & Justice. Non-resident partners include Resounding Harmony and the Peace Project.

We can't do everything, but we ALL can do something. We encourage you to do something to promote peace and justice in the world. Whether you are a person of faith or someone who has no professed religious or spiritual faith, it is important for you to work to overcome cynicism and complacency and take personal responsibility for making peace and doing justice. We would love for you to get involved with Hope for Peace & Justice as our partner in this great work. Look for more information about our programs at the following websites:

- **H4PJ.org** to sign up for you copy of the daily *Liberating Word*.
- **Art4PJ.org** to learn about Art for Peace & Justice.
- **PeaceHouseDallas.org** to learn about programs and events of our peace and justice partners.
- **ProgressiveRenewal.org** for church growth resources and to learn about the work of our leadership consultants.

Hope for Peace & Justice
5910 Cedar Springs Road
Dallas, TX 75235-6806
(214) 351-1432

Rev. Michael S. Piazza is a spiritual visionary, author and social justice advocate who currently serves as President of Hope for Peace and Justice, a non-profit ministry whose mission is equipping progressive people of faith to be champions for peace and justice. He also is the co-director and co-founder of the Center for Progressive Renewal, which is renewing Progressive Christianity by training new assertive leaders, supporting the birth of new liberal/progressive congregations, and by renewing and strengthening existing progressive churches. Under his courageous leadership as senior pastor and later dean, the Cathedral of Hope in Dallas, Texas made religious history by reclaiming Christianity as a faith of extravagant grace, radical inclusion and relentless compassion while becoming the world's largest liberal Christian church with a predominantly lesbian, gay, bisexual and transgender outreach.

A native of Georgia, Rev. Piazza has served in ministry for more than three decades, pastoring churches in Texas, Georgia, Oklahoma and Florida. He holds Bachelor degrees in history and psychology from Valdosta State College in Georgia and a Master of Divinity from the Candler School of Theology, Emory University in Atlanta.

The Center for Gay and Lesbian Studies in Religion and Ministry at Pacific School of Religion presented Rev. Piazza with its "Leading Voice" award in 2010. The "Advocate" magazine named Rev. Piazza one of the most influential people in the gay and lesbian movement (August 1999). His published books include *Liberating Word, A Daily Reflection for Liberals, Volume One: The First Testament*; *Gay by God: How to be Lesbian or Gay and Christian* (formerly *Holy Homosexuals*); *Queeries: Questions Lesbians and Gays have for God; The Real antiChrist: How America Sold its Soul*; and *Prophetic Renewal: Hope for the Liberal Church*, designed to help restore vitality to liberal congregations. Rev. Piazza and his partner Bill have been together since 1980 and have two daughters.